Teaching the
American
Language to
Kids

TALK

★★

Charles E. Merrill Publishing Co.
A Bell & Howell Company

R. B. Dever

Indiana University

★★

Columbus   Toronto   London   Sydney

Published by Charles E. Merrill Publishing Co.
A Bell & Howell Company
Columbus, Ohio 43216

This book was set in Times Roman, Helvetica, Jana, and Delphian.
The production editor was Jan Hall.
The cover was prepared by Will Chenoweth.

The research underlying this book was supported, in part, by grant #OEG 9-242178-4149-032 from the U.S. Office of Education, Bureau of Education for the Handicapped, to the Center for Innovation for Teaching the Handicapped. Contractors undertaking such projects under government sponsorship are encouraged to express freely their professional judgment in the conduct of the project. Points of view or opinions stated do not, therefore, necessarily represent official Office of Education position or policy.

International Standard Book Number: 0-675-08437-7
Library of Congress Catalog Number: 77-077089

1 2 3 4 5 6 7 8 9—82 81 80 79 78

Printed in the United States of America

To John D.,

who made mincemeat out of my assumptions

Preface

TALK is a result of my diverse (some would say "strange") background. Academically, I earned my bachelor's and master's degrees in Latin. Thus, from the very beginning of my academic career, I have been involved in language and the teaching of languages. The TALK method is a response to the question I asked myself as a graduate student in the area of exceptionalities back in 1963—can the methods used to teach people a foreign language also be used to teach a first language? Since then I have been developing the complete system, and the answers I have found to my question are presented in the pages that follow.

The TALK method was developed within a humanistic scholar's framework, i.e., study a problem and attempt to understand the total system so that it can be manipulated. This method requires a great deal of observation and reflection, as well as informal testing of thousands of small hypotheses. Such methodology is good for literary research but it is fraught with danger for anyone working in the behavioral sciences; one must be very confident before publishing. As soon as the ideas are published, the humanist becomes open to the scrutiny of the academic community under whose sharp eyes all houses of straw must be blown away.

TALK is on relatively safe ground, however. First, there is no question that patterns of English can be taught, as Lee, Yoder and Miller, Crystal and his associates, and a whole group of researchers in Kansas have been demonstrating for years. The question is not whether or not language can be taught, or even whether or not the TALK method is the "right" way to do it. There is no such thing as "the right way" to teach. There are only ways that are useful or not useful. Some methods are good for teaching some children and not for teaching others, and some methods can be comfortable for some teachers to use but not for others. I believe TALK is useful because of its systemic ties to the language itself. Perhaps it is a bit more useful than most existing methods.

I believe teaching methodology to be relatively unimportant. For me, the really important contributions of this book are the use of a tagmemic grammar as a tool in language instruction for developmentally disabled children, and the system of assessment that is based on the developmental sequences in Chapter 6. The inclusion of tagmemic grammar is due to the patient teaching of Dr. Peter Fries, now at Central Michigan University. I gratefully acknowledge his influence in Chapters 3 through 5 and his comments on Chapters 1 and 2. As to the system of assessment, the data which support and flesh out the analysis of the developmental sequences are from the good labor of others. What I have done is to provide an organization. Since the existing data is now systematized, it can be carried around inside the head of anyone who understands the system: no charts or tables are really needed to know the significance of the data that children provide us with while they speak. The observation checklist found in Appendix A is good for recordkeeping, but it is unnecessary for the purpose of actually making an assessment of a child's current functioning. I am able, for example, to walk into a classroom of TMR children, and within the first 30 minutes of listening to them, know what I have to teach about half of

them, and usually what it is I would teach if I were to begin a language lesson in the next hour. The rest of the class usually takes a little longer, but not much. I firmly believe that anyone else can learn to do the same thing with a little effort. My students are usually surprised to find out how true this is.

Very often I will find a group of preadolescent or teenaged (ages 12–14) TMR children who have developed beyond anything that TALK is capable of teaching them. This is both pleasing and disheartening. It is pleasing because their teachers are usually the type of people who believe that low-functioning children can learn if only the teacher works hard enough at teaching them. It is disheartening because children who can subordinate clauses have by no means completed their learning of the language, and we do not yet know enough about developmental sequences to go beyond this point in our teaching. I have tried to suggest in Chapter 2 some areas which might prove to be fruitful for further research, I hope that energetic researchers will pick up on these ideas and try to see what they can find out.

R. B. Dever
Indiana University

Acknowledgments

The lesson plans in TALK were derived from hundreds of hours of work that took place over a seven-year period in a number of classrooms. Not only were a number of adults involved in their development, there were also a sizable number of children who had to put up with efforts that were, at times, fumbling (to say the least). To all of these people, the teachers, their children, their administrators, and my university students, I can only say "thank you" and try to mention some of them.

Without the children, of course, nothing would ever have been done. The schools from which they came were the St. Coletta School, Jefferson, Wisconsin; the school of the Stone Belt Council, Bloomington, Indiana; the Monroe County (Indiana) Community Schools Corporation; the Wayne Township Joint Services Program, Indianapolis, Indiana; the Indianapolis, Indiana, Public Schools; the Indiana School for the Deaf, Indianapolis, Indiana. I have also had a great deal of feedback by mail from a number of people around the country whose classrooms I could not visit. The teachers, administrators, parents, and the children of these schools have been extremely cooperative. I am grateful for their assistance.

In 1968 I published an article suggesting that something like TALK might be possible in teaching language to educable mentally retarded children. Karla Flink, then a teacher at St. Coletta School, read that article and suggested that we try it out in her classroom for trainable mentally retarded children. At the time I thought that working with such low-functioning children would be fruitless and was very reluctant even to try it. She was insistent, however, and I agreed—only to be presented with the first suggestion that it was indeed possible to teach English as a first language to low-functioning children. It is impossible to say how grateful I am to this group of children. They taught me a profound truth: it does not matter what labels you use with such children—they are still children and will learn the same things that all children learn if the conditions are made right.

The next year I went to Indiana University, and, in two seminars, met some students who insisted that they learn *how* to do something; reading through the literature was not enough for these people, and they forced me to leave the ivory tower and to out where the action is. Together we made up lesson plans, taught from these plans and video-taped the lessons. As a group and individually, we watched the tapes over and over again, looking for the things that worked and the things that did not. We discovered a great deal this way, and I must thank not only Becky Brown, in whose class this all took place, but also the members of those two seminar groups: Mona Ballard, Lizette Burns, Gerry Gorman, Martha Long, Normandie Mindheim, Judith Scott, Nancy Schultz, Renee Utt, Phyllis Venturella, Becky Walkden, Richard White, Brenda Williams, Susan Cross, Karen Davidenkoff, Ellen Heston, Jill Morgan, Patricia Roy, Charla Shryock, Ruth Terpstra, and Carolyn Webb.

Since the first two seminar groups I have had a number of university students to whom I owe a great deal. These students have found me to be obscure, pedantic, irascible, and sometimes even interesting; however, they have never ceased to be a source of inspiration to me. They made many, many transcripts and have stayed with me all the way from those first halting attempts to understand, until now, when it has become easy. I owe them as much as I owe the teachers who opened their classrooms to me. Without either of these groups I would never have been able to come as far as I have with my ideas.

Connie Lautner, working for the Stonebelt Council for Retarded Citizens, also used the early materials in the spring of 1970. She gave me a detailed account of what she did and what happened when she did it. This account was invaluable and had a strong influence on the materials that were written in the following year.

In the summer of 1970, Becky Brown worked as my assistant with a group of very young TMR children who had never had lessons in what we were then calling *TERC* (Teaching English to Retarded Children). Again we taped all of the lessons, criticizing and learning as we went along. Also in this summer, Miriam Cox asked me if she could try the program with some children in the training school at Moose Jaw, Sasketchewan, Canada. I agreed to work with her and was lucky enough to observe her in action. I discovered that I was indeed able to pass on what we knew about TERC. The hard work of both of these people made the summer very productive.

The winter of 1970–71 was the time in which we were able to do a great deal of polishing of the materials. It was also the time in which we found that we could work with many different kinds of language disabled children using the same methods for all. Four people contributed a great deal to our methodology at this time: Joyce Ellsberry, speech and language therapist in the Wayne Township Joint Services Program; Julia Hosek, speech and language therapist in the Indianapolis Public Schools; Judith Whitemarsh, teacher at St. Coletta School; and Sr. Loretta Wilson, also a teacher at St. Coletta School. Miss Ellsberry and Mrs. Whitemarsh appear as the teachers in our training film. Their markedly contrasting teaching styles illustrate how adaptable the method is to the personal teaching style of individual teachers.

Miss Ellsberry and Miss Hosek also demonstrated to me the wide applicability of TALK; as speech therapists they were concerned with a wider range of children than just those classified as TMR. They began including in their program any child with a language problem and to them I owe the necessity of having to change the name of the materials from TERC to TALK.

Mrs. Jean Dover, Miss Ellsberry's aide, appears in the film as the prototype of the ''perfect'' aide for the program. I learned a lot from watching her and hope that all teachers are lucky enough to have such a person working in their classrooms. To all four of these people I owe a great deal—they ''polished'' the method for me and helped develop a wide range of techniques for the day-to-day operation of the program. Their creative efforts are submerged so deeply in the lessons that I could not possibly label their specific contributions.

During this period two other people helped me in ways that I cannot overstate: Bill Twyford and David Fortune. Mr. Twyford was my research assistant in the spring of 1970, and Mr. Fortune was my assistant in the winter of 1970–71. They wrote many of the Experimental I and II lessons, doing much of the initial development work for me, giving the program its rough written start.

The winter of 1971–72 was another period of development, and several people must be mentioned as having contributed a great deal to TALK. The first of these is Elaine Smith, a teacher in the Indianapolis Public Schools. I gained a number of insights from watching her class in action and from conversations with her afterwards about what was going on. I owe her more than she probably realizes. My research assistant, Dennis DeLoof, also contributed a great deal during this period.

The third revision was completed in the fall of 1972. Joseph Strain, especially, deserves mention here in a very special way. The things that resulted from the beautiful interactions I had with him resulted in the Experimental III materials. Without his input, TALK would be a quite different program than it is now.

In the winter of 1974–75, I was invited by Alfred Lamb and Jesse Smith, the Director and Associate Director of the Indiana School for the Deaf, to try to teach a pedagogical form of sign language to normally intelligent deaf children. I learned a great deal from the three teachers who did this work: Jan Fuerher, Pam Hofer, and Natalie Wilson. Most of all they taught me that, in the final analysis, the teaching of English as a first language is the same no matter what form it takes.

I would like to mention the person who has had the greatest effect on these materials, probably without knowing it: my friend and teacher, Dr. Peter Fries, a linguist who is currently at Central Michigan University. He demonstrated to me the value of a tagmemic grammar in applied work of this nature. It took him a long time to get me to realize what he was really talking about, but everything I have done in the past several years has been directly influenced by his thinking and by his gentle persuasion.

The Instructional Development Laboratory in the Center for Innovation in Teaching the Handicapped, Indiana University, was also invaluable in the structuring of the Experimental III Materials. This group was led by Dr. Sivasailam Thiagarajan, and the help given me by Renie Adams on the Experimental III materials was well-done and deeply appreciated.

I would also like to thank Robert and Lynn Grody, who made our training film. It is a good movie because of their ability to understand what I was doing and to capture it on film.

Finally, I would like to express my deep appreciation to the other workers in the field on whose labors I have drawn so heavily. Chief among these would be Laura Lee and her associates at Northwestern University, and all of the other people in applied English linguistics whose methods I have adapted to teaching English as a first language. Dr. Lee's data filled in the gaps of my logical analysis, and without the work she and her colleagues have done, I would never have been able to work out the sequences in the detail necessary to adequate programming. Dr. Charles Fries and Dr. Robert Lado, and the many English teachers around the world who were also influenced by these men, have served both as endless sources of ideas and as ceaseless inspirations. To these and to all of the others whose work has become so ingrained that I no longer understand that it is not mine, I offer appreciation and thanks.

To all of these people, the ones I have named and the ones who have faded from my memory, I express my gratitude. If any children are ever helped by TALK, they deserve the credit; I have been only the instrument for bringing their work together in one place. Only the problems that remain can be fully attributed to me.

CONTENTS

Contents

TABLES

FIGURES

Teaching the
American
Language to
Kids

TALK

PART 1

Background

CHAPTER 1

Introduction

In recent years, courts of the land and state legislatures have been developing laws requiring all children to be served by the public schools regardless of the degree or type of handicapping conditions they might have. These actions mean that children with tremendous physical, social, and/or cognitive problems are now entering the schools. TALK (Teaching the American Language to Kids) was designed to help teachers and clinicians to work with children who have developmental language problems.

TALK was developed within the discipline of Applied English Linguistics. The program is designed to teach English as a first language in much the same manner in which it has been taught as a second language for many years. It has been used to teach children who have been called *mentally retarded, deaf, hard-of-hearing, language-delayed,* and a host of other things. The children it can assist, whatever they are called, have in common the fact that they are developmentally disabled in the area of language. That is, their language development has not kept pace with their chronological age. Note that not all handicapped children have language problems. There are many children, however, who have not developed their command of American English at a rate commensurate with that of their peers. To these children the language must be taught directly. TALK presents one way for doing this.

This book will discuss a number of issues. One set of answers will be provided to the problems of the definition of language and how children normally develop their command of it. In doing so, the assumption will be made that language-handicapped children are no different from normal children in the course of their development (an assumption never shown to be false). The book will then consider a method for developmentally classifying the utterances made by all children. This method will provide teachers and language therapists with a way to use the current language behavior of language-handicapped children to predict the future course of development. The major goal of the enterprise is to provide a method by which a teacher or a therapist will be able to sequence a teaching program.

Finally, the text will discuss how all of these steps can be done systematically. The result will be an assessment technique that will allow the practitioner—whether he works in the classroom as a teacher, in the clinic as a therapist, or in the laboratory as a researcher—to place the child in a developmental sequence. Once this is accomplished, the last part of this text will present a method for teaching language-handicapped children to speak the language.

Although many people have spent a number of years in developing the TALK teaching method, it must be noted at the outset that TALK lessons are not the only possible way to teach children with language disabilities. Certainly, those children who function below certain levels in development *must* be taught by some other method. Accurate assessment, however, gives teachers instructional power. The assessment technique provided in TALK is truly powerful, and it may well prove to be TALK's most useful aspect in the final analysis.

Applied Linguistics vs. Psycholinguistics

This book is written from the standpoint of the applied linguist. Since applied linguistics is a little-known (albeit much-practiced) discipline, our first task is to define terms.

The first term to consider is *linguistics,* a discipline that concentrates on developing theories of the structure of language. Linguists are theoreticians by trade, and they often function as if the language(s) they analyze have little or nothing to do with people in the flesh. Indeed, there is much to recommend the linguist's point of view, since languages exist before any one person is born into a language, and continue to exist long after that individual dies and ceases to speak that language. It may be true that there are languages which have only a single surviving speaker, and that those languages die when that speaker dies (Bloomfield, 1933); however, this fact does not mitigate the independence of languages existing as systems outside of individual speakers. When a child is born the system is already there to learn, and the child's task is to find out how to use it. The theories provided by linguists are valuable because they can provide lenses through which the rest of us can view the subject matter: the language to be taught.

Linguists have developed many different theories of language systems, but educators and psychologists working in the area of language development typically are conversant with only a few of them. In recent years, for example, transformational theories (Chomsky, 1957, 1965) have been heavily used in psychology and child development, but this group of theories does not represent the only possible way to think about the system that underlies a language. Indeed, there are many genres of theories being expounded by linguists, and each has its uses.

Psycholinguistics is basically part of the larger discipline of psychology. Psycholinguistic researchers often use the theories developed by linguists to develop experimental paradigms which will yield information about the way people process or learn language. Like the general field of psychology, psycholinguistics can be subdivided into two basic schools of thought: cognitive and behavioral. By and large, the cognitive psycholinguists find the framework of a transformational grammar extremely useful. Psycholinguistic experimental paradigms are designed to find out what knowledge people need in order to process or develop a language, and transformational grammars naturally lend themselves to the prediction of behavior. On the other hand, the behavioral psycholinguists, like their counterparts in general psychology, often think in Skinnerian terms in that they focus on stimulus control, antecedent variables, consequents and responses. Researchers in this group attempt to discover connections between stimuli and responses. Many behavioral psychologists who work with language variables would object vehemently to being called psycholinguists, but nonetheless, they are psychologists working in the area of language. Like the cognitive psycholinguists, the main research thrust of the behaviorists is in attempting to derive theories about how people operate within the context of language behavior. Therefore they are properly thought of as being psycholinguists.

Applied linguistics is neither of the above. Unlike both linguists and psycholinguists, the derivation of explanatory theories is not a major preoccupation for workers in this field. Rather, applied linguists are interested in the pedagogy of language, i.e., how to teach someone to speak a language who does not now speak it. Applied linguists usually rely on the theories developed by linguists to provide them with basic information about the language(s) they wish to teach. They also rely on the theories and data developed by the psycholinguists to provide them with the information necessary to sequence objectives and to develop a teaching methodology. The primary thrust for an applied linguist is in changing behavior in specific people, not in developing explanatory theories.

Both psycholinguists and applied linguists are oriented toward behavior in people, but the research questions they ask are quite different; and in fact, they are complementary. For example, the psycholinguist usually asks questions like *how,* and *why,* while the applied linguist tends to ask questions like *what, when,* and *in what sequence.* Again, this distinction goes back to the difference in goals between the two groups: the psycholinguist wishes to explain or predict human behavior, whereas the applied linguist wants to change it, i.e., to teach people to speak a language. Thus, workers in the two disciplines see people from different perspectives. The psycholinguist sees people as constituting the research group that will be a source of experimental data which can be interpreted and which will lead to a greater understanding of how and why people do the things they do. The applied linguist sees people as a group that needs to increase functioning within a specific society. To do this they will have to increase their ability to use a language. This difference stems from the fact that the applied linguist sees a language as a tool that people use to carry on the affairs of a society whereas the psycholinguist sees it as the dependent variable in an experimental paradigm.

The psycholinguist can choose to study responses to any aspect of any language, existing or invented. The applied linguist, on the other hand, must make an attempt to take the entire language being used by a group of people into account because he wants his students to become fluent speakers of that language. To attain fluency, people need to learn a great deal about the target language. The psycholinguist, however, is able to build up evidence piece-by-piece and does not have to consider the entire language all at the same time. In this respect, then, the psycholinguist has it just a little easier, because there never has been, nor will there ever be, a complete description of any language. Languages are simply too complicated for this to be done, and the applied linguist often finds himself flying in the dark with no instruments to guide him.

Workers in the two disciplines get into different arguments with their colleagues. For example, although the proponents of the cognitive and behavioristic camps in psycholinguistics might get into arguments with each other over whether or not a specific theory should be used, most of their arguments are not across positions, but within positions. The bulk of their debates concern the proper way in which to interpret research data and how to form their theoretical constructs. Applied linguists, on the other hand, are much more likely to argue over which descriptive theory is the most useful for organizing programs, or which is the proper method to use in teaching a particular feature of a language.

Finally, the training of psycholinguists and applied linguists is usually quite different. Psycholinguists are usually first, and foremost, psychologists. There are some psycholinguists who were first trained as linguists, but these tend to be in the minority. Interestingly enough, few applied linguists have been trained as educators in spite of the fact that it is a pedagogical discipline. Rather, most applied linguists are first trained as theoretical linguists; then they take jobs as teachers of English to speakers of other languages, or as teachers of foreign languages in universities and schools of language throughout the world. There is, however, a rapidly growing group made up of people trained either as educators or as speech clinicians. These workers are interested in the problem of first language learning as faced by children who are language handicapped. It is in this genre that the present text falls.

Figure 1.1 presents in schematic form the relationships expressed previously. Arrows indicate direction of information flow. Note the direction of information between people

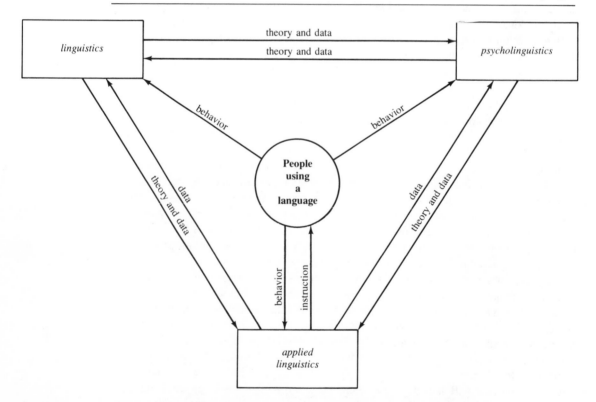

Figure 1.1. Linguistics, psycholinguistics and applied linguistics in relation to people using a language.

and the various disciplines: Whereas the linguist and the psycholinguist use people as the source of their data, the applied linguist's primary aim is to make an input into people. This, of course, is the pedagogical task.

The above portrait of linguistics, psycholinguistics, and applied linguistics might seem overdrawn because pure examples of each are not easily found. Note that workers in the three disciplines are invariably academics, and academics are notorious for wearing more than one hat. In practice, linguists often cross over into the area of psycholinguistics and applied linguistics and vice-versa. From the point of view of the disciplines per se, however, the definitions presented are accurate.

As an applied linguist who was basically trained as an educator, I feel that facing up to the question of how to teach English as a *first* language will allow us to make a great deal of progress with children often seen as hopeless. Although teaching this group requires a great deal of work, the results can certainly be worth the effort. To do this, however, we must recognize the fact that English is a language, and like any other language, it must be learned. Children everywhere seem to develop language in similar ways (Brown, 1973). Therefore, it should be possible for us to make generalizations about the sequences in which children learn the language that will allow us to assess the level at which any child is currently functioning. If we can do all of this, we can develop a good teaching program. It is this view that puts TALK in the context of applied English linguistics.

The Task of Teaching

Teaching does sometimes "just happen." More often, however, good teaching is the result of hard work. A consistently good teacher not only knows what to teach and how to teach it, but also when to teach it and to whom. The very best teaching is generally the result of having followed a three-part rule:

> *A teacher must be able to state, in terms of behaviors, exactly what it is the child should do upon completion of the teaching.*

Broad, sweeping statements of goals simply are not sufficient to cause learning to take place. If a teacher does not know what *behaviors* the child should exhibit as a result of the teaching efforts, any behavioral changes observed will be either (*a*) a result of the accidental coincidence of what the child needs with what the teacher happens to do, or (*b*) simply a natural development that would have occurred even if the teaching had not been done. As applied to the teaching of "language," it is not enough to say that we want a child to "improve his language." A teacher must be much more specific and say not only what is meant by the term *language,* but also what is meant by *improve.* The teacher must be able to state what the child should be able to *do* when the teaching is over that he does not do now. Not only this, it must be stated well enough to allow us to observe the child's behavior and make a judgment as to whether or not the teaching has been successful.

> *The teacher must be able to state, again, in behavioral terms, what it is the child does now and where this places him in relation to normal development.*

A behavioral statement, of course, is the end product of assessment. If the teacher can state with assurance how far from the behavioral goals the child is currently functioning and the sequence that child will follow in reaching the goals, that teacher will know where to begin teaching and how much to teach.

> *The teacher must figure out a way to get the child from where he is currently function-ing to where he should be functioning.*

This is the actual teaching act, and at this point there are an infinite number of possible methodologies to use. If the first two steps have been done well, it should be possible to find a way to get the child to exhibit the desired behaviors.

Teaching is thus both a science and an art. The first two parts of the three-part rule deal with the science of teaching, i.e., the quest for the knowledge of what to teach, when to teach it, and how much of it to teach. The third part is the art of teaching and involves the ability of a good teacher to figure out a way to cause a change in behavior. Methodology may vary from child to child and for any single child over time. It requires a sensitive teacher who knows what has to be taught and who has the means to tell when the child is making progress. Although the teacher can use an existing methodology such as the one found in Chapter 8, he must have a large bag of tricks and be ever-ready to drop a method that is not working in favor of another method. He may wish to create his own method. Any teacher must be far more concerned with the science of teaching than with the art; if we can find out what a child needs to learn, we can surely find a way to teach it.

In keeping with what was said above, then, the first thing that must be done is to establish what to assess. Only when the teacher has a clear idea of what to assess can he figure out how to carry out the task. As a start, then, let us turn to the matter of definitions.

Definitions

Mention of the word *language* seems to open one of the biggest cans of worms in education. It has been used to refer to everything from babbling to thought itself. While it is easy to see that language is used during events such as classroom lectures, it is difficult to justify the notion that it lies behind the ability to tell the difference between a square and a triangle. Yet items dealing with the latter are typical in existing language tests and teaching programs. This indicates that, until we can get the term down to a behavioral concept, we will never really find it useful in either assessment or teaching programs.

One of the more common confusions seems to involve the differences in the scope of the term *communication* and that of the term *language*. Therefore, let us first turn to a consideration of these two terms.

Language and Communication

Communication is simply the transmission of information. If a sender transmits some bit of information to a receiver who receives it, communication takes place no matter what the mode of transmission is—nor who or what the sender and/or receiver happens to be. The message may be anything which needs to be transmitted, and it may be coded in any form. In this sense, *communication* is a term which has had a wide range of manifestations; it includes not only *languages* such as English, German, and Japanese, but it also includes things such as Morse code, ''body language,'' and even the dance that bees do to tell other bees where to find nectar-bearing flowers. Many other things are included in the term; in each of these cases, as long as information is transmitted, communication takes place. The communication may be between human and human, between human and animal, between animal and animal, or between nature and human or animal. The only essential element is that information somehow gets transmitted. If it does, communication occurs.

Communication may be *direct* or *indirect*. In direct communication the sender and receiver are in immediate contact with each other. In indirect communication, however, the sender and receiver are displaced with respect to time and/or place, and the communication is placed (and often stored) in some kind of secondary code such as writing, Morse code, smoke signals, etc. The secondary coding systems usually involve the changing of communication modalities, e.g., from auditory stimuli to visual stimuli.

In the present framework a very constricted view is taken of the term *language*. Here it will refer to *a language*[1] (Dever, 1966). Any language is simply one of the many tools for communication. Note that there are indeed many ways to communicate: rabbits, for example, communicate by thumping their hind feet when there is danger present; in another example, our stomachs communicate the fact that we are hungry to our brain at the appropriate times. These are not examples of language, however.

All languages are very special forms of communication. They are spoken by people, and they exist to give people a tool to carry on the affairs of their society (Francis, 1958). All languages are cultural tools. This fact means that they are used for discourse and they exist only within a cultural context. The tool of a language is used, specifically, as a vehicle for carrying thought efficiently from one mind to another. Discourse is the only reason for the existence of any language.

Because there are different things to talk about in different societies, there are different languages (some 4,000 of them, according to Bloomfield, 1933) in use around the world. In France most of the people speak French, and in most parts of the Phillipines people speak Tagalog. In part of South America many people speak Qechua, and in part of India people speak Urdu. In this country most people use American English. It is true that there are children in this country who are in an environment where, for example, everybody speaks Spanish or some other language, such as one of the North American Indian tribal languages. It is also true that some of the children in these environments have language development problems. Unfortunately, TALK will be unable to help the teacher who has problem cases of this type. In the main, children with language problems in this country are growing up in an environment in which American English is spoken, and it is only with the development of spoken American English that we will be concerned.

The better a person knows his native language, the more potential he has for carrying on the affairs of his society. In fact, the degree to which a person learns the language of a society may well determine the upper limits of his ability to participate in that society. American English is the language used to carry on the affairs of the modern-day American society. In order to be able to participate in the running of the society a person must have some command of the language; note that there appears to be a very strong correlation between the ability to use the language and the possession of power. This fact is even reflected in our IQ tests: scores on IQ tests are correlated with social status, and the subtests with the greatest correlation to overall IQ scores are the vocabulary tests (Jensen, 1969). Note, too, that vocabulary is only a minor aspect of the language as a whole. The

---

[1]When we use the term *a language* as constituting the whole meaning of the term *language,* it means that we exclude all other tools of communication from consideration. Only human beings use a language (Hockett, 1960), and most languages are spoken only (Francis, 1958). The single exception to this rule is the sign language used by deaf people. This reference to the spoken language means that writing will be excluded from the view of language in this book as will be all systems of animal communication. The terms *assessment* and *teaching* will refer only to problems of development in spoken English. The methods can be extended to sign language only when one of the pedagogical forms of signed English (Moores, 1974) is the system being learned by deaf children.

fact that we test "intelligence" by assessing it, however, reflects the importance of language itself to our society.

System

Every language is a system, yet educators have only recently begun to cope with this fact. American children are usually told, for example, that a noun is "a person, place, or thing." In spite of the lip service paid to this definition, native speakers of American English "know" that it is stated backwards. We can rarely say why or how we know this, but that we "know" it can be demonstrated. The following example was presented to me some 15 years ago. I am unable to state its original source, but it illustrates this point quite well:

(1.1) The mum mum mumly mummed a mum's mum.

In the nonsense "sentence" in (1.1), the reader is asked to look at the third "word" and categorize it as one of the parts of speech. Native speakers usually recognize it as being a noun, but is it a person? A place? A thing? Obviously, it is none of these; but then, how do we know that it is a noun? How too, do we know that the fourth "word" is an adverb, and the fifth a verb? The reason is that we, as native speakers, know the *system* which constitutes the language. We "knew" what nouns were long before we learned the definition of a noun as being a "person, place or thing," because we could use them in the proper places. More than likely, we could not label the nouns as such, but we rarely misused them, i.e., we knew their functions.

Our knowledge of the system also tells us that we could substitute real words for each of the "mums" in the above "sentence." Because of this, we recognize the sentence in (1.2) as being essentially the same as the nonsense sentence:

(1.2) The bad boy deftly stole the lady's purse.

Now the definition of a noun as a "person, place or thing," makes sense, because *boy, lady* and *purse* are members of the categories listed in the definition of a noun. Making sense does not always mean that the definition is good, however, because we also "knew" that there are other major problems with this kind of definition. For example, consider the fact that many words can be categorized as one part of speech at one time, and as another part of speech at another. Ask anyone what part of speech the word *blue* is, and the typical response will be that it is an adjective. Yet, in (1.3) it is a noun:

(1.3) Give me two blues and a red.

In this example *blue* is, indeed, a noun because it functions as the head of the noun phrase and is inflected for plurality (see Chapter 4). Its meaning has little do with its function, a point the reader would do well to keep firmly in mind. We generally think of the word *blue* as being an adjective because it usually functions as a noun modifier (*a blue sky*), and as such, it can be inflected for comparative (*bluer*) and superlative (*bluest*) (Francis, 1958). Nevertheless, there is nothing inherently "adjective" about the word per se. Changes in context can change its use as a part of speech. The point is that the old definitions are meaning-based: anytime we try to define grammatical categories (such as parts of speech) on the basis of meaning, we develop definitional problems. Grammar and meaning are governed by different rules in any language, and we must clearly distinguish them in our thinking before we try to teach them.

Other examples could be given to demonstrate that all the traditional meaning-based definitions have problems, yet native speakers of English have no trouble in identifying the parts of speech in any American English utterance. Why? Because we, as native speakers of the language, learned the system of the language long before we learned the definitions, and the system identified the privileges of occurrence of each part of speech, i.e., where each part of speech will be allowed to fall in an utterance. Since we already knew the system, we were able to accept the definitions as they were given to us; we could ignore the exceptions to the definitions easily by identifying them as being exceptions, e.g., we could identify nouns even when they were not "persons, places, and things," in much the same manner that we identified the third "mum" in (1.1) as being a noun.

Without the system there is no language, yet explaining what *system* means is very difficult. Some person (the source is again unknown) once used an analogy that may help. In this analogy, a language is like a machine, such as a watch, an internal combustion engine, or a steam-driven generator. A machine with all its parts in place will work for us and do a more efficient job. We could take the machine apart and lay all of the parts out on some surface so that all of them were clearly visible. We could then label each part and describe the function of each part. No matter how well we labeled the parts of the machine, however, nor how well we described the functioning of each part, we would not have the machine itself until we put all of the parts together in the correct relationships to each other. It is the *system of relationships among the parts* that makes the machine functional. So it is with a language. Each word in a language does little by itself, but all the words working together give us a fine tool for communication. Children have to learn not only the various words of the language, but also the relationships and interworkings among the various words, i.e., they have to learn the *system* of the language. To say it yet another way, languages are not only collections of words, they are also sets of interrelated rules for stringing together words in a way that allows us to communicate meaningfully. The whole, in the case of any language, is definitely greater than the sum of its parts, and it is the system that makes it greater.

Rules

Each language, as stated previously, is a system of closely knit "rules." These "rules" are simply patterns of behavior that occur over and over. Knowledge of the rules allows us to say things we have never said before, and to understand things we have never heard before. To illustrate: It is easy to make up a sentence which most people have never heard before but which will instantly be understood by virtually every native speaker of the language over a certain minimum level of development. For example, there are not many people who have heard the following sentence before:

(1.4.) The boy with the fish is hiding behind the chair.

Although it may be possible that someone, somewhere has spoken the sentence (1.4), almost nobody can admit to having heard it spoken. Yet, at the same time, everyone to whom it has been presented has had no difficulty in understanding what it means. Technically, this is true because a language is *productive*, i.e., users of a language are able to produce novel utterances and understand other novel utterances. The thing that allows us to do this, of course, is the system of rules which constitutes the language itself. When we teach a language to children we must concentrate on the teaching of the *system* in order to do the job adequately.

Describing Languages

Grammars

The system of rules for ordering words in a language is called a *grammar*. It is important to note that the word *grammar* is ambiguous. As pointed out by P. H. Fries (personal communication), (*a*) we can speak of the grammars which the speakers of a language actually learn (intuitive grammars), and (*b*) we can speak of the grammars which grammarians write (formal grammars). Intuitive grammars are probably much more complex than formal grammars, i.e., native speakers of a language intuitively know far more about that language than any grammarian has been able to account for so far. Formal grammars have received a great deal of attention in psychology and education lately, largely because of the work of Chomsky (1957, 1965, and elsewhere). Unfortunately, there is very little or no information about intuitive grammars; in fact, such information will never be available and we are limited to educated guesses in this area: intuitive grammars are locked inside the minds of people and are inaccessible to view. The language *behavior* of people is accessible, however, and observation of the regularities of that behavior allows us to write a formal grammar.

For our purposes, it is also important to point out that the formal grammars invented by grammarians are just theories or inventions that attempt to account for how a language operates. They are not statements of people as they actually function (Chomsky, 1968). Too often there is little or no distinction drawn between the invented models of a language and the functioning of people in that language. This fact has resulted in some misplacement of energy in the study of the learning of a language (Dever, 1972b). Any formal grammar can do no more than provide us with a system for observing or organizing behavior. To try to ascribe anything more to any theory is to accept the theory as truth. This would, of course, be mysticism, not science. A grammar must be chosen for its utility, not for its popularity or currency.

Semantics

Every language not only has grammar, it also has a set of semantic rules. Whereas a grammar is a set of rules for sequencing words, semantics is the system of rules governing meaning. Most of us tend to think of meaning in relation to the *lexicon,* or the vocabulary of a language. However, as important as the meaning of individual lexical items may be, the meaning of words is not the only form of meaning. The word *book,* for example, has one meaning, and the word *worm* has another meaning. Combine them and together they have a totally different meaning: *bookworm* means *an avid reader of books* (one who "devours" books). Embedded in larger contexts these words, like most words, can take on totally different meanings. In talking about a contemporary with a known aversion to reading, for example, we might say sarcastically, "He is a real bookworm, that one is." The point is, that the entire context is part of the meaning system, and there are a number of levels of meaning. There is meaning on the word level, on the phrase level, on the clause and sentence levels, and on the discourse level. All are affected by context, which also has meaning. In short, there are as many levels of meaning as there are levels of grammar. Because the language has both grammar and semantics, both must be taken into account when teaching.

When all is said and done, it is the overt behavior of the child with which we must concern ourselves. We cannot speak of what goes on inside a child's head (intuitive grammar) simply because that is not available to us for inspection. We can only observe what a child does, and then attempt to order and classify the behaviors found so that we can make predictions of what the child will naturally learn to do next. In the present context, it is the behavior of the child in relation to his use of the patterns of American English to which we must attend. The methods of assessment and teaching presented in this text rely on a tagmemic grammar of English.

Tagmemic theory was first developed by Dr. Kenneth Pike and his colleagues of the Summer Institute of Linguistics (e.g., Elson & Pickett, 1965; Liem, 1966; P. H. Fries, 1972). Tagmemics has been found very useful in describing previously unknown languages from many different parts of the world; in fact, more languages have been described by tag-memicists than by grammarians of any other stripe. The specific form of tagmemic theory that will be used is the one presented by P. H. Fries (1964, 1966, 1968, 1970a, 1970b, 1972, 1973a, 1973b), who has concentrated most of his investigations on the study of the structures of American English. To both of these men, Pike and Fries, the method of assessment presented in this book owes a great deal.

A basic notion in tagmemic theory is the distinction between *form* (what occurs) and *function* (the role it plays). It is sometimes helpful to think of functions as providing slots for forms to fill. Many different forms can fill the same function in a language, and the same form can fill different functions. To illustrate the slot-like nature of functions, consider the following example:

(1.5) *Little toys* are in the box.

The italicized portion of sentence (1.5) is a noun phrase (form) that plays the role (fills the function) of *subject* in the sentence. The specific form chosen for the slot is irrelevant. That is, we could have chosen any one of the following subjects, none of which would alter the subject function itself:

(1.6) *Many big toys* are in the box.

(1.7) *Half a dozen rubber toys* are in the box.

(1.8) *Most of the toys I see* are in the box.

(1.9) *Toys* are in the box.

In each of the examples (1.5) through (1.9), the constructions of the individual noun phrases are quite different; yet they are still noun phrases, and each fills the subject function. This is because, as far as the grammar is concerned, noun phrases are *mutually substitutable* in filling the subject function. As a matter of fact, we could also fill the subject function with constructions other than noun phrases:

(1.10) *Mary* is in the box.

(1.11) *It* is in the box.

The subject in (1.10) is filled by a proper name, and in (1.11) it is filled by a pronoun phrase. Both of these are constructed differently from noun phrases (Fries, 1972), yet both can fill the subject function equally as well as can the noun phrase.

The view taken in this book is that both form and the functions filled by the forms must be considered. The assessment system that will be presented in Chapter 7 is based on the hypothesis that children must learn the functions of the various constructions of English sentences before they can learn the forms that can fill them. To illustrate briefly, children must learn the functions of the clause (subjects, predicates, objects, etc.) before they can learn the constructions that fill those functions (the noun phrase, verb phrase, etc.). Similarly, they must learn the functions of the verb phrase (head, modal, etc.) before they can learn the forms that fill those functions (verbs, can/could, etc.). The tagmemic grammar used in this text is an excellent vehicle for such an idea because it provides a way to think about the relationships between various forms and the functions they can fill.

Hierarchical Units of Analysis

We will have to consider the fact that not all grammatical constructions are the same. Sentences are different constructions from words, for example, because sentences have different grammatical patterns. The fact that sentences typically have larger grammatical patterns does not necessarily mean that they are any more important; it simply means that we have to consider them separately from words. In fact, we can look at the grammar of English as constituting a hierarchy.

Morphemes, or the smallest units of language that have meaning (Francis, 1958), can be words or they can be only parts of words. The word *dog,* for example, is both a single morpheme and a single word. The word *dogs,* however, is a single word with two morphemes, (*dog + -S*) and the word *blueberries* is a single word with three morphemes (*blue + berry + -S*), and so on.

Phrases can consist of a single word, as in (1.9) or they can be very complicated, as in the italicized noun phrase in (1.12):

(1.12) *Only the first three brass doorknob handles over there* . . . (fell off).

A clause can consist of a single word as long as it contains a verb phrase:

(1.13) *Go!*

Or they can be made up of a number of phrases:

(1.14) *The man / gave / his wife / some bubble gum.*

Sentences are made up of one or more clauses. The clauses in sentences, when there is more than one clause, can be single words:

(1.15) *Go / jump.*

Or they can each be as complicated as any isolated clause:

(1.16) *The little old lady might have seen the big vampire bats / that had been flying swiftly through the night.*

Discourse, or the back-and-forth interplay between speakers, can be made up (at least in part) of combinations of morphemes, phrases, clauses, and sentences. All of this is represented in Figure 1.2. Keep this figure in mind while working through the description of the language and the method of assessment. It would be well to spend at least a short time considering it.

Figure 1.2 represents the units of analysis of English as a set of nested boxes, one set within another. Each lower unit will be subsumed within the higher units as they are discussed. Note that two kinds of meaning are inherent in each layer of the hierarchy: grammatical meaning and semantic meaning. We can talk about each of these kinds of meaning separately, but we never really use one without using the other. That is, people say little or nothing that is either purely grammatical or purely semantic in nature. Grammar, we must remember, is simply the rules for ordering words, while semantics is the meaning that accrues to both the parts and the whole. The problem is that we know far more about the grammar than we do about semantics. It turns out to be most efficient to talk about both the language and language development in terms of the grammar and bring in semantics where we can, than it is to try to handle it the other way around (Crystal, Fletcher, & Garman, 1975). Therefore, the assessment method will be presented in terms of the grammar rather than in terms of semantics. Eventually, we may find that the learning of the language has more to do with semantics than it does with grammar (as suggested by Bloom, 1970). When and if this is worked out we may have to change our approach, but for the present we can still be relatively efficient if we couch our assessment procedures in grammatical terms and try to bring semantics in where we can.

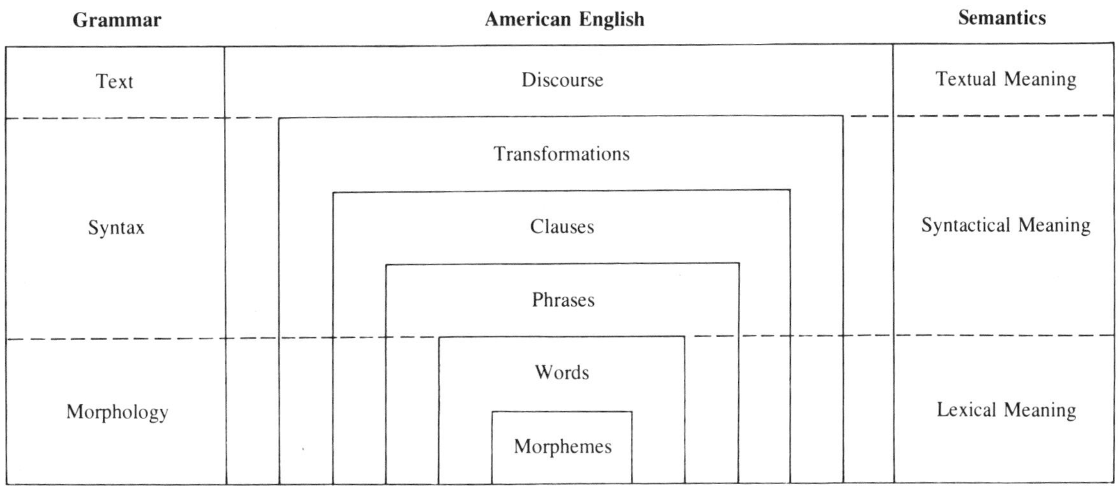

Grammar	American English		Semantics
Text	Discourse		Textual Meaning
	Transformations		
Syntax	Clauses		Syntactical Meaning
	Phrases		
	Words		
Morphology	Morphemes		Lexical Meaning

Figure 1.2. The hierarchy of English.

Assessment of Language

The State of the Art

The current status of language assessment procedures is that most available techniques do not help the teacher or the clinician who wants to know what to do with little Johnny when the instructional program begins tomorrow. It may be true that there are a lot of tests on the market, and that many people are doing things that they call "language assessment." Not many of these things are truly helpful to persons trying to structure programs for real children, however (there *are* exceptions, as will be noted later). It need not be this way once we get over the initial conceptual problems.

Rosenberg (1971) was one of the first to find that assessment of the language-handicapped child was in a categorical state of non-knowledge. He made the point that a useful assessment instrument would have to be based on an adequate characterization of what it is a child acquires when learning a language. The place to begin, of course, when testing anything, is to decide what you want to find out. Most test and assessment procedure developers, with the exception of Lee and her associates (Lee, 1974), and Crystal and his associates in England (Crystal et al., 1975) seem to have ignored this precept. A glance through almost any test or assessment procedure that is currently available gives one the impression that American English has little or nothing to do with language development: Most test of "language" include things like digit-span subtests, which require the child to remember sequences of 2, 3, 4, or more numbers. Such a subtest is irrelevant to language assessment. A test of digit span in a "language assessment" device is a test for the memory of numbers, not a test for knowledge of the language. It may be true that the language is *used* while presenting stimuli or in giving responses, but saying that this is testing language is like saying that an assessment of knowledge of music ability can be carried out with a pure tone audiometer. While it may be true that the ability to produce beautiful music may include the ability to produce pure tones, knowledge of music does not depend on being able to hear them. Beethoven, who was deaf, provides a good example to illustrate this point. There are children in the world who cannot remember where they have just been, but who have the ability to produce the grammar of the language at nearly the level of a normal child of the same age (this book is dedicated to one such child). For such a child to be tested on language ability with a test of digit span would be a waste of the child's time and the examiner's. It would tell nothing of what is needed in order to structure a language teaching program. Note that a test of digit span may provide certain kinds of useful information: many children do have memory problems and we must find out that they exist. Such knowledge can help us conceive of the teaching act as more than just language instruction. But we must also be realistic in asking what it is we are trying to test.

There are a few formal tests of language extant that do deal totally with knowledge of American English. The developers of these tests must be admired for their efforts and their accuracy in identifying the problems, but there are serious doubts about the ability of many of these tests to tell teachers what they need to know. One of the best examples of this is the test of inflectional morphology developed by Berko in 1958, and the tests that have been modeled on it (e.g., Chappell, 1968). This test attempts to elicit data on whether or not a child can produce the inflectional endings of English, such as the noun plural or the verb past inflection. Berko used nonsense syllables as names for little creatures that she developed, such as the "wug" (Figure 1.3). In testing for the plural, the wug is shown to a child and the child is told, "Here is a wug." Then the child is shown

Figure 1.3. A wug.

Source. From "The Child's Learning of English Morphology" by J. Berko, *Word*, 1958, *14*, 153. Reprinted by permission of Johnson Reprint Corporation.

two of them and is told, "Now there is another one. There are two of them. There are two _____." The child is supposed to fill in the blank with the properly inflected form. The theory behind this test is that the child who knows the plural morpheme will produce it by saying *"wugs"* (/wəgz/). A child who does not know the inflection, however, will say something else or nothing at all. Dever and Gardner (1970) compared responses obtained

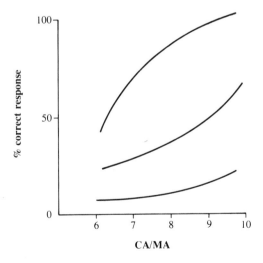

Figure 1.4 Percentage of correct response by normal and retarded children to items on Berko's test of morphology. (Composite graph)

Source. Adapted from numerous graphs in "Performance of Normals and Retardates on Berko's Test of Morphology" by R. Dever and W. Gardner, *Language and Speech*, 1970, *50*, 162–181.

from normal and mildly retarded children matched on both chronological age (CA) and mental age (MA) on this test. They got remarkably regular curves for each item—curves that were similar to those presented in Figure 1.4. However, in another study (Dever, 1972a) a group of children who would be the equivalent of the MA sample in the first experiment were tested. Their responses on the test items were compared to the use of the same features in their conversational free speech. There was no correlation between the two. That is, if a child responded correctly to a test item, he would have been expected regularly to produce that inflection in his free speech. Further, if the paradigm is a good paradigm, we would expect a child who responded incorrectly on a test item to have difficulty with that item in his free speech. This did not happen. Figure 1.5 presents graphically what actually did happen. Children who responded correctly to a test item usually used it correctly in their free speech. However, children who responded incorrectly to the test item also used it correctly in their free speech. Thus, an incorrect response to a test item told little or nothing about what the child ordinarily did while talking.

It should be noted that the Berko paradigm attempts to elicit a very low level of grammatical complexity. Inflectional morphology carries very little grammatical information in English; and, in fact, there is no information carried by inflectional morphology that cannot be carried in another way by the language. Plurality, for example, can be carried by numbers or other noun phrase determiners, e.g., *two* and *many*. But inflections lend themselves particularly well to test paradigms by their regular nature and by the fact that there are many different vocabulary items to which each inflection can be attached. If such a low level and ostensibly easy-to-test grammatical feature cannot be tested, what of the more complicated features of the language? What happens, for example, when we try to determine by using a test how well a child can use the very important forms of BE (*am, are, is, was, were, be, been, being*) in all of their complicated settings?

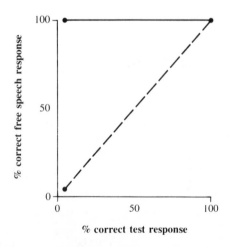

Figure 1.5. Typical obtained correlation between responses to items on Berko's test of morphology and actual usage in free speech.

Source. Adapted from tables in ''A Comparison of the Results of a Revised Version of Berko's Test of Morphology with the Free Speech of Mentally Retarded Children'' by R. Dever, *Journal of Speech and Hearing Research,* 1972a, *15,* 169–178.

Attempts to assess the ability to use a language on the basis of responses to items on a formal test are probably a waste of time and money for the practicioner faced with real children. Formal test results are not likely to yield any useful information for the person who needs to know how to structure an efficient teaching program. Indeed, if the results of the study on the Berko paradigm are generalizable to other tests of language (a hypothesis which cannot presently be demonstrated), we would probably find many more ''language-handicapped'' children than actually exist. In addition, we would be doing a lot of teaching to children who already know how to use what is being taught. From my classroom observations, this is exactly what happens all too often.

The complicated nature of the language presents another set of problems. Most of the useful methods for assessing language development stop at too low a point in the sequence of development to be of much use in the public school classroom. The bulk of these are observation systems that look for such things as babbling, single-word utterances, and two-word utterances. These instruments never progress to the point at which they could be used to program a child's lessons beyond the 1½–2-year level of development. However, the system developed by Crystal and his associates (Crystal et al., 1975) is a very nice exception in that it can assess development up to about the age of a normal 4–5-year-old child. Although their system and mine were developed independently, they are very similar.

The Developmental Sentence Scoring System, or *DSS,* (Lee, 1974) is also a very interesting and useful instrument. It consists of a set of eight categories within which features are scaled in terms of the order of appearance during normal development. It requires the making of a transcript of a child's conversation with an adult. The transcript is scored for the features as they appear in the scale. One category of scores is that of ''Indefinite Pronouns or Noun Modifiers.'' Within this category, for example, the pronoun *it* is given a score of 1 if it appears in a transcript, while the determiner *all* is given a score of 2, because it normally appears in a child's speech at a later point in time than the pronoun *it*. Other features are scored similarly. The scores for all of the sentences in the transcript are added up and divided by 50 (the number of sentences used in scoring), and the result is the *DSS* score. This score can be used to compare children across time, or to compare groups of children one with another. The instrument has validity and reliability (Koenigschnecht, 1974) and is quite useful for things such as record keeping and assessing the efficacy of language programming. There is no question as to its applicability in the context of the learning of American English. It does have the drawback of being difficult to interpret when trying to find out what to teach next to a child, however. For programming purposes, other methods are more useful.

In summary, with the exception of the Lee scale and the Crystal et al. system, there still appears to be little or no argument to Rosenberg's (1971) contention that assessment and testing of language are not being done very well. Yet, if the three-part rule for good teaching is to be taken seriously, assessment of current functioning is absolutely critical. The burden for developing an adequate assessment system thus rests with the program developer. TALK is largely a statement of procedures for assessing the development of the use of American English that will result in behavioral objectives. In other words, TALK is mainly concerned with the science of teaching English as a first language. The methodology presented in Chapter 8 and the lesson plans can help add to the teacher's ''bag of tricks'' and they have been found to be very useful by a number of teachers. The major emphasis of TALK, however, is on (*a*) the language, and (*b*) assessment of language development. In the chapters that follow, we will go into these matters in detail.

CHAPTER 2

The Task

In learning a language, a child is placed under two sets of constraints: those imposed by the physical world that govern the use of the language, and those imposed by the rule-structured nature of the language. In the case of the physical world, there are a set of requirements which, if not met, will cause problems to appear during the learning of the language. These requirements will be the topic of the first part of this chapter. In the case of the second set of constraints, there are certain sequences in which the language must be learned which, if violated, will result either in the learning not taking place or in the learning of splinter skills. The existence of these sequences and a general theory of what they are like will be the topic of the second part of this chapter.

Language Problems of Childhood

Most children seem to learn their native language simply because they are human (Lenneberg, 1967; McNeill, 1966; Olson, 1971; Brown, 1973; and others). There are always a few, however, who do not learn to speak it at the level of their peers, and some who do not learn to speak it at all. More often than not, the reason the latter two groups exist can be found in the *physical requirements* for learning a language. If these requirements are not met, learning will not take place at the rate which would ordinarily be expected. In order to understand these requirements, let us schematically represent the situation in which a

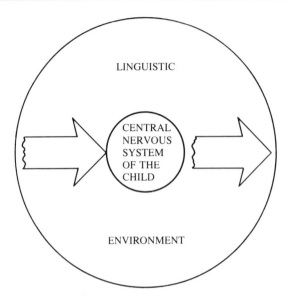

Figure 2.1. Schematic diagram of the conditions necessary for learning a language.

child normally finds himself at birth, and the conditions which must be present in order for the language to be acquired (Figure 2.1).

There are four physical requirements for the learning of a language: (*a*) there must be a *linguistic environment;* (*b*) there must be an *input* to the organism; (*c*) the language-learning "circuits" in the *central nervous system* of the organism must be relatively intact; and (*d*) the child must be able to make a linguistic *output.* Let us consider each of these requirements in turn to see what effect disruption at each of these points can have.

Condition #1: The Environment

Somehow the primary linguistic data must potentially be available to the child. These data consist of the language that is spoken by the people in the child's linguistic community. If they are not made available to the child he will probably have a language problem. There are two major things that can happen to the primary data, and the effect on the child's language learning will be different for each.

One thing that can happen is that the child may not be in a position ever to have contact with a language. There are some cases, for example, where children have been totally isolated from other people by being locked up in an attic or a cellar, and who seldom or never have anyone to talk with. These children are usually language-delayed and may never have learned anything at all about the language. They are also usually classified as being *retarded.* Perhaps the most famous case of this type is the one which Jean-Marc Gaspard Itard described when he took Victor, the "wild boy of Averyon," into his house in 1799 to try to "civilize" him (Humphrey and Humphrey, 1962). Itard was quite disturbed over the fact that he did not teach Victor what he set out to teach him, and recent psycholinguistic theory posits an explanation as to why this happened. Lenneberg (1967) notes that, if a child receives an insult to the central nervous system before the onset of puberty which results in aphasia, or loss of language-speaking ability, the ability of the child to relearn language depends on the length of time before puberty that the insult is incurred. If the insult is suffered very early in life, most, if not all, of the language will readily be relearned. If it takes place shortly before or sometime after puberty, however, little or no language will be relearned by the child. By extension, then, it can be argued that there are sensitive periods in life beyond which the learning of a language becomes extremely difficult, perhaps impossible. Victor, for example, was judged to be about 12 years old when found, and was "mute" (alinguistic) at the time; he reached puberty while being taught by Itard. Evidently the child had never learned a language, and quite possibly, if Lenneberg is correct, it was too late to begin doing so. Indeed, Itard, despite his Herculean efforts, never quite succeeded in his attempt. This suggests that there may indeed be a sensitive period beyond which point a language cannot be learned.

Another recent case along the same general line (Curtiss, Fromkin, Krasken, Rigler, & Rigler; 1974), however, suggests that the latter hypothesis may need revision. This is the case of Genie, a child who was isolated until the age of 13, and who, at the age of 14, began to develop language normally. At the least, this case places the question of sensitive periods for language development into the "unanswered" category. It is likely, however, that the longer the delay, the greater the magnitude of teaching difficulty.

The second thing that can happen to the linguistic environment is a common occurrence among minority children, including many Blacks, American Indians, Mexican-Americans, Puerto Rican-Americans, and many other groups too numerous to name. That is, the child can be born into an environment where the people speak a language other than one required for functioning in the schools. For many, if not most, of the children in this situation there may be no language development problem per se. Rather, the problems they have with American English are probably those faced by children the world over who speak a language that is not the language spoken by the culture-at-large. Their problems are further intensified by the fact that they are often objects of discrimination. The effect of being placed into this situation is that the language of the majority could be much harder to learn because of a lack of interaction with majority group members. Linguistic isolation is found in many forms. No matter what form it takes, however, it always effects the learning of the language.

Condition #2: The Input

It is often the case that the child's environment will contain the necessary stimulus potential for learning a language. However, because the child has a sensory problem that prevents the language input, the primary language data never reach the language-learning circuits so that the language can be learned. In effect, this generates somewhat the same problem as being isolated. A good example of this problem is found in the child who is born deaf. Deafness has much the same effect as does linguistic isolation, i.e., the deaf child cannot hear the primary spoken linguistic data even though they are present in the environment. Therefore, he does not interact linguistically with other speakers. Such a child has great difficulty learning the system of rules which allows productivity in the use of the language. A child who does not learn a language as well as his peers will be unable to carry on the affairs of his society as well as they do. Since the "business" of a child's society includes going to school, the effects of this problem show up in school. Deaf children are typically linguistically and academically retarded, although the incidence of actual mental retardation among the deaf is not very different from that which would be expected from a random sample of the population (Moores, 1970).

Condition #3: The Central Nervous System

The third requirement for learning a language is that the organism must be relatively intact, at least in those portions of the central nervous system in which the language is learned and processed. If it is not, the learning of the language can be slowed or (possibly) erratic. The sequences of development of the language are usually not very different from that of the normal child at a similar level of general cognitive and social development, at least in relation to the system itself.

Central nervous system variables may result in several different kinds of language problems.

The Child who is Language-Delayed

For the first few years of their lives some children, for one reason or another, do not say much, or in some cases, nothing at all. They may appear to be physically and/or intellectually normal in all other respects. Often they appear to comprehend most of what is said to them. Many of these children eventually speak. It can be quite startling when some suddenly begin to talk as if they had been talking throughout their entire lives. One of the possibilities for the cause of such a delay might be an auditory-perceptual problem. That is, just as some children are born with visual-perceptual problems such as figure-ground disturbances, some children are probably born with auditory-perceptual problems which cause them to interpret the things they hear very differently from the way most people interpret them (Morehead & Ingram, 1976; Cromer, 1976). The result is that learning will be slow. Many such children give the impression that they are either deaf or hard-of-hearing.

It might be very difficult to distinguish this type of problem from that of general retardation, or from those caused by hearing problems per se: auditory perceptual problems can have the same effect on language learning as would input or processing problems (Menyuk & Looney, 1976).

The Child who is Retarded

Children who have had some damage to their central nervous systems from one source or another develop with marked slowness. These children will sometimes (not always) have certain physical stigmata, such as those associated with Down's syndrome, hydrocephaly, or other problems. Many retarded children appear to be physically normal. All of them share the same feature, however: They generally behave as if they were much younger children in their intellectual and social development. Commonly, they are also retarded in their language development. That is, they speak American English not as normal children of the same chronological age would speak it, but as a younger child would speak it. It is not uncommon to find children who are in their early "teens," for example, who still speak in an infantile manner. It should be noted that linguistic retardation is not a *necessary* accompaniment to mental retardation, however. I have personally known mentally retarded children whose development of the grammar was normal or near-normal. The fact that there is a strong correlation between mental retardation and linguistic retardation should not lead us astray and cause us to assume that *all* retarded children have language problems, or, conversely, that all children with language problems are retarded.

The Child who is Aphasic

Aphasic children's language sometimes appears more or less bizarre. They generally have experienced an insult to the central nervous system which results in some specific problem or set of problems. For example, some asphasic children block associations in such a way that, although their syntactic patterns appear to be relatively normal, they cannot think of a specific vocabulary item which they need at the time they need it. Others may block out function words and use a very high ratio of content words, etc. There are, in short, a number of different forms of aphasia, although it is rare to find a child who actually is afflicted with this condition.

The Child who is Echolalic

The echolalic child is another whose language behavior might seem bizarre. Such children tend to repeat the things that are said to them in what is apparently a noncomprehending manner. Some of these children repeat back everything said to them and some repeat only some of the things said to them as if they were echolalic only part of the time. Premack and Premack (1974) point out that some echolalic children repeat only things said immediately preceding their echolalic behavior, while others seem to have a delay in making their response that may be several minutes to several days or weeks long. The latter usually go around saying things that are totally irrelevant to the context. The author's limited contact with both types of echolalic children suggests that the echolalic responses have little or nothing to do with language development. One case involved a boy whose repetitions were immediate and perfectly formed in the adult grammar. This child was eventually taught to use English sentences meaningfully, but in the beginning stages of the process, he lost his apparent ability to use the adult grammar and began to speak in an infantile manner. He subsequently had to progress through the normal sequences.

All of the groups of children mentioned have problems in developing their language. These problems vary in two ways: They have problems either in learning the language system itself, or in organizing what it is that they have learned so that they can produce English clauses, sentences, and discourse. Therefore, they must be taught the language, and their disabilities thus present problems in applied English linguistics. Their specific problems generate questions of *how* to teach, not *what* to teach. In most cases the assessment procedures will be the same across all of the problems discussed. It is not possible to predict, however, which methodologies will work for one child or another without knowing the specific child.

Condition #4: The Output

There is one other group of children, as shown in Figure 2.1, who have language-connected problems. These are the children who have some form of motor output problem.

At first glance, children with only output problems may not seem to have problems with the learning of the language itself but, rather, in making themselves understood. For a great many of them, this is likely to be true. The children in this category are those children with motor problems of such a degree that there is some interference with the output of their utterances. At the least, this problem results in the listener having to make an extraordinary effort to understand what they have said. Children in this category have production problems such as those generated by cleft palate, stuttering, or cerebral palsy. If the motor interference were not present, it is possible that many of these children might not be seen as having any problems at all.

Learning a language, being an interactive process (Brown & Bellugi, 1964), may not take place if the linguistic adults in the environment cannot understand the child well enough to carry out their modeling and interactive functions. In addition, not being understood *may* result in a motivational problem, i.e., such children may come to the point that they give up trying to communicate in a language. Such children might fail to learn what children of their age normally learn because they do not make the attempt to try to say things the way an adult would say them. Practice seems to be important in learning the language, and thus, some children with motor output problems may not progress as quickly as they should. Admittedly, this is speculative, but I have known children in whom this might be the case—children who seem to be normal or near-normal intellectually, but who have severe motor problems in the vocal tract and who just do not learn as much about their language as they should relative to their chronological age. In this sense, it is possible that motor problems can result in something like the linguistic isolation experienced by deaf children. Thus, children with output problems *may* present a language-teaching problem in addition to the speech-therapy problem that they usually present.

According to the model presented, then, there are a number of different kinds of first language-learning problems that can be experienced by children. Any or all of these problems *could* be experienced by any one child. If more than one condition is disrupted, the teaching problems are multiplied. The child who is retarded and deaf, for example, has problems beyond those of the child who is simply either retarded or deaf; and the child who is both retarded and who cannot be understood because of motor output problems presents a problem of tremendous magnitude. However, none of the problems we will find in language-handicapped children are ever hopeless. Any child can be taught *something* as long as we are willing to try to teach. The greater the problem, the greater the need to be precise in what we do when we teach (Gold, 1976). It is only by understanding the task so that the child's current functioning can be accurately assessed that we will be able to plan adequately for efficient instructional input.

Note that in all of the above, nothing was said about the child with visual-perception problems, or with cognitive-development problems, such as difficulty in discriminating a circle from a square. Rather, the concentration is totally on the learning of American English as a language. Many of the things that other workers might see as "language" problems simply are not discussed in the pages that follow. Again, it is worth restating that we will reap benefits from this constriction of the field of definition—it will allow us to be precise in what it is we are trying to teach. Problems such as those generated by visual-perception problems, and those of not knowing how to discriminate objects are best handled in the context of other disciplines; for example, the former might be categorized as a *learning* disability and the latter as a *cognitive* problem. For such problems different assessments are required and different things must be taught.

These then, are the kinds of problems that can arise from the physical requirements of learning and using the language. Let us now turn to a consideration of the fact that, because any language is a system, learning a language also requires a system.

The Child's Learning of American English

The ideas presented to this point provide a tool to organize the language instruction of the learner. In addition, they can also provide us with the tools for the future development of an entirely new concept of how children learn language—a theory that has the potential to describe development all the way into adulthood.

For example, I was in my office when my wife and 3-year-old daughter came to pick me up. My research assistant, Mr. S., was there when they came in. I introduced my daughter to Mr. S. The ensuing conversation went like this:

(2.1) Child: Mr. S., do you work here?
      Mr. S.: Yes, but I have to go home now.
      Child: Where do you live at home?
      Mr. S.: My house is on the other side of Bloomington.
      Child: I live in Bloomington.
      Mr. S.: All the time?
      Child: (After a short pause) What time is it?

While this may not be an exact transcript of the conversation, it is close enough to illustrate what happened. Note very carefully what it is she talked *about* each time she said something. The conversation seems to follow a pattern of the child taking whatever it was that Mr. S. said last in time and using that as the focus for the next thing she said. On the surface, the conversation seems to flow smoothly for awhile, but at the very end the child went off on what was apparently an entirely new subject. It can be argued, however, that she was being entirely consistent within her own framework *if* the focus for her next utterance was that which was said immediately preceding her utterance. Of course she did not understand the gales of laughter that erupted from the adults in the room at that moment.

The second incident came later during that week when my two boys, ages 7 and 10, went to the movies. When they came home they came in to raid the refrigerator. I was in the kitchen at the time and asked them how they liked the movie. The 7 year old began a scene-by-scene recounting of the film beginning with the first scene of the movie. He was doing pretty well until he got to about the twelfth scene when he was interrupted by something, got confused and lost his place. In trying to remember what happened next, he entirely forgot where he was in his narration, and went all the way back to the beginning and started over again. At this point, the 10 year old could not stand it any longer. He broke into the conversation and said, "It was about a boy who lost his father and took his dog and went to find him." The 7 year old said, "Yes," and went blithely on with his scene-by-scene recounting, apparently unable to stop the thing once he had it in motion.

This incident shows two more levels of sensitivity to the *topic of conversation*. Whereas the younger girl had to take whatever was at hand to talk about, the 7 year old was able to follow a connected story but had to do it all in sequence. The oldest child, however, was able to rise to a level of abstraction that was far above either of the first two children. The fact that the 7 year old was able to agree with the older boy's abstraction may or may not have meant that he was almost ready to be able to abstract concepts.

Learning Language: A Theoretical Point of View

Every child must learn to carry on discourse. Halliday (1970) calls the learning of discourse *text*, or *the use of language that is relevant to the situation*. The ability to maintain text varies from little ability at very young ages to much greater ability as the person grows older. This variance in ability is well illustrated in the previous examples. Whereas the 3-year-old girl was able to maintain text at only a very rudimentary level, the 7 year old could recount a movie scene-by-scene (intermediate level). On a higher, sophisticated level, the 10 year old could make an abstraction of the movie as a whole. All three of these levels are illustrations of variations in the learning of discourse, which requires text. Discourse, as was said in Chapter 1, is the only reason for the existence of any language and is what we all must learn to do if we are to carry on the affairs of society.

Knowledge of the various levels of discourse and their sequences of development is not currently available, but enough is known about what a child has to learn to be able to lay out the task, at least in a rudimentary form. We can take, as an example, the construction of some of the components of the paragraph to illustrate some of the concepts that the child must learn at an early age.

Table 2.1 presents two paragraphs. Both paragraphs in the table contain exactly the same information on the surface; indeed, they almost have exactly the same vocabulary. But most people who read them react differently to each—that is, most people feel that the first paragraph seems to generate a picture of poor Mr. Abernathy doing things that indicate that he is very sad, while the second does not. The question is, why should this be so, given the fact that the same information is presented in both paragraphs? It is obvious that word order has something to do with it, but this is not an adequate response. There is more to it, and we can be relatively specific in exposing the mechanisms involved.

There is a complex interaction between grammar and semantics in the two paragraphs. These interactions will cause most people to say that the first paragraph is about Mr. Abernathy's turnips, while the second is about Mr. Abernathy. In the first paragraph our attention is focused on the place that turnips have in Mr. Abernathy's life and the terrible thing that befell them; in the second paragraph, however, the place turnips have in Mr. Abernathy's life is never brought out. That is, the second paragraph simply is a reporting of an event in Mr. Abernathy's life. Therefore, we do not experience any sense of calamity upon reading it.

Table 2.2 shows how this is done. Note that the first clause in both paragraphs has exactly the same construction. That is, *Mr. Abernathy* fills the grammatical function of *subject, didn't like* fills the function of *predicate,* and *children* fills the function of *direct object. Mr. Abernathy* also fills the semantic function of *actor* (the ''doer'' of the action) in the clause; *didn't like* the semantic function of *action;* and *children* the semantic function of *patient* (the undergoer of the action). In addition, on the discourse level, the clause is about *Mr. Abernathy (topic),* and *didn't like children* is what is said about the topic *(comment).*

A similar analysis can be made of the second clause in the first paragraph, but note that the topic of this clause does not coincide with the grammatical subject as is true of the first clause. That is, *his turnips* is the topic of the clause, while *he cared for lovingly* is now the comment. *His turnips* actually fills the grammatical function of the direct object of the clause. Compare this situation to the corresponding clause in the second paragraph, where the grammatical subject, actor, and topic functions are all filled by *he.* Carrying this

---

Table 2.1. Illustration of the Task

I	II
Mr. Abernathy didn't like children.	Mr. Abernathy didn't like children.
His turnips he cared for lovingly.	He cared for his turnips lovingly.
Every single one of his turnips was attacked by worms.	Worms attacked every single one of his turnips.

Table 2.2. Grammatical and Semantic Relationships of the Abernathy Paragraphs

I	**Mr. Abernathy**	**didn't like**	**children.**	
Grammar:	Subject	Predicate	Direct Object	
Semantics:	Actor	Action	Patient	
Discourse:	Topic	Comment		

	His turnips	**he**	**cared for**	**lovingly.**
Grammar:	Direct Object	Subject	Predicate	Adverbial
Semantics:	Patient	Actor	Action	Manner
Discourse:	Topic	Comment		

	Every single one of his turnips	**was attacked**	**by worms.**	
Grammar:	Subject	Predicate	Complement	
Semantics:	Patient	Action	Actor	
Discourse:	Topic	Comment		

II	**Mr. Abernathy** **He** **Worms**	**didn't like** **cared for** **attacked**	**children.** **his turnips** **every single one** **of his turnips.**	**lovingly.**
Grammar:	Subject	Predicate	Direct Object	Adverbial
Semantics:	Actor	Action	Patient	Manner
Discourse:	Topic	Comment		

analysis further, note that, in the third clause of the first paragraph, the semantic actor function has been separated from the grammatical subject function by casting the clause in the passive voice. That is, *every single one of his turnips* fills the grammatical function of subject, but semantically it fills the patient function, or "item that undergoes" the action. Again, this is not the case in the corresponding third clause of the second paragraph in which the grammatical and semantic functions of subject and actor and the topic of the clause again coincide in *worms*.

The effect of the separation of the topic and actor from the grammatical subject in the first paragraph can be analyzed. Context is important. For example, in our culture everyone is supposed to love children, but Mr. Abernathy does not. He loves turnips instead. By making *his turnips* the topic of the second clause in the first paragraph we juxtapose them physically to *children* in the first clause, and thus equate the two. That is, because *his turnips* is the topic of the clause, they stand out as being important to the clause, and because of the unusual coincidence of direct object and topic, our attention to the turnips is unusually heightened and *turnips* now becomes the focus of our attention.

Evidently turnips are as important to Mr. Abernathy as children are to everyone else, and probably in his opinion anything that happens to his turnips is as important as anything that could happen to the children of everybody else. Then, in the third clause, in which *every single one of his turnips* appears as the topic of the clause (reinforcing *turnips* as the topic of the paragraph), our expectation of the importance of the turnips is heightened. When we find out that his "children" were eaten by worms, we understand how devastated Mr. Abernathy feels. This effect is heightened by the separation of the actor from the grammatical subject, which, as Halliday (1970) points out, has the effect of emphasizing the actor as the doer of the action. Note, too, that this emphasis is made even stronger by features such as phonological stress in the paragraph when it is read aloud.

None of these ideas come through in the second paragraph. Here, by maintaining the coincidence of grammatical subject, actor, and topic functions all through the paragraph we signal that nothing really out of the ordinary is taking place. Thus, the second paragraph simply reports an incident that has little or nothing that is unusual about it. In the second paragraph the focus is all on Mr. Abernathy. The regularity of the functions make this only a weak emphasis and we feel that the second paragraph is a simple recounting of an event that is not very extraordinary.

These two paragraphs illustrate a very important fact: Any child who is to learn American English must learn not only the grammatical functions that allow words to be strung together in patterns understood by others, he must also learn the semantic functions of the language on both the clause and discourse level. In addition, he must learn how to manipulate both grammatical and semantic functions independently in order to be able to control the communicative properties of the language. For the educator, the lesson to be learned is that concentrating on only the semantic or the grammatical functions has definite limitations. In order to produce a truly good set of instructional materials, the full set of grammatical and semantic functional relationships will have to be recognized, utilized, and taught.

We must bear in mind the fact that the grammatical functions of subject-predicate-direct object, and the semantic functions of actor-action-patient, are not the only grammatical and semantic functions of the clause. Even in the little example provided above, note that nothing was said about the adverbial *lovingly,* which carries both the semantic function of *manner* and the grammatical function of *adverbial modifier* in the second clause. Nor was anything said about the semantic functions on the phrase or word level. There are a number of other grammatical and semantic functions to be considered and taught, and all are important. The educational problem is one of finding out how to organize our thinking so as to maximize our potential for teaching. The following section attempts to provide the beginning of such an organization. Although we cannot pretend that it responds adequately to the need we have to recognize, assess, and teach everything, it may be a beginning step in the right direction.

The Topic-Comment Concept

In searching for an overall organizing concept within which to construe the totality of language development, there is an instructive analogy in the construction of a well-written novel (Figure 2.2). Provided that it is well-written, a reasonably sophisticated reader can summarize a novel with a topic-comment[1] statement. For example, one might say Sol-

---

[1]The terms *topic* and *comment* are being used here in such a way that they are roughly equal to the terms *theme* and *rheme* as used by tagmemicists, e.g., Halliday (1970).

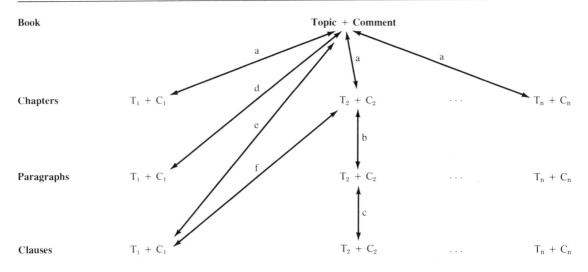

Figure 2.2. Topic + comment organization of a novel.

zhenitsyn's *One Day in the Life of Ivan Denisovich* is about a man (topic) who is tenacious in regard to life itself (comment). But there is obviously more to the book than this, and if we would look further we would find that each individual chapter of the novel could be analyzed in exactly the same manner. That is, a topic-comment statement can also be made about each individual chapter by the sophisticated reader. It is probable, however, that when this analysis was completed, none of the topics and none of the comments of the individual chapters would be the same as the topic and comment of the novel as a whole. At the same time, however, the aggregate of topics and comments of the individual chapters and the systemic relations among them would constitute the topic and comment of the novel as a whole, and each of these would have its place within the novel.

There are also reciprocal relationships, i.e., the topics and comments of a book's individual chapters are partially determined by the topic and comment of the book. That is, the significance of an individual chapter often is seen differently after the entire book has been read than while reading it.[2] In Figure 2.2 the relationship between the chapters and the novel as a whole is represented by the arrows marked *a*. These are drawn as double arrows indicating the two-way relationships that exist.

A similar relationship holds between the topics and comments of paragraphs within a chapter and the topic and comment of the chapter. (To prevent cluttering of the diagram only one line has been drawn to represent each of these and the following relationships.) The relationships between the topics and comments of the individual paragraphs and the topic and comment of a chapter are represented by the single line marked *b,* a double-headed arrow representing the reciprocal relationship. On this level there is an additional relationship between the topics and comments of individual paragraphs and topic-comment of the novel as a whole (*d*). Thus, the topics and comments of all the individual paragraphs taken together along with the relationships among them constitute the topic and comment of the book. This is also a reciprocal relationship; the individual paragraphs can mean one thing *out of* context and quite another thing *in* context.

[2]This fact has long been recognized by the discipline of literary criticism: It is only by reading and rereading a novel that "the full meaning" of the novel and its parts can be discerned by a critic.

Finally, the individual clauses each have a topic and a comment. The topic and comment of the paragraphs are derived from the topics and comments of the clauses within the paragraph just as is true of the Abernathy paragraph. The relationships between the paragraphs and their clauses are represented by the arrows marked *c*. There are also reciprocal relationships between the clauses, the paragraphs, the chapters, and the novel. These are represented by the arrows marked *d, e,* and *f.*

What we have represented in Figure 2.2 is very close to a model of what a child has to learn when he learns a language because the parts of a novel have analogies in daily language usage. Each clause a person speaks has a topic and a comment, but each topic and comment on the clause level is affected by the context within which it is found. That is, each topic and comment of an individual clause is affected by the topic and comment of the monologue (what one person says before another begins to speak) within which it is found, and each topic and comment of the monologue is affected by that of the conversation within which it is found. Likewise, each topic and comment of monologues (or paragraphs) is affected by the role(s) that a person may be playing at the moment, by the message(s) the person has to transmit while playing those roles, and by the life-style of a person. The topics and comments of clauses, monologues, and conversations are all affected by each other in the same kind of reciprocal relationships that exist between clauses, paragraphs, chapters and the novel. The learning of these relationships constitutes the learning of discourse.

As previously mentioned, one of the major aspects of learning discourse is learning *topic maintenance* or *text* (Halliday, 1970). This is the use of language that is relevant to the situation. Text is required in monologues and in conversations. It also must be maintained from situation to situation. As one grows older, one learns how to maintain text with greater skill. This statement is illustrated in the examples given in the beginning of this section: that is, the conversation of the 3 year old is analogous to the clause in a novel; the conversation of the 10 year old is analogous to the novel as a whole; and the conversation of the 7 year old is someplace between these extremes (a paragraph or chapter).

Stages of Learning

All language learning is organized along the discourse functions of topic and comment, and as learning nears completion at one topic-comment level, children reorganize their learning set and begin to learn how to use the topic-comment of the next higher level of abstraction in discourse. The very lowest topic-comment unit is that of the expression of an event, and children spend their first years learning this unit. The very highest level of topic-comment probably occurs, if it is reached, sometime after the age of leaving high school if existing data can be so abstracted (e.g., Hunt, 1970). At all points there are successively higher levels of topic-comment organization and successively more sophisticated levels of discourse, such as the event, the monologue (or paragraph), or the conversation. Each of these levels of discourse has grammatical and semantic interactions which can be discovered.

The Clause

The clause is the first semantic and grammatical organizing unit of learning discourse; it is a matrix within which children carry out the learning of phrases, morphology, and sentence-level transformations. An understanding of how it develops, therefore, is crucial to the structuring of any language program for low-functioning children.

The clause is first learned as a set of grammatical and semantic functions. All lower-level constructions (units of analysis), i.e., the phrase, words, and morphology, are learned within the context of the clause as functions (roles) of the clause or functions of those constructions that fill clausal functions. Once this learning is underway, the manipulations of the clause are learned, i.e., questions, coordinations, subordinations, and passive. Once the clause is largely under control the next higher topic-comment organizer can be brought into play and the learning of discourse will continue. If it is not brought under control, learning will not progress beyond the level of the clause.

TALK: A Task Analysis of the Learning of the Clause

The sequences in which English clause constructions must be taught are available to logical analysis. The hierarchical structure of tagmemic theory provides an extremely useful tool for such an analysis. The sequences found in the TALK assessment system and lesson plans are a direct result of having done a hierarchical task analysis.

A good task analysis has two major aspects: a *content* task analysis, in which the behaviors that the learner must exhibit are analyzed; and a *process* task analysis, in which the things that the instructor must do to cause the learner to learn are analyzed (Gold, 1976). In TALK, the content task analysis is presented in Part II. This part contains (*a*) the grammar of English sentences (Chapters 3, 4, and 5), and (*b*) the statement of the sequences in which they are best taught (Chapter 6). The sequences are stated in terms of prerequisites, i.e., patterns appearing early in the sequence must be learned prior to patterns appearing late in the sequence. The process task analysis is presented in Part III. This part contains (*a*) the system for analyzing the developmental status of children's language (Chapter 7), and (*b*) the TALK teaching method (Chapter 8). The last section of the book, Part IV, contains the TALK lesson plans.

The fact that TALK was constructed using task analysis is an important footnote to the assessment system presented in Chapter 7. Gold has stated (personal communication) that a learner typically brings some knowledge with him into the learning of a task. The teacher must discover how much of the behavior the learner can exhibit and teach only those behaviors that remain to be learned. This notion gives a very special meaning to the term *assessment,* because in a task analytic framework, *no* statements are made about the learner. Our attention is focused on the *task* and on discovering which parts of it must still be learned.

In the case of teaching English as a first language, as would be true for any instructional situation, goals and objectives must be stated in terms of the task itself. Learner variables provide information on *how* the task is to be presented but tell us nothing about *what* to teach. For example, in the case of a deaf child, although the task might most profitably be presented visually, the task of learning the rules of the language is the same as it is for a hearing child. To return to the idea of the science of teaching for a moment, if the teacher can find out *what* a child must learn next, a way can be found to get the child to learn it. In this framework, task analysis has been shown to be an important and useful tool that increases instructional power (Gold, 1976; Levy, Pomerantz, & Gold, 1975).

The Following Chapters

The following Chapters (3, 4, and 5) will describe American English. It is only when the teacher, clinician, or researcher has such a description that it will be possible for them to make an accurate assessment of what it is the child knows. If you are already aware of a tagmemic description of English, skip the next three chapters. For those who need instruction on the necessary concepts, however, the following chapters should prove valuable. They provide an analysis of what adults do when they use the clause and sentence patterns of American English. They also provide a description of these patterns and establish the goals for a language program.

PART 2

Content Analysis

PART 2

Content Analysis

CHAPTER 3

Concepts of American English I
The Sentence

In order to find out how to assess the development of American English we must make sure that we know something about content. What is it that we are trying to assess? Part II will present some concepts of the grammar and semantics of adult American English.

It will not be necessary for us to develop an extremely detailed grammar. A general assessment of how well each child can use sentences, the phrase, and certain aspects of inflectional morphology will be sufficient to (a) place all children, e.g., in a class of trainable mentally retarded children, into appropriate language groups for instructional purposes; (b) properly sequence the goals of the language program; and (c) assess the ongoing effectiveness of the program. If we were to develop a very detailed grammar not only would we probably get bogged down in specifics, but we would also fall victim to a curve of diminishing returns on what we could say about a child's grammatical behavior and what we could do with the information. Even if we could find out all there is to know about a child and what he needs to learn (which we cannot), we would not have the time to teach him everything he must learn. In teaching language, as in teaching all major facets of human existence, the child must do some of the work himself. We can only help him to become more efficient in his learning by establishing guidelines for him and by pointing out the major things to be learned.

Even though we really do not need to go very deeply into the grammar of American English to obtain the tools that will be useful for instructional purposes, many readers will be forced to go more deeply into a grammatical description of the language than they have ever done before. It may be that you will find many of the following concepts new and different. If you should find the following chapters on English either difficult or tedious (or both), you should keep in mind the fact that *an assessment cannot be carried out if you do not know what you are trying to assess.* You can make a serious assessment only when you have a firm grip on the subject matter. Past experience indicates that the most efficient way to approach the task is to familiarize yourself thoroughly with the following concepts of English grammar before you try to use them.

The first level in the hierarchy of English grammar with which we will be concerned is that of the clause. There is reason to believe that it is the first major organizing unit for the learning of language (Chapter 2), i.e., children behave as if they use the clause as a matrix within which they can (*a*) organize the learning of phrases and morphemes, and (*b*) develop higher-level units in the hierarchy: transformations and discourse. This fact makes the clause a prime organizer in the presentation of the language concepts that are needed for the assessment procedure presented in Chapter 7.

The discussion of clause that follows is a simplification of the work done by P. H. Fries (1968, personal communications), Elson and Pickett (1965), Liem (1966), and the chapter on tagmemics in Gleason (1965). The interested reader is referred to these sources for further information. Quirk, Leech, Greenbaum, and Svartik (1972) were also found to be of very great help in writing this chapter.

Clausal Functions

English sentences consist of one or more clauses. A clause is a construction that contains one and only one verb phrase. All English clauses contain natural groupings of words that play certain roles in the clause. These groupings are the *clausal functions:* subjects, predicates, objects, complements, and adverbials. That is, some groupings play the clausal role of subject, some groupings play the clausal role of predicate, etc. Some of these functions are *obligatory* and are required for the existence of the clause, and some of them are *optional* and do not have to appear for a clause to exist. We will be most concerned with the obligatory functions, because a child *must* learn them if he is to use the clause to organize his subsequent learning.

To illustrate natural groupings in clauses, consider three different clauses of varying lengths.

(3.1) John opened the door.

(3.2) The old man didn't open the garden door.

(3.3) Men with small hands might not have opened some heavy old castle doors.

Each of the above examples presents a transitive declarative clause, and each naturally subdivides into three groups. Native speakers of English intuitively recognize this, and most would agree that the groupings are as follows:

Subject	*Predicate*	*Direct Object*
(3.1a) John	opened	the door.
(3.2a) The old man	didn't open	the garden door.
(3.3a) Men with small hands	might not have opened	some heavy old castle doors.

Each of the groupings in the examples have an internal integrity, i.e., they form units. These units are the *clausal functions* (subject, predicate, direct object, etc.). While it is true that the units can be further subdivided, any subdivision that is carried out beyond this point would be a subdivision of the fillers of a function, not of the clause. That is, the three clauses in (3.1)–(3.3) have now been broken down as much as possible *on the clause level*. Each of the clausal functions in the examples is obligatory in the particular clause type used; if we remove one of the functions from any of the three examples we would no longer have a clause, as illustrated in the following examples:[1]

(3.1b) *Opened the door. (subject removed)

(3.2b) *The old man the garden door. (predicate removed)

(3.3b) *Men with small hands might not have opened. (direct object removed)

In each case, we can see that when we delete an *obligatory* function we destroy the clause as a clause. This is not the case if an *optional* function, such as an adverbial, is deleted from a clause. This is illustrated by the clause found in (3.4):

(3.4) Winifred saw Samuel yesterday.

In this case there are four natural groupings, the last one of which is an adverbial:

	Subject	*Predicate*	*Direct Object*	*Adverbial*
(3.4a)	Winifred	saw	Samuel	yesterday.

When we say that a function is optional we mean that it may or may not appear at the option of the speaker. The adverbial function in (3.4) is optional, and its deletion does not change the basic clause in any significant way:

(3.4b) Winifred saw Samuel.

Subjects, predicates, and direct objects are obligatory in declarative transitive clauses—the speaker *must* use them. These three functions are not obligatory in all clauses, however, and this affects the way clauses develop during the language-learning period. In order to illustrate what the differences are, let us turn to a discussion of the three basic clause types.

Three Basic Clause Types

There are three basic clause types: transitive clauses, intransitive clauses, and equative clauses. Each of these have declarative, question, and imperative variations. This fact is illustrated in Table 3.1.

There are several things to note about Table 3.1. The first is the fact that declaratives, questions, and imperatives are simply variations of the basic clause. That is, the declara-

---

[1]The asterisk (*) appearing before an example is a convention used by linguists to denote an impossible construction in a language. This convention will be followed in this book.

Table 3.1. The Three Basic Clause Types Appearing in Declarative, Question, and Imperative Form

Clause Type	Declarative	Question	Imperative
Transitive	John loves Mary.	Does John love Mary?	Love Mary (John)!
	Algernon could drive the car.	Who could drive the car?	Drive the car (Algernon)!
	Richard will open the door.	What will Richard open?	Open the door (Richard)!
Intransitive	Everybody will get up.	Will everybody get up?	Everybody get up!
	John went.	Did John go?	Go (John)!
	Mary Lou swims.	What does Mary Lou do?	Swim (Mary Lou)!
Equative	You must be a doctor.	Must you be a doctor?	Be a doctor!
	He is a fat man in the play.	Is he a fat man in the play?	Be a fat man in the play!
	Josephine was silly.	Was Josephine silly?	Be silly (Josephine)!

Note. Words in parentheses are vocatives (a semantic function). They are set off only to indicate the possibility of their inclusion, not to indicate that they must appear.

tive "John loves Mary," the question "Does John love Mary?" and the imperative "Love Mary!" are just different forms of the same transitive clause. Thus we can discuss the major clause types as one issue, and consider the general relationships between declaratives, questions, and imperatives as a separate issue. As such, all examples of the basic clause types in this chapter will be of declarative clauses. Questions and imperatives will be discussed separately as variants of basic constructions, not as separate types.

The second thing to note about Table 3.1 is the fact that not all clauses in the table must contain subjects. In all imperative clauses the subject is optional, not obligatory. It may or may not appear, at the option of the speaker.[2] For example, it appears in only one of the imperatives in Table 3.1. In the other imperatives the "person addressed" is a vocative (something like an attention-getter); it is not a subject. The only imperative with an expressed subject is found in the first intransitive imperative given in the table ("Everybody get up!"). Some readers will react to the statement that the subject is optional in imperatives by saying that there is a subject, but that it is "understood." The reader must always keep in mind the fact that we are operating within the confines of a descriptive grammar, and what does not appear may not be described. Because the subject may or may not appear at the speaker's option, we simply consider it to be an optional function. Thus, since the subject function may, but does not have to, appear in the imperative, we must consider it to be optional in English clauses.

The third thing to note about Table 3.1 is that, while some clauses have objects or complements, this is not true of all clauses. Objects or complements simply do not exist in

---

[2]The option to include the subject is often exercised when providing emphasis, e.g., "You get out of here with those muddy shoes!"

the basic intransitive clause, for example. We must conclude that, like subjects, they are not required for the existence of English clauses.

We now have two facts: (*a*) subjects are optional in imperatives, and (*b*) objects and complements are optional in many clauses. These facts allow us to draw the conclusion that the only function that *must* appear in *all* English clauses is the predicate. Thus, the general rule for the construction of the English clause is presented in (3.5):

$$(3.5)\ \text{English Clause} = \pm\ \text{Subject} + \text{Predicate} \pm \begin{Bmatrix} \text{Direct Object} \\ \text{Complement} \end{Bmatrix}$$

This rule is read, "An English clause consists of (=) an optional (±) subject, an obligatory (+) predicate, and an optional (±) direct object or a complement. All English clauses are simply variants of this rule. Thus, all clauses *must* have a predicate, and they may or may not have one or more other functions. Since the predicate is the only function common to all English clauses, clause types can be defined in terms of the predicate. Further, since the head is the major obligatory function of the verb phrase (see Chapter 4), typing of clauses can be carried out in terms of the verb that fills the head slot of the verb phrase filling the predicate slot. There are three general types of verbs in English: transitive, intransitive and equative; therefore, there are three basic clause types in the language. They are classified according to the type of verb in the predicate.

Transitive, Intransitive, and Equative Clause Types
Transitive Clauses

Transitive clauses are probably the most common clauses in English. All transitive declarative clauses in English take the following general form:

(3.6) Transitive Declarative Clause =

   + Subject   + Predicate   +Direct Object

(somebody or something)   (verbs)   (somebody or something)

Note the mneomonic device in (3.6) that can be used to test a clause to see if it is transitive. If, in a clause, "somebody or something verbs somebody or something," it is a transitive clause.

Some examples of the basic transitive declarative clause are presented in Table 3.2. In this table, as in all tables in the book that present the grammar of a construction, we will follow the form for tables developed by P. H. Fries (1972). Across the top of the table will be listed the *functions* (roles) of the construction; in the center of the table will be presented some examples of the *forms* the construction can take; and across the bottom of the table will be listed either the *fillers* or *filler classes* that can play the various roles of the construction. Thus, from Table 3.2 we can see that the transitive declarative clause has the obligatory functions (top line) of *subject,* filled by (bottom line) pronouns, personal nouns (names), or noun phrases; *predicate,* filled by transitive verb phrases; and *direct object,* filled by pronouns, personal nouns, and noun phrases. As in most English clauses, the adverbial function is optional. All of the examples in Table 3.2 follow these rules. A few tables in this chapter will include the optional adverbial function, as in Table 3.2. Keep in

Table 3.2. The Basic Transitive Clause

Functions:	+ Subject	+ Predicate	+ Direct Object	± Adverbial
	John	loves	Mary.	
	We	grow	vegetables	in the summer.
	Only the two of them	will have completed	their work	by then.
	Some little boys with ideas of their own	hate	oatmeal	passionately.
	The old ladies upstairs	can't stand	raucous police dogs.	
Filler Classes:	Personal Noun Pronoun Noun Phrase	Transitive Verb Phrase	Personal Noun Pronoun Noun Phrase	Adverb Prepositional Phrase

mind the fact that adverbials can always be used in English sentences even though they will not always be specified in the examples given.

The distinguishing feature of almost all transitive clauses is the fact that they can be made passive.[3] This is not true of the other two major clause types. In the passive voice, the general form of the transitive clause is turned around so that the action goes in the other direction. Thus, whereas the action goes from left to right in the active (3.6), it goes from right to left in the passive (3.7):

(3.7) Passive Transitive Declarative Clause =

+ Subject   + Predicate   ± Passive Complement

(somebody or something) (is verbed)   (by somebody or something)

This situation is further illustrated in Table 3.3, in which each of the examples found in Table 3.2 is cast in the passive voice. Note that the direct object of the active voice transitive clause becomes the subject of the passive voice version of the same clause. In addition, the subject function of the active clause in Table 3.2 becomes a complement which can be deleted at the speaker's option in the passive.

Transitive Clause Subtypes

Not all transitive clauses take exactly the form given in Tables 3.2 and 3.3. Like all of the major clause types in English, the transitive clause has a number of subtypes. It would be presumptuous to claim that the following is a complete presentation of all the possible

---

[3]The only exceptions to this feature are those clauses with verbs like *have* and *resemble*; see Table 3.7.

Table 3.3. Passive Forms of the Basic Transitive Clause

Functions:	+ Subject	+ Predicate	± Passive Complement	± Adverbial
	Mary	is loved	by John.	
	Vegetables	are grown	by us	in the summer.
	Their work	will have been completed	by only the two of them	by then.
	Oatmeal	is hated	by some little boys with ideas of their own.	
	Raucous police dogs	cannot be stood	by the old ladies upstairs.	
Filler Classes:	Personal Noun Pronoun Noun Phrase	Transitive Verb Phrase	Personal Noun Pronoun Noun Phrase	Adverb Prepositional Phrase

variations of any of the basic clauses. There is neither the room nor the necessity to present an exhaustive listing of all of the possible subtypes, and certain liberties have been taken in the interests of brevity. Nevertheless, because it is instructive to note that there are other forms that any clause type can take, we will list several for each.

TRANSITIVES WITH INDIRECT OBJECTS. One subtype of the declarative transitive clause contains an indirect object function. Table 3.4 shows its construction. All clauses in this subtype contain verbs from a class that act like *give*. The filler class for the predicate listed at the bottom of the table indicates this idea. Note that some clauses found in this subtype can have two different passives, and that either the direct object or the indirect object can become the subject of the passive.

(3.8a) He was given money by her.

(3.8b) Money was given him by her.

For some other clauses in this subtype, however, the indirect object cannot become the subject in the passive, it can only become a prepositional phrase. For example,

(3.9) A taxi was called for her by him.

(3.10) An edifice was built to the general by the town.

The point is that we could go a lot further in breaking the transitive clause down into subtypes, because clause subtypes have additional subtypes. Transitive clauses with indi-

Table 3.4. Transitive with Indirect Object

Functions:	+ Subject	+ Predicate	+ Indirect Object	+ Direct Object
	He	called	her	a taxi.
	Joseph's wife	has made	him	a sweater.
	She	gave	him	money.
	The town	built	the general	an edifice.
	The executive board	assigned	the new president	a secretary.
	The whole office	sent	the birthday boy	a very large card.
Filler Classes:	Personal Noun Pronoun Noun Phrase	Verb–*give*	Personal Noun Pronoun Noun Phrase	Personal Noun Pronoun Noun Phrase

rect objects, for example, have at least two subtypes: one has two passives, the other has only one. The type that has one passive has at least two further subtypes: one in which the prepositional phrase in the passive begins with *for* (3.9), and one which begins with *to* (3.10). Obviously, we could get even more detailed about subtypes, but such details would serve no useful purpose in this text.

TRANSITIVES WITH OBJECTIVE COMPLEMENTS. Another subtype of the transitive clause has an objective complement. The construction of this subtype is presented in Table 3.5. Note that the objective complement function gives additional information about the direct object. The word *complement* comes from the Latin word *complere,* meaning *to fill out* or

Table 3.5. Transitive Clause with Objective Complement

Functions:	+ Subject	+ Predicate	+ Direct Object	+ Objective Complement
	He	called	her	a fool.
	They	thought	him	smart.
	His parents	named	him	Frank.
	People in brick houses	consider	people in glass houses	crazy.
	Three-fourths of the people	elected	that man	president.
Filler Classes:	Personal Noun Pronoun Noun Phrase	Verb–*call*	Personal noun Pronoun Noun Phrase	Personal Noun Adjective Phrase Noun Phrase

to complete, and both subject and object functions can be complemented in English clauses. Thus, in the first example in the table, it is *her* (the object) that is being called *a fool. Her* is the direct object, and can become the subject when this clause is cast into the passive.

Note how the objective complement differs from the direct objects that are found in the subtype previously presented in Table 3.4, even though they look the same at first glance:

(3.11) He called her *a taxi.*   (direct object)

(3.12) He called her *a fool.*   (objective complement)

In example (3.11), *taxi* does not complement *her,* whereas in example (3.12), *fool* does. We know this fact because *fool* in example (3.12) cannot become the subject of the passive equivalent, while *taxi* in example (3.11) can:

(3.11a) A taxi was called for her by him.

(3.12a) *A fool was called for her by him.

Thus the clauses found in Table 3.4 and those found in Table 3.5 are different constructions and must be classified as separate subtypes in spite of the fact that they may appear to be the same at first glance. There is a very important point here. In attempting to teach a construction to a child, there are times when we could insert an example of a construction that is quite different from the one we are attempting to teach. When this happens, the results can be disastrous to the lesson. You must be *very* careful to use the right examples during instructional activity or you can cause confusion.

TRANSITIVES WITH TWO OBJECTS. Another subtype of the transitive has two objects. Its construction is presented in Table 3.6. The fact that this subtype actually has two

Table 3.6. Transitive Clauses with Two Direct Objects

Functions:	+ Subject	+ Predicate	± Direct Object	± Direct Object
	She	taught	me	Latin.
	Everyone	asked	John	the question.
	The company	pays	him	money.
	Algernon	owes	his bookie	several hundred dollars.
	They	showed	him	my wallet.
Filler Classes:	Personal Noun Pronoun Noun Phrase	Verb–*teach*	Personal Noun Pronoun Noun Phrase	Personal Noun Pronoun Noun Phrase

objects means that either one can become the subject of the clause when it is cast in the passive voice:

(3.13a) Latin was taught me by her.

(3.13b) I was taught Latin by her.

Not only this, but either object (not both) can be deleted without changing the basic transitive clause:

(3.14a) She taught me.

(3.14b) She taught Latin.

Note how different this subtype is from the transitive clauses with indirect objects (Table 3.4). Although some indirect objects can become the subject of the passive clause, they cannot be left out of the clause in the same way as can either of the objects in Table 3.6. Note, too, how easy it would be to confuse this subtype with those that have objective complements:

(3.15) They made her mad. (objective complement)

(3.16) They taught her math. (two objects)

When we delete *mad* from (3.15), we get a very different meaning from that of the original, but this is not true when we delete *math* from (3.16).

TRANSITIVES WITH NO PASSIVE. The final example of transitive clauses is found in Table 3.7. This is the maverick transitive clause because it has no passive voice even though it has a direct object. The verbs in this class are called "verb–*have*"[4] because *have* is the most common of the group.

Summary: Transitive Clauses

All transitive clauses have direct objects. Some transitive clauses can also have indirect objects, some others can have objective complements, and some can have two objects.

---

[4]There are several verbs in English which have multiple meanings and which function in multiple constructions. *Have* is one of these. It can have any of the following meanings (C.C. Fries, 1948):

a. *Obligation.* "I have to work tonight."

b. *Causation.* "They had him bring lunch."

c. *Necessity.* "They have to eat supper sometime."

d. *Possession.* "He has a lot of gall."

e. *Obtain.* "You can have a bargain at Macy's."

f. *Completed Action.* "We have done it again." (Auxiliary in the perfective function of the verb phrase.)

Of all of these, only *e* (meaning *obtain*) can be made passive: "A bargain can be had at Macy's." The others function only in the active voice. Only the auxiliary *have* (f) is not a transitive verb.

Table 3.7. Transitive Clause with No Passive

Functions:	+ Subject	+ Predicate	+ Direct Object
	People with several yachts	obviously have	money.
	She	lacks	all semblance of respect.
	A terrible accident	befell	the entire company.
Filler Classes:	Personal Noun Pronoun Noun Phrase	Verb–*have*	Personal Noun Pronoun Noun Phrase

Almost all can appear either in the active or the passive voice. When you are unsure as to whether a clause is transitive, another good test, in addition to the mnemonic device given in (3.6), is to try to make the sentence passive and listen for whether or not it "sounds" right to you. If it does not, it is most likely *not* a transitive clause. Native speakers of English have a fine sense of grammaticality and teachers must learn to trust it.

Intransitive Clauses

Intransitive clauses, in their basic form, are probably the least frequent clauses in English (Quirk, et al., 1972). Most often, they take the following form in the declarative:

(3.17) Intransitive Declarative Clause = + Subject + Predicate

(somebody or something)   (verbs)

Again, note the mnemonic device given in (3.17): If in a clause, "somebody or something" simply "verbs," it is probably an intransitive clause.

Table 3.8 gives some examples of the forms that this clause type can take. From Table 3.8 we see that the fillers of the subject of the intransitive are just like those of the

Table 3.8. The Basic Intransitive Clause

Functions:	+ Subject	+ Predicate	± Adverbial
	Mary	swims.	
	The Jones boys	may have failed.	
	Everyone with number two	fall in	over by the wall.
	The bright kid	understood	immediately.
	The door	closed	loudly.
Filler Classes:	Personal Noun Pronoun Noun Phrase	Intransitive Verb Phrase	Adverb Prepositional Phrase

transitive: they can be pronouns, proper nouns, or noun phrases. Unlike transitive clauses, however, the verb that functions as head of the verb phrase is an intransitive verb. Also, there is no direct object. Consequently, there can be no passive form of the clause:

(3.18) *Is swum by Mary.

Note that there are some verbs that can be either transitive or intransitive at the option of the speaker. We can say, for example:

(3.19) He understood the question.   (transitive)

(3.20) He understood.   (intransitive)

Again, the reader must be cautioned that, when working within a descriptive grammar, only that which appears may be described. Transitivity, in this sense, occurs only when there is a direct object. Usually, this direct object can function as the subject of a passive clause. If a direct object is not present in the adult grammar, the clause is not transitive.

Intransitive Clause Subtypes

Like the transitive clause, the intransitive has a number of subtypes.

INTRANSITIVES WITH SUBJECTIVE COMPLEMENTS. As presented in Table 3.9, some intransitives have a subjective complement, i.e., the complement refers to the subject of the clause. Like all intransitive clauses, there is no passive possible for this subtype, e.g., we cannot say,

(3.21) *Fat is seemed by them.

Table 3.9. Intransitive Clauses with Subjective Complement

Functions:	+ Subject	+ Predicate	+ Subjective Complement
	Bulldogs	look	fierce.
	My son	is getting	very tall.
	The music in the hall	sounded	quite foreign.
	Our students	seem	more tired than usual.
	They	will become	doctors.
	She	resembles	Jane.
	It	weighs	three pounds.
Filler Classes:	Personal Noun	Verb–*seem*	Personal Noun
	Pronoun	Verb–*become*	Pronoun
	Noun Phrase	Verb–*weigh*	Noun Phrase
			Adjective Phrase

There is some question as to whether the ''verb–*seem*'' group of this subtype is a kind of intransitive clause or a variant of the equative clause (see next section) because of the nature of the subjective complement (see Gleason, 1965). However, because of the unique nature of the verb BE found in the equative clause, we will consider equative clauses as being in a class by themselves for assessment and instructional purposes. Therefore, we will consider all of the clauses like those in Table 3.9 to be intransitive.

Note that, for some verbs in this category, nobody really does anything:

(3.22) Jane resembles Marilyn Monroe.   (verb–*seem*)

However in other cases somebody does do something:

(3.23) He became famous.   (verb–*become*)

The complement of clauses in the verb–*weigh* group appears to be related to a different determiner in the noun phrase than most of the others in Table 3.9 (see Chapter 4). Both the predicates and complements of clauses in the verb–*seem* group, for example, are related to modifiers in the noun phrase:

(3.24) Bulldogs look fierce. ⟺ Fierce-looking bulldogs[4]

But only the complements of the verb–*weigh* are related to modifiers in the noun phrase:

(3.25) The box weighs three pounds. ⟺ The three-pound box

Most verbs in the verb–*seem* group will allow only adjectival complements. They will not allow noun phrases to appear in the complement nor will they allow adverbs of manner. The verb–*weigh* group will admit only noun phrases of measure to appear in the complement, and the verb–*become* class will admit any of the filler classes listed in the table as complements. In all instances, the subject and the complement of these clauses refer to one and the same thing, however, and there is no passive possible.

INTRANSITIVES WITH INDIRECT OBJECTS AND ADVERBIAL COMPLEMENTS. The other example of intransitive clause subtypes is presented in Table 3.10. The clauses in this table resemble the transitive clauses with indirect objects found in Table 3.4; but again, like all intransitive clauses, these have no passive. They have an indirect object, but the function that appears to be like the direct object found in the clauses in Table 3.4 is actually an adverbial complement to the verb that tells us ''how much,'' ''how long,'' etc. These complements cannot serve as the subject of the same clause in the passive voice:

(3.26a) *Plenty was cost me by it.

This fact is also true of the indirect object in these clauses.

(3.26b) *I was cost plenty by it.

---

[4]The double arrow is a convention used by Gleason (1965) to indicate that two or more constructions are related to one another. A slash through the arrow (⟺̸) indicates a nonrelationship.

Table 3.10. Intransitive Clause with Indirect Object and Adverbial Complement

Functions:	+ Subject	+ Predicate	+ Indirect Object	+ Adverbial Complement
	That gift	cost	me	plenty.
	His new coat	will last	him	years.
	The job	took	him	too long.
Filler Classes:	Personal Noun Pronoun Noun Phrase	Verb–*cost*	Personal Noun Pronoun Noun Phrase	Adjective Phrase Noun Phrase of Measure

Summary: Intransitive Clauses

In general, intransitive clauses have no passive voice because they have no object to fill the subject function in the passive.[5] Again, one test for finding out whether or not a verb is intransitive is to try to cast the adult form of the clause into the passive. If it works, the clause is transitive. If it does not, it is something else. This works not only for those verbs that are always either transitive or intransitive, but also for those that can be either (e.g., *understand*).

Equative Clauses

Equative clauses are those clauses in which the verb–BE fills the head function of the verb phrase in the predicate and in which there is a subjective complement. In equative clauses the subject and the complement have approximately equal status; they both refer to the same thing. The verb–BE in these clauses acts to equate the subject and the complement. Clauses like these have been called "A = B" clauses by some grammarians (e.g., Sweet, 1957).

There is no passive possible for equative clauses, partly because semantically they express states of existence rather than actions. Thus, because there is no action, the action cannot be turned to go in the opposite direction as it can for transitive clauses.

(3.27) Equative Declarative Clause =

+ Subject   + Predicate   + Subjective Complement

(somebody or something) *is / am / are / was / were / be* (somebody, something, somewhere or sometime)

Again, note the mnemonic device that can be used as a test for the equative clause.

---

[5]This statement will have to be modified in Chapter 5 to account for the semantic aspects of the transitive clause, because casting a clause into the passive involves manipulations of both grammatical and semantic features.

The equative clause has three general subtypes. Examples of each appear in Tables 3.11, 3.12, and 3.13. The difference between these three subtypes is found in the fillers of the complement function. In Table 3.11, all of the complements are adjectival (adjective-like) in nature; in Table 3.12 they are nominal (noun-like); and in Table 3.13 they are adverbial (adverb-like). They are differentiated by the differences in their relationships to other clauses.

EQUATIVES WITH ADJECTIVAL COMPLEMENTS. These clauses (Table 3.11) have complement fillers that are related to the adjective modifiers found in noun phrases (see Chapter 4):

(3.28a) The boy is *nice*. ⟺ The *nice* boy (went home)

(3.28b) The fact is *difficult*. ⟺ The *difficult* fact (prevented us from understanding)

EQUATIVES WITH NOMINAL COMPLEMENTS. The complement fillers of this subtype (Table 3.12) are nouns. They tend not to have much of a relationship to the noun modifiers in the noun phrase:

(3.29a) That man was *Mr. Jones*. ⟺̸ *Mr. Jones* that man . . .

(3.29b) This lamp is a *product*. ⟺̸ *This *product* lamp . . .

This rule is not absolute, however, because there are a few noun complements in equative clauses that can function as noun modifiers:

(3.30) The girl is a *servant*. ⟺ The *servant* girl (brought food)

Table 3.11. Equative Clause with Subjective Complement I

Functions:	+ Subject	+ Predicate	+ Subjective Complement I	± Adverbial
	John	is	very tall	now.
	The boy down the hall	was	kind of nice.	
	That fact	will be	rather difficult.	
	His presence	might not have been	very complimentary	in our house.
Filler Classes:	Personal Noun Pronoun Noun Phrase	Verb-BE	Adjective Phrase	Adverb of Time or Place Prepositional Phrase

---

Table 3.12. Equative Clause with Subjective Complement II

Functions:	+ Subject	+ Predicate	+ Subjective Complement II
	John	is	a doctor.
	He	was	a virtuous reprobate.
	This lamp	may be	a product of his handiwork.
	This whole group	will be	teachers.
	All of them	were	granola lovers.
Filler Classes:	Personal Noun Pronoun Noun Phrase	Verb–BE	Personal Noun Pronoun Noun Phrase

Note also that the adjective modifiers in noun phrases can usually be recast into equative clauses (see Chapter 4) as in (3.31):

(3.31) The *big* boy ⟺ The boy is *big*.

but that noun modifiers in noun phrases cannot always be recast into equative clauses:

(3.32) The *hospital* garden ⟺̸ *The garden is *hospital*.

EQUATIVES WITH ADVERBIAL COMPLEMENTS. The third subtype (Table 3.13) has an adverbial complement. This is the only clause type in English in which an adverbial is obligatory. Remove the adverbial and you destroy the clause:

(3.33a) The man is here.

(3.33b) *The man is.

Table 3.13. Equative Clause with Subjective Complement III

Functions:	+ Subject	+ Predicate	+ Subjective Complement III
	A man	is	here.
	Three soldiers in centurion costumes	are	out behind the barn.
	This parcel	should have been	in there.
	All the brothers	were	in their places.
	It	is	three o'clock.
Filler Classes:	Personal Noun Pronoun Noun Phrase	Verb–BE	Adverbial of Place Adverbial of Time

The adverbial in this subtype is related to a post-noun modifier that appears in the noun phrase (see Chapter 4):

(3.34) The man is *here*. $\Longleftrightarrow$ The man *here* (wants to see you)

Finally, note that the optional adverbial found in all equative clauses is restricted to time and place adverbials (see section on semantics, p. 61). Like the verb-*seem* intransitives, they do not admit adverbs of manner (which tell "how"). We cannot say, for example:

(3.35) *He is a doctor *rapidly*.

In all equative clauses, the complement is a subject complement. That is, the complement refers to the subject. This is the reason why the complements of equative clauses can be used as modifiers of the head of noun phrases, as in (3.34) and the other examples in this section.

Summary: Equative Clauses

Equative clauses express A = B relationships between the subject and the complement in the clause. The complement can be noun-like, adjective-like, or adverb-like in nature. All, however, have in common (*a*) an equative relationship between the subject and the complement, and (*b*) the fact that they cannot be made passive.

Thus, the differences between the three subtypes of the equative clauses are not so much in the distribution of the functions as they are in the relationships that those functions have to other constructions.

Question and Imperative Forms of Clauses

Earlier it was stated that the declarative, question, and imperative clauses were all simply variants of the basic clause types, and that all clauses and their subtypes could be found in any of these forms. It is interesting to note that the basic transitive, intransitive, and equative clause types appear in their adult form at different points in developmental time while the children are learning the language. It is also interesting to note that the imperative, declarative, and question variants of these clause types also reach adult status at different times, which means that each of the boxes in Table 3.1 (p. 40) has its own timetable for reaching adult status. The reason for both of these facts lies in the relative complexity of the various types and their variants. Obviously, intransitive clauses are structurally more simple than transitive clauses simply because the basic intransitive clause does not require an object. They appear in their adult form before the transitive does. For other reasons, the equative clause appears to be more difficult than the transitive clause and will appear in its adult form at a later point in time than does either the transitive or the intransitive clause types. Similarly, imperative clauses in all verb types are less complex than are the declarative clauses and will appear in adult form at an earlier point in developmental time. Question clauses are more complex than either declarative or imperative clauses and appear in adult form later than both of them.

Thus, it is important to know what it is we are talking about when we begin to think about the way a child learns the language. Let us now, therefore, turn to a brief discussion of imperative and question clause types.

Table 3.14. Examples of Imperatives

Declarative	Corresponding Imperative
Somebody walks to the store.	Walk to the store!
Somebody threw that book away.	Throw that book away!
Somebody is a man.	Be a man!
Somebody asks John if the oranges are green.	Ask John if the oranges are green!
Somebody told me what color the ribbon is.	Tell me what color the ribbon is!
Somebody tells Mary to read her book.	Tell Mary to read her book!

Imperative Clauses

Most active declarative clauses have corresponding imperatives. Typically the subject is not usually expressed in the imperative, because, semantically, most imperatives are commands addressed directly to someone who is in the presence of the speaker. When the subject of a clause is the person who is being spoken to, there simply is no need to express it grammatically—the context takes care of that. There are only a few situations in which the imperative subject will be expressed in English, and these will be outlined in the following. For the most part, however, it does not appear. Some examples of declaratives and their corresponding imperatives are presented in Table 3.14. In each of the declaratives in this table, a dummy subject has been used.[6] Actually, the "somebody" could be any subject at all, e.g., *the boy with the green hair*. In any case, no subject is expressed in any of the imperatives in the table. In addition, note that the verb phrase in each of the imperatives contains only the head function, and that it is tenseless, i.e., we can say, "Go!" to someone, but not "Went!" Because there is no tense, none of the optional verb phrase functions (Chapter 4) may appear in the imperative.

Note that Table 3.14 presents examples of transitive. intransitive, and equative clauses. Also, note the last three imperative examples in Table 3.14; these forms have proven to be extremely useful in eliciting questions and imperatives from children in a teaching program and show up in the lessons for TALK. The point is that the relationships between grammatical constructions can become very useful in a teaching sense. That is, since declaratives, imperatives, and questions are related, we should think of those relations not only as being things to be taught, but also as teaching tools. Remember, all three of these forms can include the subtypes discussed under declarative clauses.

Sometimes imperatives do express the grammatical subject when we want to provide some emphasis or when we are addressing several people. Gramatically, however, the following subjects are not obligatory:

(3.36) You get out of the house with those muddy shoes!

(3.37) Everybody go back to the wagon train!

Note that declaratives and questions can also give commands; they are not the exclusive province of the imperative. *Command* refers to meaning, and the definition of *imperative*

---

[6]A dummy will be used often throughout these chapters.

is in grammatical terms, not semantic. If a command is given in a declarative, it is no less a declarative. For example, declaratives are often used as commands in the military or in large corporations when presenting directives:

(3.38) All personnel will cease this practice immediately.

Note (*a*) that (3.38) does not address anyone directly, and (*b*) that both tense and an auxiliary appear in the verb phrase. Neither of these can occur in an imperative as defined previously, and thus (3.38) is a declarative. To show that it is even possible for a question to give a command, consider the elementary school principal who goes to a classroom and says to one of the children, "Wouldn't you like to come with me?" No child would dare refuse, and semantically, it is a command. Grammatically, however, it is a question.

There are a few declaratives which have very limited corresponding imperatives. In each case the verb in the predicate semantically involves an action or a state over which the person addressed usually has no willful control. For example, the declarative

(3.39) John is tall.

has no useful corresponding imperative. We find it useless to say,

(3.40) *Be tall!

simply because we have little or no control over how tall we can be. There is always the example of the stage director who tells an actor to be tall, i.e., to play the part of a tall person, but this example only points up the fact that we have to go through mental convolutions to find a situation in which we can use such an imperative, and that the situations in which it could be used are extremely limited and unlikely to occur. For all practical purposes, in teaching children with limited command over the language, these imperatives cannot exist.

Summary: Imperatives

The grammatical construction of most imperatives is very much like that of declaratives except that the subject does not have to be expressed in the imperative, and the verb phrase contains only a tenseless verb. Generally, the only exceptions to this are found when heavy emphasis is being given to the imperative. In these cases the subject appears. When the subject of the imperative appears, it always refers to the person or persons being addressed.

Questions

In this section we will talk about some of the types of questions that can appear in English, but we will not go into their construction. A detailed presentation of questions requires that we talk about relationships called *transformations* that involve functions of the verb phrase. This discussion will wait until Chapter 5.

In general, there are three types of questions: *yes/no* questions, *wh-* questions, and tag questions. Construction of each of these has its own set of rules and will be considered separately.

Yes/No Questions

Some questions always call for an answer that has either a *yes* or a *no* in it. These responses may occur singly or they may be elaborated upon at the option of the person

Table 3.15. Examples of Declaratives with Corresponding *Yes/No* Questions

Declarative	Yes/No Question
That is a lovely hat.	Is that a lovely hat?
Rover loves doggy biscuits.	Does Rover love doggy biscuits?
Wilfred may go to the bathroom.	May Wilfred go to the bathroom?
She has finally seen Paris.	Has she finally seen Paris?
Alice was thrown off the horse.	Was Alice thrown off the horse?
He was catching dragonflies.	Was he catching dragonflies?

responding. In any case, the person asking the question expects, at the least, to hear either a *yes* or a *no* as a part of the response. Examples of this type of question are presented in Table 3.15. Note that there are a number of different forms that *yes/no* questions can take and that they all have a corresponding declarative. In each case, however, the verb, or part of the verb phrase, is moved to a position in front of the subject of the clause. How this occurs will be elaborated on in more detail in Chapter 5.

Wh- Questions

Unlike *yes/no* questions, *wh-* questions require something other than a *yes* or a *no* in the response. In fact, they require some specific bit of information, such as "where?" or "how?" Note that all but one *wh-* question in Table 3.16 begins with a word that begins its spelling with a *wh-*. Note, too, how the responses to these questions will differ from the *yes* or *no* responses in Table 3.15; where the *yes/no* questions seek affirmation or denial, *wh-* questions seek some bit of information from the respondent. In Chapter 5 we will find that the form of the *wh-* question itself specifies what the response is supposed to be.

Tag Questions

Tag questions are conversation-makers. They consist of a declarative with a part of a *yes/no* question tagged onto the end. The interesting thing about these questions is that they do not really seek to find anything out. Rather, they look for agreement with

Table 3.16. Examples of Declaratives with Corresponding *Wh-* Questions

Declarative	Wh- Question
That thing is a dog.	What is that thing?
Mrs. Jones threw the salesman out.	Who did Mrs. Jones throw out?
We put it under his bed.	Where did we put it?
Wally ate it this morning.	When did Wally eat it?
You kiss a porcupine very carefully.	How do you kiss a porcupine?
The boy on the left took the cookie.	Which boy took the cookie?
He left because he was heartsick at the prospect.	Why did he leave?

Table 3.17. Examples of Tag Questions

That's a new hat, isn't it?

You love me, don't you?

You didn't eat it, did you?

You won't go in there, will you?

---

something that the speaker has said. Examples of this type of question are presented in Table 3.17. Note particularly the responses that would be given to the examples in this table. It would be difficult to respond with anything other than agreement to the questions as they are asked, because the person asking the question phrases it in such a way that he expects agreement in the response. The function of these questions seems largely to be conversational in nature.

Summary: Questions

In general, there are three types of questions: *yes/no, wh-,* and tag. Each is classified in terms of the response it seeks: "*yes/no* question seeks either a *yes* or *no;* a *wh-* question seeks a bit of information, and a tag question seeks agreement. Each has its own set of construction rules. These rules will be elaborated upon in Chapter 5.

Semantic Aspects of the Clause

This section will be intentionally brief. The topic of the section is largely tangential to the aim of the text, i.e., to present a method for assessing the development of grammar. Nevertheless, at various times we will be forced to make some minor excursions into the semantic aspect of the language, and it seems appropriate to mention a few things about the semantics of the clause before we close the chapter.

Information in this section is taken largely from P. H. Fries (1973b, n.d.) and Brown (1973). Because of the differences in theoretical orientation of these two authors, and because it is necessary to remain brief, some liberties have been taken in both terminology and conceptual interpretation. The reader who wishes more depth should consult these sources for more detailed information and extensive bibliographies.

The information which follows will be divided into two sections: the semantics of the predicate function and the semantics of other functions of the clause. Because of the orientation of this text, such a presentation seems both logical and efficient. Because the predicate function is central to the English clause, we will turn to it first.

The Semantics of the Predicate Function

The definition of verbs that most of us learned in junior high was that they "express action or states of being." This rule is obviously a statement about semantics (meaning) and not about the grammar (sequences of words), as it was intended to be. However in terms of semantics, it is quite true. That is, the predicate function of the English clause can express either *action* or *state*. Semantically, action can be expressed in either transitive or intransitive verbs in the predicates, while state can be expressed in transitive, intransitive, or equative verbs.

Action

The term *action* means just what it says: the predicate of the clause is one in which an action is expressed. Action, by its very nature, must be *observable,* but note that such observability is not necessarily that to which behavioristic psychologists refer when they use this term. That is, the action may be observable only to the "doer" of the action. For example, all of the following clauses contain semantic action. (The clauses are marked for grammatical clause type.)

    (3.41) The terrorists *blew up* the dam.   (transitive)

    (3.42) Some of them *observed* her carefully.   (transitive)

    (3.43) The door *opened.*   (intransitive)

    (3.44) Nearly everyone in the room *listened.*   (intransitive)

Notice how each of these sentences makes a statement about an action, but that in (3.42) and (3.44) the action is likely to be unobservable. It is very difficult to tell when someone is observing something because we can all look at something without seeing it or we can listen to something without hearing it. Only the "doer" of the action can say for sure whether he is actually listening or observing, as any teacher can freely attest. These require acts of the will to separate them from simple body posture. Nevertheless, when they occur they are actions, i.e., somebody *does* something. Semantically, we would classify the predicates in (3.41) to (3.44) as expressing action.

State Propositions

State propositions, on the other hand, have no actions involved in them. Rather, they make a statement about the way things are. Equative clauses, by the very nature of the verb BE, invariably contain state propositions:

    (3.45) My wife *is* now at home, thank God.   (equative)

    (3.46) Maximilian *was* pretty short.   (equative)

State propositions are not limited to the equative clause. They can also be found in both transitive and intransitive clauses:

    (3.47) I always *wanted* a dog.   (transitive)

    (3.48) He *owns* three cars.   (transitive)

    (3.49) Josephine *seems* very lucky.   (intransitive)

    (3.50) Wyatt *understood.*   (intransitive)

Note how, in all six examples just given, there is no action. Rather, predicates in (3.47)–(3.50) express state, or "the ways things are." No action actually occurs when we "want" or "own" something, or when we "understand." In addition verbs like *seem* (see Table 3.9) act very much like BE in terms of both the grammatical and semantic functions that they can fill—both take subjective complements, and both express state.

The Semantics of Other Functions of the Clause

In the following list of clause-level semantic functions, note that the semantic functions are not tied to grammatical functions in any rigid way. There may indeed be a correlation between some of the grammatical functions and certain semantic functions, but grammar and semantics are separable. This fact may eventually prove to be important in the development of child language; right now, in fact, it is possible to demonstrate that the separation of certain grammatical functions from certain semantic functions does indeed take place at specific points in development (see Chapter 6).

The clausal semantic functions which will be discussed in the following are the actor, instrument, dative, patient, time, location, manner, and accompaniment.

Actor

The actor is typically animate, i.e., it possesses life. Very often it coincides with the grammatical subject of an action proposition:

(3.51) The *bugs* killed the poor strawberries.

(3.52) That foolish *kid* spent the last penny.

It is not always the case, however, that the actor coincides with the grammatical subject. In the case of the passive voice, for example, the actor coincides with the passive complement:

(3.53) The poor strawberries were killed by the *bugs*.

(3.54) The last penny was spent by that foolish *kid*.

Sometimes the actor is inanimate, especially when natural forces are involved:

(3.55) *The frost* killed the poor strawberries.

(3.56) The *wind* blew down the flagpole.

Instrument

The instrument function is similar to the actor function except for the fact that it usually refers to an inanimate object used by the actor to effect the action.

(3.57) The *bat* hit the ball.

(3.58) The road was widened by the *bulldozer*.

In both of these examples the actor is not stated. In its place is the inanimate object that was used by the actor to effect the action. Neither a bat nor a bulldozer is able to carry out the action by itself: both need an animate being to cause the action to occur. There are times, though, when an animate being can be both an actor and an instrument:

(3.59) Boss Tweed used *people* to further his own ends.

In (3.59), *people* fills two functions. One is that of patient ("undergoer": see following) of the action of being "used," and the other is that of instrument used in "furthering the ends" of Boss Tweed. The fact that a form can fill two functions at the same time is not unusual in English subordinates (P. H. Fries, 1970b); note that *people* in this clause fills the grammatical functions of both the direct object of *used* and the subject of *further*.

The instrument can also coincide with the adverbial function:

(3.60 She rode in on her *broom*.

(3.61) He opened the door with the *key*.

(3.62) They kept time with a *drum*.

Patient

Like the labels for most semantic functions, the word *patient* is a very graphic term. It refers to the "undergoer" of the action; as in medical terminology, the patient is someone who is operated on. This condition is clear from the following examples:

(3.63) John ate the *apple*.

(3.64) They stood poor *Joe* against the wall.

In these examples the patient is shown as coinciding with the grammatical direct object of the clause. This is not always the case. In intransitive clauses, for example, we very often find that the patient coincides with the subject function. In the following examples the head noun in the subject undergoes the action:

(3.65) The *seawall* withstood the storm.

(3.66) An *arm* rose up.

The patient function also coincides with the grammatical subject in passive-voiced clauses:

(3.67 *Joe* was stood against the wall.

(3.68) The *fan* was turned on at once.

Dative

Dative is one semantic function that does not have a graphic name. The dative is the recipient of an action, which is quite a different role from being the patient, or the "undergoer" of the action. In the following examples in which the dative coincides with the indirect object, the patient can be seen to coincide with the direct object:

(3.69) Barnhorst bought his *son* a radio.

(3.70) Evelyn brought *him* luck.

Note, however, that the dative can also be found in the direct object or subject.

(3.71) I liked the *play*.

(3.72) *I* tasted the pepper in the soup.

In example (3.71) the direct object does not undergo any action, but does *receive* action of some sort: it is the action of positive affect. In (3.72) it is the subject that receives the action of tasting the pepper, i.e., *pepper* expresses the patient function.

The dative can also be expressed in prepositional phrases that are difficult to classify in terms of the grammar being presented in this text. Quirk et al. (1972) call them *adjuncts,* which means that they are optional ''add-ons'' to the clause. These adjuncts, however, can carry the semantic function of the dative:

(3.73) Ed built a dollhouse for his *daughter*.

(3.74) A memorial was erected to his *memory*.

Time, Place, Manner, and Accompaniment

Several semantic functions (time, place, manner, accompaniment) have been grouped together because they generally coincide with the adverbial function. In general, they respond to the questions *when, where, how, with whom,* or *with what.* These responses are illustrated in the following examples:

Time: ''When?''

(3.75) They met at *three o'clock*.

(3.76) I'll see you *then*.

(3.77) *When that happened,* they agreed.

Place: ''Where?''

(3.78) Everybody looked *up the pipe*.

(3.79) *There* they saw a mouse.

(3.80) I'll meet you *under the oak trees*.

Manner: ''How?''

(3.81) They ate their grapefruit *carefully*.

(3.82) *Wishfully,* they thought of the old days.

(3.83) He assembled it *with great precision.*

Accompaniment: ''With whom?'' or ''With what?''

(3.84) She went home *with Naomi's husband.*

(3.85) He ran *with his dog.*

(3.86) My aunt went shopping *with my wife.*

Exceptions to the coincidence of these functions with adverbials occur for the functions time and place. Both of these functions can coincide with the grammatical subject, as illustrated by the following:

(3.87) *London* is foggy.   (Where?)

(3.88) *My tent* sleeps three people.   (Where?)

(3.89) *Yesterday* was a holiday.   (When?)

(3.90) *Three o'clock* is the meeting time. (When?)

In addition, both time and place can coincide with the complement function of the equative clause:

(3.91) Three men are *here.*   (Where?)

(3.92) It is *time to go.*   (When?)

"Empty" Subjects

The last topic to be discussed in this section is the ''empty'' subject. There are a number of times when the subject appears in a sentence, but it has no immediately apparent reference to anything:

(3.93) *It* was raining.

(3.94) *There* was a dog there.

Look closely at these two sentences and ask the questions ''What was raining?'' and ''Where was a dog?'' The answers, obviously, cannot be gleaned from (3.93) and (3.94) in the same way that the answer to the question ''Who are here?'' can be found in example (3.91). This is because the subjects are empty, i.e., they are dummies that play a semantic and grammatical role; by themselves they have no meaning.

The role that they play is in discourse. Typically, the topic of a sentence is in the first function to appear in the sentence (recall Mr. Abernathy in Chapter 2). Sometimes, when we wish to provide emphasis, we will remove a function or a construction from its normal position in the sentence. As a result, the listener focuses on that function or construction because it is not where it is expected to be. In the previous examples our attention is focused on the complement function in each sentence: the complement actually becomes the topic of the clause, and our attention to it is heightened by the use of the dummy in the subject. In reality, the dummy subject *is* the topic, but we are forced by the fact that it is a dummy to search further in the sentence to find out what it refers to. The grammar of these dummies is beyond the purpose of this book, and so nothing more will be said about them at this time.

Summary

A number of semantic functions coincide with the grammatical functions of the clause. It should be clear by now that there is more to semantics than just the meaning of words (which is semantics on the morpheme level), and that not everything that could be said about the subject has been said. We will have still more to say about semantics on the phrase level when we talk about the noun phrase and the verb phrase, but even that will leave much unsaid. At this point I have attempted to do little more than provide a brief introduction to vocabulary used in research that is just now getting started. This work, however, is sure to continue to develop in the future. The study of child language development is also moving in the direction of the development of meaning, and there is no question about the importance of semantics to those of us who must structure language development programs. For the present, however, we will still find that it is easier to follow the development of grammar across time than it is to try to couch everything in terms of semantics. (See also Crystal et al., 1975, who present a very strong argument for building assessment and teaching programs based on grammar rather than semantics.)

CHAPTER 4

Concepts of American English II
Phrases, Words, and Morphemes

This chapter presents the grammar of constructions below the clause in the hierarchy (Figure 2.1, p. 22). Verb phrases, noun phrases, and prepositional phrases are important constructions because they fill clause functions. Therefore, a major part of this chapter will be devoted to these grammatical constructions. In addition, because no discussion of a language would be complete without at least a brief discussion of morphemes and words, the final pages of this chapter will be addressed to this topic.

The information in this chapter is adapted from several sources. Most of the grammar of the verb phrase and noun phrase has been adapted from information presented by P. H. Fries (1972; personal communications). The discussion of morphemes and words is taken largely from Francis (1968), LeFevre (1970), and Quirk et al. (1972). The statements on semantics were taken from Quirk et al. (1972), Fries (1974), and Brown (1973). The interested reader is referred to these sources for further information and extensive bibliographies.

The Verb Phrase

The predicate function, which is filled by the verb phrase, is central to the existence of the English clause (see Chapter 3), and is crucial to the system of assessment presented in this book. Therefore, this chapter will begin with a presentation of the construction of the verb

Table 4.1. The English Verb Phrase

Verb Phrase Functions

Subject	+ Tense	± Modal	± Perfective	± Continuum	± Passive	+ Head	Direct Object, or Passive Complement
He	(pres)					throws	a ball.
He	(past)					threw	a ball.
A ball	(pres)				is	thrown	by him.
A ball	(past)				was	thrown	by him.
He	(pres)			is		throwing	a ball.
He	(past)			was		throwing	a ball.
He	(pres)		has			thrown	a ball.
He	(past)		had			thrown	a ball.
He	(pres)	can				throw	a ball.
He	(past)	could				throw	a ball.
A ball	(pres)			is	being	thrown	by him.
A ball	(past)			was	being	thrown	by him.
I	(pres)		have	been		throwing	a ball.
I	(past)		had	been		throwing	a ball.
You	(pres)	will	have			thrown	a ball.
You	(past)	would	have			thrown	a ball.
A ball	(pres)		has		been	thrown	by him.
A ball	(past)		had		been	thrown	by him.
We	(pres)	shall		be		throwing	a ball.
We	(past)	should		be		throwing	a ball.
A ball	(pres)		has	been	being	thrown	by him.
A ball	(past)		had	been	being	thrown	by him.
You	(pres)	may	have	been		throwing	a ball.
You	(past)	might	have	been		throwing	a ball.
A ball	(pres)	will	have	been	being	thrown	by him.
A ball	(past)	would	have	been	being	thrown	by him.
Filler Classes:	Present Past	May Can Shall Will Must	HAVE -en	BE -ing	BE -en	STEM	

phrase (VP). It happens that the VP is an easy construction to understand, largely because the functions of the VP do not have a lot of fillers.

The construction of the English verb phrase is presented in Table 4.1.[1] This table is laid out in the same manner as those for the clause types found in Chapter 3. Across the top of the table are listed the obligatory (+) and optional (±) functions of the phrase in the linear sequence in which they appear in the phrase. The filler classes for these functions are listed across the bottom. In the center of the table are examples of how the functions of the VP can appear singly or in combination with the other functions. The only VP function that has been left out of the table is the negative. Inclusion of this function would have complicated the table unnecessarily, and later it will be covered separately. To read the table, choose any horizontal line and read from left to right; when you do, you will find a complete English clause with two or more VP functions expressed. The verb phrases found in the table get increasingly complicated as they approach the bottom of the table. The last two examples would represent the longest possible transitive VP in English if they were negated.

Obligatory Functions

Inspection of the top line of Table 4.1 reveals that there are only two obligatory functions of the verb phrase. That is, in English verb phrases, only the tense and head functions must be expressed; all other functions appear at the option of the speaker.

Tense

Tense is a grammatical concept that is independent of actual time, i.e., tense and time are two totally different things. *Time,* according to the dictionary, refers to "measured or measurable duration." It has reality in that it has an external reference, i.e. all time can be measured in terms of the speed of light, which is an eternal constant.

Tense, however, cannot be measured; in fact, it varies from language to language. It is a grammatical concept that often *refers* to time, but is not measured in terms of time. Strangely enough, past tense in English can be used actually to refer to future time [see (4.23) for one possible example] and present tense can refer to past time [see (4.22) for one example]. While it is true that past tense is *correlated* with past time, the correlation is not perfect, and the two concepts (tense and time) must be separated in our thinking.

Some languages have a number of tenses. Latin for example, has six, as shown in Table 4.2. When tense is applied in Latin, as in all languages, the verb undergoes a change. In Latin, something is added to the stem. Consider the examples in Table 4.2. In each case a change takes place in the verb itself, and we can see that six different grammatical tenses can be expressed in Latin. (Note that the tense markers are underlined in the table.) Because English has only two tenses, an auxiliary is required to express many of the same Latin time references found in Table 4.2. In fact, the translations given in this table show that more than one auxiliary is sometimes required to form the English equivalent to the Latin. Unlike Latin, English verbs have no future tense. Time relationships, like future, are indicated by changes made elsewhere in the English VP.[2]

---

[1] We will refer to this table again and again throughout the section on the VP in this chapter. You might find it helpful to place a bookmark at the table so that you can return to it easily.

[2] The stem of the English verb is seen here as being the present tense form. There have been arguments raised to the effect that there actually is no "present" tense (Trager & Smith, 1957). Those who make this argument claim that there is only "past" and "nonpast" tenses. Either view is acceptable in the present framework.

Table 4.2. Latin Tenses and Their English Equivalents

Tense	Latin Example	English Equivalent
Present	Appell<u>at</u>	He calls.
Imperfect	Appella<u>bat</u>	He called.
Future	Appella<u>bit</u>	He will call.
Perfective	Appella<u>vat</u>	He has called.
Past Perfect	Appella<u>verat</u>	He had called.
Future Perfect	Appella<u>verit</u>	He will have called.

As was stated previously, tense must appear in the English VP.[3] It does not always appear in the head function, i.e., tense is a movable function. If one or more auxiliaries are used in a VP, tense is attached to the first auxiliary that appears. This fact can be seen in Table 4.1, p. 66. In the first two examples in the table, tense is attached to the stem: *throws* versus *threw*. In all of the other examples in the table, however, the stem is tenseless. Note that we do not find verb phrases like those in (4.1)–(4.3) in English. Tense can occur only once in a VP, and it must be attached to the *first* form that appears in the verb phrase:

(4.1) *A ball *is threwn*.

(4.2) *He *was ranging* a bell.

(4.3) *He *might saw* a doctor.

When more than one auxiliary appears in a VP, it is always the first auxiliary appearing in the phrase that is inflected for tense:

(4.4) A ball $\left\{ \begin{array}{c} is \\ was \end{array} \right\}$ being thrown.

(4.5) You $\left\{ \begin{array}{c} will \\ would \end{array} \right\}$ have thrown a ball.

(4.6) She $\left\{ \begin{array}{c} may \\ might \end{array} \right\}$ have been throwing a ball.

Head

The head function of the VP is filled by a verb stem. The stem alone inflected for tense can constitute the VP; it can also appear in its tenseless form when it is preceded by one of the optional VP functions (modal, perfective, continuum, passive or negative; see following).

---

[3]An exception to this will be made in the chapter on transformations (Chapter 5) when we discuss the infinitive VP. In this verb phrase, which only appears in subordinate clauses, tense is never expressed. The point that tense does not appear in the imperative VP has already been made in Chapter 3.

In any case, the head function must be filled in some way or there is no VP. The verb stem that appears can be any transitive or intransitive verb, or the equative verb BE. If the verb is intransitive or equative, no passive function can appear in the VP; only transitive verbs can be made passive.

Optional Functions

The functions of the verb phrase other than tense and head shown in Table 4.1, p. 66, are optional and are used by the speaker only when he wants to use them. These functions are the *modal,* the *perfective,* the *continuum,* the *passive,* and the *negative.*

Modal

The modal auxiliaries are *may, can, will, shall,* and *must.* Their past tense forms are: *might, could, would,* and *should* (*must* has no past tense form). If a modal appears, it invariably occurs first in any VP and tense must be attached to it.

Semantically, modal auxiliaries express moods such as ability, permission, intent, willingness, and obligation, among others. Their use results in clauses such as the following (a most incomplete listing):

(4.7) Alfred
$\left\{ \begin{array}{l} may \\ might \\ can \\ could \\ will \\ would \\ shall \\ should \\ must \end{array} \right\}$
eat the apple
$\left\{ \begin{array}{l} \text{(because he likes apples)} \\ \text{(tomorrow if the mood strikes him)} \\ \text{(because he has strong teeth)} \\ \text{(if he could find it)} \\ \text{(when he wakes up)} \\ \text{(under any circumstances)} \\ \text{(if I have anything to say about it)} \\ \text{(because it's good for him)} \\ \text{(or else)} \end{array} \right\}$

Perfective

The perfective has a *discontinuous filler* because part of it appears in one place and part in another. For this reason we use the shorthand notation at the bottom of Table 4.1 to represent the filler class of this function, i.e., HAVE -*en* represents the entire filler of the perfective function. The HAVE part represents the auxiliary that always appears in this function. The capital letters indicate that it can appear as one of three forms: *have, has,* and *had.* The first two are the present tense forms. Which one is used in the verb phrase depends on what the subject of the clause happens to be. *Has* is used when the subject is *he, she, it,* or any word for which one of these can be substituted, e.g., *John, The green door, My best pipe,* etc. *Have* is the present tense form that is used with all other persons and numbers that fill the subject. This is illustrated by (4.8) and (4.9):

(4.8)
$\left\{ \begin{array}{l} \text{He} \\ \text{She} \\ \text{It} \\ \text{John} \\ \text{The green door} \\ \text{My best pipe} \end{array} \right\}$
has disappeared.

(4.9)
$$\left\{\begin{array}{l} \text{I} \\ \text{You} \\ \text{We} \\ \text{They} \\ \text{Both of my best pipes} \end{array}\right\}$$ *have* disappeared.

Had, the past tense form of this auxiliary, has only one form that appears with all subjects alike:

(4.10)
$$\left\{\begin{array}{l} \text{He} \\ \text{She} \\ \text{It} \\ \text{I} \\ \text{You} \\ \text{We} \\ \text{They} \\ \text{Everybody} \\ \text{Some of my worst enemies} \\ \text{All of the best people} \\ \text{Both} \\ \text{None} \end{array}\right\}$$ *had* gone by the time I got there.

The other part of the filler of this function is represented by the symbol *-en*. This symbol stands for any of the past participle forms of the stem in whatever form it may appear. The past participle is irregular and takes many forms. [See (4.169) below.] There are good historical reasons for the differences in these forms. Any native speaker of English will have no trouble in recognizing them when they appear, however. The point is, we need a shorthand way of talking about all of them at the same time, and whatever notation we choose will be quite arbitrary. The use of *-en* to refer to all of the past participial forms is simply the notation chosen here. Note that this inflection may not always be attached to the verb stem that fills the head function. The little dash in front of the *-en* symbol indicates that it *must* be attached to something, and that something is "whatever appears next in the VP." It may be the stem [(4.11) and (4.13)], the auxiliary of the continuum (4.12), or the auxiliary of the passive (4.14).

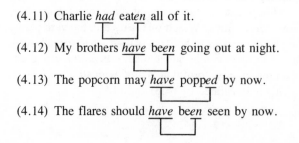

(4.11) Charlie *had* eat*en* all of it.

(4.12) My brothers *have* be*en* going out at night.

(4.13) The popcorn may *have* popp*ed* by now.

(4.14) The flares should *have* be*en* seen by now.

Finally, note the linear sequence of the perfective. If a modal appears, the perfective must follow it. If any other function of the VP appears, the perfective function precedes it.

Semantically, the perfective function of the verb phrase has two major time relationships. For the *present perfective,* i.e., when the auxiliary is inflected for present tense, the time indicated can be one stretching from the indeterminate past to some point up to the present:

(4.15) Solly *has* liv*ed* in Indonesia for ten years.

(4.16) Margaret says she *has* be*en* married all her life.

The present perfective can also indicate completed action at an indefinite time in the past or at some time in the future:

(4.17) Jenny Lou *has* se*en* the Eifel Tower.

(4.18) Margo will *have* eat*en* her breakfast by 9 A.M.

The *past perfective,* i.e., when the auxiliary is inflected for past tense, indicates completed action prior to some point of reference in past time:

(4.19) Igor *had* gon*e* to Rome before they got out of bed.

Continuum

The shorthand notation for the entire filler of the continuum function is BE *-ing*. Like the perfective filler HAVE *-en,* it is discontinuous, i.e., the BE stands for the auxiliary, and the *-ing* stands for the present participial form of the stem (see section on morphology in this chapter). The BE auxiliary, however, is more complicated than HAVE because it has the five forms that appear in Table 4.3 as well as the tenseless form *be*.

In terms of its linear position the BE auxiliary must follow the perfective and any modal that may appear, and it precedes the passive and head functions. It will follow any modal

Table 4.3. Forms of the English Verb BE

Number	Person	Present	Past
singular	I	am	was
	you	are	were
	he, she, it	is	was
plural	we	are	were
	you	are	were
	they	are	were

if there is no perfective, or it appears first in the VP if there is neither modal nor perfective to precede it. Examples similar to the following can be found in Table 4.1, p. 66.

(4.20) I $\left\{ \begin{array}{c} am \\ \underline{was} \end{array} \right\}$ go*ing* home.

(4.21) We will *be* see*ing* them tomorrow.

(4.22) Norris has *be*en fish*ing* all day.

(4.23) I would have *be*en go*ing* today, if I hadn't broken my leg.

Note that when tense is attached to either the modal or perfective function, the form of the auxiliary in the continuum that appears is *be,* not one of the personal forms (*am, are,* etc.). This is the tenseless form of BE, and it must be used if tense is attached to another function in the VP. This is shown in (4.21), where the modal carries tense; in (4.22), where the perfective carries tense; and in (4.23), where the modal again carries tense. In addition, when the perfective and the continuum appear together in the same VP, the *-en* of the perfective filler is attached to the BE of the continuum filler, and the *-ing* of the continuum goes to the end of the next form in the string:

(4.24) I *have be-en go-ing.*

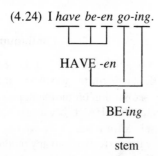

HAVE *-en*

BE-*ing*

stem

(4.25) Winston *had be-en see-ing* spots before his eyes.

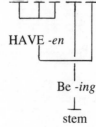

HAVE *-en*

Be *-ing*

stem

Semantically, the continuum refers to ongoing, incomplete, or indefinite action. This action may take place in reference to any time, present, past, or future:

(4.26) My kids *are* bugg*ing* me. (present time)

(4.27) Mama *was* kiss*ing* Santa Claus. (past time)

(4.28) I'll *be* see*ing* you. (future time)

Passive

The passive is a very complicated function and more will be said about it in Chapter 5 when we deal with transformations. For the present, only those grammatical aspects of the passive relevant to the transitive verb phrase will be considered.

The passive can appear only when the VP contains a transitive verb. In a very real sense, therefore, Table 4.1, p. 66 is applicable only to transitive verb phrases. The passive function must be deleted from the table completely when thinking about intransitive and equative verb phrases. Like the perfective and continuum, the passive VP function is discontinuous. It has, as a filler, the auxiliary BE and the past participial form of the verb (which we denote with *-en,* just as we did for the filler of the perfective function). Since it is the last optional function that can appear in the verb phrase, its auxiliary will always fall immediately before the verb stem when it is used, and its inflection will always be attached to the verb stem. All functions other than the head, when they appear, will precede the passive function.

The auxiliary BE is just like the auxiliary in the continuum function. That is, the BE responds to changes in the subject for person, number, and tense (4.29), and it is tenseless when another auxiliary appears (4.30)–(4.32). BE will also have attached to it any inflection that belongs to a previous discontinuous filler as shown in (4.30)–(4.32).

(4.29)

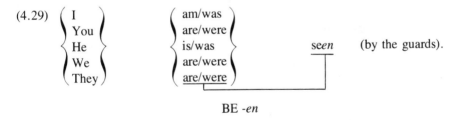

BE *-en*

(4.30) The paper *was be-ing writ-ten* (by the author's son).

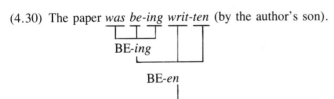

(4.31) That fact *has be-en know-n* (by everyone).

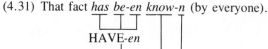

HAVE-*en*

BE-*en*

stem

(4.32) The building *had be-en be-ing discuss-ed* (by the architects).

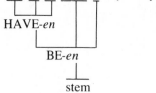

HAVE-*en*

BE-*ing*

BE-*en*

stem

Finally, note that the subject for the passive is not the same as the subject for the active. A glance at Table 4.1 shows that in each case where the passive is used, the subject of the passive clauses would be the direct object of the active clauses. The technical aspects of this will be discussed in Chapter 5.

Negative

The negative was not presented in Table 4.1 because it would have made the table too complicated to read. Basically, it is applied to the VP in a very simple manner: It is attached to whatever carries tense. There are, however, three conditions under which this happens.

Condition #1: Verb Phrases with Auxiliaries

When one or more of the optional functions appears in the VP, the negative is attached to the auxiliary that carries tense. This rule is shown in the following examples:

(4.33) Mayor McNaughton $\left\{ \begin{array}{c} has \\ has\ not \end{array} \right\}$ switched to the Democrats.   (perfective)

(4.34) Lucinda Fluckmeyer $\left\{ \begin{array}{c} may \\ may\ not \end{array} \right\}$ be the best actress ever.   (modal)

(4.35) John $\left\{ \begin{array}{c} is \\ is\ not \end{array} \right\}$ sleeping here tonight.   (continuum)

(4.36) Mr. Tannenbaum $\left\{ \begin{array}{c} was \\ was\ not \end{array} \right\}$ thrown in the water.   (passive)

Since tense is attached to the first auxiliary in the VP, if more than one auxiliary appears, the negative is attached to the first one.[4]

Condition #2: Equative Verb Phrases with No Auxiliaries

When the verb phrase contains the equative verb BE and has no auxiliaries in it, the negative filler *not* is simply attached to the verb stem:

(4.28) I $\left\{ \begin{array}{c} am \\ am\ not \end{array} \right\}$ too sick to go to work.

(4.39) They $\left\{ \begin{array}{c} were \\ were\ not \end{array} \right\}$ home.

*Condition #3: Transitive and Intransitive Verb Phrases
with No Auxiliaries*

When transitive and intransitive verbs appear and there are no auxiliaries to carry tense, an auxiliary must be supplied to carry negation. To do this we use a dummy auxiliary, often called the "dummy DO." It appears before the verb in all cases, and its only purposes are to carry tense, person, third singular markers, and the negative when there is no auxiliary:

(4.40) He calls her "mother."
He *does not* call her "mother."

(4.41) We see the light.
We *do not* see the light.

(4.42) George fell off the stage.
George *did not* fall off the stage.

Look at the differences between (4.40), (4.41), and (4.42). In the first example, the form of the dummy is *does* (third singular subject, present tense). In the second example, the form of the dummy is *do* (other than third singular subject, present tense). In the third example, the form of the dummy is *did* (past tense, all subjects).

The negative can be contracted to most tense-carrying auxiliaries, the dummy, or to the main verb, BE. This is simply a phonological rule: Remove the vowel from the negative and unstress the negative syllable.

(4.43) John *isn't* sleeping here tonight.

(4.44) Mayor McNaughton *hasn't* switched to the Democrats.

(4.45) Lucinda Fluckmeyer *can't* be the best actress ever.

(4.46) We *aren't* all in this together.

---

[4]The rare exception to this rule occurs when special emphasis is given to the negative, i.e., at times the negative can be taken out of its normal position and placed immediately before the verb: "He will be not working." Note the stress and intonational changes that accompany this act.

(4.47) He *doesn't* call her "mother."

(4.48) George *didn't* fall off the stage.

There are a few exceptions to this rule. We do not contract some forms of the modal auxiliaries. It is possible to use contractions like *mightn't, shant,* and *mayn't,* but it is rare actually to hear this done. We also do not contract the first person singular of BE. That is, (4.49) and (4.50) are English, but (4.51) is not:

(4.49) He $\left\{ \begin{array}{c} is \\ isn't \end{array} \right\}$ a bear.

(4.50) We $\left\{ \begin{array}{c} are \\ aren't \end{array} \right\}$ going.

(4.51) I $\left\{ \begin{array}{c} am \\ *amn't \end{array} \right\}$ too old for comfort.

Historically, the word *ain't* comes from the attempt to use a contraction for the first person singular negation of BE. The idea that this is a "bad" word is a social class judgment, not a grammatical rule. Some dialects now use it for all present tense persons and numbers of the negated BE.

Summary: Verb Phrase

The English verb phrase is a construction that can be summarized with the formula presented in Table 4.4. This formula is read: The verb phrase consists of (=) an obligatory (+) tense function that may or may not have negation attached to it; an optional modal filled by *may, can, shall, will* or *must;* an optional perfective function filled by HAVE-*en;* an optional continuum function filled by BE-*ing;* an optional passive function filled by BE -*en;* and an obligatory head function that is filled by a verb stem. Tense is attached to the first function that appears in the verb phrase and may require the dummy DO in transitive and intransitive clauses if there is no other auxiliary. The perfective, continuum, and passive functions are discontinuous, i.e., the auxiliary appears in one place and the inflection is attached to the next element in the string. The DO,

Table 4.4. The English Verb Phrase

$$VP = \left\{ + \text{Tense:} \begin{bmatrix} \text{Present} \\ \text{Past} \end{bmatrix} \pm \text{Negative:} \begin{bmatrix} \text{DO not} \\ \text{not} \end{bmatrix} \right\} \pm \text{Modal:} \left\{ \begin{array}{c} \text{may} \\ \text{can} \\ \text{shall} \\ \text{will} \\ \text{must} \end{array} \right\} \pm \text{Perfective: HAVE -}en$$

$$\pm \text{Continuum: BE -}ing \pm \text{Passive: BE -}en + \text{Head: verb stem } V_t \left\{ \begin{array}{c} V_i \\ V_{BE} \end{array} \right\}$$

HAVE, and BE auxiliaries change forms to agree with the subject of the clause in terms of person, number, and tense. The stem that fills the head function can be a transitive verb, an intransitive verb, or the equative verb BE.

The Noun Phrase

Noun phrases fill the clause-level functions of subject, direct object, indirect object, and complement. They can also fill the head function in prepositional phrases (see the following) as well as play other roles in English clauses. Thus they are very important constructions in English. Noun phrases are also very complicated constructions, partly because they have many functions, and partly because most noun phrase (NP) functions each have several filler classes.

Table 4.5 presents the grammar of the English noun phrase (P. H. Fries, 1972).[5] As we can see from this table, the only obligatory function of the NP is the head, i.e., the only filler a noun phrase needs is a noun.

Proper Nouns and Pronoun Phrases

Note that proper nouns (names of persons, places, or things, such as *John, Antarctica,* or *the Smithsonian Institution*) and pronouns do not fit into Table 4.5 because they are not noun phrases.

Proper nouns are not noun phrases because they cannot be modified the way nouns are modified. We do not hear phrases such as the following:

(4.52) **Merely* the third Oklahoma . . .

(4.53) **Each tall George Bernard Shaw* . . .

Pronouns and pronoun phrases present a similar situation. The following are not noun phrases because the heads of the phrases are not filled by nouns:

(4.54a) *She* ate it all up.

(4.55a) *Three of them* got away.

(4.56a) *The both of them* are in the pit.

Many times we think of pronouns as being only personal, possessive, or reflexive pronouns; but actually, a pronoun can be anything that takes the place of a noun (*pro* is Latin for *for*). The examples (4.54a), (4.55a), and (4.56a) all contain pronoun phrases. One way we can tell that they are pronoun phrases and not noun phrases is to try to make the head of the phrase plural. If this does not work, the word is probably not a noun, and the phrase is not a noun phrase.

(4.54b) **Shes* ate it all up.

---

[5] Again, you may wish to mark the place where this table is found because it will be referred to often in discussing the NP.

Table 4.5. Construction of the Noun Phrase

± Limiter	± Determiner$_1$	± Determiner$_2$	± Determiner$_3$	± Loose-Knit Modifier	± Close-Knit Modifier	+ Head	± Restrictive Modifier	± Nonrestrictive Modifier
		the		large		men		
		my				men	in the room	
	all	the			rubber	erasers		on my left,
	both	the	two			boys,		
		the	several	long-playing		records		
			three	brand new	car	doors		
		these		yellow	notebook	paper		
		John's				thousands of people		
		the				both of them		
		our				duty to succeed		
	almost half	the		new	motor-driven / steamship	era		
		our neighbor's		new	long-playing	record		
		the			men's store	cabinet	in the corner	
Only	Quantity phrase	Possessor phrase	Numeral phrase	Adjective phrase	Nominal phrase	Noun	Adverbial	Adverbial
Just		Indefinite article	Numeral comparison phrase		Genitival phrase	Complex nominal	Adjective phrase	Adjective phrase
Even		Definite phrase	Quantifier phrase				Prepositional phrase	Prepositional phrase
At least								
Particularly								
Especially								
Merely								

Source. Adapted from *Tagmemic Sequences in the English Noun Phrase* by P. H. Fries. Santa Ana, Calif.: Summer Institute of Linguistics, 1972. Reprinted by permission.

(4.55b) **Threes of them* got away.

(4.56b) **The boths of them* are in the pit.

This test does not work with mass nouns (words like *milk, sand,* or *police*). Native speakers should have no difficulty recognizing these words, however. Just in case, another test is to try to use the optional modifiers of the noun phrase (see the following sections) in the phrase. Since the major feature of pronoun phrases is the fact that they are not constructed like noun phrases, they will not sound right when the optional modifiers are added:

(4.54c) **The big she* ate it all up. (det.$_2$ * and close-knit modifier)

(4.55c) **Seven three of them* got away. (det.$_3$)

(4.56c) **The two both of them* are in the pit. (det.$_3$)

Because the optional prenoun modifiers cannot be used in the phrases in the above examples, the constructions are not noun phrases. Rather, they are pronoun phrases. They fill the same clause-level functions that a noun phrase can fill, however (e.g., subject of the clause).

Obligatory Functions

As stated previously, the only function that must be filled in a noun phrase is the head function. All other functions are optional.

Head

As shown in Table 4.5, the head must appear in order for a noun phrase to exist. At the least, it must contain a noun. Clearly, then, a noun phrase can consist of a single word:

(4.57) *Waitresses* are women.

(4.58) *Pictures* hung everywhere.

Complex Nominals

The head function can also be filled by more than a single word. Complex nominal constructions that can fill the head function behave exactly as a single word would behave in the head slot. Their construction is illustrated in Table 4.6. You can see that the complex nominal construction itself has two functions: (*a*) a head filled by a noun; this word can be inflected for plural (*torrents of sound*); and (*b*) a completion that begins with the words *of, that,* or *to* and ends with either a clause or a phrase.

As stated before, complex nominals behave as if they were a single word. The entire construction fills the head function of the noun phrase. This means that (*a*) the complex nominal may appear all by itself with none of the other functions of the noun phrase present (just as can any head); or (*b*) it can be modified by any of the optional NP modifiers of the head, just as is true of any other head of a NP.

---

[6]Defined on p. 82.

Table 4.6. Construction of the Complex Nominal

+ Head	+ Completion
threshold	of hearing
torrent	of sound
surface	of the water
number	of people
duty	to succeed
wish	to be someplace else
desire	to gain entry
need	to win
fear	that he would fail
understanding	that he would inherit everything
possibility	that they did not understand
fact	that they were there

(4.59) *Duty to succeed* is sometimes more important than life itself.

(4.60) *All their desires to be someplace else* were in vain.

Note that Table 4.6 shows both phrases and whole clauses filling the completion function of the complex nominal. At this point it is best not to say much about the use of clauses in this slot, since this topic will be handled in Chapter 5. The whole group of *of* completions, however, requires a few comments. There are two classes of *of* completions. The first is illustrated in the following examples:

(4.61) A new *frame of time* is needed.

(4.62) The *city of New York* went broke.

In these examples, the head of the complex nominal represents an entire class of things, and the completion represents the specific member of that class to which the speaker is referring. Thus, there are many "frames," but *frame of time* is a specific member of that class. There are also many cities of which *New York* is only one member of the class. Note how this opens up the possibility of metaphor:

(4.63) The *torrent of sound* . . .

(4.64) The *threshold of hearing* . . .

In (4.63) we have a metaphor in that the word *torrent*, which usually refers to water, refers here to sound. In (4.63) a *threshold* is part of a doorway, but here it refers to the point at which we begin to hear a stimulus that has previously been too soft or too low in frequency to hear.

The second group of *of* completions are almost the opposite of the first. This situation is illustrated by the following:

(4.65) A *cube of ice* fell on the floor.

(4.66) The *top of the morning* to you.

In both of these examples, the head of the complex nominal refers to a part of the unit that the completion refers to. Thus, *ice* is the whole, while *cube* is the part; and *morning* is the whole while *top* is the part. Table 4.6 gives additional examples.

Optional Functions

The other functions listed in Table 4.5 are optional; they do not have to be expressed. The table reflects the normal sequencing of these functions. In fact, this sequence is actually what defines the functions. However, the order of some may be permuted by the speaker when he feels that strong emphasis is needed. In addition, some of the functions can be repeated and some may appear only once in the NP. These variations will be illustrated as appropriate.

Limiter

The limiter function is filled by one of only a small group of words. These words are listed at the bottom of Table 4.5. If the limiter is used, it will appear first in the NP, and it can appear only once in any individual NP. Some examples of its use are the following:

(4.66) *Only* a few men came to the party. (the rest stayed home)

(4.67) *Even* the least of them will be saved. (along with everybody else)

(4.68) *Especially* the last ones should be warned. (because they are the ones in the greatest danger)

Carefully observe that most of the words that fill the limiter function can also function as adverbs, and that confusion as to which function they fill is possible. Note that changes in meaning will accompany changes in function for the words that are italicized in the previous examples:

(4.70) A few men came *only* to the party. (They did not go to the other places: adverb)

(4.71) The least of them will be saved *even*. (In spite of all of the problems this causes: adverb)

(4.72) The last ones should be *especially* warned. (Take particular care to warn them: adverb)

Adverbs not only function differently grammatically (they fill clause-level functions whereas the limiter fills a noun phrase function), they also communicate different meanings. That is, limiters can modify only the head in the noun phrase, while adverbs modify either adjectives or the head verb in the verb phrase (but not the head of the NP).

The result is that the meaning of the message communicated changes along with the change in function.

Determiner₁

The determiner₁ (det.₁) is filled by a quantity phrase that always has the possibility of being followed by a det.₂ (Table 4.5). This phrase may be a single word or a group of words, but in each case the head of this quanity phrase is a word from the following list:

(4.73) all   half
       both   double
                twice
                one-fourth
                etc.

If there is no limiter, the det.₁ will be the first function in the noun phrase when it occurs, and it will occur only once in any single NP. It can be qualified, as in the following examples:

(4.74) *Almost all* the people there were sober.

(4.75) *Slightly less than one-tenth* the population knows what is going on.

Determiner₂

The det.₂ function can be filled by a definite phrase, an indefinite article, or a possessor phrase (Table 4.5, p. 78). It will appear first in the NP if there is no limiter or det.₁, and it usually precedes all of the other NP functions when it appears. It need not appear at all, however:

(4.76) Lovely sounds filled the air.

(4.77) Men came over to us.

Definite Phrases

Definite phrases constitute one filler class of the det.₂ and consist of a definite article (*the*), a demonstrative pronoun (*this, that, these, those*), or a phrase containing one of these (Table 4.5). It results in NPs such as the following:

(4.78) $\begin{Bmatrix} The \\ That \\ This \end{Bmatrix}$ boy you were talking to is very nice.

The definite phrase can be more than one word. For example, the demonstratives and the definite article can be intensified by the use of *very*.

(4.79) $\begin{Bmatrix} The \\ These \\ Those \end{Bmatrix}$ *very* people who said they wouldn't, did, in fact, eat the stuff.

Indefinite Articles

Indefinite articles form a second class of fillers of the Det.$_2$ function. These are listed in (4.80):

(4.80) $\begin{Bmatrix} A\ (an) \\ Any \\ Each \\ Every \\ Some \\ No \end{Bmatrix}$ man is an island.

For both definite and indefinite articles, we can find instances in which adjective intensifiers can be placed in front of the article of the det.$_2$ for the sake of providing emphasis. In fact, there are even times when the adjectives themselves can appear before the indefinite article:

(4.81) He comes from *quite a* good family.   (adjective intensifier in front of article)

(4.82) This is *too difficult a* task to do. (adjective phrase in front of article)

These are unusual instances, however, and ordinarily the linear position of the det.$_2$ is fixed between the det.$_1$ and the det.$_3$ as shown in Table 4.5.

Possessor Phrases

Possessor phrases are the third filler class of the det.$_2$ function. These possessors may be as simple as a possessive pronoun:

(4.83) *His* job was getting him down.

(4.84) *My* feeling is that it is too much for him to handle.

Possessives can also become very complicated, however. One form of the possessor is the genitive inflection (-'s) that is attached only to noun phrases. The entire possessor noun phrase then functions as a det.$_2$ for the head noun in another noun phrase:

(4.85)

NP		
D$_2$		Head
NP	Genitive	
The boy	's	bicycle

was stolen last night

Not only this, but the possessor phrase is repeatable, i.e., it can be nested over and over again, noun phrase within noun phrase. Each time it recurs, the det.$_2$ genitive inflection is attached to another noun phrase. Figure 4.1 shows how this works. Each individual level

									Clause	
								Subject		Predicate
								NP		VP
					Det.$_2$				Head	
			NP				Genitive			
		Det.$_2$			Head					
	NP			Genitive						
Det.$_2$			Head							
NP		Genitive								
Det.$_2$	Head									
My	wife	's	brother	's	daughter	's	boyfriend			came in.

Figure 4.1. Noun phrases nested within the possessor filler of the determiner$_2$ function.

Source. Adapted from *Tagmeme Sequences in the English Noun Phrase* by P. H. Fries. Santa Ana, Calif.: Summer Institute of Linguistics, 1972. Reprinted by permission.

in the figure is a noun phrase, and all but the top level contain a noun phrase within a noun phrase. As we rise through successive levels in the figure, each noun phrase can be inflected for possession, and the '*s* genitive inflection makes each NP act as a separate det.$_2$. Thus, the entire NP in one box becomes part of a det.$_2$ in the box immediately above it. The process can be repeated as often as the speaker wishes to repeat it, and each time the same thing occurs. Many functions of many constructions are capable of being repeated in much the same manner. It is this possibility for "nesting" that enables us to say that there is no such thing as "the longest clause" in English. As soon as you produce whatever you think would be the longest clause or sentence, you would find that some function or other could be repeated and the clause or sentence becomes longer than it was. In the present case of the det.$_2$, it is even possible to embed another whole clause within

			Clause	
			Subject	Predicate
		NP		VP
	Det.$_2$			Head
	NP		Genitive	
The man I saw yesterday			's	briefcase	disappeared.

Figure 4.2. Noun phrase with subordinated clause inflected for possession in a determiner$_2$.

Source. Adapted from P. H. Fries, ibid.

the noun phrase and to inflect it for possession, as shown in Figure 4.2 (the embedded clause in Figure 4.2 fills the restrictive modifier function: see the following and Chapter 5). The NP *The man I saw yesterday* is inflected for possession and functions as a det.$_2$ for the head noun *briefcase*. The NP *The man I saw yesterday's briefcase* fills the subject function of the entire sentence.

Noun phrases can become very complicated. It is small wonder that it takes years for children to learn some of the complications.

Determiner$_3$

The det.$_3$ is filled by either a *numeral phrase,* a *numeral comparison phrase,* or a *quantifier phrase* (Table 4.5). It follows the limiter, det.$_1$, and det.$_2$ functions if they appear and precedes all other functions of the NP if they occur.

(4.86) *Three* men came in.

(4.87) The other *three* men came in.

(4.88) The *three* big men came in.

There are special cases, however, when the loose-knit modifier (see following section) can precede the det.$_3$ for the sake of providing emphasis:

(4.89) Those big *three* men came in.   (emphasis, adjective out of its normal position)

The three filler classes of the det.$_3$ are as follows:

Numeral Phrases

Numeral phrases can consist of a single number (4.90) or they can be qualified numbers, as shown in (4.91) and (4.92).

(4.90) *Thirty* people blocked his view.

(4.91) *Almost seven hundred* fruitflies filled the jar.

(4.92) *Nearly twenty-five* windows were open that day.

Numeral Comparison Phrases

Numeral comparison phrases do not count anything. Rather, they assume a point of reference and compare a number to that point. For example, the following have points of reference:

(4.93) *More than twenty* people attended the rally.

(4.94) *Far fewer* chickens *than the hundred we expected* fell off the bus.

Note that the comparison phrases in the det.$_3$ can be discontinuous, i.e., part can appear in one place and part in another, just like the discontinuous fillers in the verb phrase. In

(4.94) the head of the NP appears between parts of the det.$_3$ function. Perhaps the complicated nature of this construction reflects the difficulty children have in learning how to conserve quantity, as Piaget has pointed out (Flavell, 1963).

Quantifier Phrase

Using quantifier phrases, we can talk about numbers of things without actually using numbers:

(4.95) $\left\{ \begin{array}{c} Some \\ Many \end{array} \right\}$ men were there.

Note the possibility of confusing the word *some* that fills the det.$_3$ slot with the same form that is an indefinite article and can fill the det.$_2$ slot:

(4.96) *Some* man was there. (det.$_2$ filler)

The quantity word can also be qualified:

(4.97) $\left\{ \begin{array}{c} Very \\ Awfully\ few \\ Many \end{array} \right\}$ races were run that day.

(4.98) *Hardly any* sand got in her boots.

(4.99) *Rather little* milk was consumed at the picnic.

Some people get stuck on the difference between the quantity phrase filler of the det.$_1$ function and the fillers of the det.$_3$. Two comments are relevant here: (*a*) the items in the det.$_1$ quantity phrase come from a very restricted list (see 4.73); and (*b*) it is always possible to have a det.$_2$ follow a det.$_1$, but almost never can a det.$_2$ follow a det.$_3$. For example, only one of the following utterances is grammatical:

(4.100) *All* the people had a good time. (det.$_1$)

(4.101) *Many the people had a good time. (det.$_3$, if the article is deleted)

Loose-Knit Modifier

The loose-knit modifier (LKM) is filled by an adjective phrase. (See Table 4.5, p. 78.) There are a number of subtypes of this filler, but all are adjectival in nature, i.e., all characterize the head noun in some way. Also, most loose-knit modifiers can be restated as complements in a Type I equative clause (see Chapter 3). In addition, most can be inflected for comparative and superlative (see the following section on morphology). Thus, all of the following are adjectival in nature, and each of the italicized words in the left-hand column are loose-knit modifiers.

(4.102) The *old* lady $\Longleftrightarrow$ The lady is *old*. (*older, oldest*)

(4.103) *Complete* knowledge $\Longleftrightarrow$ The knowledge is *complete*. (*more complete, most complete*)

(4.104) His *quick* moves $\Longleftrightarrow$ His moves are *quick*. (*quicker, quickest*)

Note how different all of the above are from those words that are close-knit modifiers (CKM) (see also section which follows):

(4.105) *Hospital* gardens... $\Longleftrightarrow$ *The gardens are *hospital*.

(4.106) The *pool* bottom... $\Longleftrightarrow$ *The bottom is *pool*.

The italicized words in (4.105) and (4.106) do not characterize the head nouns in the same way as do the words found in (4.102)–(4.104) because the words in the first group are adjectives, while those in the second group are both nouns (i.e., they can both be inflected for plurality, for example). While it gets a little more complicated than these examples might indicate, the examples (and the relations they present) show the essential differences between loose-knit and close-knit modifiers: loose-knit modifiers are adjectival in nature and close-knit modifiers are nominal.

Loose-knit modifiers can be repeated for as long as we can keep track of them:

(4.107) It was a *long, hot, dry, windy, brown, distasteful* summer.

The filler of the LKM is an adjective phrase. The simplest of these phrases contains just an adjective, such as *young, various,* or *recent*.

(4.108) The *old* man

(4.109) *Free* particles

Loose-knit modifiers can be repeated, and when they are repeated, each adjective in the string modifies the head noun in the noun phrase. Observe that the following phrases remain grammatical when the second LKM is deleted:

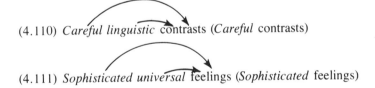

(4.110) *Careful linguistic* contrasts (*Careful* contrasts)

(4.111) *Sophisticated universal* feelings (*Sophisticated* feelings)

Many adjective phrases are more complicated than these examples. Adverbs, for example, can modify the head of the adjective phrase. In contrast to the previous examples, see how removal of the adjective makes the phrase ungrammatical:

(4.112) An *especially unflavorable* influence (*An *especially* influence)

(4.113) *Systematically misleading* data (*Systematically* data)

In (4.112) and (4.113) the entire phrase fills the LKM function, whereas in (4.110) and (4.111) there are two separate adjective phrases, and thus, two separate loose-knit modifiers.

Most adjective phrases can also contain intensifiers. They usually consist of words like *very* or *truly*.

(4.114) *Truly systematically misleading* data

(4.115) *Very sophisticated universal* feelings

The intensifiers and qualifiers used in this manner are all part of the adjective phrase, i.e., they tell us things like *how much* and *to what degree* the adjective phrase applies.

Ordinals

Included in the category of adjective phrases would be the ordinal numeral phrases:

(4.116) The *first* boy in line smiled broadly.

Unlike other adjectives, however, ordinals cannot be repeated,

(4.117) *The *first second* boys

but they can be modified by cardinal numerals when the cardinal numeral precedes the ordinal:

(4.118) The *six first* swimmers swam in the final heat. (loose-knit modifier)

Note, however, what happens when the ordinal numeral is first:

(4.119) The *first six* swimmers got medals. (determiner$_3$)

In (4.118) the reference is to the six swimmers who were first in several heats, but in (4.119) the reference is to the six swimmers who beat everybody else in one race. These examples demonstrate that, when combined with cardinal numerals, the ordinals are loose-knit modifiers only when they follow the cardinal numeral. When they precede the cardinal numeral, they are part of the det.$_3$.

Ordinal phrases, like all adjective phrases, can be qualified, but only to a limited extent because of semantic constraints. We can say:

(4.120) The *very* $\left\{ \begin{array}{l} first \\ last \end{array} \right\}$ house on the block is mine.

(4.121) He lives in the *very next-to-the-last* house on the block.

but we cannot say:

(4.122) *He lives in the *very ninth* house on the block.

Derived Adjectives

Another group of adjective phrases are those whose adjectives are formed by derivation from another part of speech (see the following section on morphology). There are three derivations to be considered: *-ing* adjectives, *-en* adjectives, and the adverbial adjectives.

1. *-ing adjectives* are those that are related to the continuum function in the verb phrase. They are formed by adding *-ing* to a verb. They then fill the loose-knit modifier function as do other adjectives. This is shown in the following examples:

(4.123) The *running* water ⟺ The water is *running*.

(4.124) The *increasing* mass ⟺ The mass is *increasing*.

2. *-en adjectives* are those that are related to either the passive or the perfective functions in the verb phrase. In either case, the adjective is formed by taking the past participial form of the verb and placing it in the loose-knit modifier slot:

(4.125) *Unwritten* Viking traditions ⟺ The Viking traditions *are unwritten*.

(4.126) The *closed* book ⟺ The book *was closed*.

(4.127) The *slipped* disc ⟺ The disc *has slipped*.

3. Another group of derived adjectives are those that are derived from adverbials.

Manner adjectives are related to adverbs of manner (those that tell "how" something happens).

(4.128) The *slow* traffic ⟺ The traffic moves *slowly*.

(4.129) The *rapid* fish ⟺ Fish swim *rapidly*.

Adverbial adjectives are those adjectives that are related to other adverbs that end in *-ly*, as in the following:

(4.130) An *absolute* nut ⟺ An *absolutely nutty* man.

(4.131) A *spotless* white ⟺ *Spotlessly white* clothes.

(4.132) A *complete* bookworm ⟺ He is *completely* a bookworm.

Close-Knit Modifiers

The close-knit modifier (CKM) function of the noun phrase is filled by a nominal phrase or a genitive (Table 4.5).

Just as the loose-knit modifier is adjectival in nature, the close-knit modifier is nominal, or noun-like in nature; i.e., it can be inflected for singular or plural:

(4.133) A *peach* basket

(4.134) The *careers* seminar

The CKM always follows the LKM (if there are any) and immediately precedes the head function (Table 4.5). When it appears, the CKM is repeatable:

(4.135) The *state tree surgeons'* association

In this example, the association is both one that functions on a state-wide basis, and one that is composed of tree surgeons. Both of these CKMs modify the head noun of the noun phrase.

Like the adjective phrase that fills the LKM function, nominal phrases can consist of more than one word. In these cases, the noun in the nominal phrase can be modified:

(4.136) The *blue collar* worker

The words that precede the noun in a nominal phrase may be either nouns, as in (4.135) or (4.137), or adjectives, as in (4.136).

(4.137) The *hospital garden exit door* handle (came loose)

(4.138) The *brown bag* lunch

Genitival Phrase

The other filler of the CKM function is a genitival phrase. This phrase could be confused with the genitive in the det.$_2$, except for the fact that the genitive in the CKM has nothing to do with possession. There is a distinct difference between the genitives in the following examples:

(4.139) The *man's* store burned down.

(4.140) The *men's* store burned down.

In (4.139), a store owned by a specific man burned down, but in (1.140), we are told that a store for men burned down, not a store owned by men—it could, in fact, be a store wholly owned by women or children. The genitive in (4.140) indicates "type of store," not possession. Only (4.139) contains a det.$_2$; (4.140) contains a CKM.

Derived Nouns

Many fillers of the CKM are nouns that are derived from other parts of speech. There are two major classes of these: (*a*) -*ing* nouns and (*b*) -*en* nouns.

1. -*ing nouns* look much like the -*ing* adjectives, but they are related to the gerund (see Chapter 5) rather than the continuum.

(4.141) *Jamming* transmitters ⟺ Transmitters for jamming

(4.142) *Shopping* centers ⟺ Centers for shopping

There are also a group of two-word -*ing* nouns:

(4.143) *Ocean-going* steamships ⟺ Steamships that go on the ocean

(4.144) *Man-eating* sharks ⟺ Sharks that eat men

2. -*en nouns* are related to the passive function of the verb phrase. Like -*en* adjectives, they use the past participial form:

(4.145) *Downtrodden* people ⟺ The people are downtrodden.

(4.146) *Controlled* emotions ⟺ The emotions are controlled.

Post-Noun Modifiers

There are two post-noun modifiers, *restrictive* and *nonrestrictive,* in the NP. We will not say much about them in this chapter. For the most part, they are complicated modifiers because they are often filled by a clause:

(4.147) The boy *who ate the bacon* went home sick.

It is best to wait until Chapter 5 to talk about this class of fillers of these functions. Less complicated phrases, either adverbials or adjectical phrases, also fill the exact same functions.

Restrictive Modifiers

One of the post-noun modifiers is called a *restrictive modifier* of the head noun. The terminology is due to the fact that restrictive modifiers specify the head noun, and in one way or another differentiate it from all other possible members of the semantic class indicated in the meaning of the noun. The following are restrictive modifiers; note how they all answer the question ''Which *noun?*''

(4.148) The man *in the black suit* followed us.

(4.149) The car *near the lamp post* was demolished.

(4.150) This cow *here* is a good one.

Restrictive modifiers can be adjective phrases, as in the following examples:

(4.151) That hill *yonder* is the one we will climb.

(4.152) The town *twenty miles back* was the one we wanted.

Many of these adjective phrases will be formed just like the ones found in the loose-knit modifier, i.e., there are *-ing* and *-en* adjective phrases that can function as restrictive modifiers:

(4.153) The crocks *containing the beer* are the ones I want. *(-ing)*

(4.154) It is a dream *come true*. *(-en)*

(4.155) The theories *shown false* were discarded. *(-en)*

Nonrestrictive Modifiers

There is one other kind of post-noun modifier, called a *nonrestrictive modifier*. This modifier is constructed very much like the restrictive modifier, except that instead of delineating the head noun from all other members of that class, it simply provides more information about the head noun. Very often the head noun doesn't need any more specification because we already know which one it is—perhaps we have been told earlier in a conversation, or perhaps we just know. In any case, when it is used, the nonrestrictive modifier supplies us with more information. Like the restrictive modifiers, the nonrestrictive modifier function can be filled by clauses, adverbials, or adjective phrases:

(4.156) Albert, *who was wearing a black suit,* looked great.

(4.157) Francine, *from the back of the room,* shouted something sweet.

(4.158) This man, *so powerful,* wept like a baby.

(4.159) That little boy, *skipping along,* reminded me of someone I knew.

(4.160) The paper, *driven by the wind,* flew to the top of the tree.

Note the commas that appear in each example above. These do not appear with the restrictive modifiers when they are written down. They indicate the nonrestrictive nature of the modifier. They also reflect the fact that the spoken nonrestrictive modifier has an intonational contour that the restrictive modifier does not. Indeed, it is often true that the only way we can tell whether a post-nominal modifier is restrictive or nonrestrictive is by listening to whether or not it is set off from the rest of the clause by the intonational contour. Try reading the following examples aloud, and listen for the difference in intonation:

(4.161) The story with all its attendant problems looked good.

(4.162) The story, with all its attendant problems, looked good.

Example (4.161) contains a restrictive modifier, while (4.162) contains a nonrestrictive modifier.

Summary: Noun Phrase

The English noun phrase is a complicated construction. Partly this is due to the fact that it has many functions and many fillers of those functions. Partly, the NP is complicated due to the ability of some words and phrases to act as fillers of several different functions. In the following examples, observe how the same word appears in three different functions (note the stress changes):

(4.163) Ónly the man came in. (limiter)

(4.164) The man *only* cáme in. (adverbial)

(4.165) The man ónly came in. (restrictive modifier)

Other noun phrases, moreover, can be embedded within the det.$_2$ and the close-knit modifier, which means that some functions can occur several times, each within a different noun phrase.

The rule for constructing the NP is presented in Table 4.7. This is presented in the same manner as the rule for the VP (Table 4.4); it is a summary of Table 4.5, p. 78 and all that

Table 4.7. The English Noun Phrase

$$
NP = \pm \text{Limiter:} \begin{Bmatrix} \text{only} \\ \text{merely} \\ \text{just} \\ \text{even} \\ \text{at least} \\ \text{particularly} \\ \text{especially} \end{Bmatrix} \pm \text{Determiner}_1 : \text{Quantity Phrase} \pm \text{Determiner}_2 : \begin{Bmatrix} \text{Possessor Phrase} \\ \text{Indefinite Article} \\ \text{Definite Phrase} \end{Bmatrix}
$$

$$
\pm \text{Determiner}_3 : \begin{Bmatrix} \text{Numeral Phrase} \\ \text{Numeral Comparison} \\ \text{Phrase} \\ \text{Quantifier Phrase} \end{Bmatrix} \pm \text{Loose-Knit Modifier: Adjective Phrase}
$$

$$
\pm \begin{matrix} \text{Close-Knit} \\ \text{Modifier:} \end{matrix} \begin{Bmatrix} \text{Nominal Phrase} \\ \text{Genitival Phrase} \end{Bmatrix} + \text{Head:} \begin{Bmatrix} \text{Noun} \\ \text{Complex Nominal} \end{Bmatrix}
$$

$$
\pm \text{Restrictive Modifier:} \begin{Bmatrix} \text{Adverbial} \\ \text{Adjective Phrase} \\ \text{Prepositional Phrase} \end{Bmatrix} \pm \begin{matrix} \text{Nonrestrictive} \\ \text{Modifier:} \end{matrix} \begin{Bmatrix} \text{Adverbial} \\ \text{Adjective Phrase} \\ \text{Prepositional Phrase} \end{Bmatrix}
$$

has been said in the preceding section. It is read as follows: The English noun phrase consists of an optional limiter filled by the words *only, merely, just, even, at least, particularly, especially;* an optional det.$_1$ filled by a quantity phrase; an optional det.$_2$ filled by either a possessor phrase, an indefinite article, or a definite phrase; an optional det.$_3$ filled by a numeral phrase, a numeral comparison phrase, or a quantifier phrase; an optional LKM filled by an adjective phrase; an optional CKM filled by a nominal phrase or a genitival phrase; an obligatory head filled by a noun or a complex nominal; an optional restrictive modifier filled by an adverbial, an adjective phrase; or a prepositional phrase; and an optional nonrestrictive modifier filled by an adverbial, adjective phrase or a prepositional phrase.

Some Semantic Aspects of the Noun Phrase

One of the interesting things about semantics is the fact that meaning is not necessarily tied to grammatical function. In Chapter 3, for example, we saw how the semantic actor function can coincide with either the grammatical subject or object function. But even this is not the whole story, and the actor function can provide us with good examples of some of the complexities involved.

We will very often find that the actor is contained in a noun phrase. Just as often as not, it will be expressed in the head of that noun phrase:

(4.166) The *professor* teaches students.

The head has no monopoly on the actor when it does appear in the noun phrase, however. Here is an example in which it appears in a LKM:

(4.167) *Professorial* teaching of students

and in the det.$_2$:

(4.168) The *professor's* teaching of students

In short, semantic functions are moveable. P. H. Fries (1972; personal communications) has shown some of the range of possibilities for manipulation of semantic functions within the noun phrase. In this section I will provide a very rough synopsis of some of his work just to illustrate the possibilities available. For a more complete presentation the interested reader should consult Fries's grammar of the noun phrase (1972). Once more I must state that the main thrust of TALK is the development of grammar, not of semantics.

Illustrations of Complexity in the Relationships between Grammar and Semantics

One of the grammatical fillers of the det.$_2$ function is the possessor. This function can carry a number of semantic functions, and possession is far from being a simple matter. Through the genitive inflection we may indicate *alienable* possession, or those things that can be separated from their owners:

(4.169) *Maxine's* castle (Maxine owns a castle.)

(4.170) The *general's* medals (The general has medals.)

We may also indicate *inalienable* possession, or those things that cannot be separated from their owner without destroying the possession itself:

(4.171) *Ralph's* toes

(4.172) *Mendenhall's* life

Not only are these types of possession expressed by the possessive filler of the det.$_2$, but semantic relationships that have nothing to do with possession are also expressible, such as *source:*

(4.173) The *reporter's* story (The reporter wrote the story.)

(4.174) *Altman's* movie (Altman made the movie.)

or *actor:*

(4.175) The *sailor's* request (The sailor made the request.)

(4.176) The *elephant's* charge (The elephant charged.)

patient:

(4.77) The *prisoner's* release (They released the prisoner.)

(4.78) The *Forsyths'* story (The story is about the Forsyths.)

or even *time:*

(4.179) *Yesterday's* newspaper (The newspaper that appeared yesterday.)

(4.178) *Tomorrow's* generation (The generation that will appear at a future time.)

There are many more examples that could be given. The loose-knit modifier can express attribute, action, time, modality, and place, and the close-knit modifier can express, among other things, agent, patient, time, place, measure, and purpose. The point is that there is great complexity to learning a language that we are just now beginning to sort out. With all of our sophistication in our ability to develop methods for teaching children with developmental disabilities, we are still just scratching the surface. Such fantastic complexity, even on the phrase level, leads us to believe that we would be able to do little teaching indeed were it not for the fact that we can get along by actually doing a lot less than we believe we do. The children, even the lowest functioning ones, still must sort out most of the data by themselves. The most we can do is to provide them with some direction and help them look for the next logical area of concentration.

Prepositional Phrases

Prepositional phrases have two functions: the *relator* function, filled by a preposition, and the *axis* function, filled by a noun phrase, an adverb, or another prepositional phrase

Table 4.8. Construction of the Prepositional Phrase

Functions: +	Relator	+	Axis
	in		the water
	at		that time
	with		great care
	without		any profit
	due to		his stopping
	about		then
	for		after the movie
Filler Classes:	Preposition		Noun Phrase
			Adverb
			Prepositional Phrase

(which means that we can nest them). The prepositional phrase construction is shown in Table 4.8.

The list of prepositions filling the relator function in the prepositional phrase is finite, and appears in Table 4.9. Note that the preposition itself does not have to be a single word such as *in* or *on*. It can, in fact, be two words, or even what is called a *phrasal preposition,* which consists of two prepositions with a word like *regard,* or *behalf* between them.

The prepositional phrase can fill a number of different functions, both on the clause level and on the phrase level. We have already seen, for example, that a prepositional phrase can fill the adverbial function in a clause (Chapter 3). The most common semantic functions filled by these phrases are *time* (tells when), *place* (tells where), and *manner* (tells how):

(4.181) Mr. Windle was sitting *by the window*. (place)

(4.182) Mr. Windle was sitting *at four o'clock*. (time)

(4.183) Mr. Windle was sitting *with great dignity*. (manner)

These functions can appear singly, as in the previous examples, or they can be combined:

(4.184) Mr. Windle was sitting *by the window with great dignity at four o'clock*.

The linear sequence these functions usually have is:

place–manner–time

Sometimes the adverbial of time can precede the adverbial of manner, but this occurrence is relatively unusual. Neither time nor manner usually precede the adverbial of place:

(4.185) *Mr. Windle was sitting *at four o'clock with great dignity by the window*.

Table 4.9. English Prepositions

Single-Word Prepositions

about	before	during	opposite	through
above	behind	except	out	under
across	below	for	over	unlike
after	beneath	from	per	up
against	beside	in	regarding	upon
along	between	like	round	until
amid	beyond	near	since	unto
among	concerning	of	toward	with
around	considering	off	till	within
as	despite	on	to	without
at	down			

Two-Word Prepositions

across from	down from	off of	together with
along with	due to	onto	up to
along side of	except for	out of	up with
apart from	inside of	outside of	
away from	instead of	over to	
back of	into	throughout	

Phrasal Prepositions

in regard to	by means of	on top of
on account of	in addition to	in behalf of
in spite of	in front of	on behalf of

Two other semantic functions that prepositional phrases can fill are those of *instrument* (what is used to carry out the action) and *accompaniment* (that which is in the presence of the actor):

(4.186) Players are supposed to hit the ball *with the bat*. (instrument)

(4.187) O'Rourke sat *with his beer*. (accompaniment)

We have also seen, in the section on the noun phrase in this chapter, that the prepositional phrase can fill the completion function of a complex nominal that fills the head function of a noun phrase:

(4.188) The state *of the art* was deplorable.

We have also seen how prepositional phrases can fill restrictive and nonrestrictive modifier functions in the noun phrase:

(4.189) The man *in the rear* sat down. (restrictive modifier)

(4.190) The lady, *with her poodle*, got right on the elevator. (nonrestrictive modifier)

Table 4.10. The English Prepositional Phrase

$$\text{Prepositional Phrase} = +\text{ Relator: Preposition} + \text{Axis:} \begin{cases} \text{Noun Phrase} \\ \text{Adjective Phrase} \\ \text{Adverb} \\ \text{Prepositional Phrase} \end{cases}$$

Summary: Prepositional Phrases

Prepositional phrases have the functions of relator, filled by a preposition; and axis, filled by a noun phrase, an adverb, an adjective phrase, or another prepositional phrase. This is presented in Table 4.10. Prepositional phrases can fill adverbial and adjunct functions on the clause level, or they can fill restrictive and nonrestrictive modifier functions, and head completion functions in noun phrases.

Morphology

Some early childhood educators seem to treat certain aspects of morphology as being most of what there is to a language. In the present system, however, morphology occupies a relatively minor position in the hierarchy relative to the sentence and discourse. If we think in terms of importance to communication, it appears that phrase, sentence, and discourse rules are certainly more important than morphology. In the balance, however, is the fact that words consist of morphemes or combinations of morphemes, and this makes morphology an important subject. Without words, a language does not exist. In spite of the fact that morphology occupies a low-level position in the language, we certainly must attend to it in our teaching. Therefore, we will take the last part of this chapter to present a few facts about English morphology. Most of what is said in the following discussion is taken from Francis (1958) and LeFevre (1970). The interested reader is referred to these sources for further information and detail.

Overview

Morphemes are groups of sounds that carry meaning and fill functions on the word level. A word is composed of morphemes; sometimes a word can be a single morpheme, sometimes it can be made up of several morphemes. For example, the word *dog* is a single morpheme carrying the meaning of *canine animal.* The word *dogs,* however, has a slightly different meaning. It still carries the semantic reference to *canine animal,* but with the addition of the morpheme for grammatical plurality it now means *more than one canine animal.* In the first instance we had one morpheme (*dog*); in the second we have two morphemes (*dog + plural*). It is important to look at *words* not as individual units but as constructions made up of the parts we call *morphemes.* Each of the parts carries meaning, either semantic or grammatical (or both).

A *free morpheme* can stand alone, and will often serve as a base to a *bound morpheme.* The latter must be attached to a free morpheme or to another bound morpheme. In the example given in the previous paragraph, the morpheme *dog* is a free morpheme: we can use it in a normal sentence ("I see a dog.") The morpheme *plurality* is a bound morpheme, however, because it cannot appear all by itself. Base morphemes are usually free, as stated previously. Bound morphemes, however, are usually either *inflections* or *derivational morphemes.*

Inflectional Morphemes

When we were in grade school, most of us learned that plurals are formed by adding an *s* or an *es* to the end of nouns. This statement actually refers to the writing system, not to the language itself. In terms of sound there is a little more to the system; not only is the rule for pluralization a little more complicated, but also the same rule for forming some inflections holds for forming others, e.g., noun plurals, possessives, and the third singular verb inflection all have the same phonological rules.

Unlike some other languages, like Russian, there are only a few inflections in American English (see Table 4.11). Note that inflectional morphemes, unlike most other morphemes, carry mostly grammatical meaning, and only a modicum of semantic meaning. Plurality, possession, past, third singular, comparative, superlative, etc., are all largely grammatical concepts. In this sense, inflections are unlike other morphemes, most of which carry a heavier semantic load.

Noun Plurals

Nouns can be *count* nouns or *mass* nouns.

Count Nouns

Count nouns are those that can be inflected for plural with the noun plural inflection [S_1]. Most of these are regular, i.e., they do not change their base when being inflected. Given the base form of a regular noun, the phonological form of the plural can be predicted with total accuracy. That is, the sound of the plural is determined by the final sound of the base.

Table 4.11. English Inflections

Morpheme	Symbol	Example	Used On	Signals
Plural	{S_1}	two chairs	nouns	"more than one"
Genitive	{S_2}	the dog's bone	nouns	possession
Third Singular	{S_3}	He throws	verbs	third person singular subject
Past	{T}	They poured	verbs	past tense
Past Participle	{-en$_1$}	broken	verbs	completed action
Passive	{-en$_2$}	driven	verbs	passive voice
Present Participle	{-ing}	wishing	verbs	incomplete action
Comparative	{-er}	bigger	adjectives	degree
Superlative	{-est}	biggest	adjectives	degree

Note. Brackets { } are used as a shorthand notation to indicate a morpheme. Sometimes an abstract symbol will appear in the brackets. This stands for a number of forms that function, morphologically, the same way. Thus, {-er} indicates comparison, both in the form *faster* and in the form *more definite*, i.e., both forms are comparatives. A numerical subscript indicates that there are several morphemes that have the same physical form, and the number indicates which morpheme is being discussed.

There are three forms to the regular plural, /-s, -z/, and /- ɨ z/. The /-s/ sound is attached to all regular bases ending in unvoiced sounds except those ending with /-s, -š/, or /-č/. The /-z/ is attached to all regular bases ending in voiced sounds except /-z, -ž/ or /-ǰ/. The /-ɨz/ sound is attached to all regular bases ending in /-s, -z, -š, -ž, -č, -ǰ/. Examples of regular plurals appear in (4.191):

(4.191)

/-s/	/-z/	/-ɨž/
cat/cats	iron/irons	judge/judges
book/books	dog/dogs	church/churches
clip/clips	vow/vows	wish/wishes
kite/kites	pen/pens	class/classes

Plurals for irregular nouns, on the other hand, are unpredictable. There are several classes of these, as can be seen in example (4.192):

(4.192)

-en	base + vowel change	base + consonant change	no change
ox/oxen	foot/feet	knife/knives	deer/deer
child/children	goose/geese	wife/wives	moose/moose
	louse/lice		

Mass Nouns

Mass nouns have no distinction between singular and plural. These are words such as *sand, police,* and *lightning.* Some of these nouns pattern with the third singular form of the verb:

(4.193) The sand *is* on the beach.

(4.194) Lightning *strikes* tall places.

Others pattern with plural verbs:

(4.195) The police *are* at the door.

Note that neither the singular forms nor the plural forms have a one-to-one correspondence with reality. Like tense, plurality is a grammatical concept that may be correlated with reality, but does not necessarily reflect it. In (4.193), for example, there is more than one grain of sand on any beach, while in (4.195) there may be only one policeman at the door. In either case, both clauses will still be grammatical.

Genitive

The genitive is completely regular and appears only on nouns. It follows the same phonological rules as those for the regular plural. That is, the genitive $\{-S_2\}$ has the sounds of *-s/, /-z/,* and *-iz/;* like the $\{-S_1\}$, which sound appears depends on the final sound of the word being inflected. This is true for both singular (*horse's*) and plural (*horses'*) forms.

Verb Third Person Present Singular

The third singular inflection {-S$_3$} is almost completely regular; it appears on verbs when the subject is *He, She, It,* or something for which these pronouns can substitute (*George, The little old lady down the street, My broken back,* etc.). It follows the same phonological rules as those for the noun plural and the genitive. The only exceptions to the regularity of this inflection are the verb *say* and the verbs and auxiliaries *do* and *have*. That is, these verbs, if they were regular, would appear in the third singular as:

(4.196) *He $\left\{ \begin{array}{l} \text{/seyz/} \\ \text{/hævz/} \\ \text{/duz/} \end{array} \right\}$ it.

But we actually hear:

(4.197) He $\left\{ \begin{array}{l} \text{/sez/} \\ \text{/hæz/} \\ \text{/dəz/} \end{array} \right\}$ it.

About the only times we hear *does* or *has* pronounced as in (4.196) are those times when someone is trying to be funny (*Jane dooz it.*) or when we meet a child who has learned the regular third singular forms, but who has not yet learned irregular forms for *say, do,* or *have.*

Verb Past

Most verb past inflections {T} are formed with the sounds /-t/ (used on regular verbs ending in all voiceless sounds except /-t/); /-d/ (used on regular verbs ending with all voiced sounds except /-d/); and /-id/ (used on all regular verbs ending with /-t, -d/). The examples in (4.198) show these rules in action:

(4.198)

/-t/	/-d/	/-id/
wish/wished	listen/listened	flit/flitted
hook/hooked	toss/tossed	glide/glided
kiss/kissed	fan/fanned	putt/putted
flip/flipped	pull/pulled	pad/padded

There are a number of irregular verbs, however. In general, there are five forms which take irregulars (Lefevre, 1970). Examples of these are shown in (4.199):

(4.199)

Base Vowel Change + /-t/	Base Vowel Change + /-d/	Final Voiced Consonant + /-t/	Base Vowel Change	No Change
sleep/slept	sell/sold	burn/burnt	ride/rode	put/put
teach/taught	flee/fled	spill/spilt	freeze/froze	hit/hit
buy/bought	hear/heard	bend/bent	drink/drank	set/set
go/went	have/had	build/built	shake/shook	rid/rid

Past Participle and Passive

The forms of the past participle $\{-en_1\}$ and passive $\{-en_2\}$ inflections are exactly the same. Some are formed exactly like the past tense, e.g., *listened/listened, heard/heard,* while others are irregular. Examples of the types of forms of past participles appear in (4.200):

(4.200)	*Base*	*Past Tense*	*Past Participle*	
			Same as Past	*Different*
	drop	dropped	dropped	
	roll	rolled	rolled	
	sleep	slept	slept	
	teach	taught	taught	
	hit	hit	hit	
	put	put	put	
	go	went		gone
	ring	rang		rung
	choose	chose		chosen
	draw	drew		drawn
	eat	ate		eaten

Present Participle

The present participle $\{ing\}$ is completely regular and appears as /-ing/ on all verbs:

(4.201)   listen/listening
flit/flitting
wish/wishing
hit/hitting
sleep/sleeping
sell/selling
burn/burning

Comparative and Superlative

The $\{er\}$ $\{est\}$- inflections appear on adjectives and adverbs, and are completely regular when they are used. Some examples are:

(4.202) *Comparative*	*Superlative*
bigger	biggest
finer	finest
smokier	smokiest
quieter	quietest
slower	slowest

For words of three syllables or more, however, we generally prefer to use *more* or *most* rather than the above inflections. These are simply alternate forms for the inflections, e.g., we prefer to say *more beautiful* rather than *beautifuller* or *beautifullest.*

Derivational Morphemes

English has a highly developed derivational morphology. A derivational morpheme is a bound morpheme attached to another morpheme which will modify or change the meaning of the original form. It often changes the part of speech as well. For example, through the use of derivational morphemes, the noun *friend* can be changed to the adjective *friendly* and the verb *vote* can be changed to the noun *voter.*

One of the differences between inflectional morphemes and derivational morphemes that must be learned by a child is the fact that derivational morphemes can be strung out almost indefinitely, whereas inflectional morphemes cannot. With few exceptions, only one inflectional morpheme per word is allowed. Consider the famous word, *antidisestab-lishmentarianism,* for example. The base morpheme is *establish,* and the rest of it is made up of derivational morphemes. Although there is a popular legend that this is "the longest word" in English, we could add derivational morphemes to it if we wished. Through the use of *prefixes* (affixes attached to the beginning of a word) we could, for example, create the word *proantidisestablishmentarianism* should we need it, or even *neoproantidisestab-lishmentarianism.* There is room for *suffixes* (affixes placed on the end of a word), too: *antidisestablishmentarianistic.* Note, however, that once we inflect a word (e.g., for plurality), we can add no further inflections or derivational suffixes: *antidisestablishmen-tarianisms.* The only exception to this is when the genitive inflection and the irregular plural appear together, e.g., *men's.* In these instances both appear: the plural in the vowel change and the genitive attached to the end of the word.

Morphemes, by and large, carry meaning. Base morphemes carry semantic meaning, the kind of meaning that we find listed in dictionaries. The example used in the last paragraph can be continued here: the base morpheme *establish,* according to the dictionary, carries the meaning "*To* bring into being on a firm or permanent basis." Derivational affixes also carry semantic meaning, however. *Anti-,* for example, carries the meaning of "against," or "opposing," and when combined with *establish* results in *anti-establish,* which means "Opposed to bringing into being." Meanings can be specified for each of the derivational morphemes in English. When derivational morphemes are added to a base morpheme the meaning of the resulting "word" depends on the combined meaning of all its morphemes.

There are hundreds of derivational morphemes in English. Most are used to form nouns, verbs, and adjectives. Only a very few are used to form adverbs. Examples of the latter are the *-ly* ending ("quick*ly*"), *-way/-ways/-wise* ("length*wise*"), and *-where* ("some*where*"), but most derivational affixes are used to form nouns, verbs, and adjectives. It is impossible in this space to make a complete list of all derivational morphemes because there are too many of them. Table 4.12 presents a small number of derivational suffixes. It does not even begin to show the complexity of the derivational system, however.

In addition to derivational suffixes (which follow base morphemes), there are derivational prefixes (which precede base morphemes). These prefixes are almost as complicated as the suffixes. Only a few examples can be given here.

Adverbs.
a- as in "*a*gape" and "*a*fire"

Verbs.
in- as in "*in*fer"
de- as in "*de*fer"
re- as in "*re*fer"

Table 4.12. Examples of Derivational Suffixes

Function	Suffix	Examples
To make nouns from verbs	-age	leakage, breakage
	-er	worker, runner
	-ment	employment, movement
To make nouns from adjectives	-cy	fluency, vacancy
	-dom	freedom, boredom
	-ism	Americanism, nationalism
To make verbs from nouns	-ate	vaccinate, chlorinate
	-en	lengthen, strengthen
	-ify	liquify, classify
To make verbs from adjectives	-en	blacken, darken
	-ify	clarify, simplify
	-ize	finalize, sterilize
To make adjectives from nouns	-an	American, diocesan
	-ar	circular, polar
	-ate	collegiate, passionate
To make adjectives from verbs	-able	adaptable, breakable
	-ent	excellent, different
	-ful	forgetful, harmful

Nouns.	Adjectives.
out- as in "*out*growth"	*in*- as in "*in*flexible"
up- as in "*up*date"	*under*- as in "*under*growth"

Except for the fact that they precede rather than follow bound morphemes, these prefixes act in much the same way as derivational suffixes.

Free Morphemes

Languages are very regular in the main, so regular that the exceptions stand out sharply. There are good, historical reasons for the existence of the irregularities, a large portion of which are in the morphological system. The fact is that they give trouble to children learning their language. At this point we will take a short space to say a few things about some irregulars and some of the multiple-form entities in order to present some idea about what has to be taught to many children.

BE

Most English verbs have two forms, past and present. Some add a third form, the past participle. Thus, we have verbs like *turn/turned/turned* and *sing/sang/sung*. There is one verb which not only has different forms for past, present, and past participle, but it also changes for person and number; this verb is BE. Table 4.3, p. 71 has already presented the various forms of BE as it appears both as a main verb and as an auxiliary.

Pronouns

English nouns, unlike nouns in many other languages, do not change form when they are used to fill object functions as opposed to subject functions, nor do they usually reflect gender. Many pronouns, however, are different in that they do reflect differences in function and gender. Like nouns, they also reflect changes in number. There are two classes of pronouns that do this: *personal pronouns* and *possessive pronouns*. We will also discuss three other groups of pronouns: *reflexives; some, no,* and *any;* and *one/none/body.*

Personal Pronouns

Personal pronouns are used to take the place of entire noun phrases and can fill clause-level functions such as subjects or objects. They can also fill the axis function of prepositional phrases or do whatever else noun phrases can do. In general, they are simply a ''shorthand'' for NPs.

(4.203) *He* shot *her.*

(4.204) *We* all went with *him.*

Personal pronouns have many forms, as listed in Table 4.13.

Possessive Pronouns

Some possessive pronouns take the place of the noun phrases that are inflected for possession in the det.$_2$, while other possessive pronouns function as noun substitutes in filling clause-level functions. The possessives that fill clause-level functions are used as follows:

(4.205) The box is *mine.*

(4.206) *Hers* is the one on the left.

The possessives that fill the det.$_2$ function are a little different, however:

(4.207) *My* box is that one over there.

(4.208) *Her* box is under mine.

The forms of the two sets of pronouns are listed in Table 4.14.

Table 4.13. English Personal Pronouns

Person	Subject Forms		Object Forms	
	Singular	Plural	Singular	Plural
1st	I	we	me	us
2nd	you	you	you	you
3rd	he, she, it	they	him, her, it	them

Table 4.14. English Possessive Pronouns

Person	Noun Substitutes		Determiner$_2$	
	Singular	Plural	Singular	Plural
1st	mine	ours	my	our
2nd	yours	yours	your	your
3rd	his, hers, its	theirs	his, her, its	their

Reflexive Pronouns

Reflexive pronouns "reflect" or refer to another clausal function in a sentence, usually the subject:

(4.209) *I* saw *myself* in the mirror.

(4.210) *We* sent *ourselves* a letter.

The construction of these pronouns is interesting. For the third person reflexives, the objective form of the personal pronouns is combined with *self* or *selves* (for plural):

(4.211) himself
herself
itself
themselves

But for the other persons, we use the det.$_2$ possessive combined with *self* or *selves*:

(4.212) myself
yourself
ourselves
yourselves

In some cases the use of these pronouns is obligatory in a construction:

(4.213) Look out for *yourself!* (cf. *Look out for you!)

But in other cases it can be optional:

(4.214) Holding a towel around *her(self),* she opened the door.

Finally, they can be used to provide emphasis to a statement:

(4.215) I wouldn't kiss her *myself.*

Some, No, and Any

These words are used pronominally (except *no*) by themselves, or in combination with *one*, *thing*, or *body*.

(4.216) $\left\{\begin{array}{l} some \\ any \\ no \end{array}\right\}$ $\left\{\begin{array}{l} one \\ thing \\ body \end{array}\right\}$

Note that there are nine different combinations of the above six forms, e.g., *someone*, *nobody*. Note also that each of the words in the left-hand column in (4.216) has been listed as an indefinite article filler of the det.$_2$ function (4.80).

Some is more specific that *any* or *no*. That is, the reference is to something definite in the first group of the following examples, whereas it is more vague in the second group:

(4.217) Give me *some*.

        Somebody open the door.

        Something was in the water.

But:

(4.218) *Any* you find are yours.

        Anybody open the door.

        Nobody was there.

        Nothing was in the water.

Note how they work in conversational combinations or when we form questions on declaratives:

(4.219) *Somebody* left his lunch here. I looked, but I couldn't find *anyone* who would claim it.

(4.220) I saw *somebody*. Did you see *anybody?*

One/None

The pronouns *one* and *none* are used to make references across sentences in ways very similar to personal and possessive pronouns.

(4.221) Have you seen this picture? Yes, I really like that *one*.

(4.222) This little pig had roast beef. That little pig had *none*.

In addition, these pronouns can have the same indefinite quality that *some* and *any* have in that they can refer to people in general:

(4.223) *One* never cries in this house.

(4.224) *None* were found to carry the banner into battle.

Not only this, but *one* can combine with *self* to form an indefinite reflexive and can combine with *some* and *no* to form a pronoun like *somebody* or *anything:*

(4.225) One takes care of *oneself* any way one can.

(4.226) $\left\{ \begin{array}{l} Some\ one \\ No\ one \end{array} \right\}$ was eating my porridge.

Contractions

In conversational English we often contract morphemes. That is, instead of saying, "I am going," we usually say, "I'm going." Typically these contractions occur with BE, the negative, and *will*, although they can and do occur in other places. The contractions for BE, the negative, and *will* are so often used that they have been formalized in the writing system:

(4.227) *We're* going.

(4.228) I *couldn't* open it.

The contractions for BE occur as shown in Table 4.15. Note that only the present tense forms can be contracted—for past tense we always use the full form: there is no contracted form for *I was, We were, It was,* etc.

The negative is interesting because there are different ways to contract it to pronouns. We can say, for example, "You're not" or "You aren't"; "He's not" or "He isn't"; "We're not" or "We aren't"; "They're not" or "They aren't." Note, however, that we can only say "I'm not" and "He doesn't." There are no forms in English like *"I amn't." We also contract the negative to *do, can, could, will,* and *would.*

Will is the one modal that is contracted: *I'll, you'll, he'll, she'll, it'll, they'll, George'll,* etc.

We use other contractions in conversation that do not have the legal status in writing that are held by the previous examples. We often contract vowels in speech, for example.

Table 4.15. BE Contractions

	Uncontracted Forms		Contracted Forms	
	Present		Present	
Person	Singular	Plural	Singular	Plural
1st	I am	we are	I'm	we're
2nd	you are	you are	you're	you're
3rd	he, she, it is	they are	he's, she's, it's	they're

This is called *elision:*

(4.229) I c'n do it. (I can do it.)

We can also elide consonants and even whole words, as in:

(4.230) J'eat yet? (Did you eat yet?)

We have to teach the major contractions so that children will sound "natural" when they speak. Children will learn contractions such as those in (4.229) and (4.230) by themselves, eventually.

Concluding Statement

The reader should realize that morphology has not been explored in depth here, and in fact, many facets of morphology were not even touched on. We did not, for example, discuss parts of speech: prepositions, nouns, verbs, etc. Some of these items appear as part of the discussion on syntax in other places in the book. Much more space is required to do justice to the topic of American English than we have available, and the reader is urged to consult some of the good references cited when additional information is needed.

CHAPTER 5

Concepts of American English III
Transformations

In the present framework, a transformation is simply a rule expressing the grammatical relationship between two or more related utterances. This is quite different from the concept of transformations as used by transformational grammarians, and it is also much more limited in scope. The only transformations with which we will be concerned are those stating the relationships (*a*) between declaratives and questions, (*b*) between active and passive voice, and (*c*) between clauses in coordinate and subordinate relationships. We will take up each of these in turn. The basic information in this chapter is taken from P. H. Fries (1964; 1973a; 1972; personal communications), and Quirk et al. (1972). Also helpful in formulating the chapter were Chomsky (1957) and Gleason (1965). The interested reader will wish to refer to these sources for more information.

Questions

The general rule stating the relationship between all questions and their corresponding declarative clauses is that *tense appears before the subject in questions,* whereas it *follows* the subject in declaratives. There are three general conditions under which this occurs: (*a*) in any clause with auxiliaries in the verb phrase, (*b*) in equative clauses with no auxiliaries in the verb phrase, and (*c*) in transitive and intransitive clauses with no auxiliaries in the verb phrase. Note the similarities between the conditions in the formation of questions and those for the negative function in the VP.

Yes/No Questions

Yes/no questions are those that can be answered with either a *yes* or a *no,* as was stated in Chapter 3. This simple response may be elaborated upon by the respondent, but any elaboration is optional as far as the grammar is concerned.

Three General Conditions for Questions

Clauses Containing Auxiliaries in the Verb Phrase

Any verb phrase, whether it be in a transitive, intransitive, or equative clause, can contain one or more auxiliaries. When this happens, the auxiliary that appears first in the phrase will carry tense (see Chapter 4). In questions, this tense-carrying auxiliary will appear in the slot immediately in front of the subject. Table 5.1 shows this relationship. The first line of this table contains a declarative clause in which the modal carries tense. The

---

Table 5.1. Tense Movement in Clauses with Auxiliaries

Declarative clause:	That vase could break.
Tense goes in front of the subject:	That vase — could — break.
Question:	Could that vase break?

Table 5.2. Clauses with Auxiliaries and their Corresponding *Yes/No* Questions

Declaratives	Questions
The family in the green house *is* mov*ing*. BE -ing	*Is* the family in the green house moving?
They *have* brok*en* their lease. HAVE -en	*Have* they broken their lease?
Igor *could* be dead by Tuesday. MODAL	*Could* Igor be dead by Tuesday?
Martha *has been* see*ing* a new boy. HAVE -en BE -ing	*Has* Martha been seeing a new boy?
He *might have been being* watch*ed*. MODAL HAVE -en BE -ing BE -en	*Might* he have been being watched?

---

second line shows the tense-carrying auxiliary dropping out of its declarative position following the subject and moving toward its position in questions. The third line shows this move completed, and the question now appears in its adult form.

This relationship holds true for all clauses with auxiliaries. Table 5.2 contains a number of clauses of different types, each with one or more auxiliaries, and each with its corresponding *yes/no* question. In each case, the relationship expressed in Table 5.1 holds true, i.e., the tense-carrying auxiliary follows the subject in declaratives, but precedes it in questions.

Equative Clauses with No Auxiliaries

If the clause is an equative clause with no auxiliaries, the verb BE carries tense. When this happens, the verb itself appears in the position in front of the subject to form the question. This situation is shown in Table 5.3. The first line in this table contains a declarative clause. The second line shows the tense-carrying BE dropping out of the position following the subject and moving toward the front of the clause, and the third line shows this move completed. The question now appears in its adult form.

Table 5.4 contains a number of equative declarative clauses with their corresponding *yes/no* questions. In all cases, note that the relationship expressed in Table 5.3 holds true. Observe how none of the clauses in Table 5.4 contain any auxiliaries in their verb phrases. When an equative clause contains one or more auxiliaries in the verb phrase, the rule governing clauses with auxiliaries (Tables 5.1 and 5.2) applies.

Transitive and Intransitive Clauses with No Auxiliaries

The third general situation is found in a clause that contains either a transitive or an intransitive verb with no auxiliaries in its verb phrase. In this situation tense must still

---

Table 5.3. Tense Movement in Equative Clauses with No Auxiliaries

Declarative clause:	His little girl is very smart.
Tense goes in front of the subject:	His little girl very smart. is
Question:	Is his little girl very smart?

Table 5.4. Declarative Equative Clauses with No Auxiliaries and their Corresponding *Yes/No* Questions

Declaratives	Questions
That lady *was* my wife.	*Was* that lady my wife?
Even the little ones *were* tall.	*Were* even the little ones tall?
Bulldogs *are* fierce.	*Are* bulldogs fierce?
The bill collector *is* here.	*Is* the bill collector here?
The time for dancing *was* yesterday.	*Was* the time for dancing yesterday?

appear before the subject of the clause, but transitive and intransitive verbs do not act like the verb BE in equative clauses, i.e., the verb does not move. We do not find question clauses such as the following in English:

(5.1) *Throws John the ball?

(5.2) *Ran the boy?

Instead of the verb moving, what happens is that a dummy auxiliary appears to carry tense and person markings. This dummy is DO, the same dummy that is used to carry tense and person in negation (see Chapter 4). Table 5.5 shows the declarative/question relationship in these clauses. Again, the first line in the table shows the declarative clause, and the second line shows tense being removed from its position following the subject. The third line of the table shows how a slot is created for tense to appear before the subject and illustrates why a dummy is needed—tense per se has no overt manifestation, and needs something to which it can be attached. The last line shows the dummy appearing in the slot before the subject. The question now appears in its adult form.

Table 5.6 shows a number of different clauses requiring the dummy DO when they are in the question form. Note that the dummy has three different forms: *do, does,* and *did.* The first two are present tense forms, and the third is the past tense form. When the subject is *he, she, it,* or anything for which these pronouns will substitute, the third person

---

Table 5.5. Tense Movement in Transitive and Intransitive Clauses with No Auxiliaries

Declarative clause:	The cat in the hat watched carefully.
Tense goes in front of the subject:	The cat in the hat watch____ carefully. ← _ _ _ past _ _ ↗
Tense before subject:	(past) the cat in the hat watch carefully?
Question:	Did the cat in the hat watch carefully?

Table 5.6. Declarative Transitive and Intransitive Clauses with No Auxiliaries and the Corresponding Yes/No Questions

Declaratives	Questions
Mighty oaks *grow* from little acorns.	*Do* mighty oaks grow from little acorns?
He *wants* his supper.	*Does* he want his supper?
We *throw* the coach in the water after the meet.	*Do* we throw the coach in the water after the meet?
The kid with the ice cream *looked* sticky.	*Did* the kid with the ice cream look sticky?
We really *named* him Sue.	*Did* we really name him Sue?

singular present form *does* is used. All other persons of the subject will require *do* in the present tense:

(5.3)

$$Do \begin{Bmatrix} I \\ you \\ we \\ they \end{Bmatrix} hear\ that\ noise?$$

(5.4)

$$Does \begin{Bmatrix} he \\ she \\ it \\ George \\ the\ boy\ in\ the\ rear \end{Bmatrix} hear\ the\ noise?$$

Wh- Questions

Wh- questions are so-called because most begin with a word that is spelled with *wh-: who, what, where, when, why, which, whose,* and *how.* We also have to include in this group of words the phrases that have *wh-* words in them, e.g., *what kind of, under what circumstances.* These questions ask for a bit of information rather than the agreement or disagreement that *yes/no* questions seek. Moreover, the particular bit of information requested is specified by the *wh-* word that is used. The *wh-* transformation requires

1. Some part of the corresponding declarative is not known by the speaker.
2. In his question, the speaker uses a *wh-* word to replace the part of the declarative that is unknown.
3. The respondent is required to respond with only that part of the declarative that was replaced by the *wh-* word in the question.

These requirements are illustrated in Table 5.7. In this table, the last column contains a response that would be typical if the question should occur during a conversation. Note the relationship between the underlined portions of the declaratives, the *wh-* questions, and the minimal obligatory responses.

Table 5.7. *Wh-* Words as Replacements

Declaratives	Corresponding *Wh-* Questions	Minimal Required Responses
You went *out.*	*Where* did you go?	Out.
That is *a dog.*	*What* is that?	A dog.
Harry left the party.	*Who* left the party?	Harry.
They climb mountains *because they are there.*	*Why* do they climb mountains?	Because they are there.

Table 5.8. Functions Replaced by *Wh-* Words

Wh- Word	Function(s) Replaced	Example
Who	Subject	*Jane* left early. *Who* left early?
Who(m)	Object/Complement	We saw *Fred*. *Who(m)* did we see?
What	Subject	*The book* fell down. *What* fell down?
What	Object/Complement	It was *a brick*. *What* was it?
Where	Adverbial of Place	They went *home*. *Where* did they go?
When	Adverbial of Time	It happened *yesterday*. *When* did it happen?
How	Adverbial of Manner	He disappeared *quietly*. *How* did he disappear?
Which	Det.$_2$	*That* tree is the biggest. *Which* tree is the biggest?
Which	Loose-Knit Modifier	*The litle* girl hurt herself. *Which* girl hurt herself?
Which	Restrictive Modifier	The pipe *on the left* is still lit. *Which* pipe is still lit?
Why	*Because* Coordinate Clause	She smiled *because she was happy*. *Why* did she smile?

Wh- words replace parts of clauses or phrases. Table 5.8 lists the *wh-* words and shows most of the declarative functions they replace. Note that some *wh-* words replace clausal functions, some replace phrasal functions, and *why* replaces an entire clause in a coordinate sentence. The functions replaced by the *wh-* word, of course, are precisely those which must appear in the response if it is to make sense. Parenthetically, note that it is possible to elaborate on the obligatory response. That is, just as it is possible to elaborate the response to a *yes/no* question, the question in (5.5a) can be responded to with either of the responses in (5.5b):

(5.5a) Q: *Where* did you go?

(5.5b) $\left\{ \begin{matrix} Out \\ I \ went \ out. \end{matrix} \right\}$

The same three general conditions hold for *wh-* questions that hold for *yes/no* questions: that is, tense movement occurs differently in (*a*) any clause with auxiliaries, (*b*) equative clauses with no auxiliaries, and (*c*) transitive and intransitive clauses with no auxiliaries. These rules apply:

Table 5.9. *Wh-* Question in All Clauses with Auxiliaries

Declarative Clause:	You could have killed him with that rock.
1. Unknown:	You could have killed him with _____?
2. *Wh-* replacement:	You could have killed him with (what) ?
3. *Wh-* replacement is placed at the front of the clause:	You could have killed him with ⌐ ? ⌐ — _ _ what _ — — ‾
4. Tense is placed before the subject:	What you have killed him with ? ‾ could ‾
Question:	What could you have killed him with?

1. If the clause contains one or more auxiliaries, the first (tense-carrying) auxiliary moves to the position before the subject.
2. If the clause is equative, and if there are no auxiliaries, the verb BE moves to the position before the subject.
3. If the clause is transitive or intransitive and contains no auxiliaries, the dummy DO appears before the subject to carry tense and person markers.

Wh- questions have a four-part relationship to their corresponding declaratives. This relationship is shown in Tables 5.9, 5.10, and 5.11. In each case the same thing happens:

1. Something is unknown.
2. A *wh-* word fills the function of the unknown.
3. The *wh-* word is placed at the front of the clause.
4. Tense is placed in the position between the *wh-* word and the subject.

The final clause in each table is the adult form of the question.

Table 5.10. *Wh-* Question in Equative Clauses with No Auxiliaries

Declarative Clause:	The lady over there is the queen.
1. Unknown:	The lady over there is _____?
2. *Wh-* replacement:	The lady over there is (who) ?
3. *Wh-* is placed at the front of the clause:	The lady over there is ⌐ ? ‾ — —who ‾
4. Tense is placed before the subject:	Who the lady over there ⌐ ? ‾ is _ _ ‾
Question:	Who is the lady over there?

Table 5.11. *Wh-* Questions in All Clauses with No Auxiliaries

Declarative Clause:	Nelson Eddy sang to Jeanette MacDonald sweetly.
1. Unknown:	Nelson Eddy sang to Jeanette MacDonald _____?
2. *Wh-* replacement:	Nelson Eddy sang to Jeanette MacDonald (how) ?
3. *Wh-* is placed at the front of the clause:	Nelson Eddy sang to Jeanette MacDonald ↙ ? how
4. Tense is placed before the subject:	How ___ Nelson Eddy sing to Jeanette MacDonald? — past
Question:	How did Nelson Eddy sing to Jeanette MacDonald?

There is one apparent exception to the rule that tense moves before the subject of the clause. It turns out not to be an exception after all. When the *wh-* word replaces the subject (or any part of the subject), it cannot move. It is already in the initial position. Because it cannot move, nothing else happens, i.e., tense does not move. The whole clause simply keeps the word order it had before the *wh-* replacement occurred:

(5.6) *Evelyn* had a new hat.

(5.6a) *Who* had a new hat?

Who and *what* are not the only possible *wh-* words with which this "exception" can occur. *Which,* for example, can replace either the det.$_2$ or the loose-knit modifier in a noun phrase which fills the subject function. In this case, as well as in those similar to (5.6), there would be no *wh-* movement and no tense movement:

(5.7) The *loose* knot came untied.

(5.7a) *Which* knot came untied?

When *which* replaces a restrictive modifier that is in a subject function, the *wh-* word moves to the front of the clause, but there is no tense movement:

(5.8) The boy *on the left* broke the window.

(5.8a) *Which* boy broke the window?

Tag Questions

The third type of question is the tag question, named thus because part of it is a *tag* that is placed onto the end of a regular declarative.

Tag questions are a little like *yes/no* questions in English in that they can be answered with either a *yes* or a *no*. They are formed by adding, to a declarative clause, a tag which is the negation of the statement found in the declarative. That is, if the declarative part of the

Table 5.12. Examples of Tag Questions

Declarative	Tag Question
John hurt his elbow.	John hurt his elbow, *didn't he?*
John just couldn't write that term paper.	John just couldn't write that term paper, *could he?*
Ivan is not allowed to stomp around the palace.	Ivan is not allowed to stomp around the palace, *is he?*
The girls were wearing shoes.	The girls were wearing shoes, *weren't they?*

tag question is positive, then the tag will be negative, and *vice versa*. Some examples of tag questions appear in Table 5.12.

Note that the tag part of the question is like an abbreviated *yes/no* question clause:

(5.9) John hurt his elbow, *didn't he* (hurt his elbow)?

Pronouns used in the tag correspond to the nouns found in the declarative part of the tag question in person, number, and gender. In addition, as was noted above, sometimes the tag is positive and sometimes it is negative, depending on whether the verb phrase in the declarative clause that precedes the tag is negative or positive. Finally, note the fact that there is a semantic difference between *yes/no* and tag questions: a *yes/no* question seeks a bit of information, e.g.,

(5.10) Q: Did John go home?   *A:* $\begin{cases} \text{Yes.} \\ \text{No.} \end{cases}$

The responses to the following tag questions, however, show that the tag question looks for agreement:

(5.11) *Q:* John went home, didn't he?   *A:* Yes.

(5.12) *A:* John didn't go home, did he?   A: No.

In this respect, tag questions are almost rhetorical in nature. Like the subject of the weather, they are typically used simply for the sake of making conversation.

Negation in Questions

It is easy to make a negative question—the only thing that has to be done is to negate the declarative and then make a question out of it. Although it is a simple matter grammatically, the semantic result is not what we might expect. Table 5.13 shows why. Note that the question that corresponds to the positive declarative would be answered with a *yes* because the lamb does have white fleece in the related declarative. The answer to the negative question is also *yes,* however, which does not correspond to the information given in the negative declarative. Semantically, negative questions are often quite dif-

Table 5.13. Declarative and Question Negatives Compared

Question Form	Declarative	Question	Response
Positive	Mary's lamb has white fleece.	Does Mary's lamb have white fleece?	⎧ Yes. ⎫
Negative	Mary's lamb doesn't have white fleece.	Doesn't Mary's lamb have white fleece?	⎨ No. ⎬ ⎩ Yes. ⎭

ferent from other questions in that they usually expect simple agreement as a response, not information. In this respect they are very much like tag questions.

Summary: Questions

There are three general types of questions in English: *yes/no* questions, *wh-* questions, and tag questions. Grammatically these are differentiated by the responses they evoke in the person answering the question: *yes/no* questions elicit a response that, minimally, contains a *yes* or a *no; wh-* questions all begin with a *wh-* word that replaces a clause or a part of a clause, and the minimal response to the question contains the part of the clause that was replaced by the *wh-* word; tag questions are simply declaratives with part of a *yes/no* question tagged on at the end of the declarative—they require a *yes* or a *no* as part of the response. Which of these is required is specified by the question itself, i.e., whether or not the tag has a negative in it.

The one thing common to all questions is the movement of the tense to the slot in front of the subject of the clause, except in the case of the *wh-* questions in which the *wh-* word replaces part of the subject function. *Yes/no* questions move only tense. *Wh-* questions move tense, but also place a *wh-* word at the front of the clause. Tag questions either negate or affirm the declarative that precedes the tag, and tense movement appears in the tag itself.

Passive

In any language there are usually a number of different ways to say something. The passive voice is a device that helps us to be more flexible in our expression of what we want to say. The word *voice* is a grammatical term that refers to the difference between active and passive. In the active voice, the grammatical subject does something (or "acts upon" something else), and the action goes from left to right:

(5.13) John found a large object.

— direction of action →

The passive voice allows us to take exactly the same statement and turn it around so that the action expressed goes in the other direction. The grammatical subject has something done to it:

(5.14) A large object was found by John.

← _____

direction of action

The relation between active and passive voice is very complicated. It appears only in transitive clauses, it involves two different levels in the grammatical hierarchy (Figure 2.1), and it involves semantic rules as much as it does grammatical rules. It is small wonder that the passive is one of the last clausal transformations to be learned by children.

Phrase Level

The verb phrase function of passive has already been discussed in Chapter 3. Briefly, the filler of the function is BE-*en;* in terms of its linear position, the passive is always the last function in the verb phrase to appear before the head. It takes forms such as the following:

(5.15) *is* throw*n*

⌐_____⌐

BE -*en*

has *be*en se*en*

⌐_____⌐

BE -*en*

is *be*ing flogg*ed*

⌐_____⌐

BE -*en*

Clause Level

At the same time that the BE -*en* filler is used, changes take place on the clause level. The filler of the direct object function in the active voice appears in the front of the passive

---

Table 5.14. The Passive Transformation

Active Declarative:	*Hedda Hinkle* sang *a beautiful love song.*
Direct object becomes subject; VP passive function filled:	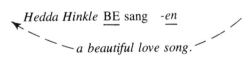
Subject becomes agent; *by* added:	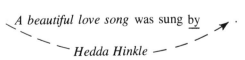
Passive:	*A beautiful love song* was sung by *Hedda Hinkle.*
Passive agent deleted:	*A beautiful love song* was sung.

Table 5.15. Grammatical and Semantic Relationships in Active and Passive Voice

Active Voice:	**Mrs. Hammerstein**	**grows**	**lovely vegetables.**
Grammatical Functions:	subject	predicate	direct object
Semantic Functions:	actor	action	patient
Passive Voice:	**Lovely vegetables**	**are grown**	**by Mrs. Hammerstein.**
Grammatical Functions:	subject	predicate	passive agent
Semantic Functions:	patient	action	actor

clause to fill the function of the passive subject. The phrase that fills the subject function in the active voice appears at the end of the passive clause and fills the function of optional passive complement. Finally, the preposition *by* is inserted before the passive complement. At the option of the speaker, the passive complement can be deleted. This transformation is illustrated in Table 5.14. Note that the meaning of the clause does not change. Whatever the event narrated in the active clause, the same event is narrated in the passive clause, but the direction of the action is now reversed, i.e., something or somebody now has something done to it by something or somebody.

Semantics

One of the most common ways of providing emphasis in English is to take something out of its "normal" (most frequently occurring) position and put it someplace else. The active is certainly more common than the passive in English (except in certain academic circles). Placing the direct object of the active clause into the subject position is certain to provide it with more emphasis than it would have had. There is more to it than just this, however, because the passive voice transformation is partially semantic in nature.

The active transitive clause has an actor/instrument-action-patient relationship. That is, somebody or something does something to somebody or something. In the active voice, the *actor,* or "the doer of the action," and the grammatical subject coincide, while the *patient,* or "the acted upon," and the direct object coincide. When cast into the passive voice, however, the semantic and grammatical functions of the active clause are separated, and the patient coincides with the grammatical subject of the passive. This means that not only have grammatical functions been taken out of their normal position, but they have also been separated from their "normal" semantic coincidences. In addition, in the passive it is also possible to delete the actor entirely, leaving the patient as the major focus of the clause. The net effect of this is to place the patient, or the recipient of the action, in a heightened focus in the clause. These correspondences are shown in Table 5.15.

Alternate VP Filler

In addition to BE *-en,* we often find the passive function of the VP filled by GET *-en,* as in the following:

(5.16) Glasses *get* brok*en* when they are left lying about. (present tense)

(5.17) His glasses *got* brok*en* in the struggle. (past tense)

This colloquial filler of the passive function in the verb phrase is fairly common. As in (5.16) and (5.17), it often appears with the agent deleted; but it is certainly possible for it to appear, as in (5.18):

(5.18) The leaf *got* toss*ed* about (by the wind).

One problem with identifying this filler lies in the fact that it is so easily confused with another construction that looks very similar, but which can have no actor. There is no way, for example, to add an actor to the following clauses:

(5.19) The meeting *got* bogg*ed* down in confusion.

(5.20) They *got* dress*ed* when the police came.

Neither (5.19) nor (5.20) is in the passive. Rather, GET functions as filler of the head of the VP in an intransitive clause. The word that looks like a verb is a subjective complement. The complement is filled by an adjective derived from a verb. These adjectives include *gone, done, dressed,* and *lost.* Note how similar the active (5.20) is to the passive in (5.21), for example:

(5.21) They *got* arrest*ed* when the police came.

GET, then, is like so many other verbs in English, for example, DO, BE, and HAVE. It is one of those forms that can have more than one meaning and can fill more than one grammatical role with the separate meanings.

Summary: Passive Voice

The passive voice is an alternate form for the declarative. It gives emphasis to the semantic patient by placing it in the front of the clause while separating it from the grammatical object. It is a complicated construction because it involves changes on two levels of the grammatical hierarchy (clause and phrase levels) in addition to manipulations of semantic functions. These changes occur all at the same time in its formation. On the phrase level, the BE-*en* passive function appears; on the clause level, the active subject becomes the passive complement, the active direct object becomes the passive subject, and the positions of these functions in the clause change. Semantically, the actor is separated from the grammatical subject and can be deleted at the speaker's option. Finally, the patient is separated from the grammatical direct object. The action, rather than going from left to right in the printed clause, now goes from right to left in the passive.

The BE auxiliary in the passive VP function has all of the forms of BE as fillers. The alternate form GET (*get/got*) can also be used in the same slot.

Coordinates and Subordinates

We will consider two general types of sentences in this section: coordinated clauses and subordinated clauses. The latter will be further broken down into *wh-* subordinates and infinitive subordinates.

Coordinated Clauses

Two or more clauses can be conjoined with conjunctions. In the resulting sentence, both clauses will have equal grammatical status, i.e., neither will assume a minor position in relation to the other, and the removal of the conjunction(s) will not change the meaning of either of the original clauses. Thus, two clauses could be conjoined as in any of the following examples:

(5.22) Roger eats it $\left\{\begin{array}{l} and \\ but \\ so \\ because \\ although \end{array}\right\}$ Fanny makes it.

Not all conjunctions consist of a single word. Sometimes more than one conjunction is used, one appearing at the beginning of the first clause and one appearing before the second clause:

(5.23) $\left\{\begin{array}{l} Either \\ Both \\ Just\ as \end{array}\right\}$ he comes $\left\{\begin{array}{l} or \\ and \\ so \end{array}\right\}$ I must go.

The clauses in (5.22) and (5.23) are all declaratives. In addition, it is possible not only to conjoin questions and imperatives, but also to mix declaratives, questions and imperatives in coordinate sentences. This is illustrated in Table 5.16.

In all of the examples given thus far, the conjoined clauses are all readily identifiable as being distinct clauses. Quite often, however, it is possible to combine functions in the conjoining process. When this happens, the distinctiveness of the two clauses begins to blur. As examples of this blur, consider the following two clauses:

(5.24) Ziggy put gas in his car.

(5.25) Ziggy left the area.

It is possible to conjoin the clauses in (5.24) and (5.25) simply by using a conjunction:

(5.26) *Ziggy put gas in his car* and *Ziggy left the area.*

Table 5.16. Examples of Clause Types in Coordinate Clauses

Mary plays the piano *and* Charlie dances.	Declarative + Declarative
Take this bread *and* eat it.	Imperative + Imperative
Can you sit up *or* does it hurt too much?	Question + Question
Take the check to the bank *and* they will cash it.	Imperative + Declarative
Martha has nice handwriting, *but* does she make sense?	Declarative + Question
Raise your arm *or* is it really immobile?	Imperative + Question

---

The sentence in (5.26) sounds awkward, however, because the subject is repeated. Whenever the subjects of the two clauses to be conjoined are identical, as is true in this case, we usually delete the subject of the second clause:

(5.27) *Ziggy put gas in his car* and *left the area.*

This way of saying it sounds much more natural to us, and in fact, we do it all the time, not only for identical subjects, but also for identical objects, complements, and adverbials. Examples of some combinations are shown in Table 5.17.

Combinations can occur for all identical functions, a situation which sometimes results in conjoined clauses that have everything but the predicates combined. For example, consider (5.28):

(5.28)   Mary washed the dishes. Mary dried the dishes.

When we finish combining identical functions, we get the following sentence:

(5.29) *Mary washed* and *dried the dishes.*

The following do not have coordinate relationships between clauses because there is only one predicate in each of the sentences:

(5.30) *Mary and Phyllis* ate supper.

(5.31) The *red and white* pennant fluttered in the breeze.

The only point to be made here is that the use of conjunctions does not necessarily result in conjoined clauses. It is only when two or more verb phrases appear in a coordinated construction that clauses are conjoined. Subjects (5.30) and modifiers in the NP (5.31) can be conjoined, but conjoining them is not the same thing as conjoining clauses. Personal observation leads me to believe that children often will correctly conjoin noun phrases before they conjoin clauses. That is, I would expect to find children saying things like:

(5.32) Johnny and Billy came in.

Table 5.17. Examples of Deletions in Coordinated Clauses

Clauses Conjoined	Sentences	Deletions or Combinations Made
Charlene made a cake. Charlene cleaned up.	*Charlene made a cake* and *cleaned up.*	Subjects
Francisco took the picture. Betty Jo liked the picture.	*Francisco took the picture* and *Betty Jo liked it.*	Objects
Frank ate his supper. Frank drank his supper.	*Frank ate* and *drank his supper.*	Subjects and Objects

before they say things like:

(5.33) Johnny came in and Billy hit him.

The reason for this is probably to be found in the fact that the manipulation of clauses is more difficult (in a developmental sense) than is the manipulation of phrases within an established clause function.

Subordinated Clauses

Conjoining results in the formation of sentences in which the conjoined clauses have approximately equal grammatical status in the sentence. Subordination results in the formation of sentences in which one clause in the sentence is "subordinate" to another, i.e., a subordinated clause is one that is inserted into a slot in another (the "dominant") clause. For our purposes there are two major forms of subordination: (*a*) *wh-* subordination; and (*b*) infinitive subordination. We will discuss each of these in this section.

Wh- Subordination

There is a type of subordination which usually has either a *wh-* word (*who, whose, what, which, when, where, why, how, whoever,* along with a number of others) or *that* as part of the subordinate clause. This word, however, can often be deleted. Thus, both of the following sentences contain the same *wh-* subordinate, but (5.35) has deleted the *wh-* word. Note that (5.34) is recoverable from (5.35):

(5.34) The man $\begin{Bmatrix} whom \\ that \end{Bmatrix}$ *I saw* was tall.

(5.35) The man *I saw* was tall.

In *wh-* (and infinitive) subordination, we will always find (*a*) a *matrix* clause and (*b*) an *insert* clause. The matrix clause is one in which a clause or phrase function has been left blank, and the insert clause goes into the blank. The matrix, of course, is what many people call the "dominant" clause, and the insert is often called the "subordinate" clause.

Some *wh-* inserts fill clausal functions, and some fill functions in the noun phrase. That is, insert clauses can fill the functions of subject, indirect object, direct object, complement, or adverbial in a clause matrix. In Chapter 4 we hinted that insert clauses can also fill the functions of Determiner$_2$, completion in the complex nominal, restrictive modifier, and nonrestrictive modifier in noun phrase matrices. In this section we will consider separately inserts on the clause level, and inserts on the phrase level.

Insert Clauses Filling Functions on the Clause Level

In order for a clause to be an insert and fill a clausal function in another clause, the matrix must first have a blank function. For example, a matrix may have a blank object function:

(5.36a) Donahue knew *(object)*.

Given this matrix we can now insert an entire clause into the blank:

(5.36b) Donahue knew *(that) she was coming*.

When we insert a declarative (*she was coming*) into a matrix function as in (5.36b), the *wh-* word is an optional "introducer," and the speaker can use it or delete it as he chooses. When the *wh-* word *replaces* something in the insert, however, the *wh-* word cannot be deleted. Suppose we take the same matrix:

(5.37a) Donahue knew *(object)*.

Now suppose that, instead of the simple declarative used in (5.36), the insert contains an unknown. In this case, we would replace the unknown with a *wh-* word:

(5.37b) *(Somebody)* broke the beer bottle. $\Longleftrightarrow$ *who* broke the beer bottle?

Now the insert can go into the blank function in the matrix:

(5.37c) Donahue knew *who broke the beer bottle*.

In the example just given, the subject of the insert was replaced by a *wh-* word. In forming *wh-* questions, you will remember, the *wh-* word that replaces a subject is already at the beginning of the clause and is not moved for the question. When any other function is replaced by a *wh-* word in a question, however, the *wh-* word is moved to the front of the clause. The same thing happens with *wh-* inserts. To illustrate, we will first set up a matrix clause with a blank object:

(5.38a) Eloise Rappaport saw *(object)*.

Now we will set up an insert clause with an unknown complement:

(5.38b) That was *(something)*.

If we replace the unknown with a *wh-* word, it must be moved to the front of the clause before the insert can be placed into the matrix (note that, unlike *wh-* questions, tense does not move in the insert):

(5.38c) That was *what* $\Longleftrightarrow$ *what* that was

The insert can now be placed into the blank in the object:

(5.38d) Eloise Rappaport saw *what that was*.

Table 5.18 shows a number of examples of clauses functioning as direct objects. Note that any *wh-* word or *that* can introduce a direct object insert, and that the number of examples in Table 5.18 is inadequate to the task of presenting a complete list of the possibilities.

The process of inserting *wh-* inserts into other functions of the clause is very much like that for inserting clauses into the object function. For example, the following shows how an insert clause fills a subject function:

(5.39) *Matrix: (Subject)* is definitely true.
       Insert: you said *(something)*. $\Longleftrightarrow$ You said *what* $\Longleftrightarrow$ *what* you said
       Subordinate: What you said is definitely true.

Table 5.18. Examples of Insert Clauses Functioning as Direct Objects

Don't you understand *which is the correct response?*

I don't have *what you are asking for.*

We all heard *who you swore at that time.*

She said *what we were thinking.*

Don't you know *whose that is?*

The president never knew *what was going on.*

All this time you thought *(that) we were going.*

Nobody understood *(that) he called them fools.*

Everybody saw *(that) Miss Funkhauser had left.*

In a similar manner, indirect object, complement, and adverbial functions can be filled by subordinated clauses as shown in the following examples:

(5.40) She gave *whoever was there* the money. (indirect object)

(5.41) That was *who came to the party.* (complement)

(5.42) Lula May Smith dropped by *when everyone else had gone.* (adverbial)

There are three things to note about the clauses that fill the adverbial function. In the first place, they are often introduced by words such as *where, when,* or *how,* but just as often they can be introduced by a preposition as is true of other adverbials. This is true especially when the semantic functions of accompaniment or instrument are being filled by the adverbial. For our purposes, it is convenient to include these under the category of *wh-* subordinates.

(5.43) Auchingloss liked to dance *with every girl he met.*

Secondly, adverbial functions that are filled by clauses are moveable, just as are other adverbs:

(5.44a) John was flirting with Mary *when her husband walked in the door.*

(5.44b) *When her husband walked in the door,* John was flirting with Mary.

Finally, a matrix in one sentence could just as easily be an insert in another sentence when precisely the same two clauses are used:

(5.45a) I went home *when it was dawn.*

(5.45b) It was dawn *when I went home.*

Clauses that Fill Functions in Noun Phrases

RESTRICTIVE AND NONRESTRICTIVE MODIFIERS. In Chapter 4 we saw how the head noun function could be modified by a restrictive or a nonrestrictive modifier. Briefly, a restrictive modifier differentiates the head noun from all other members in its class, while a nonrestrictive modifier simply adds a bit of information about the head noun. The nonrestrictive modifier is set off by intonation contours in speech and by commas in writing, while the restrictive modifier is not:

(5.46) The boy $\left\{ \begin{array}{c} that \\ who \end{array} \right\}$ *was in the hall* smiled. (restrictive modifier)

(5.47) Alice, *who was in the hall,* put on her brightest smile. (nonrestrictive modifier)

In the above examples, (5.46) is a restrictive modifier because it differentiates *the boy* from all other possible boys in the world: it was the boy who was in the hall who smiled, not just any boy. In (5.47), however, *Alice* is already specified by the fact that we have named her. We do not have to distinguish her from all other persons in the world, but for some reason the speaker feels that it is important to tell the listener that Alice was in the hall at the time she smiled. This is simply additional information. It is supplied, in this case, by a nonrestrictive modifier. Note that any head noun can have a nonrestrictive modifier. If, in the context of the previous conversation, a nonspecific noun [such as the head of the noun phrase in the subject in (5.46)] had previously been specified to the listener, a nonrestrictive modifier could be used:

(5.48) The other day I met a young boy who was enrolled at the Maritime Academy. I was coming out of my office, and the boy, *who was in the hall,* smiled.

In (5.48) the insert in the last sentence is identical to the one in (5.46) except for the commas (and the intonation pattern when spoken). It is a nonrestrictive modifier, i.e., the context of the paragraph has already identified the specific boy, and the modifier of the head noun just adds a little bit of information about where the boy was when he smiled.

Both restrictive and nonrestrictive modifiers can function either as modifiers of heads of noun phrases in the subject function or heads of noun phrases in the object function of clauses. Examples (5.44) to (5.48) inclusive contain modifiers of head nouns within the subject function. The following examples are modifiers of the head of the NP that fills the object function:

(5.49) Lucy spoke to the man *who left.* (restrictive modifier)

(5.50) Lucy spoke to the man, *who left.* (nonrestrictive modifier)

In Tables 5.19 and 5.20, note how the insert is formed. In order for an insert to fill the restrictive modifier function, one of the nouns in the insert must refer to the same thing as one of the nouns in the matrix. In the case of Table 5.19, the object of the insert and the subject of the matrix have identical references, and the insert can be used as a restrictive modifier. Before it is inserted, however, the noun of the insert is replaced with a *wh-* word, which is moved to the front of the clause. At this point it can be inserted. Because the *wh-* word in the insert refers to the same thing as the noun being modified in the

---

Table 5.19. Formation of Restrictive and Nonrestrictive Modifiers of the Head Noun in the Subject Function of the Matrix

Matrix:	*The little boy* ran away.
Insert:	I know *the little boy.*
Wh- Replacement:	I know $\begin{Bmatrix} \text{who(m)} \\ \textit{that.} \end{Bmatrix}$
Wh- Movement:	$\begin{Bmatrix} \text{who(m)} \\ \textit{that} \end{Bmatrix}$ I know.
Insertion:	The little boy $\begin{Bmatrix} \text{who(m)} \\ \textit{that} \end{Bmatrix}$*I know* ran away.
Optional *Wh-* Deletion:	The little boy *I know* ran away.

---

matrix, the *wh-* word is optional and can be deleted or retained as the speaker chooses. Note, however, that if the insert is an equative clause, as in Table 5.20, we cannot delete the *wh-* word without changing the meaning of the sentence entirely. In equative inserts, the deletion of the *wh-* word is not an option. To illustrate this, consider the following examples:

(5.51a) Randolph found the man *who was in charge.* (restrictive modifier)

(5.51b) Randolph found *the man was in charge.* (direct object)

Example (5.51a) contains a restrictive modifier, but (5.51b) contains an object insert. Note how we must recover the *wh-* word for (5.51b):

(5.51c) Randolph found *that the man was in charge.* (direct object)

When equative clauses fill the restrictive modifier slot, any deletion must include the predicate of the insert, i.e., we can delete the *wh-* word in such a case, but we must also delete the predicate:

Table 5.20. Formation of Restrictive and Nonrestrictive Modifiers of the Head Noun in the Direct Object Function of the Matrix

Matrix:	He introduced *the man.*
Insert:	*The man* was in his class.
Wh- Replacement:	$\begin{Bmatrix} \textit{That} \\ \textit{Who} \end{Bmatrix}$ was in his class.
Subordination:	He introduced the man $\begin{Bmatrix} \textit{that} \\ \textit{who} \end{Bmatrix}$ *was in his class.*

(5.51d) Randolph found the man *in charge*. (restrictive modifier)

Now (5.51d) is exactly like the restrictive modifiers discussed in Chapter 4.

The table showing the construction of the noun phrase in Chapter 4 (Table 4.5, p. 78) states that both a restrictive and a nonrestrictive modifier can appear n the same noun phrase. This is true, but it is also true that the order of the two modifiers is fixed. If both appear in a single NP, the nonrestrictive modifier must appear after the restrictive modifier:

(5.52) The man *you met yesterday, who was in the airplane,* was Mr. Nicely.

In (5.52) the first post-noun modifier is a restrictive modifier, and the second is a nonrestrictive modifier. The order cannot be changed without changing the order of modification: the second clause will become a restrictive modifier if it changes places with the first. Either of these functions can be repeated in much the same way that the loose-knit modifier can be repeated:

(5.53) The lady *we saw under the lamppost who hailed a cab* was Mrs. Rockefeller. (repeated restrictive modifiers)

(5.54) The sale at Gregorio's, *which sells men's clothing, which also sells rowboats,* is a very good one. (repeated nonrestrictive modifiers)

All of the *wh-* words can be used to introduce subordinates that fill restrictive or nonrestrictive modifier functions. In the previous examples we have seen *who* and *which*, but others are quite possible:

(5.55) The place *where they sell water* is run by Gypsies.

(5.56) The reason *why I am telling you this* is that I like you.

All of the *wh-* words used in restrictive and nonrestrictive modifiers replace a part of the insert clause. They have the same meanings as when they are used to replace part or a *wh-* question (see Table 5.8, p. 116). That is, *who* replaces a noun that refers to a person, *why* replaces a *because* coordinate clause, etc. As in most subordinates, the word *that* is simply an alternate form for many of the regular *wh-* words:

(5.57) The girl $\begin{Bmatrix} who \\ that \end{Bmatrix}$ married him turned out to be a jewel.

(5.58) The time $\begin{Bmatrix} when \\ that \end{Bmatrix}$ you came was noted in the log.

Note that the word *what* is not used in most of the standard dialects to begin a restrictive or a nonrestrictive modifier:

(5.59a) *The box *what I showed you* is the one I want.

Standard dialects prefer *which* or *that* in this case:

(5.59b) The box $\left\{ \begin{array}{c} which \\ that \end{array} \right\}$ I showed you is the one I want.

It is possible to confuse the restrictive and nonrestrictive modifier NP functions with adverbial modifiers of the predicate. There are two tests that will help you tell whether a construction is a restrictive modifier or an adverbial modifier of a verb phrase. (*A*) If the construction has no verb, try to expand it to find out whether or not it is an insert clause. In the following examples, (5.61) is a restrictive modifier, but (5.62) is not:

(5.61) The guy *in the hall* was pretty noisy. $\Longleftrightarrow$ The guy *who was in the hall* was pretty noisy. (restrictive modifier)

(5.62) The guy was noisy *in the hall* $\overset{\longleftarrow}{\longrightarrow}\!\!\!\!|$ *The guy was noisy *that was in the hall*. (adverbial of place)

The addition of *that was* in (5.62) changes the meaning of the original clause. The modifier tells where the *guy* was noisy, not which *guy* was noisy. Consequently, it is an adverb, not a restrictive modifier of a head noun. The insert in (5.61) retains its original meaning when expanded, however, and is a restrictive modifier.

(*B*) The second test is to try a *wh-* question, i.e., restrictive modifiers answer the question, *which (noun),* while adverbials answer questions like *where, when, how, with whom,* or *with what*. Thus (5.61) answers the question *which guy* while (5.62) answers the question *where was the guy noisy?*

COMPLEX NOMINALS. Another place in the noun phrase where we will find clauses is in the complex nominal filler of the head function (see Chapter 4). These insert clauses can be either *wh-* inserts or infinitive inserts; we will discuss only the *wh-* inserts here. Actually, they are rather simple in terms of their construction—a clause is merely inserted into the completion function of the complex nominal (see Chapter 4) along with the word *that*:

(5.65) The announcement *that we were leaving* came too late.

(5.66) The discovery *that the world was round* was electrifying.

In both of the above examples, the *wh-* insert clause fills the completion function. That is, words such as *announcement* and *discovery* are too vague to be used without giving more information about them. In Fries's terms, the completion function of the complex nominal is ''optional but indispensable'' (P. H. Fries, 1972). That is, we can choose not to use the complex nominal, but somehow we must convey the information that is contained in it. If we do not use the complex nominal we *must* find some other means of getting the information to the listener. The *wh-* completion is one of the options available to us for supplying the information.

POSSESSORS. We have also seen that entire clauses can be inflected for possession and fill the det.$_2$ function of the noun phrase (Chapter 4, Figure 4.2). That is, the italicized clause in (5.67) fills a det.$_2$ function:

(5.67a) *The girl I love*'s heart belongs to me.

Note, however, that the object of the insert clause seems to precede the subject. This is not actually the case, because *I love* functions as a restrictive modifier of *girl* in the following manner:

(5.67b) *Matrix:* The *girl's* heart belongs to me.
   Insert: I love the girl.
   Subordinate: The *girl I love the girl's* heart belongs to me.

Since English prefers not to repeat fillers (cf. coordinations, for example), the second *the girl* is deleted, and the result is as in (5.67a). Many people, when seeing sentences such as (5.67a) written down, will deny that they can occur in English. Sentences such as this are perfectly good constructions, however, and we use them quite often in speech.

Infinitive Subordination

Clauses that have infinitive verb phrases are subordinated in much the same way that *wh*-clauses are subordinated, except that they do not fill the restrictive or nonrestrictive modifier functions in English. Much of what will be said following, therefore, will be repetitious of the preceding.

The Infinitive Verb Phrase

The construction of the infinitive verb phrase is slightly different from that of the ordinary verb phrase: it is presented in Table 5.21. As can be seen in this table, the infinitive verb phrase, like the ordinary verb phrase, contains the obligatory head function filled by a verb stem, and the optional functions of perfective, continuum, and passive (in the case of infinitive VPs, with transitive verbs). Unlike the ordinary verb phrases, however, the infinitive VP has no tense function. Thus, infinitive verb phrases such as the following are impossible in English:

(5.68a) *to threw

Table 5.21. Construction of the Infinitive Verb Phrase

Functions:	± Marker	± Perfective	± Continuum	± Passive	+ Head
	to				see
	to			be	seen
	to		be		seeing
	to	have			seen
	to		be	being	seen
	to	have		been	seen
	to	have	been		seeing
	to	have	been	being	seen
Filler Classes:	to	HAVE *-en*	BE *-ing*	BE *-en*	STEM

(5.69b) *to had gone

(5.70a) *to were going

In order to make the above phrases sound right, we must remove tense:

(5.68b) to throw

(5.69b) to have gone

(5.70b) to be going

Note also that the infinitive VP is marked by the infinitive marker *to*. Usually this marker is obligatory, but sometimes it can be deleted at the option of the speaker, and sometimes it *must* be deleted from the infinitive VP. Because it is optional in some phrases, the marker function is labeled optional (±) in Table 5.21.

Finally, infinitive VPs cannot contain a modal. There are no infinitive VPs such as the following in English:

(5.71) *to may go

(5.72) *to can be seen

Infinitive Clauses as Subordinates

The relation of the infinitive VP to the sentence is always that of insert. The only time infinitive clauses can be matrix clauses is when they are already subordinated to another clause. They fill the functions of subject, direct object, or complement in a matrix clause, or completion of the complex nominal in a noun phrase. Some of these relationships are illustrated in Table 5.22. As in *wh-* subordinates, the matrix has a blank slot which is filled by the clause containing the infinitive VP. The clause to be inserted appears in its infinitive form. Once formed, the infinitive is simply used to fill the blank function in the matrix (the obligatory subject deletions shown in Table 5.22 are explained in the text following).

Infinitive clauses can fill either subject or complement functions in equative clauses; and in fact, they can even do both at the same time. In this case, aphorisms such as the following are the result:

(5.73) *To know me* is *to love me*.

(5.74) *To seek* is *to find*.

Like the *wh-* inserts in complex nominals, the infinitive complex nominal inserts are "optional but indispensible." That is, if the information contained in the completion does not appear in the head of the NP, it must be given someplace else.

Thus, infinitive clauses are subordinated in just about the same way that *wh-* clauses are subordinated. The major differences between infinitive subordinates and *wh-* subordinates are (*a*) Infinitive verb phrases have their own special construction rules; and (*b*) Infinitive clauses cannot function as restrictive and nonrestrictive modifiers of the head noun in a

Table 5.22. The Infinitive Clause as Insert

Object Insert

Matrix:	Jerrold wants (*something*).
Insert:	Agatha marries him. ⇔ Agatha *to marry* him
Subordination:	Jerrold wants Agatha *to marry* him.

Subject Insert

Matrix:	(*Something*) is my heart's desire.
Insert:	I climb mountains. ⇔ I *to climb* mountains
Subordination:	*I to climb mountains* is my heart's desire.
Obligatory Subject Deletion:	*To climb mountains* is my heart's desire.

Complement Insert

Matrix:	That thing is (*something*).
Insert:	It opens cans. ⇔ It *to open* cans
Subordination:	That thing is *it to open* cans
Obligatory Subject Deletion:	That thing is *to open cans*.

Complex Nominal Completion Insert

Matrix:	His *duty* was plain.
Insert:	He succeeds. ⇔ He *to succeed*
Subordination:	His *duty he to succeed* was plain
Obligatory Subject Deletion:	His *duty to succeed* was plain.

noun phrase as is possible for *wh-* clauses, nor can they fill adverbial functions. Instead, the infinitive insert can fill only subject and object clause functions and the completion of the complex nominal function in noun phrases.

Deletions in Infinitive Subordinates

As is true of coordinated clauses, identities in the infinitive insert and matrix clauses are deleted. If the subjects of the two clauses are different, both must appear in the sentence. When the subjects of both the matrix and insert clauses are identical, however, the subject of the insert is deleted. These relationships are illustrated in both Tables 5.22 and 5.23.

The same deletions occur when the subject of the infinitive is a dummy and the infinitive clause functions as the subject or object of an equative clause. The examples in (5.73) and (5.74) show this deletion. The process of deleting these subjects is shown in Table 5.24. Note how these inserts begin with dummy subjects. If only one infinitive appears in an equative, it can fill either subject or object functions. Thus, the infinitive can be moved about for the sake of providing emphasis:

(5.75) All he wanted was *to be left alone*.

Table 5.23. Deletions of Subjects in Infinitive Inserts

All Functions Different: No Deletions

Matrix:	John waits for (*something*).
Insert:	Mary moves out of the house. ⇔ Mary *to move* out of the house
Subordination:	John waits for *Mary to move out of the house.*

Identical Functions: Deletion Required

Matrix:	Max wants (*something*).
Insert:	Max buys a house. ⇔ Max *to buy* a house
Subordination:	Max wants *Max to buy a house*
Obligatory Subject Deletion:	Max wants *to buy a house.*

(5.76) *To be left alone* was all he wanted.

If two clauses are inserted into an equative clause matrix (see Table 5.24), the subjects are identical and both are deleted. The result is an aphorism.

The infinitive marker is also deleted in some instances. Such deletion is required when one of the following verbs fills the head function of the predicate in the matrix:

(5.77) See, feel, have, look at, hear, make, let, listen to, etc.

This situation occurs only when the matrix verb is in the active voice. When it is passive, the marker appears. The following examples illustrate this concept:

(5.78a) She saw *him leave.* (active matrix)

(5.78b) He was seen *to leave.* (passive matrix)

(5.79a) They made *him appear before the grand jury.* (active matrix)

(5.79b) He was made *to appear before the grand jury.* (passive matrix)

Of course, not all of the verbs in the list in (5.77) are transitive, and not all can be made passive. In the active, however, all delete the infinitive marker.

Table 5.24. Deletions in Infinitive Inserts in Equative Clauses

Matrix:	(*Something*) is (*something*).
Insert #1:	(*Somebody*) falls in love. ⇔ (*Somebody*) *to fall* in love
Insert #2:	(*Somebody*) knows madness. ⇔ (*Somebody*) *to know* madness
Subordination:	(*Somebody*) *to fall in love* is (*somebody*) *to know madness*
Obligatory Subject Deletion:	*To fall in love* is *to know madness.*

Because there is no tense in the infinitive VP, there is nothing to which tense can be attached when the infinitive verb phrase is negated. When an infinitive is negated, the negative word *not* appears in front of the entire infinitive verb phrase:

(5.80) He wanted *not to see her at all.*

In the case of verbs like *need* (in the sense of "is required to") and *dare,* the marker is deleted in the negated form, and we find sentences such as the following:

(5.81) We need *to go home for lunch.*

(5.82) We need *not go home for lunch.*

Finally, the verb *help,* when it fills the head function in the predicate of the matrix clause, is in a class by itself. When this verb appears, the infinitive VP of the insert clause can appear in its full form, the subject can be deleted, the marker can be deleted, or both can be deleted at the option of the speaker. This is illustrated by the following:

(5.83a) Marsha helped *them to build it.*

(5.83b) Marsha helped *to build it.* (infinitive subject deleted)

(5.83c) Marsha helped *them build it.* (infinitive marker deleted)

(5.83d) Marsha helped *build it.* (infinitive marker and subject deleted)

Gerunds as Alternative Infinitives

A gerund is like a verb with only the *-ing* inflection of the BE *-ing* present. It is used only in insert clauses that act like an infinitive. Therefore, we can look at them as being alternate forms of the infinitive. The difference between infinitive verb phrases and verb phrases with gerunds is that gerunds can have no auxiliaries. That is, we find no verb phrases like the following in English:

(5.84) *can *running*

(5.85) *have *seeing*

(5.86) *might have *looking*

Gerunds, like infinitives, are tenseless. They are subordinated as shown in Table 5.25. Note how similar infinitives and gerunds are:

(5.87) Mabel likes Herbert $\left\{\begin{array}{l} to\ pose \\ posing \end{array}\right\}$ for pictures.

(5.88) It was sad $\left\{\begin{array}{l} to\ think \\ thinking \end{array}\right\}$ of John having all that fun.

One interesting difference between infinitives and gerunds, however, is the fact that gerunds can be "possessed" in much the same way as the head of a noun phrase can be

---

Table 5.25. Gerund Inserts

Matrix:	John likes (*object*).
Insert:	John fishes. ⇔ John *fishing*
Subordination:	John likes *John fishing*
Obligatory Subject Deletion:	John likes *fishing*.

''possessed.'' In this sense, they are like nouns:

(5.89) *His leaving* was a cause for rejoicing among the troops.

(5.90) *John's graduating* was a disaster.

Note, in both of the above examples, that the gerund verb phrase is still the predicate in an insert. In the case of (5.89) and (5.90), we find subject inserts, but notice that we can find object inserts as well:

(5.91) They all resented *my punishing the cat.*

Summary: Coordinates and Subordinates

Some sentences contain two or more predicates, each of which are in separate clauses that have been combined in one of several ways. One method of combination is that of coordination. In coordinated sentences, clauses are connected by conjunctions and the original clauses have equal status in the resultant sentence.

Another method of combination is that of subordination, which can be either *wh-* or infinitive subordination. When clauses with *wh-* replacements are subordinated, a function of an insert clause is replaced with a *wh-* word, just as in *wh-* questions, and the *wh-* word is moved to the front of the clause. Unlike questions, however, tense does not move. The clause is then inserted into a matrix, where it can be used to fill the clausal functions of subject, direct object, complement, and adverbial, or noun phrase functions of restrictive or nonrestrictive modifiers, det.$_2$, or complex nominal completion. When declaratives are subordinated, the *wh-* word simply serves as an introducer; it does not replace a function. It can be deleted. In infinitive subordination, the VP in the insert must first be made into an infinitive or a gerund before it can be inserted. Once this occurs, however, infinitive clauses can fill either subject, object, or complement functions in matrix clauses, or the complex nominal completion function in the head of noun phrases.

Summary

Transformations are statements of grammatical relationships between related constructions. This is a different view of transformations from that found in other grammars, but for assessment and teaching purposes it turns out to be quite useful. The relationships, as stated in this chapter, can be used as the basis for scaling developmental sequences that will allow us to (*a*) figure out where a child is functioning in terms of development and (*b*) construct teaching paradigms that will help a child who has developmental problems. The manner in which this can be done will be the topic of Chapter 6.

CHAPTER 6

The Development of the Sentence

The last three chapters contained an analysis of *what* a child born into the community of speakers of English must learn. Obviously, he cannot learn it all at once: some of the content of Chapters 3, 4, and 5 must be learned before the rest can be learned. This chapter contains the result of a hierarchical task analysis of the prerequisites to the complete development of the adult forms of English sentences. It sets forth a logical order for teaching the obligatory clause functions, the phrase functions, and the transformations. Data from other sources have been drawn upon to support and flesh out the analysis. The result is a very detailed hypothesis on the normal sequence of acquisition of English grammar in the first few years of life.

Many details presented in this chapter, especially those dealing with the developmental sequence of the VP and the transformations, have relied upon the work of Lee and her associates at Northwestern University. (Her book is a valuable resource and is strongly recommended.) Also helpful has been the work of Miller and Yoder (1974), Menyuk (1971), McNeil (1966, 1970), Olson (1971), and Brown (1973). Although the statement of the sequence must still be couched in the terms of a hypothesis, my observations and those of my students lead me to believe that the sequence reflects reality rather well. It can serve as a guide to a teacher in planning for the instruction of children with developmental language disabilities.

In the search for understanding the sequence of acquisition of adult sentence patterns, the hypothesis states that children must first learn the basic clause functions (subjects,

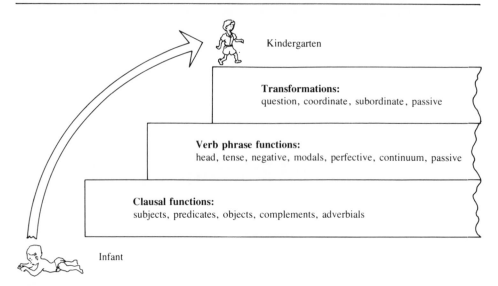

Figure 6.1 General sequence of acquisition of the sentence patterns of English.

predicates, objects, and complements). These functions, when learned, are used to organize the rest of the learning involved. That is, once learned, the clause functions serve as matrices within which children structure the learning of phrases, morphology, phonology, and upon which they build the more complex learning, such as that required for the transformations (see Figure 6.1).

Once the child starts to get the clausal functions under control, we begin to observe the development of the verb phrase functions that are prerequisite to the development of the transformations (coordination, questions, subordinations, and passive). Once the child begins to use the first completely filled VP functions, the first transformations begin to appear in his speech. As new learning takes place on the clause level, more potential for learning at other levels in the hierarchy develops (see Figure 2.1). Learning on the highest level usually begins before the learning of the lower levels is complete.

In order to structure an adequate language program for a child, it is necessary for the teacher to find out where in this sequence the child is currently functioning. The sequence presented in the following section (*a*) lays the foundation for the discussion in Chapter 7 on how to do an adequate assessment, and (*b*) provides a sequence for a good language instruction program.

Five Stages in Clause Development

As children grow, their clause development goes through five major stages (Table 6.1). **Each of the basic clause types—transitive, intransitive, and equative—moves from one stage to another independently.** As functions from other levels in the hierarchy (Figure 2.1) are added to the child's linguistic repertoire, each of the clause types reaches the highest level of development for specific transformations. It is most important to note that neither the child nor the entire language move from stage to stage. Each clause type develops independently, and it is often the case that development of the three major clause types is spread over two or even three stages at times. It is not at all rare, for example, for a

Table 6.1. Schematic Description of the Acquisition and Elaboration of the English Clause

Stage	Grammar	Semantics	Discourse
I. Babbling	No grammar	No meaning	No text
II. Holophrastic	a. No grammar	a. Substantives	a. Topic in environment, comment spoken. No text.
	b. No grammar	b. Relations	b. Topic in environment, comment spoken. Rudimentary text.
III. Preclausal	a. Pivot-open constructions	a. Relation-substantive constructions	a. Topic added or comment elaborated.
	b. One or more obligatory grammatical and semantic function missing.	b. One or more obligatory grammatical and semantic function missing.	b. Topic and comment elaboration. Longer text.
IV. Clausal	All obligatory grammatical and semantic functions present.		Initial separation of topic from grammatical subject in *wh-* questions.
V. Major Transformations	Position shifts, deletions, additions.	Separation of actor from grammatical subject.	Topic manipulated independently from grammatical subject.

child to exhibit some Stage V intransitive questions while his transitive declaratives and questions are at Stage IV and all his equative clauses are at Stage III. The nine boxes in Table 3.1 (Chapter 3, p. 40) must each be considered separately when analyzing the developmental status of a child's language.

Stage I: Babbling

In the babbling stage the child simply produces a lot of sounds. These sounds are not random; as development proceeds through the babbling stage, the child increasingly produces English vowels and consonants in accordance with his increasing physiological competence. In addition to producing vowel and consonant sounds, the infant also seems to begin modeling[1] the intonational patterns of the language being spoken around him. These intonation patterns appear to be among the very first features of English that a child imitates. Whether the child's utterances are "language," in the sense that they are "American English," cannot be claimed.[2] However these utterances do communicate needs and desires (Halliday, 1972). Because of the currently assumed lack of structure of these utterances, this stage must be considered to be essentially prelinguistic.

Stage II: Holophrastic

Soon the normal baby begins to say things.[3] His first English utterances are generally made up of single words, e.g.:

(6.1) Mama

(6.2) Kitty

Here, in these first single-word utterances, which have been called *holophrastic* (McNeil, 1970), the child makes semantically complete utterances that contain the discourse functions of both *topic* and *comment* (see Chapter 2). The utterance itself appears to be the comment, while the topic is unstated and must be sought in the child's external or internal environment. For example, a child might say:

(6.3) Banana (or its infantile equivalent)

and it could have any one of the following meanings (and more):

---

[1]Such modeling is not necessarily imitation of a specific parental stimulus pattern. Rather, the baby seems to be trying to imitate the general idea of intonation patterns, not one specific instance. This also seems to be true of most linguistic imitation, no matter at which level it occurs. It may even be true, in fact, of most kinds of childish imitation. At the age of four or five, for instance, many children will take a pencil and scribble all over a piece of paper and insist that they are "writing." In effect, this is an imitation of "what adults do" rather than of "what an adult did": this is what is meant here by the term *modeling*.

[2]This statement may have to be modified. Halliday (1972, 1973a, 1973b) is in the process of identifying semantic functions that appear in the babbling stage. Before long it may be possible to identify a Stage Ia (no meaning) and a Stage Ib, in which meaning can be discerned even though English words do not appear.

[3]For some children there is a severe break between the babbling stage and the stages which follow (Menyuk, 1971). When it occurs it is marked by silence; the children in whom it occurs simply stop making noises.

(6.3a) that the child sees a banana

(6.3b) that the child is identifying an object as being a banana

(6.3c) that the child wishes to have a banana

(6.3d) that the child has lost sight of a banana that has just dropped from his hand

In each of these instances we can readily identify the topic of the utterance: In (6.3a) and (6.3b) the banana is visible to the child and the topic of his comment is most probably the physical object itself. Note that the comments of (6.3a) and (6.3b) are different, however, and that adult clauses with equivalent meaning would be different. In (6.3c) and (6.3d) the object may or may not be visible to the child, and the topic could be quite different from either of the first two utterances. In (6.3c) it is likely to be an internal state (e.g., the child's hunger or his desire for the taste of a banana), while in (6.3d) the topic is probably the lack of the banana. One thing clearly demonstrated by this is the fact that the total meaning of the child's utterance cannot be understood until we know the context in which the utterance is made. Discourse, or the back and forth flow of conversation, requires both a topic *and* a comment. Since the topic, at this stage, is in the environment, the utterance has relatively little communicative value until the topic is identified by the listener. In order for us to understand the topic of the child's utterance and what his comment about that topic really is, we must be present when the utterance occurs.

Thus we can see that the structure of adult discourse appears to be present in rudimentary form from the time the child utters his first word. In the first part of this stage, however, there seems to be little or no text, i.e., the child seems largely to communicate with himself. When he wishes to communicate with others he slips back to the forms of babbling he has been using prior to the use of his first word (Menyuk, personal communication). After awhile, however, the child will begin to respond to an utterance made by somebody else, for example:

Adult: Do you want some more milk?
Child: Milk (or, perhaps, *more*).

This is the most rudimentary form of text, and it usually begins to occur while the child is still making holophrastic utterances.

The child's holophrastic utterances, even at this early point in development, have clause-level semantic meaning. The first class of semantic functions to appear are generally those that Miller and Yoder (1974) have called *substantives*. Substantives are those semantic functions that have an environmental referent. Examples of the first substantives to appear can be found in the first column of Table 6.2.

Again, note how a single form can fill a number of functions. The utterance "Mama," for example, can fill the semantic functions of *comment* ("Mama is here"); *vocative* ("Mama, come help me"); *greeting* ("Hi, Mama"); *actor* ("Mama just did something"); *patient* ("Something just happened to Mama"); *possessor* ("This object belongs to Mama"). The list in the first column of Table 6.2 is arranged according to frequency of usage of the substantive functions that appear in Stage IIa, i.e., the most frequently used functions are at the top of the list and the least frequently used are at the bottom.

Usually one or more substantive functions have appeared in the child's overt speech

Table 6.2. Semantic Functions Appearing in Stage II

Substantive Functions			Relational Functions		
Function	Purpose	Possible Forms	Function	Purpose	Possible Forms
Comments, greetings	Labeling of perceived events	"Mama" "Baby"	Recurrence	Comment or request	"More." "Again." That is more milk. I want some more milk.
Vocative	Attention-getting	"Mama" "Daddy"	Nonexistence	Something the child expected to find is not present	"No." There isn't any ball here but I thought there would be one.
Agent	Causer of action	"Mama" "Daddy"	Disappearance	Child has lost contact with something	"Away." "Allgone." Where did the ball go? The ball is gone.
Patient	Undergoer of action (infrequent)	"Mama" "Daddy"	Rejection	Child does not want something	"No." Take that asparagus away.
Action	Marking action	"Fall" "Catch" "Turn" "Tire"	Cessation	An action has ceased	"Stop." The top is no longer spinning.
Possession	Association of objects with objects or people	"Daddy" "Mommy" "Mine"	Existence	Something is present and the child has noticed it	"There." "Oh-oh." "Oooh!" Will you look at that thing over there!

Source. Adapted from "An Ontogenetic Language Teaching Strategy for Retarded Children" by J. Miller and D. Yoder, In *Language Perspectives: Acquisition, Retardation, and Intervention* by R. Schiefelbush and L. Lloyd (Eds.) Baltimore: University Park, 1974. Adapted with permission.

before he begins to use another class of semantic functions.[4] These are the Stage IIb functions[5] which Miller and Yoder have called the *relational* functions. Forms filling these functions do not have environmental referents. Rather, they express semantic relations of one kind or another. The second column in Table 6.2 contains a list of these functions and examples of forms that can be used as fillers. Again, note how a single form can fill different functions, e.g., the form *no* can fill nonexistence, disappearance, or rejection functions, and, at times, even the cessation function. It is worth repeating that we must be in the child's immediate environment to understand his utterances. Words used to fill the recurrence function, for example, could also indicate a comment or a request ("That is more milk," or "I want some more milk"). Further examples can be seen in Table 6.2.

As long as the child continues to speak in one-word utterances, his clausal development remains at Stage II. Those utterances expressing relational functions have been classified as Stage IIb because they generally begin to appear later, while those utterances expressing substantive functions have been classified Stage IIa because they generally begin to appear earlier. Once again, however, note that the only real distinction to be made between these two classes of semantic functions is that of semantic function itself: the Stage IIb utterances express relations while the Stage IIa utterances express substance.

Observe that all holophrastic utterances fill only semantic functions. There is no grammatical structure in them simply because there cannot be any grammatical structure until there is more than one word (remember that "rules of grammar" are simply the regularities found in stringing words together). Other than the existence of certain intonation patterns in holophrastic utterances (e.g., those for emphasis, declarative, and question), grammatical rules need two or more morphemes in sequence. Therefore, "grammar" per se cannot occur in holophrastic utterances. The genesis of the entire structure of both text and many of the clausal semantic functions are present at this stage, however. Thus, speaking purely in terms of description, semantic meaning develops first, and grammatical meaning follows. This also appears to be the case for at least some of the subsequent stages.

McNeill (1970) and Menyuk (1971) both note several other important features of holophrastic utterances in addition to those brought out by Miller and Yoder:

1. Holophrastic utterances can be imbued with emotion in that the child may simply be expressing his feelings about something. The comment he is making may be purely emotional and thus be difficult to interpret.
2. Not all children use the same holophrastic words—the fact is that there are some children who do not learn, for example, a word for *kitty* or *ball* simply because they

---

[4]I have known children whose first word represented a relational function, e.g., *more*. This illustrates the fact that distinctions within stages, e.g., Stage IIa versus IIb, are arbitrary and exist largely for classificatory convenience rather than eternal verity. However the acquisition of the major organizers, such as clausal functions and transformations, are invariant in terms of their sequence of arrival.

[5]Note, however, that the child continues to make utterances that would be classified as being at Stage IIa (and will do so all his life). This situation is a manifestation of what Brown (1973) calls *the law of cumulative complexity*. That is, anyone can (and will) say things that would be classified at a lower level of development once he has learned to do so. Even adults say things that can be classified as being indicative of Stage IIa development. We cannot allow these low-level constructions to throw us off when we try to analyze what it is a child *knows* how to do.

do not have a kitty or ball in their environment and the linguistic adults never have the opportunity to talk about them.

3. It is also true that some children will invent private words, the meanings of which are apparent only to the child and perhaps to a very few adults or older children.

4. Because phonological learning (the learning of the sounds of the language) continues to take place beyond the holophrastic stage, words used by the child in Stage II typically have not yet attained the normal adult pronunciation of the words that are found in the child's environment.

Stage III: Preclauses

Sooner or later all children begin to put two or more words together and their utterances begin to get more complex. When this occurs we say that the child's clauses begin to enter the third stage, or the stage of the *preclause*. These utterances are called *preclauses* because, while they are more complex than the holophrastic utterances which have been appearing, they do not yet have the grammatical construction of adult clauses.

Stage IIIa: Early Two-Word Combinations

When the child's utterances begin to have two or more words in them, three things happen:

1. Grammar, or the rules for stringing words together, appears.
2. The topic of the discourse begins to be expressed (for the exception to this, see the following.
3. The substantive and relational functions that appear singly in Stage II begin to be combined and more clause-level semantic functions appear.

Stage III has two different substages, which are defined largely by the approximation of the preclausal utterances for each clause type in the adult grammar. We will consider each of the substages separately.

Grammatical Relations

The first of the preclausal utterances consist of two-word combinations, as we would expect. These combinations have often been referred to as *pivot-open* combinations (e.g., McNeill, 1970; Olson, 1971). It is convenient to use this terminology in reference to the grammar of this stage simply because it allows us to make an adequate description of the grammatical features of the clause at this point in development.

Words from transcripts of children's conversations can be classified as to whether they occur relatively few times or whether they occur over and over again. Of course, some words that occur over and over for some children will occur relatively fewer times for others, but in general a pattern emerges from each such distributional analysis. The words that occur again and again in a child's speech are called *pivot-class* words, and those that occur only occasionally are called *open-class* words. The pivot-class words compose a rather small group for any one child, while the open-class words compose a much larger group. New vocabulary words are added to both groups as the child grows older, but the open-class items are added more rapidly than are the pivot-class items.

The grammatical rules written to show how these words occur in a child's speech during Stage IIIa are presented in Table 6.3. As can be seen, these rules are very weak and do not

Table 6.3. Grammatical Rules in Stage IIIa

Pivot-Open

Open-Pivot

Open-Open

tell us much about the child's use of the language. Indeed, the entire concept of pivot and open rules has come under strong attack from several quarters lately (e.g., Brown, 1973) simply because they are not very useful in analyzing a child's speech. This argument cannot be contested. The only thing that these rules say is that a child's Stage IIIa utterances consist of either a pivot and an open word (in any order), or two open-class words. This does not mean, however, that the grammar is a poor description of what occurs; it simply indicates that the grammatical rules at this point are subordinate to the basic semantic functions that are still being developed. As it turns out, a description of the development of semantic functions will still provide us with a more useful tool from the standpoint of developing instructional programs for children whose clauses are at Stage IIIa.

Discourse

Even though the grammatical categories appear to be relatively unimportant, something very important is happening in discourse: the topic of the utterance, which was previously found only in the environmental context, now begins to be expressed overtly. When two-word utterances begin to appear, the child begins to add a degree of precision to his discourse. This development continues through the next stages and beyond in much the same fashion that biological cell structure develops. The topic and comment of each clause comes to be expressed with increasing precision as the grammatical structure becomes more elaborate. Table 6.4 shows us an interesting fact about the structure of discourse at this point: The topic of the Stage IIIa utterances does not always occur in the initial position of the utterance as is true of the adult clause (Halliday, 1970). For at least a time in the preclauses, the position of the topic of the clause is variable.

Note, too, in Table 6.4, how the grammatical categories interact with the discourse functions. More often than not, the pivot-class items appear to function as comments about the open-class topics, but this is not necessarily true in all instances. This situation shows us that, although the discourse and grammatical functions of child language are interdependent and often correlate with each other, they are independent, at least to some degree. Note that this fact is true from the earliest point of grammatical development.

Children who make holophrastic and Stage IIIa preclause utterances do not maintain text for very long. One or two exchanges is about the extent of it (see Chapter 2). Even though some precision has been added to the child's utterances, communication of meaning in the preclausal stage still relies heavily on the contextual circumstances in which the utterance occurs. As in the case of the holophrastic utterances, we usually must be present to discover what the child means by what he says. Since topics and comments are still incompletely stated at this point, many of the child's utterances are quite ambiguous without context. This ambiguity is most clearly seen in the last two columns of Table 6.4 in which identical utterances have totally different meanings. The very first utterance in each of these columns comes from Bloom (1970), for example. In the first instance the little girl who said this was holding up her mother's sock, and the first word is a comment

Table 6.4. Examples of Two-Word Combinations

Grammatical Categories:	Pivot + Open	Pivot + Open	Open + Pivot	Open + Open	Open + Open
Semantic Categories:	Comment + Topic	Topic + Comment	Topic + Comment	Comment + Topic	Topic + Comment
	big boss	it door	boot off	Mommy sock	Mommy sock
	big boat	it mine	light off	Selena shoe	Selena shoe
	big bus		pants off		
		that broke	shirt off		
	more taxi	that hot	shoe off		
	more melon				
			bunny do		
	byebye plane		Daddy do		
	byebye man		Momma do		
	byebye hot				
			mail come		
	allgone shoe		Mama come		
	allgone vitamins				
	allgone egg		airplane by		
			siren by		
	no bed				
	no down				
	no fix				

Source. Adapted data from Bloom, 1970; Braine, 1963; McNeill, 1970; unpublished data from Heber.

Table 6.5. Examples of Two-Word Combinations with External Topics

Grammar: Semantics:	Pivot- Action	Open- Patient
	Take	nap.
	Take	ride.
	Got	boat.
	Got	mine.
	See	boy.
	See	hot.
	Push	it.
	Close	it.

about the sock ("This is Mommy's sock") in a possessive relationship. The second utterance occurred while the little girl's mother was putting on the girl's sock, and the second word was the comment of the utterance in an actor-patient relationship ("Mommy is putting on the sock"). Approximately the same things happened with the second set of utterances in these columns.

Not all two-word utterances contain a stated topic. There is one whole class of utterances which are good illustrations of this. These utterances contain a verb and typically fill the semantic functions of action-patient, as shown in Table 6.5. In each of the examples in Table 6.5, neither the pivot nor the open-class words can be classified as *topic*. Rather, the entire utterance seems to be a comment about an environmental topic, probably one that could be characterized with a personal pronoun: *I, we, you, they*. In terms of the grammar, many of these utterances could be either declaratives or imperatives; without context it is impossible to know. When they are declaratives they lack a stated topic.[6] Examples in Table 6.5 appear to be direct expansions of the comment of the holophrastic utterance. In this they are quite unlike the examples in Table 6.4, where the topic has been added to the holophrastic comment. What this fact indicates once again, of course, is that the grammatical, semantic, and discourse lines of development progress independently in Stage III. The grammatical development is that of the pivot-open classes occurring in all two-word combinations, while the discourse development is twofold: (*a*) the addition of the topic to the holophrastic utterance, or (*b*) the differentiation of the comment (Table 6.5). Later, about the time the language begins to reach Stage V, the child must begin to learn to manipulate the grammatical, semantic, and discourse functions independently.

Semantics

The grammatical relationships we have been talking about are still secondary to the semantic relationships which develop in this stage. That is, the semantic relationships that

---

[6]It is interesting to note that any of these examples would be classified as Stage IV transitives if they are true imperatives. Since adult imperatives express the subject function optionally, an imperative clause need not contain an expressed subject to be fully developed in a child's utterance (Table 6.1).

Table 6.6. Semantic Relationships in Two-Word Utterances (Stage IIIa)

Function	Construction		Examples of Forms
Recurrence	More, Another, Again (used as an imperative)	+ Substantive	More milk. Again beanbag.
Nonexistence	No, Away, Allgone	+ Substantive	No supper. Allgone baby.
Rejection	No	+ Substantive	No bed. No kiss.
Denial	No (appears late)	+ Substantive	No wash. No go.
Possession	Substantive + Substantive		Daddy chair. Mommy lunch.
Location	a. Substantive + Substantive b. Action + Substantive		Sweater chair. Book table. Walk store. Go store.
Existence	A, The	+ Substantive	A dog. The chair.
Attributive	Attributive + Substantive		Big train. Red book.
Dative	Action + Substantive		Give mommy. Give me.
Accompaniment	Action + Substantive		Walk mommy.
Instrument	Action + Substantive		Sweep broom.

Source. Adapted from Miller and Yoder in Schiefelbush and Lloyd, op. cit., pp. 144, with permission.

appear in the adult clause began to develop in Stage II. Although not all of the adult semantic functions are present from the very beginning, some, such as the possession and location functions, can appear in nascent form at an early time, even before the adult grammatical functions of the clause begin to appear. Early semantic functions develop largely on the clause level, and they develop independently of both the discourse functions of topic and comment and the grammatical functions of pivot-open.

The relational and substantive classes of semantic functions that first appeared in Stage II begin to be combined in Stage IIIa. The first combinations are illustrated by the first five entries in Table 6.6. In addition, the substantive relationship of *possession* is expanded, and other functions begin to appear, e.g., *location, attribution, dative, accompaniment, instrument, actor, action,* and *patient* functions.

Typically, the words that fill the relation functions in Stage II become pivot words in Stage IIIa. These words, of course, are few in number and occur frequently. The substantive functions of Stage II typically coincide with the open-class words in the grammar of Stage IIIa. The O + O combinations, however, account for most of the manifestations of the last six semantic rules appearing in Table 6.6. At this point in developmental time, the discourse functions of topic-comment, the clausal semantic functions in Table 6.6, and the grammatical functions of pivot and open are all contained in these two-word combinations. The child's task at this point is to begin to sort out these various functions.

The semantic relationships in Table 6.6 will form the basis for the development of the grammatical combinations that appear in Stages IIIb and IV. When the adult clausal functions finally do begin to appear, the child's utterances can be classified as being at Stage IIIb.

Stage IIIb: The Emerging Adult Clause

A short time after the child begins to put two words together, he begins to add more words to his combinations. The result is utterances that are three, four, and more words long. About this point the obligatory grammatical functions of the adult clause clearly emerge (subjects, predicates, objects, complements and adverbials). A number of workers (e.g., Brown, 1973; Bloom, 1970; Miller & Yoder, 1974) see these as being the continuance of the emergence of semantic functions, and they are correct in this observation. That is, in adult grammar we often see the grammatical subject coincide with the semantic actor, the grammatical predicate coincide with semantic action, and the grammatical direct object coincide with the semantic patient (see Chapter 3). The utterances of children that are made up of these coincidences can be interpreted either in terms of grammar or in terms of semantics. A teacher will find it easiest to structure a teaching program, however, by thinking in terms of the grammar because not enough is yet known about the regularities of semantic development (a point also made by Crystal et al., 1975, who refuse even to consider semantics on the single-word level). The grammatical development is regular and simple, however. When a child reaches this point, it becomes very easy to specify sequences of development in terms of the grammar for the purpose of structuring a teaching program.

Grammar

When one of the major clause types begins to move into Stage IIIb, what happens is that, while one or more of the adult grammatical functions of the clause will be present in the utterance, one or more will also be missing. For this reason, even though the child's combinations may begin to have more than two words, they remain preclausal in nature, i.e., not all of the functions of the clause appear.

Table 6.7 contains real and invented examples of Stage IIIb declaratives broken down by clause type for illustrative purposes. Close examination of this table illustrates what was said previously. It is more difficult to find examples in a child's speech of Stage IIIb intransitives with predicates missing than it is to find examples of either Stage IIIb transitives or Stage IIIb equatives with predicates missing. Whereas intransitives require the presence of only two functions to be classified as being at Stage IV, most Stage IIIb intransitives with predicates missing would probably be classified as filling Stage IIIa semantic functions when reading through a transcript. Nevertheless, children will say things similar to all of the examples found in Table 6.7. Any clause with one or more of the grammatical functions missing like the ones in Table 6.7 should be classified as being at Stage IIIb.

In a similar way, at this point in development, questions will also have one or more of the grammatical functions of the clause missing, and these, too, are classified as being at Stage IIIb. Table 6.8 lists several examples within each clause type of typical Stage IIIb questions. Again, some of these examples were invented for illustrative purposes (many are, however, from actual transcripts) but they are typical of the kinds of things that children whose clauses are at Stage IIIb will say. The problem in making judgments about Stage IIIb questions is that it is sometimes difficult to judge what is missing from a question in a transcript, especially in the case of the *wh-* questions. Probably the easiest way to handle the classification of questions, until one gets the experience that will allow instantaneous judgments, is to recast the question into its corresponding declarative form and then to make the judgment as to whether or not any of the clausal functions are

Table 6.7. Examples of Stage IIIb Declaratives

Intransitive	Transitive	Equative
(Subjects Missing)	(Subjects Missing)	(Subjects Missing)
Look in there	Pushing me	Is cat
Playing	Making a basket	Is my toy
Gone away	Dropped it	
Turn round and round	Hear a noise	
Closed	Put me in there	
	Tease Stanley	
	(Objects Missing)	(Complements Missing)
	Daddy will get	A bridge is
	Put in there	Him is
	I broke	
	Johnny find	
	You not do	
		(Predicates Missing)
		It a dog
		Katy in there
		Him my daddy
		Me a big girl
		You not very good

missing. To illustrate this point, one of the utterances in the first section of the transitive examples is

    (6.5a) What get over there?

If we recast this into its corresponding declarative form, we get

    (6.5b) *(Somebody or something)* get *wh-* over there.

Now we can see that the *wh-* word has replaced the direct object in the declarative form before it was moved to the front of the clause, and that it is the subject function that is missing from the child's utterance; it is thus a Stage IIIb transitive question. Similar operations can be done with each of the utterances in Table 6.8, and the reader should try the process until it makes sense.

    Never will we find a Stage IIIb intransitive imperative, because this construction requires only that the predicate be present. In cases when an intransitive imperative appears, all obligatory functions of the clause must be present. For example, clauses such as the following have all of the obligatory functions present:

    (6.6) Run!

Table 6.8. Examples of Typical Stage IIIb Questions

Intransitive	Transitive	Equative
(Subjects Missing)	(Subjects Missing)	(Subjects Missing)
Run now?	Push that truck?	What is?
Hurt?	Find your ball?	Is my piece?
Where play?	Why put in there?	Is nice boy?
When going?	What get over there?	Is down?
	What giving me?	
	(Objects Missing)	(Complements Missing)
	Who will do?	You was?
	When you buy?	Who is?
	Daddy find now?	
	Did Mama drop?	
	I holding?	
		(Predicate Missing)
		What that?
		Where table?
		Johnny dirty?
		Mama there?

(6.7) Smile!

(6.8) Sit down!

So, in relation to the obligatory clausal functions, when an intransitive imperative appears in a child's speech, it will automatically contain all of the obligatory clausal functions. Obviously, then, no examples of Stage IIIb intransitive imperatives can be given.

Stage IIIb basic transitive imperatives, however, would consist of only a predicate. When they appear they would take a form such as the following:

(6.9) Pick up!

That is, a Stage IIIb transitive imperative would have a predicate, but the obligatory direct object would be missing. We can also find many examples of Stage IIIb transitive imperatives among transitive clauses with indirect objects. Very often these sentences will appear with the indirect object present and the direct object missing. It is possible, however, for the direct object to be present while the indirect object is missing. These situations would be illustrated by the following:

(6.10) Give me! (direct object missing)

(6.11) Give truck! (indirect object missing)

There is a problem with the interpretation of (6.11): We interpreted the sentence as being one in which the indirect object is missing. It could be, however, that what is actually missing is a prepositional phrase carrying the dative, as in (6.12):

(6.12) Give the truck *to me*.

Problems of interpretation will always be present, but when they occur they do not pose serious problems for the purpose of setting up an instructional program. Any child will provide enough examples of each of the major clause types (and most other constructions) for us to be able to make a decision as to whether or not he must be taught the grammar. If one example in a child's speech is uninterpretable, no purpose is served by worrying about it. We simply look for other examples that will tell us what we need to know.

Semantics

The semantic development of Stage IIIb keeps pace with the grammatical development. The semantic functions of *actor, action,* and *patient* become clearly established in the child's repertoire of semantic functions (note that these functions coincide with the grammatical functions of subject, predicate, and object). Also, the *existence* function is expanded from the simple noun phrase with which it began ("A ball"; "My cookie") into the equative clause with the predicate missing ("It a ball"; "That my cookie"). Both of these expansions are carried out by combining previously existing semantic functions as in the following examples:

(6.13) Want more milk (action + recurrence)

(6.14) Put sweater chair (action + location)

(6.15) There my book (location + possession)

(6.16) It big dog (substantive + attributive)

In other words, the child develops and combines existing semantic functions in Stage IIIb. Other development occurs, for example, through the appearance of pronouns. Semantically, personal pronouns are superordinate substantives, i.e., any substantive can be represented by a personal pronoun, and in Stage IIIb we begin to see pronouns appearing, such as *he, she, it,* and *somebody,* along with the pronouns that are superordinate location functions (*there, here, someplace*) and superordinate possessives (*my, mine, your, his, hers, its*). The development of the pronouns continues for some time beyond this point, of course, but it begins in Stage IIIb.

Discourse

Text maintenance is still short and sweet in Stage IIIb, with exchanges around a topic being of relatively short length. It is rare to find conversations on a single topic that last for more than two or three exchanges when a child's clauses are at IIIb or below. More typically, conversations are limited to one exchange. That is, somebody says something, and the child says something, the conversation is over and a different one begins.

During Stage IIIb, however, we do begin to see the separation of the grammatical subject and the topic of the clause (see Chapter 2). That is, *wh-* questions, by their very nature, cannot have the topic and grammatical subject coincide except in the case where the *wh-* word replaces the grammatical subject:

(6.17) *What* do you see? (object replaced)

(6.18) *Who* is there? (subject replaced)

In (6.18) the *wh-* word has replaced the subject of the clause, and the topic of the clause is still the subject. However, in (6.17), and in most other *wh-* questions, the *wh-* word replaces some other grammatical function that must be moved to the front of the clause where it becomes the topic. Topic and grammatical subject are thus separated because the subject of the clause is no longer at the front of the clause. When children begin to use *wh-* questions, they are, in fact, beginning to learn that grammatical subject and topic can be separated. This independent manipulation of topic and subject is very rudimentary, but real. Continuance of this line of development will eventually allow the child to say some very complicated things.

There is a lot going on during what seems like a very simple period of development. In Stage IIIb, new semantic and grammatical functions are being introduced by the child, and complicated manipulations of the independent functions are beginning to occur. In spite of the fact that what the child says on this level appears to be very simple, foundations for extremely complicated utterances are being laid. The very fact that actor and grammatical subject, and topic and grammatical subject are being separated at such an early point in time is astounding, and yet it is a very normal thing to happen. The next step for the child is to put together all the grammatical functions of the adult clause and to begin to learn the constructions that fill them.

Stage IV: Clauses

Eventually the development of the clause reaches a point at which all of the obligatory functions of the clause appear in each of the basic clause types. As each clause type arrives at this point it will be classified as being at Stage IV. Since the transitive, intransitive and equative types reach Stage IV status at different times, each must be assessed separately for any one child.

A clause type that has reached Stage IV status may still not sound like an adult clause because, even though the clausal functions may be filled, the VP and NP functions and the transformations still have to be learned. It is important to note, however, that a clause type that has all of the clausal functions present is able to serve as a matrix for learning the lower-level functions and the transformations. The child now acquires a powerful set of organizing concepts that will allow him to proceed with this learning.

Grammar

Table 6.9 contains examples of Stage IV imperatives. These clauses, as was stated above, reach Stage IV status very quickly simply because they require only a predicate to be complete.

Note that while some of the imperatives in Table 6.9 sound the way an adult clause would sound, many do not. The reason some are not like adult clauses is *not* because they are incomplete *as clauses,* but rather, because their noun phrases or verb phrases have not

Table 6.9. Examples of Stage IV Imperatives

Intransitive	Transitive	Equative
Go!	Push truck!	Be quiet!
Come on!	Kiss dolly!	Be more careful!
Shut up!	Hold this!	Now be my daddy!
Look!	Pick me up!	
Look, Mommy!	Tie my shoe!	
Don't fall down!	Hold your hands out!	
Move over there!	Lookit that girl!	
	Open that up!	

fully developed. All of the obligatory clausal functions are present in each of the examples, however, and they are Stage IV clauses. This is true whether or not any optional functions (e.g., adverbials) appear.

This pattern is also true for the declaratives and questions. Table 6.10 contains examples of Stage IV declaratives, and again, notice that all of the obligatory functions of the clause are present in every case. That is, for the intransitives we can identify subjects, predicates, and direct objects, and where applicable, indirect objects; for the equatives, we can identify subjects, predicates, and complements. Even though the noun phrases and verb phrases may still be relatively undeveloped and full of "errors," all of the obligatory clausal functions are filled, and each of the clauses in Table 6.10 are at Stage IV.

Table 6.11 contains some examples of questions that are at Stage IV. Again, in each case, the obligatory functions of the transitive, intransitive, and equative clauses are present. In many instances, the verb phrase functions are also complete, but in addition, something else remains: To make an adult question, a transformation must occur, i.e., tense has to appear in front of the grammatical subject. Therefore, it is very often the case that a question has a fully developed verb phrase and still cannot be classified as being a Stage V clause because tense has not yet appeared before the subject. These clauses must be classified as being Stage IV until this transformation is finally made.

For the imperatives and most declaratives (with the exception of the passive), Stage IV is as far as the clause type *as a clause* can develop. You must remember that, in terms of clausal development, once the clausal functions are present, however nascent the form,

Table 6.10. Examples of Stage IV Declaratives

Intransitive	Transitive	Equative
Johnny runned away.	Them climbing a rock.	It is cat.
The bear come out.	I want that.	They are blue.
That baby crying.	That man pushing truck.	That's not a baby.
Somebody hanged up.	He carry duck in truck.	We is happy.
I blow with it too.	That dog step on my toe.	You are my friend.
Him sleeping.	Nobody won't get my wagon.	There the truck is.
That ball won't bounce.	Mommy give me cookie.	Here they are.

Table 6.11. Examples of Stage IV Questions

Intransitive	Transitive	Equative
(Yes/No)	*(Yes/No)*	*(Yes/No)*
I play in the street?	You do this?	That is my bear?
It might burn up?	Turn it you around?	We are here already?
It will cry?	That Smokey put out fire?	That my daddy briefcase is?
You are climbing on?	You do it again?	
We looking?	Do that is holding it?	
(Wh-)	*(Wh-)*	*(Wh-)*
You sit where?	Where you put it?	Where the bus is?
Where you reading now?	What he holding?	What that is?
Where shall we shall go?	What that ball doing?	Who those men are?
Who writing?	He break which one?	

development of the clause is complete. There is nothing more a child can learn about the existence of the clausal functions. It may still be true that he will have to learn the functions of the noun and verb phrases, and he may still have to learn to manipulate tense and the functions of clauses and phrases so that he can form questions, subordinates, coordinates, and the passive. Stage IV clauses must appear, however, before the child is ready to begin learning the transformations.

Semantics

While there undoubtedly is semantic learning that takes place in Stage IV, little is known about it at this point. By the time a child's clause types reach Stage IV status, most of the learning of the early clausal semantic functions has been accomplished. There is some separation of grammatical and semantic functions that occur before, during and after the grammatical functions are finally learned. For example, the child must learn that the patient, or the "acted upon," not only can coincide with the grammatical direct object, but it can also coincide with the grammatical subject of the clause (see Chapter 4). For example, in (6.19), the direct object and patient coincide:

(6.19) He broke *the balloon*.

But in (6.20), the patient coincides with the *subject* of the clause:

(6.20) *The balloon* broke.

By the time a child's transitive clauses reach Stage IV status, we find this sort of construction occurring regularly. While it may not be learning of semantic functions per se, it certainly must be seen as having something to do with it. Unfortunately, it is not possible to get more detailed at this point.

Text maintenance continues, of course, and conversations get longer and longer as the child learns more about his language and how to manipulate it. Concurrently, the child's cognitive sphere is becoming more differentiated and complex, and he finds himself with more and more things to talk about in his life. To do this he must learn more complex ways of expression. We must realize that text maintenance is still not very long at this point in development, however. Conversations still do not consist of more than a couple of exchanges; even then, the topic of the child's utterance tends to be taken from whatever was said by the previous speaker. [Recall example (2.1), p. 27, in which a conversation was presented between a small child and an adult.]

By the time a child's clause types have reached Stage IV status, he has begun to use pronouns and other connectives. The acquisition of these words gives him a tool with which he can pick up a topic from the previous utterance in order to make a comment about it. For example, in the following mini-conversation, the child's utterance would be nonsensical if it were not for the previous utterance:

(6.21) Adult: Mary hurt her leg.
        Child: She did?

The pronoun, of course, refers to the topic of the adult's utterance and serves to connect the two utterances in the conversation. Note, too, that the child's utterance is ellipted. That is, the only things to appear in the child's utterance are the subject of the clause and tense from the verb phrase. The entire utterance, however, must be construed to mean:

(6.22) Did Mary hurt her leg?

Due to the nature of the grammar of discourse in English, however, only a pronoun and the tense-carrying dummy DO are required to say all that there is to say in this particular situation, and the rest of the clause can be ellipted. Children whose clauses have reached Stage IV status have usually been doing this sort of thing for awhile.[7] Adult speakers of the language do it, after all, and learning how is part of the learning of discourse.

The learning of *wh-* words and their use in questions begins in Stage IIIb. It continues through the period when Stage V clauses are being formed. As stated above, *wh-* replacement and movement to the front of the clause (except in the case of subject replacement) requires a separation of topic from grammatical subject. It takes awhile to get a firm grip on this construction, and the learning of how to do it continues through the beginning of Stage IV. Again, the formation of *wh-* questions contributes to text, as can be seen from typical responses to *wh-* questions:

(6.23) Question: *What* was that?
        Answer: *A dog.*

In (6.23) the response to the question is an ellipted clause, with only the equative complement being stated by the child. The person who asks the question must realize that he

---

[7]This means, of course, that ellipted utterances may never be used to conclude whether or not a child knows a specific clause or VP construction. A missing optional grammatical construction is no reason to say that a child does not know it.

does not know this complement, replace it with a *wh-* word and then make it the topic of his question by placing it at the front of the clause. The one who answers must realize that the complement was requested and then supply it. This process is part of what is involved in the learning of text, and we see a lot of it by the time a child's clauses have reached Stage IV status.

Stage V: Transformations

As was stated previously, most declaratives and imperatives cannot go beyond Stage IV status. Once the obligatory functions are present in these clauses there is no more to be learned *about the clause.* There are four constructions, however, that require learning beyond that of the basic clausal functions: *questions, coordinates, subordinates,* and the *passive.* For each of these constructions, the basic clausal functions may be present, but the construction may not sound the way an adult's would sound. A transformation must be complete before a sentence containing it can be classified as being at Stage V.

Grammatical Prerequisites

Although we are still thinking in terms of the learning of sentences, much of the development of the Stage V constructions depends on the child's having learned the noun and verb phrase functions while his clauses are still in Stage IV. The reason for this, of course, is the fact that the transformations that are involved in Stage V require manipulation of various functions of the noun and verb phrases. That is, Stage V questions require tense to be moved to the position in front of the subject of the clause. This move does not happen until the VP functions that carry tense are learned; *wh-* and the infinitive subordinates require the existence of the clause and noun phrase functions that serve as slots for the inserts; the passive, of course, requires the learning of a new verb phrase function before it can be completed. All in all, noun and verb phrases become extremely important to the development of the sentence once the basic clausal functions required for Stage IV are learned. Once the basic clause types reach Stage IV, the clause can be used as a matrix within which this learning can occur.

VERB PHRASE DEVELOPMENT. Like the clausal functions, the verb phrase functions develop a little at a time. Lee and her associates at Northwestern University (Lee & Canter, 1971; Lee, 1974) have mapped the sequence of development of the functions of the verb phrase. This sequence is roughly presented in Table 6.12. It is the result of a great

---

Table 6.12. Sequence of Final Acquisition of Verb Phrase Functions

1. Transitive and Intransitive Head
2. Continuum
3. Equative Predicate (BE)
4. Modals and Dummy Do
5. Passive
6. Perfective

Source. Adapted from data in *Developmental Sentence Analysis* by L. Lee. Evanston, Ill.: Northwestern University, 1974, with permission.

Table 6.13. Example of the Sequence of Question Formation through Stage V

Stage II. That?

Stage III. What that?
            What's that?

Stage IV. What that is?
            What is that is?

Stage V. What is that?
          What's that?

---

deal of work on their part, and it holds true for the overwhelming majority of children. Although, as in all such sequences, there is the possibility of minor variation, the regularity of appearance of these functions in this order is such that it provides us with an excellent teaching sequence.

The sequence found in Table 6.12 is for the *completion* of learning of the listed functions. There are two things operating within the sequence that the teacher must be aware of. One is the fact that some fillers of late-developing functions will appear before the early-developing functions are under control. For example, it is not unusual for one past tense modal (e.g., *could*) to appear before any form of BE appears in the equative predicate. The second thing is that the learning of the negative is tied to the learning of each VP function. It does not appear at any specific point in the sequence, but rather appears with individual functions as they are added to the VP. More will be said about the learning of the negative in another section.

While the VP functions are being learned, the transformations are also being learned. Thus, we will hear children constructing Stage V questions with the continuum before the perfective or passive functions ever make an appearance in their speech. Once the child has the equipment to make a transformation, he will do so. As each VP function is learned, transformations that require that function will begin to be found.

The Development of Specific Transformations

In this section we will consider (*a*) questions, (*b*) coordinated clauses, (*c*) subordinated clauses, and (*d*) passives.

QUESTIONS. In general, questions go through a specific acquisition sequence. Not all children go through every step of this sequence, but no child violates the sequence even if he skips one or more steps. One example is presented in Table 6.13. The example given involves the *wh-* replacement of the complement in an equative clause.

At a very early point in development, children simply place a rising intonation contour on declarative holophrastic utterances. Further, every question a child asks prior to the point at which (*a*) tense moves in *yes/no* questions, or (*b*) *wh-* words appear in *wh-* questions, will have a rising intonation.[8]

When the child's clauses reach Stage III, he begins to use *wh-* words to represent unknown(s) in the clause. The *wh-* words begin to appear at the front of the clause before tense moves because they are the topic of the child's utterance. The intonation contour

---

[8]It is interesting to note that less than half of the *yes/no* questions used by adults have a rising intonation (C. C. Fries, n.d.)

may either fall or rise once it appears because the *wh-* word itself signals the question. *Yes/no* questions continue to have rising intonations until tense is moved, however.

In the case of the example in Table 6.13, the *wh-* word may first appear either as *what* or *whats;* in Stage III children make no distinction between them. When the question reaches Stage IV, it is normal to find the predicate remaining in its declarative position (following the subject). For example, "What that is?" is a question with the *wh-* word added and moved to the front of the clause. All the clausal functions are present, but tense has not been moved to its position before the subject. Sometimes we will even find tense duplicated; it can appear both before and after the subject, as in the second Stage IV example given, in Table 6.13. Some children may skip one or both of these substeps.

Table 6.14. Examples of *Yes/No* and *Wh-* Question Development Across Stages III, IV, and V

Condition[a]	*Yes/No*	*Wh-*
	(Stage III)	
1.	We throwing?	Who tearing?
	Make lunch?	Who got?
2.	That my ball?	Where your mother?
	Dishes broke?	Who you?
3.	You pick up?	What did?
	Mow lawn?	Where put sweater?
	(Stage IV)	
1.	We are throwing ball?	Who tearing paper?
	Mommy will make lunch?	Who got bear?
2.	That my ball is?	Where your mother is?
	Dishes are broke?	Who you are?
3.	You picked it up?	What did you did?
	Daddy did mow lawn?	Where I put sweater?
	(Stage V)	
1.	Are we throwing ball?	Who is tearing the paper?
	Will Mommy make lunch?	Who's got the bear?
2.	Is that my ball?	Where is your mother?
	Are the dishes broken?	Who are you?
3.	Did you pick it up?	What did you do?
	Did Daddy mow the lawn?	Where do I put the sweater?

Note.
[a]Conditions:
  1. All clauses with auxiliaries
  2. Equative clause with no auxiliaries
  3. Transitive and intransitive clause with no auxiliaries

Table 6.15. Lee's Sequence of Question Development

Yes/No	*Wh-*
Equative clauses with no auxiliary: BE	
	Object and complement replacements: *who, what, how much*
	Adverb of place replacement: *where*
Continuum: BE *-ing*	
	Adverb of time and manner replacements: *when, how*
Transitive and intransitives with no auxiliaries: dummy DO	
Modals: may, can, etc.	
	Coordinated clause replacements: *why, how come, what if*
Perfective: have *-en*	Possession replacement: D_2: *whose*
	Loose-knit and close-knit modifier replacement: *which*

Source. Adapted from Lee, op cit., p. 159, with permission.

Finally, in Stage V, tense moves in front of the subject; the child now forms his question the way an adult would do it. In the case of the first Stage V example in Table 6.13, a contraction must still be made. However, this contraction (and others like it) must wait for the full form of the tense carrier to appear before the subject. Thus, even though the first example in Table 6.13 sounds exactly like the last, the two are far from being examples of the same level of development.[9]

Table 6.14 contains a number of examples of questions at Stages III, IV, and V that illustrate the developmental sequences involved. Remember that there are three general conditions for questions: (*a*) all clauses with auxiliaries, in which the first auxiliary in the VP moves in front of the subject; (*b*) equative clauses with no auxiliaries, in which the verb BE moves before the subject; (*c*) clauses with transitive and intransitive verbs and no auxiliaries in which the dummy DO appears before the subject to carry tense.

Note how orderly the sequence of development is in each of the examples in Table 6.14. In all of the Stage III utterances, one or more of the clausal functions are missing; in each of the Stage IV questions, all of the clausal functions are present but tense has not yet

---

[9]This fact indicates that at no time may we use a contraction as evidence for the existence of the uncontracted form.

been moved to the position before the subject; and in each of the Stage V questions, tense has been moved, and the question appears the way an adult would form it.

Table 6.15 presents the sequence of development of the questions as listed by Lee (1974). This list includes the developmental sequence for both *yes/no* and *wh-* questions, and forms an excellent teaching sequence, even if some children normally do switch acquisition of adjacent constructions in the table. Note that neither *yes/no* nor *wh-* questions develop totally before one another, but rather they interact during development. Once the child begins to use a *yes/no* equative clause question, for example, a *wh-* equative question becomes possible. This is because the *wh-* question requires both the tense movement (as in *yes/no* questions) and the *wh-* replacement and movement.

COORDINATED CLAUSES. The coordinated clauses are simply two clauses joined by a conjunction. The development of the basic construction of the individual clauses is required before two of them can be joined in the coordinate relationship at the Stage V level. Coordinated clauses that have one or more functions missing from either of the conjoined clauses would be classified as being at Stage IV. According to Lee (1974), the first fully formed coordinated clauses do not appear until after the first Stage IV equative clauses appear. Even then they all do not appear at once because of the semantic differences among them. The first Stage V coordinated clauses are those that use *and*. The others do not appear until after the questions with the continuum have reached Stage V. At that time, the coordinated sentences using *but, so, or,* and *if* appear. The clauses that are conjoined with *because* do not appear until about the time that questions using the dummy DO and the modals appear. The sequence of appearance of the other conjunctions is unknown and probably occurs later.

The first coordinated clauses to reach adult status are those in which all functions are present in the clauses to be conjoined. Only later will identical fillers of parallel functions be deleted in the second clause. Thus, conjoinings similar to those in (6.24a) and (6.25a) appear before ones similar to those found in (6.24b) and (6.25b):

(6.24a) Johnny hit me and he ran away.

(6.25a) Mary washed the dishes and Mary dried the dishes.

(6.24b) Johnny hit me and ran away. (identical subject deleted)

(6.25b) Mary washed and dried the dishes. (identical subject and object deleted)

It is important to distinguish between clauses that are coordinated and noun phrases that are coordinated. When noun phrases are strung together with a conjunction, the result is a single clausal function (subject or object). This construction will develop before complex sentences with coordinated clauses appear. That is, the construction in (6.26) seems to develop before the construction in (6.27):

(6.26) Mary and Billy went to school. (conjoined noun phrases)

(6.27) Mary went to school and Billy went to school. (conjoined clauses)

The sentence in (6.26) is not a transformation; it involves a development within the noun phrase. The sentence in (6.27) has two verb phrases, however, and thus contains coordinated clauses. The sentence in (6.26) is a Stage IV clause, while the sentence in (6.27) is a Stage V sentence with two clauses.

SUBORDINATED CLAUSES. There are two kinds of subordinated clauses: infinitives and *wh-* subordinates. They are parallel in their construction in that each requires both a matrix and an insert (see Chapter 5). They are also somewhat parallel in their development, largely because in most instances, both *wh-* inserts and infinitive inserts can fill the same clause and noun phrase functions. They are different in many respects, however; as a consequence, each has its own course of development. Development at the Stage V level is attained when *both* insert and matrix have all obligatory clause and verb phrase functions completely filled in the sentence.

Infinitive Inserts. Adults (the author definitely included) will often form infinitives similar to those found in (6.28) and (6.29):

(6.28a) I'm gonna eat now.

(6.29a) I hafta get over there fast.

When we adults are asked to repeat what we said, however, we would probably be able to slow down and say these same sentences as they are found in (6.28b) and (6.29b):

(6.28b) I am going to eat now.

(6.29b) I have to get over there fast.

That is, for adults, "gonna *verb*" and "hafta *verb*" (and a few others) contain full-fledged infinitives, as evidenced by the fact that we can put in all of the requisite fillers when we must. Early in the development of the infinitive in children's language, however, utterances such as (6.28a) and (6.29a) appear, but the children cannot expand them so that they will sound like (6.28b) and (6.29b). This inability indicates that construction words such as *gonna verb* do not contain true infinitives for children in the early stages of development. Lee (1974) notes that there are three words that appear early in the development of the infinitive that act in this manner: *wanna, gonna,* and *gotta.* To this list I would add *hafta* and *hasta.* For a long time these words, which are infinitives in the adult form of the language, appear to fill a function that is analogous to one of the verb phrase functions, i.e., they precede a verb in a single verb phrase. Thus, for a child who uses these words and has not yet developed the infinitive, the verbs *eat* and *get* in (6.28a) and (6.29a) would function as the head of the verb phrase in a single clause.[10]

Eventually the infinitive marker *to* begins to appear in a child's language when it is obligatory (some verbs require the marker to be deleted; see Chapter 5). Once we observe clear examples of the marker, we have evidence that the child is using a true infinitive, and we can conclude that the infinitives are reaching Stage V. This evidence will occur in several places. The first is with verbs other than the ones listed previously:

---

[10]Therefore, no sentence containing the words *wanna, gonna, hafta, hasta, gotta* in the matrix can be used as evidence for a child's knowledge of infinitive inserts. Lee (1974) points out two other words that appear early, *lemme* and *lets.* These words also cannot be used as evidence for the existence of the infinitive because the marker *to* is obligatorily deleted in their adult forms.

(6.30) I like *to eat ice cream.*

(6.31) We asked *to go out.*

Another is when the subject of the matrix is third singular with *want* and *got:*

(6.32) Johnny wants *to see it.*

(6.33) She gots *to go home* (or, She's *got to go home*).

Another is when the subject of the infinitive insert is different from the subject of the matrix with *want* and other verbs:

(6.34) *I* want *you to bring that here.*

(6.35) *She* sent *him to get it.*

The point is that children will use constructions that would be interpreted as infinitives when adults use them, but cannot be so interpreted when children use them. It is only when we find unambiguous evidence for the existence of the infinitive that we can conclude that a child knows the construction.

Wh- Inserts. Some *wh-* inserts require a replacement of an unknown filler of some function, and a placement of the *wh-* word in front of the clause (see Chapter 5). To make a *wh-* question, of course, tense is also moved to the position in front of the subject, but this last step does not occur in *wh-* inserts. Here we will find some of the childish "errors" that we sometimes see at the beginning of the point in development at which a child might be just starting to use *wh-* inserts. That is, some children will use a *wh-* question as a *wh-* insert (Lee, 1974), so that the result is something like the utterances of (6.36) and (6.37).

(6.36) I know *what is that thing.*

(6.37) Can you tell me *where does the smoke go?*

Other than "errors" such as these, the development of the *wh-* insert occurs without much fanfare. Because the false infinitive insert occurs at such an early point, however, it can appear that a child is beginning to use infinitives much sooner than he uses *wh-* inserts. Actually, true infinitives do tend to appear a little sooner (but not all that much sooner) than the *wh-* inserts.

Developmental Sequences of the Subordinate Inserts. Table 6.16 presents a good approximation of the sequence of development of the infinitive and *wh-* inserts. In general, the inserts that are used as fillers of object and adverbial functions develop first, and those used as fillers of subject functions appear next. The inserts that are fillers of noun phrase functions appear later than do those used to fill clausal functions.

True contractions and deletions appear after a complete construction is learned, and this fact is as true for *wh-* inserts as it is for other constructions. Thus, the second sentence in each of the following pairs would appear later than the first (all are restrictive modifiers of object NPs—the same thing happens for subject NPs and complex nominals):

Table 6.16. General Sequence of Appearances of Inserts in Subordinate Constructions

Infinitive Objects
Infinitive Adverbials
Wh- Objects
Wh- Adverbials

Gerunds
Wh- Restrictive Modifiers in Object NP

Infinitive Subjects
Wh- Subjects

Wh- Restrictive Modifiers in Subject NP
Wh- Complex Nominals

(6.38) I saw the man *who was coming.*
I saw the man *coming.*

(6.39) Sally likes the clothes *that she gets from Schwartz's store.*
Sally likes the clothes *she gets from Schwartz's store.*

(6.40) I found someone *who is called Mac.*
I found someone *called Mac.*

This sequence for deletions is not always the case for the infinitives, however. A number of matrix verbs require that the infinitive marker *to* be deleted from the insert. Thus, sentences such as:

(6.41) Let *me see that book.*

(6.42) We saw *him leave.*

contain infinitive inserts with the marker deleted. Some of these appear very early in a typical child's development, such as the sentences with *lets* and *lemme* in the matrix. These infinitive inserts with obligatory *to* deletions cannot be used as evidence that the child knows the complete infinitive insert construction, as was noted previously.

PASSIVE. The passive is a very complicated construction because it not only contains the verb phrase passive function (filled by $\left\{ \begin{array}{c} \text{GET} \\ \text{BE} \end{array} \right\}$ *-en*), but it also requires that the grammatical subject and semantic actor be separated so that the patient can become the topic. Thus, there are both verb phrase and clausal constructions to be learned and manipulated, and it takes some time for most children to be able to do this.

The first form of the passive that most children learn is often the one with GET *-en* in the verb phrase:

(6.43) It *got taken* away.

Typically we will find that the BE *-en* filler is learned at a later time:

(6.44) It *was* tak*en* away.

There is a real problem, noted by Lee (1974) in the development of the passive. Most children will use what would be a passive in the adult language; but for the child, the construction appears to be either a simple equative or transitive declarative with GET filling the head function. For example, one of the very early and most ubiquitous examples is found in the utterance:

(6.45) It $\begin{Bmatrix} \text{is} \\ \text{got} \end{Bmatrix}$ broke.

Most children break things regularly and will say this sentence fairly early. It is difficult to interpret this as a passive when a child's clauses are just reaching Stage IV, however, because the last word in the sentence has the potential to function as a descriptive adjective. That is, *broke* seems to indicate the state that the object is in at present, not what has happened to it. Therefore, the utterance ''It is broke,'' simply seems to be an equative clause with a Type II complement. We see what seems to be exactly the same thing (except that the verb is transitive) in sentences such as:

(6.46) It is fixed.

(6.47) It got fixed.

(6.48) He is hurt.

(6.49) He got hurt.

Probably the most startling example of this will appear in one particular variation of the equative clause:

(6.50a) He is dead.

which can appear for many children as:

(6.50b) He got dead.

Those of us who have been through either deaths in the family or animal deaths that have been discussed openly in front of young children are quite likely to have run into this example. What it seems to illustrate is, that at a certain point in development, GET can be an action substitute for the equative verb BE. Examples (6.46) through (6.49) seem to be illustrative of the same thing. Lee lists a number of words that fill head functions in what could be passives for adults, but which are often either simple complements in equative clauses, or direct objects of GET for young children. Among them are included *hurt, fixed,* and *broken.* (See Chapter 5 for words like *gone, done, dressed* and *lost,* which Lee also includes in this category.) When these words are used in what appears to be passive constructions, they cannot be used as solid evidence that the child knows the passive construction. Other evidence must be found in order to draw this conclusion with confidence.

Extra-Clausal Language Development

With all the attention given to the development of the clause in this chapter, it could seem as if that was all there is to language development. This is untrue. Clausal development serves as a matrix within which other language development takes place. In fact, there are many things in the language that must be learned that are not part of clausal development. Little or nothing has been said of the development of the construction of the noun phrase, or the development of inflectional morphology, among other things. These things are not central to the learning of sentences (except for the functions in the NP which can have clauses as fillers), but they are no less important to the language as a whole. In addition, there is the whole matter of text, which has received very little attention, but which may, in fact, eventually prove to be of greater importance to understanding language learning than the clause. We will next discuss some items of interest.

Negation

Because of its central role in the development of the clause and its transformations, the development of most of the functions of the verb phrase was discussed previously. One verb phrase function that needs further explication, however, is that of the negative. At the time the verb phrase was discussed, the development of this function was passed off as simply occurring as each function developed individually. However there is more to it than this.

Even at the holophrastic stage (Stage II), children will use negations. The semantic functions of *negation* and *denial* are expressed using negative words, for example, and even though we must be in the child's immediate environment to know the exact semantic intent of the child's utterance when he makes it, these negatives do exist.

When the child begins to combine words and use sentences that are two words long or longer, interesting things begin to happen with negation. All through Stage IIIa and well into Stage IIIb, the negative is not grammatically integrated into the verb phrase. Instead, the child's entire utterance is negated. This act is in keeping with the notion that the semantic functions developed in Stage II are simply combined in the beginnings of Stage III. As a result, we begin to hear utterances such as those found in Table 6.17 at this point. Note that these negatives, all found in Stage III utterances, negate the entire clause, not just the verb phrase as is required of adult negation.

Table 6.17. Examples of Negatives at Clausal Stage III

No broke	No more whistle it
No the car going	No playing toy
Not put!	No find that
No money	No want hear him
Not big	Not you push
Not picking up	No find button

Table 6.18. Examples of Negatives at Clausal Stage IV

He no kiss you.	I don't want it.
I no want soup.	He don't see me.
I no taste them.	Don't put it there.
That is not mine.	He won't bite you.
You is not big.	Jerry won't buy me toy.
You can't find me.	I won't cut it.
Mommy can't come now.	I not eating peas.
We can't play.	It not coming now.

By the time the child's clauses move into Stage IV, the negative starts to be integrated into the verb phrase. Now the obligatory clausal functions are present, and the matrix is ready for the child to use. Table 6.18 presents examples of typical sentences that can occur at this point in development. Note several things:

1. At the beginning of Stage IV we may still see many utterances in which the negative is not yet integrated into the verb phrase. Thus sentences such as the one in (6.51) and (6.52) are not unusual:

   (6.51) No Johnny eat supper.

   (6.52) I go to bed no!

   Nevertheless, once a child develops his basic clausal functions, the negative typically becomes integrated into the verb phrase rather soon.

2. Since the verb phrase usually does not contain all of the optional functions as soon as a clause type moves into Stage IV, the negative cannot be interpreted as being attached to tense until *after* tense has developed and is being manipulated. This case presents interpretive problems when the negative appears as *can't, don't* or *won't* (see the following).

3. Since the equative clause develops so much later than either the transitive or intransitive clauses, negatives in equatives usually get placed in the complement of the equative clause before the predicate appears. This placement results in sentences such as those found in (6.53) through (6.55):

   (6.53) That not blue.

   (6.54) That no cuppa coffee.

   (6.55) There no goats.

The interpretation of *can't, don't,* and *won't* presents another problem. Children will begin to use these three negatives early in Stage IV (and sometimes sooner). The question is whether or not the use of these words really provides examples, e.g., of dummy DO and the modals with the negative attached, or whether they are simply alternate forms of *not,* i.e., is *don't* actually DO + negative, or is it a single word just expressing negation that has nothing to do with the dummy DO? In the case of all three of these words, the latter interpretation must be made until we find independent evidence for the existence of the modals *can* and *will,* and for the dummy DO. *Can't, won't* and *don't* are sometimes used for a long time before *can, will,* and *do* appear in a child's speech. During that time they must be interpreted as being simple semantic variants of the negative words *no* and *not.*

As the fillers of the various functions of the verb phrase develop, the concept of tense develops apace. As this concept develops, the negative comes more and more to sound like an adult negative, which is especially true for those functions that have discontinuous fillers, such as the continuum (BE *-ing*) and the perfective (HAVE *-en*). Normally the inflection of the continuum, for example, develops before the auxiliary appears, and we hear children saying things like:

(6.56) I not going.

Later, when the auxiliary begins to appear, the child can begin to say things like:

(6.57) I am not going.

and only later does the contraction appear:

(6.58) I'm not going.

When these fillers begin to appear in each of the VP functions, the learning of the negative becomes complete, one step at a time.

Noun Phrase

There is infuriatingly little information of the development of the noun phrase. Part of the reason for this state of non-knowledge is, I suspect, due to the lack of a good system for data gathering. Since P. H. Fries (1972) has now given us an excellent grammar of the English Noun Phrase, however, it is possible to set about gathering the needed data.

Any statements made in the following discussion about the development of the functions of the noun phrase will have to be taken with a large grain of salt. The analysis is not yet completely supported by data, and the conclusions are still tentative.

In relation to the development of the noun phrase, about the only definite thing that can be said is that the head function appears first. Of course, it is far from being fully developed when it first appears. English nouns are terribly complicated conceptually and it takes a lifetime to learn the complete system. Complex nominals, for example, probably do not begin to appear until the point at which the learning of the clause and its transformations is almost complete (and perhaps well beyond that time). In spite of all of this, the head slot in the NP *is* learned first, and the child has it available for use as a matrix for learning how to use nouns and the noun inflections.

The next function to be learned is the determiner$_2$. At a very early point in developmental time we begin to see indefinite and definite articles. They seem to develop before the transitive clauses reach Stage IV. The possessor filler of the determiner$_2$ also develops early. It takes the form of the possessive pronouns, especially *my. Your* will often appear at this time as well. At about the same time, some of the personal and possessive pronouns that can fill the head function seem to appear, i.e., *I, you, mine, yours* develop rather early, according to Lee's (1974) data, soon followed by *he, she, his* and *hers.*

Also, by the time the transitive clauses reach Stage IV, we are regularly seeing descriptive adjectives, which means that the loose-knit modifier function develops by that time. Again, all of the various filler classes do not appear immediately; just because the slot exists, does not guarantee knowledge of all the fillers of the slot. It will take the child a long time before many fillers of the loose-knit modifier are established. The earliest adjectives to appear are those that are one-half of a pair of polar descriptors: *big* or *little, far* or *near,* etc. Descriptive adjectives like *pretty* and *nice* also appear at an early time.

The determiner$_1$, the determiner$_3$, and the close-knit modifier slots seem to develop at a somewhat later time from the previous; but what that point is, or in what sequence they appear, is not known. Experience directs us to the period between the attainment of Stage IV for transitives and the attainment of Stage V for the first questions, but precise pinpointing is impossible at this time. The limiter slot also seems to develop at some point before the attainment of Stage V status for early questions.

The restrictive modifier and complex nominal functions appear late. The first restrictive modifiers seem to be adverbials, with subordinate clauses appearing quite late in the sequence. Complex nominals probably begin to develop at or about the same time that subordinate clause restrictive modifiers develop.

Table 6.19 is a hypothesized sequence of acquisition of the noun phrase functions. It does not attempt to specify the sequence in which all the fillers of the NP functions develop, but rather the sequence in which the nascent *functions* seem to appear. This limits its effectiveness as a teaching tool, but nevertheless, it can assist in structuring a program for a child with developmental problems. At the risk of becoming too repetitious, it must be stressed that the fillers of the noun phrase functions are more complex and more varied than those of the verb phrase. The result is that, even though slot for a function is established, there is still a great deal for a child to learn; it can take him some time to complete the learning of even as straight-forward a set of fillers as those for the determiner$_2$. It takes even more time for complex fillers such as those for the determiner$_3$, or the loose-knit and close-knit modifiers to be learned.

Table 6.19. Hypothesized Sequence of Order of Appearance of the Noun Phrase Functions

Stage	Function
IIIa	Head
IIIb	Determiner$_2$ Loose-Knit Modifier
IV	Determiner$_1$ Determiner$_3$ Close-Knit Modifier Limiter
V	Restrictive Modifier Complex Nominal

Inflectional Morphology

Another level in the hierarchy for which some information is available is that of inflectional morphology (Ervin-Tripp, 1966). By the beginning of Stage III, children use the correct form for at least a few of the irregular plurals and verb past. Thus it is not at all unusual for a very young child to say things like *men* and *went*. At some time prior to the attainment of Stage IV status for equative clauses, they learn the rules for forming regular plurals and verb past, and we begin to hear them say things like *mans,* and *goed*. At this point the adults near the child smile at his "mistakes," but these are not mistakes at all, of course. They are evidence of morphophonemic rules in action. That is, the child begins by learning some forms that are conceptually connected to plurality or past time. When he learns about these concepts and connects them with the grammatical rules for expressing such things, he overgeneralizes and applies the rule to *all* nouns or verbs (as the case may be) whether they are regular or irregular. Later, he begins to learn that there are exceptions to these rules, and one by one the irregulars start to reappear in their adult form.

The sequence of appearance of the regular inflections observed by Bellugi (1970) appears in Table 6.20. It must be kept in mind that these data are based on only two children.

Table 6.20 shows both the sequence of acquisition of each inflection as well as the relative frequency of each inflection in the daily speech of the mothers as they talked to the children around the house. Note that there is little relation between frequency of usage and order of appearance. Note too, that, while the order or appearance of the inflections is the same for both children, the rate of acquisition is different, and one child took a lot longer to acquire them than did the other. This kind of variation appears in all children at all levels of the hierarchy. Developmentally delayed children may show clausal development at Stage IV or even Stage V before some of these inflections appear. Note also that the

Table 6.20. Sequence of Acquisition of English Inflections in Two Children

Inflection		Age of Appearance (in Months)	
		Child #1	Child #2
{-*ing*}	(continuum)	28	19.5
{-S$_1$}	(plural)	33	24
{-T$_1$}	(past)	39	24.5
{-S$_2$}	(possessive)	39.5	25.5
{-S$_3$}	(third singular)	41	26

Source. Adapted from "The Emergence of Inflections and Negations in the Speech of Two Children" by U. Bellugi. Paper presented at the New England Psychological Association Annual Convention, 1964 (Cited by McNeill, 1970), with permission.

three {S} inflections are not acquired at the same time even though the morphophonemic rules for application are exactly the same for all three.

This sequence makes sense when seen in light of the relative degree of cognitive load presented by these inflections and the developmental hypothesis presented in this chapter. In the noun phrase, the head function is learned before the determiner$_2$, and we would expect plurality (head) to be learned before possession (determiner$_2$). Present action is more visible than any of the other concepts marked by inflections (plurality, possession, time, third singular), and the early development of the {-*ing*} would be expected. In fact, we can pin this particular inflection down quite well because it is part of the continuum function, and we know when the continuum appears (Table 6.12). The closeness of verb past and possession in the table indicates that either might occur first in some children, and there is little in the cognitive sphere that would require the verb past inflection to be learned before possession. Third singular, however, is a purely grammatical concept that has great selectivity as to where is is applied, and we would expect it to be learned last. Thus, the sequence presented in Table 6.20 appears to present us with an adequate teaching sequence for these inflections. Knowing where the continuum develops provides us with an anchor for understanding the approximate place in the overall sequence for the other inflections.

Summary

It would be presumptious to claim that this chapter says all there is to say about the sequence in which the English clause and its transformations are learned, or even that it is extremely accurate in the details it does attempt to present. Nevertheless, the sequences in this chapter can form the basis for useful assessment and teaching tools. The concepts presented also form a solid foundation for future research into the topic of how to assess and teach a child who is experiencing language development problems. The notion of the clause as the major organizing concept on the first level of language learning is a good one, yet there remains a great deal for us to learn. We still know virtually nothing about the learning of text maintenance or of the learning of semantic functions beyond Stage IIIa, for example. Yet, with all of the problems that remain, we now have a good conceptual organization for what a child must learn about the basic grammatical patterns of English, and for what we should attempt to teach when we have a child who exhibits problems. A schematic diagram (Table 6.21) of this sequence summarizes everything said in Chapter 6.

Table 6.21 is arranged so that, reading across the table, the constructions and functions in each of five areas appear in approximately the sequence we can expect to see for the typical child. Note that the table provides us with the sequences in relation to each other, i.e., a ruler laid across the page should separate what a child can do from what he cannot do.

There are, however, some caveats to the use of the table. In the first place, many constructions and functions will continue to develop long after they first appear. Articles, for example, appear quite early in a child's speech, but the determiner$_2$ is not completely filled until quite late.

Secondly, the table reflects the fact that we know more about some areas than we do about others; for example, the available data on the sequence of the verb phrase functions is much more complete (and accurate) than the data on the sequence of appearance of the noun phrase functions. Nevertheless, the table should serve well as a guide to sequencing

Table 6.21. Schematic Diagram of the Sequence of Acquisition of the Basic Grammatical Patterns of English

PRECLAUSE CONSTRUCTIONS	SENTENCE CONSTRUCTIONS	VERB PHRASE FILLERS
NO GRAMMAR		
SEMANTIC FUNCTIONS APPEAR:		
Substantive Terms		
Relational Terms		
SEMANTIC FUNCTIONS COMBINE		
GRAMMATICAL FUNCTIONS APPEAR	Intransitive Imperative (predicate)	
	Transitive Imperative (predicate–object)	
	Intransitive Declarative (subject–predicate)	
	Transitive Declarative (subject–predicate–object)	
		Continuum (*is -ing*)
	Equative (subject–BE–complement)	BE (*is*)
	Transitive Declarative (subject–predicate–indirect object–direct object)	Past inflection $\{-T\}$
		Third singular inflection $\{-S_3\}$
		Continuum (*am was* (*are were -ing*))
		BE (*am was*) (*are were*)
	Coordinated Clauses (*and*)	
		Modals (*may, can, will*)
		Dummy DO (*do, did*)
	Subordinated Clauses:	
		Modals (*must, should, could, would, might*)
	Object and complement inserts (infinitives & gerunds) (*wh-*)	
		Passive (GET *-en*) (BE *-en*)
	Adverbial inserts (*wh-*)	
		Perfective (HAVE *-en*)
	Subject inserts (infinitives, gerunds, *wh-*)	

QUESTIONS   NOUN PHRASE FILLERS

YES/NO   *WH-*

Determiner$_2$ articles
Pronouns
Determiner$_2$ possessive
pronouns

Plural inflection $\{-S_1\}$

Equative with no auxiliary   Possessive inflection $\{-S_2\}$

Loose-knit modifier

Object and complement replacements
                                             Determiner$_1$
                                             Determiner$_3$
                                             Close-knit modifier

Continuum auxiliary   Adverb of place replacements
Transitives and Intransitives
with no auxiliary
                             Adverb of time and manner
                             replacements
Modals

                             Coordinated clause replacements

Perfective
                                             Object restrictive modifier
                                             (adverbials)
                                             Object restrictive modifier
                                             (clause)
                                             Subject restrictive modifier
                                             (adverbials and clauses)
                                             Complex nominals

175

lessons for teaching the language to children with problems because, for the moment, it represents the best of our knowledge.

Finally, individual children may not stick absolutely to this sequence, but they will not violate it. I have known several children, for example, who began to insert infinitives into object slots before they began to use the equative predicate and the auxiliary of the continuum. This does not violate the hypothesis presented in Chapter 6; it only serves to point up the independence of the learning of the clause constructions and other constructions such as the verb phrase. Not only this, but some children will learn, for example, one modal, e.g., *can,* before they learn something like the auxiliary of the continuum. We can see, then, that adjacent functions within a construction may change sequence. Once more, however, if most children go through the sequences as shown in Table 6.21, then it will not do violence to a child's learning program to sequence instruction that way. That is, the sequence can be used to decide what must be taught when an assessment has been carried out. How this assessment is to be carried out will be the topic of the first chapter in Part III.

PART 3

Process Analysis

CHAPTER 7

Assessing Current Functioning

Until now we have been concentrating on the things that children must learn and the sequences in which they learn them. It is time to begin to bring it all together in relation to the task that confronts the teacher of the child who has language problems, and to show just how all of the preceding can be used to do a useful assessment.

Perhaps it would be worthwhile to stop and think about that task for just a moment. The best teachers will (a) find out what a child can do now, (b) find out what he would ordinarily learn to do next in the course of normal human development, and (c) figure out a way to get him to do that as quickly as possible. Chapter 6 provides the basic tools to accomplish the second step. We still lack a method for finding out what a child can do right now so that we will be able to place him in the developmental sequence at the right place.

By the end of this chapter I will show how this can be done with a developmental checklist. After some practice, this checklist can be used to guide the observations of a teacher who needs to know what to teach his pupils. Experience indicates, however, that a certain amount of pretraining is required for people who are not yet thoroughly familiar with the system underlying the checklist. In effect, most people seem to need a kind of "tuning up" of their observational powers before they are really ready to shortcut the process and use the checklist. Therefore, I would strongly suggest that anyone who wishes to use it should first be prepared to go through one or more complete analyses of the language status of specific children. This is to be done for no other reason than to become very familiar with the system. This chapter will present both the long and short methods of analysis. Granted that the long way is tedious and that it is very time consuming; past experience with many workshop and seminar groups leads me to believe, however, that there are very few people indeed who can go directly from Chapter 6 to the checklist and do an accurate job of assessment. The sole reason for this, in my opinion, is unfamiliarity with the concepts about which we have been talking. Anyone who works through the long method once or twice will gain the needed familiarity, however. Once this happens, you will be ready to use the short method, and you will probably agree that the effort expended on the long method was well spent and worthwhile.

The Long Method

Transcripts

The first step in doing the long method is to develop a transcript that can be analyzed and reanalyzed over and over again. This transcript should be of a child's conversation with somebody about something. The child's conversational partner may be an adult or another child. The topic of the conversation may be anything at all, just so long as it is a real conversation. Standardized formats that rely on a series of pictures about which standard questions are asked tend to elicit stereotyped responses that do not show how grammatically complex a child can really be under conversational conditions. Such formats are largely useless.

Recording Equipment and Space

Developing a good transcript is easy and will go smoothly if everything is set up correctly ahead of time. It is very important, for example, to think about the machines which will be used for recording, and the space in which the conversation is to take place.

The tape recorder should have an automatic volume control that will adjust to varying sound intensities by itself. This is an absolute necessity for recordings made in spaces where the child has some mobility and a lack of physical constraints. It is often very useful to allow the child to be somewhat mobile during the recording session, especially if he is very young. Older children are able to sit still for periods of time while in conversation, but younger ones find it much more easy to make conversation about something they are doing. Some people I have met are able to get small children to sit still and talk for rather long periods of time, but many of us find it easier to allow the child some mobility. The tape recorder has to be able to handle this. Those recorders that must be manually adjusted for sound level do not lend themselves to taping a child who is next to the machine at one moment, and halfway across the room with his back turned at the next.

The tape machine should also have good voice pickup and playback capabilities. Accurate pickup across the entire range of hearing frequencies is unnecessary, however. Also, freedom from static and hum while recording is a must, and sometimes a machine will perform better when placed on a piece of foam or folded towel so that the vibrations of the motor are dampened. Some machines perform better with an external microphone, and some better with an internal microphone. A little experimentation is usually required to learn the recording characteristics of a specific machine and how it works best.

There are some machines that have all of these characteristics but are difficult to use in doing a transcription. Accurate transcription requires that we go back and forth over specific sections of the tape many times, and it is best to have a machine with a row of buttons across the front rather than a joystick or other lever arrangement. Rewinding while using a button machine tends to be a lot faster than rewinding by moving levers.

Overall, many of the small Japanese cassette recorders possess excellent transcription capabilities. In addition, they can be run either on batteries or from an electric outlet, and they are easy on the pocketbook. A little time spent in comparing tape recorders for good transcription characteristics will pay enormous time and effort dividends in the long run.

While holding the conversation with the child, we should be in a space that is as free from extraneous noises as possible. We might get an excellent conversation going only to find that it cannot be understood when we play it back because of traffic noises or other external sources of noise such as the hum of fans. There is no need to hide the tape recorder, it can even be used as a conversation piece with some children. The best bet is to choose solid resting places for the tape recorder that will allow it to do its job well. A battery-operated machine makes it possible to record in a classroom, a broom closet, or outdoors, and from tables, desks, and the floor. Any of these situations can present itself under certain conditions. Actually, the space used is irrelevant to the analysis—any place that is relatively quiet in which the adult and child feel comfortable is going to be a good space. The essential thing when you come right down to it, is that we must be able to get the child into a conversation and record it well enough to be able to transcribe it.

Conversations

Anyone can get a child into a conversation if he is interested in what it is the child has to say. I have seen a number of people, however, who get so tied up in asking questions that they forget about the child and end up with poor data.

I personally feel that the use of standardized interview questions is a worthless technique for gathering data useful for drawing educationally relevant conclusions. The technique that most often fails is the one in which we get a set of pictures together and ask the child to "tell me what is in this picture." From such a technique we tend to get a long laundry-list set of responses that consist mainly of equative clauses, e.g., "There is a *noun*" type of response. To some children this type of thing seems to smack too much of formal tests; they tend to respond very carefully and without the full grammatical complexity of which they might be capable.

The same type of thing happens when some interviewers open the recording session the wrong way. Labov (1970) points this out beautifully with an experiment he did to find out if "nonverbal" children were truly nonverbal. Many children in inner-city schools have been identified as being "nonverbal" after someone tried to get them to talk to a tape recorder and the children remained silent. The question arose as to whether they were truly nonverbal, or whether they simply chose not to talk. Labov identified three of the most notorious "nonverbal" children in one classroom, and set up a tape recorder in the cloak room. Then he put on a coat, put a rabbit under it and went in to see the teacher while the children were all in the room. All eyes were, of course, on the coat as the mysterious lump wiggled around under it. When he was sure that he had the attention of all the children, Labov opened his coat and let the rabbit poke his head out. Then he said that he couldn't have a proper conversation with the teacher with this rabbit bothering him. What he needed was a baby-sitter for the rabbit. Every child volunteered, of course, and Labov chose the previously identified "nonverbal" children. He took them in the cloak room, turned on the tape recorder in full view of the children, and then told them that the rabbit was "very nervous." What the rabbit needed, he said, was someone to keep him calm by talking to him. Then he left the cloak room. The result was that the children evidenced complexity of speech that the school personnel found difficult to believe. Labov examined the protocols of the previous attempts and believes he knows what went wrong. Many interviewers will go to a child's room, ask for the child by name, and then take him to a space where they ask the child questions, such as "What is your name?" "What room are you in?" and "Who is your teacher?" Many children learn very quickly that what they say out loud can get them into trouble when they don't know what is going on. Under these circumstances, when the interviewer obviously knows the answers to the questions he is asking, the child must figure that there is something going on that he does not know about. The best course of action, the child believes, is to stay out of trouble by saying as little as possible. When this happens, the child gets labeled *nonverbal.*

Obviously, the technique that an interviewer uses will determine (at least in part) what he gets on the tape. There is no need to fool a child: I have always explained to a child that I am going to talk with him and record the conversation. The typical response from the child is to ask if he can listen to the tape when the interview is completed. From then on, different children need to have different interview techniques. The following is a list of some useful ones:

The TV Technique

Most children watch TV for at least a little while every day. This makes it a simple thing to say, "Did you watch TV last night (or the night before)?" Most children answer "Yes," and the next question is, "What happened on (*name of program*)?" If the interviewer is truly interested in getting the child to tell what happened, it is easy to lead him through a discussion of the program, who did what to whom and under what circumstances it was done. It helps to have watched the same program, so that when the child forgets what happened next he can be prompted by the question, "And then what did (*name*) do?"

The Howsyourdog Technique

One person I know had good success in opening an interview by asking the child, "How's your dog?" We get an amazing variety of responses to this question, all of which can open up fruitful areas of conversational exploration. Some children say that they don't have one; we can ask if they would like one, what kind they would like, and what they would do with one if they had it. Other children have had dogs that have died under various circumstances and will tell you all about it. Still others have (or have had) dogs to play with and will tell us all about the games and the good/neat/silly/stupid things that the dog does. Typical cocktail party conversations about animals are quite within the realm of conversational possibilities with children as well as with adults, and dogs are as safe as the weather.

The Inferior Technique

When a child talks with an adult he is in the position of the social inferior. This can put a lid on what it is that the child is willing to say. Labov (personal communication) points out that a child will willingly talk to someone or something that is socially inferior to him, however; puppets, Mickey Mouse dolls that light up when the child talks, and other inferiors such as small animals tend to allow a child to open up nicely. The child can be asked to tell a story to the inferior, for example; the story "Three Bears" is always good, because as Lee (1974) points out, every child in the United States seems to know this story. Even with all of its familiarity, children tend to tell it at their own level. Inferiors for the child to talk to open up a myriad of conversational possibilities, and anyone wishing to do an interview can seriously consider their use.

The Huh? Technique

Some children will resist the most valiant efforts to get them to talk, and for these children it is often helpful for the interviewer just to sit and say nothing for a rather long period of time. Allow the silence to get very heavy, and after the child begins to fidget a little, turn toward him and ask ''Huh?'' as if he had said something but not well enough to be understood. Almost invariably, the child will say something to the effect that he had not spoken, and we can ask ''Why?'' or say something to the effect that we thought he had. Once the door is open we can get a conversation going about what it is he might have said, or introduce the Howsyourdog technique.

Others

Techniques are limited only by lack of imagination and resourcefulness. What makes one child talk volumes fails miserably with another. Some children will interview us and others will drive us half mad with their own silent technique. I have gone so far as to pull a nail file out of my pocket to pare my fingernails and then ask the child if he had a knife like mine. It worked. Very young children will talk if they can manipulate objects, such as a block tower or some other toy while the interview is going on, and older children often like to talk about an exciting thing that happened to them at some point in the past. As long as a child starts talking about something, he will often continue to talk about it if he gets a little encouragement. Above all, *listen to what the child says!* Too often interviewers will be so concerned with what *they* are going to say next that they totally miss a conversation that the child tries to initiate.

What Not to Do

It is very often the case that a child who has language development problems also has a very sad home life. I learned a long time ago not to ask children questions such as ''Tell me about your father'' or ''What do you do when you go home at night?'' It is simply too easy to get yourself into a psychotherapy session that you cannot handle unless you are a qualified counselor or psychologist. Most of us are not, and it is best to stick to safe things like TV, school, animals, the weather, or actions that are going on during the interview—a picture the child is drawing, a block tower he is building, etc. The purpose of the interview is to gather data on the child's developmental language status, not to open up difficult areas in the child's private life.

Making the Transcript

The next thing to do, once the conversation is on tape, is to get it down on paper. This task is extremely difficult and time-consuming. An experienced transcriber will generally spend about four hours transcribing one hour of a child's conversation. A person who has never done it before should be ready to spend more time than this. It is especially necessary for the latter group to make the effort to do a transcription. The reason for this is that most people are amazed to find, when they finally finish their first transcript, that they have never before listened to the way in which children say what they say. It is impossible to analyze a child's level of language ability if we do not know how to listen to what they say, and the process of making a transcript helps tremendously in ''tuning'' our attention.

When complete, a decent transcript will look much like the ones found further on in this chapter. There are some things about transcript format that are important to note:

1. The child's utterances should be numbered so that they can be found quickly when needed. There are times when a child will produce several sentences in a row with no intonational break between them. In such cases, a good thing to do is to number the start of such a string, and then use letters to indicate specific sentences so that they can be found again. This will produce numbers such as 27 b, 31 a, 31 c, etc. However it is done, it is important to number the child's utterances. In using the long method of analysis, each utterance must first be classified, and then various utterances representing a single construction that are scattered through the transcript will have to be analyzed as a single unit. Thus, if we want to look at the group of utterances composed of numbers 2, 17, 21b, 49, and 122a, it will be easy to find them when they are clearly numbered. Without these numbers, however, grouping sentences for analysis becomes nearly impossible.

2. What the child says must be closely correlated with what the interviewer (or whoever else is in the environment) says before and after the child speaks. The reason for this is found in the identification of elliptical utterances (see the following section), which affect the entire analysis. Without going into this too deeply at present, the transcript must have at least two columns. One will contain what the interviewer says, and the other will contain what the child says. The two columns must be arranged so that the conversation can be read directly from the transcript without any difficulty, i.e., when the adult says something and the child follows up, it must be apparent where the adult stops and the child begins.

3. It is unnecessary to build all of the child's phonological "errors" into the transcript. It *is* necessary to represent phonology where it affects the grammar, however. Where a phonological error has no effect on the grammar, you can write out what the child says as if it were in standard adult English. To illustrate: When a child says something like *dat* for *that,* the phonological "error" does not affect the grammar; it can be written as *that.* Similarly, a child who says, *doin* for *doing* has indeed used the inflection of the continuum, and it can be represented by writing *doing.* However, a child who says *gonna* may or may not yet have developed the infinitive *to* marker, and the transcriber should represent it by writing *gonna.* If you have any doubt about how to transcribe a word, follow this rule of thumb: If there is any doubt, write it the way the child says it.

4. For some people it may be important to write the child's name, birthdate, IQ score, and other information on the transcript, but such data have no relevance to the analysis itself other than for identification purposes. I prefer to ignore such things, especially IQ data and birthdates. In terms of the analysis, the only important outcome is to decide what you must try to teach the child in the next language lesson—all those other things add nothing to the analysis.

While the form of the transcript turns out to be relatively simple, then, making it is something else. The transcriber will find that, after innumerable attempts to discover what a child has said, there will still be places that are simply unintelligible. After exhausting both yourself and your friends in an attempt to find out exactly what the child has said at such a point, and when failure has been admitted, it is best to write (*unintelligible*) to represent the utterance. Above all, do not make up data!! It is possible to analyze only what the child has actually said, and any child (and most adults, including the writer) will be unintelligible at times. The younger and the more severely retarded a child, the greater the number of times it will be necessary to find that you have to write *(unintelligible)*.

One trick that seems to help the overall transcript is as follows: When you finally are convinced that the transcript is absolutely accurate, go all the way back to the beginning of your tape and transcript, pick up a pencil, and turn on the machine with the resolution not to turn it off until you have reached the end. Follow the transcript with a pencil in your hand and make checkmarks in the margin of the transcript at the points where you find discrepancies. You will find a number of them. I don't know why this is so, but after having gone back and forth over a tape several times, running it all the way through without stopping always provides new insights and a number of corrections. It is often helpful to have someone else do this step for you. One time, a few years back, I had a number of tapes that produced almost 1,000 pages of transcript. Graduate students in speech pathology and linguistics transcribed them for me, and then I checked every one. Although the transcribers had done an excellent job, I found many errors on every single tape. Not only this, but a linguist went over the transcripts after *I* had checked them, and found even more errors in transcription! The moral: It is always worthwhile to have someone check your transcript.

In the end there should be at least six to eight pages of good transcript. This is usually plenty of data for a good analysis unless the entire transcript consists of the child answering a series of *yes/no* questions. As long as it includes good, conversational data, however, six to eight pages is plenty. Long stretches in which the adult is the only one speaking should be left out in order to make the transcript a little more compact; as long as it includes what the adult said immediately prior to a response by the child, it is all right to leave out the places where the adult spoke and the child made no response. The amount of interview time for this much data will vary from child to child. Some talky children give enough data to fill eight pages in 5 minutes, while other children require 2 or 3 half-hour sessions to produce this much. In the end, it will be the length of the transcript, not the length of the interview, that determines how long the interview should last.

The Long Method: Analyzing a Transcript

Once the conversation with the child is well-transcribed and neat, and all of the child's utterances are marked so that each one can be quickly found, the analysis proper begins. Very simply, the task is to go through the transcript time and time again, each time looking for specific functions and constructions of the language. The basic idea is to make a judgment about each of these functions and constructions in terms of the following question:

Do I have to teach the child to use *(construction or function)?*

There are several possible answers that can be given to this question in any analysis:

1. *Yes;* the child obviously must learn to do this or learn to do it better.
2. *No;* the child obviously has this construction or function under control.
3. *Not sure;* given the existing information the decision could go either way, and I will have to find out more before I can draw a conclusion that will satisfy me.
4. *No information;* on the basis of the transcript I have here, there is simply no way that I can draw a conclusion because there are no examples of this construction or

function in the transcript, nor is there any other information which I can bring to bear on the question.

In all that follows, no mention will be made of ''scores.'' Scores are self-defeating. A number is essentially meaningless to a classroom teacher unless each and every number is tied to a specific behavioral goal. No truly useful system of tying numbers to behavioral goals has ever been developed, and it is far better from an instructional standpoint to establish behavioral goals per se than it is to develop numerical scores. This is not to say that numerical scores have no usefulness, but only to say that the teacher needs a statement of behavioral goals, not numbers. Accordingly, the system of analysis presented in the following pages limits itself to the observation of behavior and the establishment of specific behavioral goals for specific children. In essence, the teacher or clinician who uses the system will make a series of judgments about whether or not a child must learn to use specific functions or constructions of English. Then, by comparing these judgments to the developmental sequence hypothesized in Chapter 6, the teacher can establish which functions or constructions should be taught first. The overall goal of the enterprise is to lay out an instructional program that reflects normal growth and development of the use of the English language. The basic assumption is that nature is the best guide to what a child should be learning.

Analyzing a Transcript

Probably the best way to demonstrate the long method of analyzing a transcript would be to go through the process step by step. Essentially, the process is one of first analyzing what the child knows about the clause, the verb phrase, and noun phrase, the transformations and a few miscellaneous constructions. Once this is complete, the child's level of usage can be placed in the developmental sequence and what must be taught next will be revealed. To show how to do this we will first need a transcript; we will use Transcript #1 (p. 189) for the following example of the long method of analysis.

Transcript #1 happens to contain a conversation between one of my students and a girl who may or may not be retarded (all names and other identifying data have been changed or deleted). Frankly, it is usually impossible to tell whether or not a child is retarded from reading through a transcript; it really does not make much difference in terms of doing an analysis anyway. Let us, though, for the sake of the exercise, assume that the child in the transcript is a twelve-year-old child who has been labeled *mentally retarded* by the school authorities. Let us further assume that we are teaching this child, and that our task is to decide what to try to teach tomorrow in the language lesson.

The first step is to make a gross judgment about the child's general level of development. Is she producing utterances that would be classified at the one- and two-word stage, or is her grammar more highly developed and at a point at which we could do a clausal analysis? A glance at the transcript tells us that she has gone beyond the one- and two-word stage; therefore, we must concentrate on analyzing the grammar.

Useful and Non-Useful Data

Before plunging in, it is important to note that we will not be able to take everything the child says into consideration. That is, some of the things people say (both children and adults) are inadmissible as evidence as to whether or not they are able to produce certain constructions. The major category of such utterances are those that are elipted, but there are other utterances that must also be ignored as well. In essence, an ellipted utterance is one which takes part of its grammar from either a previous utterance or from the environment. There are two major forms of ellipsis (Gunter, 1963):

Linguistically Conditioned Ellipsis

A linguistically conditioned ellipsis occurs when a previous utterance, produced either by the person speaking or by someone else, provides the grammar for an utterance. We see this occurring very often in the case of answers to questions (see Chapter 5), but it occurs in other places as well. In Transcript #1, the very first utterance by the child is ellipted, i.e., the adult asks the child, "What are we making?", and the child responds, "Some cake." This is perfectly good conversational usage in English, but it tells us nothing at all about how the child is able to construct any of the basic clause types (intransitive, transitive, and equative) of the language. Therefore, it will do us no good to worry over how to classify this response in terms of complete clauses, and we will ignore it when we are trying to discover what the child knows about clauses. Note, however, that this utterance *does* give us some information about the use of the determiner$_2$ in the noun phrase. When it comes time for us to try to understand something about the child's ability to construct the noun phrase, we will want to consider it. In terms of clauses, however, this utterance yields no useful information and we will skip over it when we analyze them. Utterance #95 is another good example of linguistically conditioned ellipsis. This utterance, which is grammatically an adverb of place, takes its grammar from the child's previous utterance (#94). It is useless for us to worry about whether or not this utterance "really" represents a transitive, intransitive, or equative clause, and if so, whether or not all of the obligatory functions are present. There are plenty of other utterances in the transcript that will give us the information we need, and we will ignore #1 and #95 when analyzing for the basic clausal constructions.

Environmentally Conditioned Ellipsis

An environmentally conditioned ellipses occurs when an utterance is meaningful in a specific context. Contextually ellipted utterances do not require a fully grammatical construction to communicate meaning. For example, if someone should say, "Cream and sugar?", most of us could reconstruct the context in which this "question" was asked, even though it is not a "complete" sentence in English. The regularity of occurrence of this particular utterance in our culture makes it a stark example of the kind of thing that can occur, but there are many times when we will say something that is unique to a specific situation at a specific time. In effect, environmentally conditioned elliptical utterances look very similar to Stage II and IIIa constructions, i.e., the topic is in the environment and the utterance is a comment on that environmental topic. Such is the case in the transcript for utterance #77, in which the child somehow indicates a big rock and labels it as such. Because we are working from someone else's transcript, we cannot be entirely sure what the child was trying to say. The point is that we really do not need to be entirely sure when we are trying to analyze the level of development of the child's clauses. This utterance will yield no useful information *for that purpose,* and we will simply ignore it when we analyze the clause. Note, however, that information *may* be provided for making judgments about constructions other than that of the clause. Utterance #77 is a noun phrase that contains a loose-knit modifier and a head, for example. It will be important when we try to find out what this child knows about the noun phrase.

Contractions and Elisions

In Chapter 6, we noted that contractions are inadmissible evidence as to whether or not the child knows the equative verb BE in sentences such as:

(7.1) He's my daddy.

(7.2) What's that?

We cannot use contractions for evidence for anything because at early stages in development, what appears to be a contraction may actually be a single form (such as *whats*) that is in free variation with the same form without the *-s* (*what*). That is, the child may simply be using two different forms that have no difference in meaning for him. Because of this possibility, only those utterances in which the form is fully present can be used as evidence *for* the existence of the form. If only the contracted form appears in a transcript, we have no information about the existence of that form as a productive unit in the child's speech. This statement holds true not only for the equative predicate, but also for the auxiliaries (BE in the continuum and the passive, and HAVE in the perfective); for the modals when they appear with negative contractions, i.e., *can (can't)* and *will (won't);* and the dummy DO when the negative is contracted to it *(don't)*. In each of these cases, the contracted form appears before the separated forms appear. Under these circumstances, drawing the conclusion that a child knows the auxiliaries, the equative predicate, the modals, or the dummy DO on the basis of contractions is simply impossible. We must look for other evidence.

In Chapter 6 we also noted that elisions in infinitives are also inadmissible evidence as to whether or not the child knows how to use the infinitive marker *to*. An elision is the collapse of two or more syllables into a shorter unit, e.g., *going to* is often elided and appears as *gonna*. Both adults and children elide the infinitive marker in conversation, but in the early stages of infinitive development, a child is unable to produce the marker on demand (see Chapter 6). Therefore, forms that are elided cannot be used as evidence for the existence of the form. This holds true not only for the infinitive marker, but also for elisions such as:

(7.3) Jeatyet? ("Did you eat yet?")

On the basis of such an utterance we simply cannot conclude that the dummy DO is present and must look for other evidence of its existence. Similarly, all other elisions must be ignored as constituting evidence for the existence of the form or construction involved, and we must look elsewhere for the information we need.

Other Inadmissible Evidence

Other inadmissible evidence will always be present in any transcript. The problem with conversational data is that they are rife with false starts, hesitations, dysfluencies, and other kinds of fits and starts. In addition, what Brown (1973) calls the *Law of Cumulative Complexity* will always be in effect. That is, people can (and do) say things the way they learned to say them at an earlier point in development. Utterance #77 is a good example of this, i.e., children use the spoken comment on an environmental topic exclusively at an early stage of development, but adults often use it as well. The difference is that the adult is perfectly capable of being more grammatically complex, whereas the very young child whose development is at Stage II is not. Our task, in doing an analysis, is to discover the highest level of complexity for each construction that the child is capable of producing so that we can decide what does and does not need to be taught. To do this, it is not necessary to categorize and classify each and every utterance he makes so that we have a nice, neat set of figures at the end of the analysis. Consequently, there are many times when we must ignore what the child says because it does not constitute *useful* evidence as we search for answers to the question of what we have to teach that child. In doing the analysis, we consider only the data that will tell us what we need to know. With this, then, let us begin the analysis itself.

Analysis of Basic Clause Types

The first step in the analysis is to find out whether or not the child can construct the basic clause types, i.e., intransitive, transitive, and equative. We must discover whether or not the child uses obligatory subjects, objects, predicates, and complements in the appropriate places. Because the three different constructions develop at different rates, we will do three different analyses. The first step is to read over the transcript to get a "feel" for general level of development. Next, identify where each of these constructions are found in the transcript. Once the data are found, a conclusion can be drawn as to whether or not the child knows the basic clause types.[1]

Intransitive Clauses

The intransitive declarative and imperative clauses in the first transcript are as follows.

Transcript #1

Adult	*Child*
What are we making?	1. Some cake
	2. Not that leaf in
	3. Not this in
What is that?	4. Where's the plate?
I don't know. Where is the plate?	5. Maybe down here
	6. It down here
Let's see	7. See, down pipes
	8. Want see it?
Where?	9. Right there
Oh, I see it.	10. I'm dig this
	11. See it?
Yes, I see it.	12. I didn't see it.
You didn't see it?	13. Pipes, down pipes
The pipes?	14. Yeah
	15. Want see?
Yes, I want to see.	16. I get it out?
O.K.	17. You?
O.K. Let's get the pipes.	18. The pipe
	19. The down pipes
	20. See one

---

[1]It might be worthwhile at this point to go back to Chapter 6 and place a bookmark at Table 6.21 on p. 174. The following analysis will refer to it frequently and you will need to find it easily.

Yes, it's a pretty cake.	21. This a cake
What are you doing?	22. A cake
What are they?	23. Cooking . . . cake
	24. Some rocks
What did you say?	25. Not that leafie!
	26. Not this leafie.
	27. Not this stick.
	28. Not this.
	29. I find that pipe.
	30. Find pipes.
	31. Want see it?
I want to see it.	32. Them pipes
	33. I get this in little
	34. Want see it?
Yeah.	35. It not them pipes.
	36. It not them pipes.
	37. I can't find it.
I don't know where they are.	38. To bottom . . . to bottom
Are you going all the way to the bottom?	39. Yep!
What are you going to do with the pipes?	40. Put that in there.
	41. Put that in in little
	42. Right down to bottom
	43. Maybe I can—
Your foot is in the hole, isn't it?	44. I can make feet!
	45. My foot's down there, two of them down there.
	46. And burying them!
	47. And burying them!
You're making a home for the cup?	48. You see a home?
	49. What?
	50. I bury that, that cup!
Yes, you did, Sally.	
What are you going to do now?	51. Put it in truck.
In what?	52. In truck
O.K.	53. In this truck!
All right.	54. I get it out there.
	55. Put in this truck!
	56. In this truck!
	57. I put it right there.
	58. It not fit!
	59. It not fit!
Doesn't it fit?	60. I, I cannot, not . . . hole
	61. It fit!
	62. I making this hole right there, hole, right there for bowl.
For the bowl	63. For Marcia's bowl
Whose bowl?	64. Marcia's
	65. Marcia's!
Marcia's bowl, O.K.	66. Her, I use it.
	67. Marcia, I use it.
	68. Want see?
	69. There!
There it is, you showed it to me.	70. This sand to

Yes, there's sand all over here, isn't there?
What?

Yes, I saw that big rock.
What's the matter?
There's the bowl.
Then you have to make the hole bigger.
It won't fit in there.
It fits.
No, no it doesn't. What are you going to do?

What?
Looking for the pipes again?

Is that a pipe?
Oh, O.K.
All right.

What do you want?
Where is it?

Show me where it is.
You can reach it.
Johnny lost it?

What are we doing?

Patting it, O.K.

And the sticks too, O.K.
Yes, that's where the water comes out.

Some sugar?
Where is the sugar?

Here?
Here?

Shall I get some?
Hold out your hand.

71. It's a lot (*unintelligible*)
72. I . . . feets down there
73. Feets down there
74. It's down there, here.
75. I . . . that leafie
76. I know leaf down here cause leaf down here.
77. Big rock!
78. Oh, leafs
79. Bowl there.
80. It not fit!
81. Put it in there.
82. Put in there.
83. Uh huh.
84. Put in like that.
85. Make the (*unintelligible*)
86. I can bring them pipes.
87. Them pipes
88. Yeah
89. There's a pipe.
90. Yeah
91. Put in there.
92. Can't get down.
93. Can't get down.
94. Give me that stick there.
95. Right there
96. Give me that stick!
97. That stick
98. Right over there
99. Go get it.
100. Right there
101. Johnny lose it.
102. There we go!
103. Down, get down here!
104. Cooking this
105. Cooking
106. I patting it.
107. Put that in there.
108. And sticks too
109. That . . . water comes out
110. Yep.
111. Give me . . .
112. I need some sugar.
113. I can't reach it.
114. I can't reach it.
115. Right . . . right in there
116. Right up there!
117. Right up there!
118. I show you.
119. Right in there
120. Yeah.
121. I need some sugar again.

Is that for your cake?	122. I need some sugar.
	123. Hurry!
	124. I get it.
O.K.	125. Some sugar
	126. Sugar!
	127. Sugar!
	128. That's sugar
Yes, that's sugar, isn't it?	129. Lots sugar
	130. There's some sugar!
	131. More sugar.
	132. Here's some more sugar.
	133. *(unintelligible)* this sugar
	134. Here's some more sugar!
	135. Here's some.
	136. I be back!
	137. That that policeman stockings!
Policeman stockings?	138. What's them?
They go all the way up.	139. Stockings
Do you have socks on?	140. I got little socks on.
Let me see.	141. Wanna see?
	142. See?
	143. Little socks
Yes, they're nice little socks.	144. Wanna see my other one?
Yes.	145. Them got...
	146. I got yellow
	147. I got... purple on them!
Yes, you do have purple on them.	148. And white!
And white too.	149. See
	150. White one
	151. White, purple
That's right. That's very good, Sally.	152. Stay there!
All right, I'll stay here.	153. Here's some sugar.
More sugar?	154. Not leaf
	155. Leafie in here.
	156. They're back! (referring to other children)
They're back? I don't see them.	157. Johnny talking.
	158. Johnny talking to me.
Johnny is talking to you?	159. I, I
	160. I heard... Johnny talking to
He must be talking very soft because I can't hear him.	161. What?
	162. Talking to policeman
The policeman?	163. Johnny
He is?	164. My coat dry!
It'll dry pretty soon.	165. Wanna see
	166. I can touch it.
	167. I can touch it.
You can touch it, O.K.	168. Dry!
	169. My... this sleeve wet.
	170. Them dry my sleeves.
No, they're still wet.	171. This coat wet.
	172. That's all wet.
	173. Them coat, Frank's coat

I don't know, where is Johnny's coat?
No, you don't want to sit up there, you might fall.
I'll hang on to you.
Can I hang on to here?
Let's go down and make some more cake.

Let Mary see it.

Why don't you take the bowl?
You could make a hole for the bowl.
Maybe you and Mary can both dig?

Maybe you can give her the bowl?

Worms live in the dirt.
You're going to take the worm home?

That house is your home?

Wait a minute, let Mary see it.
The worm belongs to himself.
Shall we let the worm go home?
There he goes.
If you had two, Mary couldn't have any.
Which toy?
You told her she couldn't have it.
No, not too long.
What are you going to take home?
That toy? I thought it belonged here?
Oh, that home. O.K.

Why not?

What?

174. Where Johnny coat?
175. Where Johnny coat?

176. Uh, uh, I could hang on.
177. I want hang on.
178. No!
179. Bowl's down there.
180. I can't make cake because
181. I can't make anything cause
182. I can't make cake.
183. Let's go down.
184. A worm!
185. I want it!
186. No!
187. A worm
188. I want it.
189. I want it!
190. I want that!
191. I want that cuppie!
192. No!
193. I want that cup!
194. No!
195. No!
196. I want that worm!
197. Wormee's dirty.
198. I... take worm at home.
199. Put it in bowl to
200. Take it out.
201. That my house right there.
202. Hello wormie.
203. Mary has the cup.
204. This bowl can't get out
205. My wormie!
206. My worm!
207. Put wormie down.
208. I want two.
209. Her have that toy.
210. That bowl toy.
211. Mary had this long time.
212. I going take this home.
213. This toy
214. I going take it to that home.
215. Can hold it right in my hand
216. Can hold
217. Gimme my
218. Don't give me my baby because
219. Don't give me my baby.
220. My baby too bad.
221. My baby too bad because
222. I got cup up here.
223. Me cup Mary can't get it
224. Mary... Mary can't get it.

She can't get it?	225. It up here.
	226. Gimme that bowl!
What do you want?	227. That . . . that bowl!
	228. Gimme that bowl!
All right. Are you ready for your nap Sally?	229. No!

Imperative, Stage IV: #152

Declarative, Stage III: #93, 94

Declarative, Stage IV: #58, 59, 61, 80, 102, 109, 176.

At first glance, it appears that this child's intransitive clauses are Stage IV. The question we must deal with is whether or not utterances #93 and 94 provide information that will seriously bring into question the conclusion that we do not have to teach the child to construct the basic intransitive clause type. In both of these clauses, the second of which simply repeats the first, the subject (*I?*) is missing; could this be some sort of environmental ellipsis? There are many other utterances in this transcript in which the subject is present (all of the previously listed intransitive declaratives, as well as utterances such as #12, 29, and 35). Even if #93 and 94 contained errors of some sort, it would be difficult to say that they raise any serious objection to the conclusion that this child knows the basic intransitive clause type construction. Therefore, our first conclusion is that we *probably* do not have to teach this child to use the intransitive clause type. Note that for now, this must be a tentative conclusion. Other evidence will lead us to become more or less definite in drawing it.

Transitive Clauses

The transitive imperative and declarative clauses in the transcript are as follows:

Imperative, Stage III: 55, 82, 84, 91

Imperative, Stage IV: 30, 40, 51, 81, 99, 107, 199, 200, 207, 217, 226, 228

Declarative, Stage III: 30, 46, 47, 104, 162, 198, 215, 216

Declarative, Stage IV: 10, 12, 29, 33, 37, 44, 48, 50, 54, 57, 62, 66, 67, 86, 106, 112 (and many others)

Once again, the examples at Stage IV appear to lead us toward the conclusion that we do not have to teach the basic transitive clause type. There are many examples of Stage III clauses among the transitive examples, however, and once again, we have to find out if the Stage III examples provide any serious objection to our tentative conclusion. The Stage III imperatives are missing an object (possibly *it?*), and it may be that they are examples of the Law of Cumulative Complexity. Note how this same pattern shows up in its complete form in utterances such as #8, 12, 51, 54, and 57; the utterances with missing objects can probably be discounted as providing serious negative evidence. The Stage III declaratives are all missing the subject in much the same way that the subject was missing in the Stage III intransitive declaratives previously analyzed. It is possible to see these as being environmentally ellipted, i.e., in each case the child is describing something that he is doing at the moment, and the subject is most likely *I*. It is very difficult to see how these Stage III clauses provide enough evidence to bring into serious question the conclusion that we do not have to teach the child to use the basic transitive clause type. Therefore, we will conclude that she probably knows it, and that we do not have to teach her to use it. This conclusion, of course, supports the tentative conclusion drawn on the intransitive clause construction made in the previous section. That is, because the transitive construction is learned *after* the intransitive construction, the conclusion that we do not have to teach the transitive clause implies strongly that we do not have to teach the intransitive clause.

Transitive Clauses with Indirect Objects

The imperative and declarative transitive clauses with indirect objects are as follows:

Imperative, Stage III: #111

Imperative, Stage IV: 94, 96, 218, 219, 226, 228

Declarative, Stage IV: #86 (?)

There does not seem to be enough evidence present in the transcript on which to base a conclusion about transitives with indirect objects. The only Stage III imperative (#111) is incomplete—perhaps so because, at the time, the child did not know the vocabulary item she needed to complete the sentence. The other imperatives are at Stage IV, but all of them involve the words *give me (something)*. Children (and adults) tend to say *gimme*, and for the child this may (functionally) be a single word for a child until after he learns the clause pattern with the indirect object. Therefore, these utterances with *gimme* are not good evidence for the existence of the pattern. We would find it difficult to justify the conclusion that the child knows the pattern well enough that we do not have to teach it to her. The only other example of this clause type is a declarative (#86), and this may, in fact, not contain an indirect object at all; i.e., *them* may actually be a possessive pronoun or a det.$_2$ in the noun phrase *them pipes*. Therefore, due to a lack of evidence, we can draw no conclusion about the development of this construction, and we must wait until we can get better evidence from the child. To draw no conclusion is a perfectly valid option during any part of an analysis and will force us, when we exercise it, to attend to potential examples of the construction in the child's everyday speech after we complete the analysis.

Equative Clauses

There are no equative imperatives in this transcript. The equative declaratives are as follows:

Declarative, Stage III: 2, 3, 6, 21, 72, 76, 137, 155, 164, 169, 171, 173, 220, 221, 225

Declarative, Stage IV: 71, 74, 89, 128, 130, 132, 134, 135, 136, 153, 156, 172, 179

This child's equative clauses appear to be evenly distributed between Stage III and Stage IV. Note, however, that every example of a Stage IV equative clause, with the exception of #136, has the predicate contracted to the subject. Contracted forms, as stated previously, cannot be used as evidence *for* knowledge of the equative pattern. In fact, the mass of examples of equatives with the predicates completely missing in this transcript argues overwhelmingly against the conclusion that the child has control over the pattern. The single example (#136) of an uncontracted BE does not provide convincing evidence for the conclusion that we do not have to teach the equative clause type. Therefore, we must conclude that this child does not know the equative pattern, and that we must teach it to her.

When analyzing equative clauses in a transcript, it is sometimes the case that BE is contracted in one-third of all examples, uncontracted in one-third, and in about one-third the predicate will be totally missing. A child with such a distribution may be (*a*) in the middle of the process of acquisition of the equative pattern; or (*b*) exhibiting a splinter skill as a result of having been taught the equative pattern through language programs that emphasize this construction. In either case, the conclusion would be the same: that the child has not yet learned the construction, and must be taught to use it consistently. Remember, the task is to decide what it is that we have to teach and what we do not have to teach so that we can use our time and that of the child's efficiently. If a child has not yet "nailed a construction down," so to speak, then we must help him. *When in doubt, teach it;* you can use the child's behavior during the language lessons to tell you whether or not you must continue to teach the construction you are working on.

Summary of Clause Types Conclusions

The child in this transcript probably has a handle on the basic transitive and intransitive clause types, but obviously has not yet learned to use the obligatory functions of the equative clause. Therefore, we do not have to teach her the transitive and intransitive clause types, but we will have to teach her to use the equative consistently. The transitive construction with the indirect object cannot be analyzed due to an inadequate amount of conclusive data. We would have to observe the child further until we were able to draw a conclusion. Note, however, that we could hypothesize that this construction probably must be taught. Our license to set up this hypothesis is given by the conclusion on the equative (see Table 6.21: they tend to develop at about the same time). Because we have no really good data on the transitive with indirect object, however, we must continue to regard this idea as a hypothesis and not as a conclusion.

Analysis of the Verb Phrase

Once the basic clause types are analyzed, we turn our attention to the verb phrase. In the analysis of the verb phrase, we must look not only for the existence of the VP functions, but also for "completeness of development" of the fillers of those functions. That is, many times a function will be represented by only part of the filler. When this is true, we must conclude that we have to teach the rest of it.

Modals

The evidence for the modal function of the verb phrase appears in the following utterances:

May, shall, must: No evidence.

Can: Present in #37, 43, 44, 60, 86, 166, 167, 176, 215, 216. Also present with the negative contracted in #92, 93, 113, 114, 181, 183, 204, 223, 224.

Will: Missing in #118, 124, 136, 198. Possibly also missing in #16, 33, 54 (unclear).

It is obvious that the child uses the modal *can*, but does not use the modal *will* where required. Since there is no other evidence for or against the development of the fillers of the modal function, no other definite conclusions can be drawn. The probabilities are, however, that the other modals, with the possible exception of *may,* will not be found in this child's language. This tentative conclusion is drawn on the basis of the *will* evidence; i.e., the other modal fillers tend to develop after *can* and *will.*

The fact that *can* is present is not surprising in spite of the status of development of the continuum and the equative clause (see the following section for continuum analysis). Its presence illustrates the fact that isolated fillers of some functions might appear at various times in the general sequence. The presence of one filler of the modal (or any other function) does not always mean that the function has developed. Note in Table 6.21, for example, that the modal *will* ordinarily develops at about the same time as the modal *can.* Since *will* is clearly missing from the transcript, we must conclude that the modal function must still be taught. It simply is not unusual to find either a single filler of a function developing a little out of sequence, or for the sequence of arrival of adjacent functions or constructions in Table 6.21 to vary slightly from child to child.

Note that the instances of *can* and *can't* are listed separately in the organization of the evidence. To reiterate, contracted forms cannot be used as evidence for the existence of the full form. This rule holds true not only for *can,* but also for *will* and the dummy DO as well; i.e., *can't, won't,* and *don't* cannot be used as evidence for the existence of *can, will,* and DO.

The teaching conclusion for the modals, then, is that it is probable that we must teach the modal function to this child.

Continuum

The evidence for the existence of the continuum is as follows:

-ing present, auxiliary missing: #23, 46, 47, 62, 104, 105, 106, 157, 158, 212, 214, 160, 162

Auxiliary present, *-ing* missing: #10 (?)

BE *-ing* fully present: None.

It appears that the continuum *function* is present for the child, but that she has not yet completely developed the *filler* of the function. The auxiliary is still missing, and it will have to be taught to her. In some transcripts, just as in the case of the equative clause, we will often find that all examples of the auxiliary are either contracted, missing, or only sporadically present. Again, we should not be led to believe that the child who exhibits such a pattern has a good handle on the function.

Perfective

The evidence for the existence of the perfective function is as follows:

Function missing: #140, 146, 147, 222

Function present: None.

The conclusion that the perfective will have to be taught could be drawn from the above evidence. It should be noted, however, that sentences such as "I got little socks on,"

(#140), even though they nominally require the perfective, are likely to be said this way by adults. This situation is especially true in certain dialect areas and even I tend to use *got* this way in ordinary conversation. For the child in such circumstances, we can never be sure if she is following the rules of an undeveloped grammar or if she is using a dialect feature. In other words, we simply do not have reliable evidence for the development or nondevelopment of the perfective when *got* provides us with the only evidence for the existence of the function. In the present case, however, the hypothesis that we will probably have to teach the perfective to the child is reasonable in the light of the evidence on the equative clause, the modals, and the continuum (see Table 6.21). We have already concluded that we must teach these functions, and the perfective tends to develop at a much later point in time than any of them.

Passive

There is no evidence for the existence of the passive in the transcript. Because it develops so late, however, we can conclude that we will probably have to teach it (see Table 6.21).

Negative

The evidence for the negative is as follows:

Equative clauses with no auxiliary: #35, 36, 58, 59, 80. Possibly also in #2, 3, 25, 26, 27, 28.

Clauses with auxiliaries: #37, 60, 92, 93, 113, 114, 180, 181, 182, 223, 224

Transitive and intransitive with no auxiliaries: #12, 218, 219

This child has obviously integrated the negative into the verb phrase (except in the case of the equative clause, in which the head of the verb phrase has not yet appeared). *Don't, can't,* and *won't* all tend to appear at about the same time in a child's language. Since we have examples of *can't, don't,* and *didn't,* we would expect to find *won't* upon further observation. The transcript may simply have been too short to allow it to appear.

The question that remains largely unanswered is whether or not this child has developed the negative as a function separate from the others in the verb phrase (see Chapter 6). Such separation appears to be the case for the modal *can,* since she uses both *can* and *can't.* However, we have already concluded that she has not yet developed the modal *will; will* and *won't* cannot be separate forms for this child. Note that the dummy DO is missing in #8, 15, 31, 48, 141 (?), 142(?). This fact indicates that DO and the negative are not yet separated either. The conclusion, then, is that this child has integrated the negative into the verb phrase, but that we still must teach her to attach it to tense as we teach the various verb phrase functions and their fillers.

Inflections

The evidence for the verb phrase inflections is as follows:

Past tense: Present in #12, 160, and 211, but missing in #50, 101, and 170. It could be present or missing in #51, 55, 57, 91.

Third person present singular: Present in #203, but missing in #209.

There is too little data in this transcript to allow us to draw firm conclusions about the verb phrase inflections. She may have lacked opportunity to demonstrate she could use them. There is a distinct possibility that she will have to be taught the inflections, however, since in the few instances in which they should appear, she demonstrates only sporadic control over them.

Summary: Verb Phrase Conclusions

The girl in this transcript appears to be at the beginning of the verb phrase learning sequence. Only one modal appears in the transcript, and she has not yet fully developed the continuum filler, although the function itself seems to be established. These data, coupled with the conclusions about the equative clause predicate, places development early in the verb phrase learning sequence (Table 6.21).

Analysis of the Transformations

In the analysis of the development of the transformations we search for several different things:

1. First we look at the questions to see if tense is being placed in front of the subject; and, if so, whether it occurs under all conditions.
2. In the case of *wh-* questions, we also try to discover which *wh-* words are being used and are being placed at the front of the clause.
3. In the case of the coordinates, we look for the use of conjunctions and whether the obligatory functions of the individual clauses are being filled; in addition, we look to see if the child is able to delete identical functions from the second clause, and to use relative pronouns where applicable.
4. In the case of subordinates, we look to find what functions the inserts can fill in the matrix clauses, and whether all the obligatory functions in both the matrix and insert clauses are being filled.
5. Finally, we look for passives to see if we can form a judgment as to whether or not the child knows how to form this complicated construction.

Questions

The evidence for the questions is as follows:

Yes/No Questions:
1. Clauses with auxiliaries: None in the transcript.
2. Transitive and intransitive clauses with no auxiliaries: #8, 11, 15, 31, 48, 68, 141, 144
3. Equative clauses: None in the transcript.

Wh- Questions:
1. Clauses with auxiliaries: None in the transcript.
2. Transitive and intransitive clauses with no auxiliaries: None in the transcript.
3. Equative clauses: #4, 138, 174, 175

It is obvious, from looking at these utterances, that this child is not yet moving tense in any of the questions. The only Stage V question in the transcript is in one of the equative clauses, and it has the predicate contracted (#4). All others are at Stage IV. In fact, some questions, the ones that are like little formulas in the language (''Wanna . . . ?''), are at

Stage III because they have no subjects. Even adults leave the subject out in questions like this, though. Therefore, they provide us with no useful evidence.

Note how the data on questions support the conclusions drawn for clauses and the verb phrase. That is, the equative questions follow the same pattern as the declarative equatives; and in fact, we could have drawn the same conclusion with only the equative questions as evidence. The single question with an auxiliary (#16) requires a modal (*shall? will?*) that is missing. We have already noted the lack of an independent dummy DO when we discussed the negative; in fact, the examples used as illustrations were all the same questions that are listed here (a situation which serves to point up the fact that there are many paths to the same conclusion).

The instructional conclusion, in relation to questions, is that the child is not moving tense and must be taught to do so.

Coordinated Clauses

The only clear example for coordinated clauses is #76, in which two equatives are conjoined (#180, 218, and 221 might also be coordinates). The predicates are missing from both clauses, which places this sentence below Level V. These utterances do not provide sufficient data to allow conclusions to be drawn. Because equative clauses generally develop before coordinated clauses, and because we have already concluded that the child must be taught to form equatives, we could hypothesize that she will have to be taught how to conjoin clauses. Observation should begin in which specific attention is paid to coordinates in the child's daily usage in order to obtain further information which bears on this hypothesis.

Subordinate Sentences

The data on subordinates are as follows:

Wh- subordinates: None in the transcript.

Infinitive subordinates: #8, 15, 31, 34, 68, 99, 141, 165, 212, 214

No statements can be made about the *wh*- subordinates because there is no evidence on which to base conclusions. Because of the lateness of their development, however, we could hypothesize that we probably will have to teach them (see Table 6.21). An educated guess would say that this child can probably place *wh*- insert clauses in the object of a matrix, but that when she does, we would find that obligatory functions are missing from inserts, matrices, or both. This conclusion is supported by the existing data on the status of development of the infinitive inserts. There is only one Level V infinitive in the transcript (#99), but this example has an obligatory deletion of the infinitive marker *to*. It cannot be used as evidence for the development of the infinitive. In the rest of the evidence, the marker is "present" only in #141, 144, and 165. We cannot use these as evidence for the development of the infinitive marker because *wanna, hafta, hasta, lemme,* and *lets* in the matrix provide very poor evidence for the existence of the marker (see Chapter 6). In all other examples of the infinitive, the marker is clearly missing, and the conclusion can be drawn that we probably will have to teach the infinitive construction to the child.

Passives

There are no examples of passives in the transcript, and therefore, no conclusions can be drawn about its development. Because of the lateness of the development, however, we can hypothesize that it will probably have to be taught (see Table 6.21).

Obviously, this child has not yet reached the point in development at which she can form the various transformations. Tense is not being moved in questions, coordinates are probably not yet developed, and the subordinates, if this child follows the normal sequence, will not arrive for some time yet. Although there were no examples of the passive in the transcript, we can probably assume that she does not yet know how to form it because it is one of the last constructions to arrive. Therefore, the conclusion is that we will probably have to teach her all of the constructions involving transformations.

Analysis of the Noun Phrase

The noun phrase is usually difficult to analyze simply because there are so many things to look for. It is rare indeed to find information on all of the possible NP functions in a single transcript. The most we can hope for is to get an idea of the general level of development within the noun phrase and possible trouble areas that we might start to listen for in the child's daily conversation.

Limiter

No limiters or attempted limiters appear in the transcript. Therefore, we can draw no conclusion about them.

Determiner₁

No det.₁ fillers appear in the transcript, and we can draw no conclusions about them. Do not fall into analytical traps, such as confusing the adverb of manner in #172 with the det.₁ filler *all*.

Determiner₂

The evidence for the det.₂ is as follows:

Nondefinite articles: *A* appears in #21, 22, 48, 49, but seems to be missing in #76, 180, 182.

Definite articles: *The* appears in #4, 18, 19, but seems to be missing in #41, 42, 51, 52. *This / that / these / those* appear in #2, 29, 50, 53, 55, 56, etc., but the wrong form appears in #32, 35, 36, 86, 87.

Possessor: The inflection (S₂) is used correctly in #63, 64, 65, 173, but is missing in #174, 175. The possessive pronoun is used in #144, 170, 201, 205, 206, 215, etc.

The impression to be gained from this evidence is that the child, while having learned something about the determiner₂ function, still needs to learn many fillers. The definite and nondefinite articles are still being used inconsistently and instruction appears necessary. The possessor inflection is also used inconsistently, but the first person possessive pronoun filler seems as though it might be solidly developed. No evidence exists for the other det.₂ pronouns but note how the conclusions on the det.₂ agree with the previously drawn conclusions on the clauses and verb phrase (Table 6.21).

Determiner₃

The evidence for the det.₃ is as follows:

Numerals: No evidence exists.

Comparisons: #131, 132, 134

Quantity phrases: #1, 24, 112, 121, 122, 125, 130, 135, 153. Incomplete phrase in #129.

Note that while #208 has a numeral, it is not a det.$_3$ in a noun phrase. Rather, it is a pronoun phrase, i.e., it plays the same role as an entire noun phrase even though it is not a noun. The same thing is true of the filler of the object function in #10: A word that can fill the det.$_2$ function is here filling the object function. We must not confuse fillers of one function for fillers of another, even though they have exactly the same form.

Evidently the det.$_3$ function is present in this child's language, but the degree to which its fillers are developed is still an open question. We will take a conservative stance and guess that we will probably have to teach this child to use many of the fillers of this function, even though we probably will not have to teach the function itself.

Loose-Knit Modifier

The evidence for the loose-knit modifier is as follows: #77, 140, 143, 144, 150.

On the basis of this evidence we would probably be quite willing to conclude that this child has learned the loose-knit modifier function, and that we will not have to teach it to her. It is important for us to note, however, that even though a child has learned that a grammatical function exists, that child has a lot to learn about the fillers of the function. Note in #19, for example, how this child patterns a preposition as though it were a loose-knit modifier. Learning the fillers of the loose-knit modifiers takes a lifetime, however, and there are more immediate instructional problems to worry about for this particular child.

Close-Knit Modifiers

The evidence for the close-knit modifiers is as follows: #17, 210 (?).

Although the evidence is sparse, we might hazard a guess and say that this child may know the close-knit modifier function. This conclusion is still very tentative and it is subject to change. If the slot has appeared, the fillers of this function would be rudimentary. The child still must learn a great deal about them. Again, like the fillers of the loose-knit modifier, these fillers take a lifetime to learn.

Restrictive and Nonrestrictive Modifier

None appear in the transcript and no conclusions can be drawn about them. The conclusions drawn about clauses and the verb phrase functions would lead us to believe that we may have to teach her to use restrictive and nonrestrictive modifiers, however.

Head Function

The evidence for the head function is as follows:

Head: Because the child is using noun phrases regularly, the head of the NP has developed.

Complex nominals: None appear in the transcript and no conclusions can be drawn about them.

Plural inflections: Evidence is contained in: #7, 13, 19, 24, 30, 32, 35, 36, 86, 108, 137, 140, 170, (all regular); 44, 45, 72, 78 (all irregular).

We can safely conclude that the plural inflection has developed because of the way the child uses the regular inflections on irregular plural words, such as *feets*. Her only problem now is to learn the proper forms of the irregulars; teaching irregulars will have to be done one word at a time. The complex nominal, even though we can find no negative evidence for it, will probably have to be taught because of the lateness of its arrival in the developmental sequence (see Table 6.21).

Summary: Noun Phrase

This child has evidently already learned a great deal about the NP functions. She has demonstrated that she has developed the slots for determiner$_2$, determiner$_3$, loose-knit and close-knit modifiers. The plural inflection is present in the head function. It is possible that we may still have to teach her the limiter, determiner$_1$, the post-nominal restrictive and nonrestrictive modifiers, and the complex nominal filler of the head function. Overall, the development of the noun phrase appears to be proceeding apace with the other grammatical constructions listed in Table 6.21.

Pronoun Analysis

Because pronouns are so much a part of daily conversation, we must take an interest in them. They develop early and stand out when "errors" occur, i.e., using objective forms instead of subjective forms instantly marks "baby talk" in the minds of most people. As a consequence, teachers of low-functioning children must be aware of them and assess their usage.

Personal Pronouns

The evidence for the personal pronouns is as follows:

First person: *I* occurs in #10, 12, 16, 29, 33, 37, and elsewhere. *We* occurs in #102. *Me* occurs in #94, 96, 158, 218, 219. All usages are correct.

Second person: *You* occurs in #17, 48, 118. No plural usage in the transcript, but all singular usage is correct.

Third person: *It* occurs in #6, 8, 11, 12, 16, 31, 34, and elsewhere. *He* and *she* do not occur, but the objective form *her* is substituted for *she* in #209 and possibly #66 (?). *They* occurs in #156, and the objective form *them* is substituted for *they* in #138, 145, 170. No other plurals are used in the transcript.

The child seems to have a fairly good grasp of pronouns. There is, however, a distinct possibility that she confuses the objective and subjective forms *she/her, they/them,* and possibly, *he/him.* We should begin observation for the usage of these particular forms in her daily conversation right away to see if we can identify specific problems, and we should be prepared to teach the usage of these forms when necessary.

Possessive Pronouns

There is only one place in the transcript where an attempt to use a possessive occurs— #173. This usage is in error. Observation should begin immediately to identify potential problems in daily conversation, because there is not enough information on which to base any definite conclusion.

Reflexives

No reflexives appear in the transcript and no conclusions are possible for them.

Summary: Analysis and Teaching Recommendations

Evidently this child is at the point in development where she has learned how to construct the transitive and intransitive clause types and is just now beginning the learning of the verb phrase. According to Table 6.21, these conclusions mean that we should be concentrating on teaching her to use pronouns and the continuum. Relative to the continuum, she uses the function but has an incomplete filler: The teaching of the auxiliary, then, should begin immediately. For the pronouns, the problem may simply be that she uses the objective forms where subjective forms are required, but we are not yet sure because of the lack of data. Therefore, we must begin to observe her daily conversational usage of pronouns to find out. While we are observing, we can begin teaching the BE -*ing* filler of the continuum function using the present tense third person singular form of the auxiliary. We should be ready to begin teaching the other present tense forms as soon as it is practical. Soon we will be able to begin teaching the equative clause, followed by some of the questions that are formed on the continuum and the equative.

This, then, is how the long method works. The problem is that it is difficult and time-consuming; not many teachers are likely to use it simply because there are too many other things that have to be done during the teaching day. Language, after all, is not the only thing that must be taught to children who are delayed in their language development. Such children are probably delayed in many other areas of human existence as well. No teacher who has an entire class full of low-functioning children would have the time to use the long method for each child in the class.

In response to the obvious need that teachers have for gathering and classifying data more quickly and accurately, an observation checklist was developed. The major thing that this checklist does is to speed up the method of analysis that has just been presented without losing any information that is going to affect instructional decisions.

The Short Method: Progressive Narrowing of the Range of Possible Instructional Options

After the long method has been used once or twice, an understanding of the short method can be gained easily and quickly. Using it in a typical classroom of school-aged children with language handicaps can mean that almost all the assessments can be completed by about the end of the second week of school. We will always have to worry about the occasional child who is so shy that we never hear anything at all from him, but in general, most children in a classroom can be analyzed in about this period of time. Using the short method means that the actual teaching of the language can begin early in the school year.

Whether he uses the long method or the short method, the teacher still has to accomplish the same task: to decide which (if any) constructions and functions he must teach the child and which ones the child already controls. When we use the long method of assessment, we make those decisions by looking through a transcript over and over again. In the short method, we will do away with the transcript and listen to the child as he talks.

We still must make the same decisions, however. In order to do this, the way we listen must be systematic, and a guide is necessary (see Appendix A).

The Listening Process

In the long method, only one construction or function at a time is considered during the analysis. When analyzing for the use of equative clauses, for example, all other constructions and functions in the transcript are ignored, and only the equative clause constructions are considered. Once a decision about the equatives is reached, we move on to analyze another construction. Such selective attention is also the basis for using the short method. That is, following the checklist, we listen to a child talk to people around him. As he talks, we systematically direct our attention to listening for specific constructions or functions, i.e., transitive and intransitive clauses, equative clauses, questions, subordinates, verb and noun phrase functions, pronouns, etc. When listening for a specific construction or function, everything else must be ignored until a decision can be made about the item on the checklist that is the object of our attention. As each item becomes the topic of our attention, we listen for the child's use of that construction or function, and ask ourselves:

Do I have to teach the child to use *(construction or function)?*

This question is the same one that guides the analysis in the long method. To answer it, we look for patterns just as we do in the long method: If the child consistently uses all of the obligatory functions or fillers required for the item, there is no problem and the construction or function does not have to be taught. If the child is inconsistent in his use of the obligatory functions or fillers, i.e., if sometimes he uses them and sometimes he does not, then the child is probably somewhere in the middle of learning the construction or function, and it must be taught. If the child never uses it, one of two possibilities exists: either (*a*) the child does not know the item and it must be taught; or (*b*) the child knows it and just never has the opportunity to use it in the presence of the analyst. If we decide that the first is the case, we must teach the item. If, however, we decide that the second possibility may be the case, then we must devise a way to find out whether or not he knows the item. Formal tests are not much help in doing this (see Chapter 2). Several devices *are* available, however, that can help us elicit constructions and functions in a natural setting. They can provide us with a great deal of useful information.

Straight Questions

One of the things we might try to do is to ask the child a question straight out in the hope that we will elicit the construction or function we are analyzing. Thus, if we are trying to find out if the child knows how to use the negative in equative clauses with no auxiliaries, we might do something such as hold up a piece of paper and ask him:

(7.4) Is this a pencil?

If we have chosen the proper vocabulary item to use in the question, we should elicit a negative response from the child. If the child replies with a sentence that has an "error" in it, we get valuable information for the analysis:

(7.5) That not a pencil.

A reply like the one in (7.5) would give us a bit of evidence suggesting that the child has not yet developed the equative predicate because the negative must be attached to tense in equative clauses with no auxiliaries. In the case of (7.5), there is nothing to attach it *to*.

There is a real problem inherent in trying to use this elicitation device, however. Instead of getting a response like the one in (7.5), we are far more likely to get a shake of the head or a simple "No" from the child. That is, we have asked a *yes/no* question, and ellipted responses are not only perfectly acceptable in informal situations, they are also highly likely to occur. Therefore, straight questions as elicitation devices are not likely to have a very high payoff. There is nothing wrong with trying them, however, just to see what happens.

Repetitions

Another thing we might do is to present the child with a sentence and ask him to repeat it. This technique has been used by a number of researchers, e.g., Menyuk (1969). The justification usually given for the use of this technique is that if the sentence is long enough to discount memory as a factor, a child must know the grammatical pattern before he can repeat it. Otherwise, he will conform to his own system of grammar, and will thus make "errors" of one kind or another. That is, if you say to a child:

(7.6) Say, "The little girl is sitting under the big elm tree."

the child will not be able to repeat it accurately unless he knows all of the constructions and functions involved. The child who does not know them will make "errors" which can be analyzed.

The problem with this device is not in interpreting the responses with "errors," but in interpreting accurate repetitions. It seems fair enough to assume that the child who makes "errors" in his repetition will provide you with useful data for doing an analysis. Unfortunately, there are many children who are very good parrots. That is, some children just seem to have a knack for having sentences go in their ears and out their mouths with never a stop between. Echolalic children, of course, do a great deal of this. Many children who are never labeled *echolalic,* however, seem to be able to repeat sentences that would indicate they are functioning higher than they really are.

There may be, in fact, no way to resolve this problem. It may be that we will have to rely on data elicited through repetitions or partial repetitions (see the following section). Repetitions do indeed provide a fast way to elicit constructions and functions that we might not otherwise have a chance to observe; it is a fact that the opportunity to use some constructions and functions just does not present itself very often, and we may reach the point of desperation. Certainly we can get valuable information if the child's repetition has "errors" in it. Nevertheless, if at all possible, it is best to try to minimize repetitions as eliciting devices because of the interpretive problem inherent in them.

It is probably better to use one of four other elicitation devices that we have found useful in structuring pattern drills in the TALK lessons. These devices are useful because they not only direct the child to produce a specific response, they also provide him with all of the information he needs to make the response, if he is able. Not only this, but repetition can often be removed as a factor in the interpretation of the child's responses.

Each of the elicitation devices detailed in the next section has two parts: (*a*) a *directive,* which is given by the person doing the analysis; and (*b*) a *response,* which is made by the child. In general, the procedure involves three people, although it can sometimes be done with just two. In the procedure, the person doing the analysis tells the child to go over to someone else and say something to that person. The third person may be an aide who can note directly what the child says and report it to the analyst, or he can be another child. There are obvious problems in either case. If an aide is to hear what the child says, then the aide must be aware of the range of possibilities for the response so that an accurate report can be made. If the response is to be made to another child, the analyst must unobtrusively observe it; such observation can be a real problem in some instances, especially if the child being addressed is across the room and the child making the response has his back turned to the observer. The thing to do, of course, is to pick the third party carefully so as to facilitate the gathering of information, not to hinder it. A third possibility is to tell the child to make his response directly back to the person giving the directive. This mitigates the observation problem, but it tends to make the situation less natural and more like a test. In any case, whether we use an aide, another child, or have the child direct his response to the analyst, we must first find a situation that is natural for making the desired response. The best data come from responses that are elicited in an unforced, natural manner.

Each of the directive-response pairs set forth in this section involves a *conversion.* That is, the adult directs the child to say something. In order for the child to be able to say it, he uses the utterance that the adult presents to him but must make a change of some sort in it. In some cases this change involves a *position shift,* such as the tense movement that is required in changing a declarative into a question; in some cases it is the *addition* of a function or a filler, as in negation; and in others, it is the *deletion* of parts of a construction, as can happen when an insert clause is made an independent clause.

It is important to make the child's response seem like a natural thing for him to do, i.e., we try to make it seem as though we are doing anything but giving the child a test. Especially in the case of retarded people, I feel that the test situation is detrimental to performance level because of the effect of the test situation itself, i.e., retarded people know that they do not do well on tests. The result is something like "learned helplessness" (e.g., Dweck, 1975; Floor & Rosen, 1975) in test-taking behavior. In effect, learned helplessness is an attitude toward oneself that results in behavior that is at a level below the person's ability to produce. The directives presented here try to remove the test atmosphere by using events from the normal flow of the day to elicit information from the child. The result of this technique is much more useable information than we can obtain from formal tests.

The Four Directives

"Tell (name) to (CLAUSE)"

This directive is a useful device for eliciting an imperative. We might be interested in listening to the construction of the imperative itself at times, because many imperative constructions do not appear very often in daily conversation. For example, suppose we wish to find out if the child can form an equative imperative. We could give him the following directive (D) in the attempt to elicit the response (R):

(7.7) D: Tell those guys to be quiet.
      R: Be quiet (you guys)!

Note how this directive requires the response to be changed from the infinitive to an independent imperative. On the surface it looks like a simple repetition task, but the child who carries out the directive has to be able to separate the two clauses before he can make the response. If there is any question in your mind after the child makes the response properly (assuming that he does do it), then it is always possible after a short delay to say to him "Tell them again."

Many times we find a child who could be having problems in the construction of the noun phrase, and we need to find out if he can use certain low-frequency noun phrase functions, such as the restrictive modifier. It is quite easy to use this device to elicit such constructions:

(7.8) D: Tell Mary to use the paint *in the closet.*

(7.9) D: Tell Miss Jones to find the puzzles *that we need.*

We could also use this device to investigate the use of other noun phrase functions, such as the complex nominal filler of the head function. That is, we could tell the child something like:

(7.10) D: Tell Francine to put the fish food on the *top of the water.*

Thus, any noun phrase function can be inserted into this directive (or any of the others that are presented in the following section).

Note how easily this directive can be used within the flow of natural events during the classroom day. That is, the classroom events per se are used as the topic of the directive (also true of the other directives). The classroom topic approach is a very important feature of the directives because they lack similarity to formal test procedures; any depressant effect formal tests might have on performance is mitigated by the use of the directives.

"Tell (name) wh- (CLAUSE)"

This directive relies on the construction of the *wh-* subordinate insert. In making the response, the child must take the subordinated clause of the directive and reconstruct it so that it can be used independently. For example, suppose we wish to know if the child can use the equative construction. We might use one of the following directives:

(7.11) D: Tell Harold where the book is.
       R: The book is there (Harold). (Or: Here is the book.)

(7.12) D: Tell Jane that she is late.
       R: You are late (Jane).

Note that in (7.11) a question is used as the *wh-* insert and the child is required to replace the *wh-* word with an adverbial. The directive in (7.12) has a declarative insert which requires the child to change the subject from the third person (*she*) to the second person (*you*) with a concomitant change in the verb. Thus, in both of these examples the child is required to make more than one change in the directive when he makes his response. These responses are more desirable than those in which only a single change is required, e.g., those in which the matrix clause is deleted and the insert clause retains the form it has in the directive. For example, suppose we had used the following directive:

(7.13) D: Tell Johnny that this is the place.
       R: This is the place (Johnny).

Like the first directive that uses the imperative, the response to (7.13) requires the child simply to delete the matrix. The response in (7.13) borders on repetition because its directive uses an insert in which there is no *wh-* replacement. An accurate response by the child must be interpreted with due caution. However, both the imperative directive and this form are one step removed from straight repetition, and both are preferable to it.

Note how we can use this device like the other three devices to elicit verb phrase and noun phrase functions that do not occur very often:

(7.14) D: Tell Miss Jones when the juice *has come.* (perfective)

(7.15) D: Tell Miss Jones that *only* the boys go to the gym. (limiter)

Again, even though these directives require partial repetitions, it is quite possible that if they are tried, they will provide hints that a function or construction has not yet developed.

"Ask (name) if (CLAUSE)"

By requiring the child to take a declarative and couch it in question form (moving tense), we remove any objection that could arise from using a construction that is partially repeated. This third directive does just that, by eliciting *yes/no* questions:

(7.16) D: Ask Frank if he found his wallet.
         R: Did you find your wallet (Frank)?

This device is especially good for observing verb phrase functions because any VP auxiliary can be elicited:

(7.17) D: Ask Sally if she *will* ride the bus tonight. (modal)

(7.18) D: Ask Miss Jones if she *has seen* the pins. (perfective)

(7.19) D: Ask Maria if she *is looking* in the right place. (continuum)

Thus, not only can we observe the movement of tense in *yes/no* questions, this directive allows us to observe the form of the fillers of the verb phrase functions as well. As with the other directives, we can also elicit noun phrase functions:

(7.20) D: Ask Albert if *both* the girls got lunch. (det. ₁)

(7.21) D: Ask Jenny if her *second* page is done. (LKM)

"Ask (name) wh- (CLAUSE)"

Like the previous directives, this one elicits questions, but in this case they are *wh-* questions, not *yes/no* questions. Note that the directive supplies the *wh-* word, but leaves tense movement up to the child making the response:

(7.22) D: Ask Miss Jones *what* this is. (complement replacement)

(7.23) D: Ask Marvin *which* picture he saw. (LKM or restrictive modifier replacement)

This directive can ask for any *wh-* replacement, and it can include any of the three conditions for tense movement, just as can the previous directive.

All in all, the four directives just presented can prove to be very handy when it comes time to find out whether or not a child can use a specific construction or function. In one way or another we can get the child to try to use any construction or function used in English sentences and to insert any filler into any slot. Note that such insertion includes subordinate inserts as well as the simpler ones. That is, as long as we can elicit all of the clause or noun functions, we can just as easily use insert clauses in those functions as we can any other filler:

(7.24) D: Tell Miss Jones to get the chair *in the hall.*
      D: Tell Miss Jones to get the chair *that is sitting in the hall.*

The interpretation of the responses to any of the directives requires the same cautions that we must observe in any analysis. That is, one response never "proves" anything. It is only when a consistent pattern emerges that we can draw any firm conclusion. Otherwise, we have little more than data that are suggestive of a hypothesis. When a pattern does seem to emerge, however, we should not hesitate to draw the conclusion that we must teach the child the things with which he is having problems. We should not waste time trying to teach the things he appears to have gotten under control. Again, if there is any question about whether or not to teach something, be conservative. It is better to try to teach something that the child may or may not know and be wrong than it is *not* to teach it and be wrong.

The Checklist

The checklist presented in Appendix A is, in essence, a data sheet for the content task analysis in Chapter 6. It focuses on the structures that are critical in the early years of language learning, and it has two major uses: (*a*) to help the teacher find what it is the child knows and what he needs to learn (analysis); and (*b*) to keep records of the child's progress from the time that teaching begins.

Analysis

The checklist is arranged along the general lines of development of the constructions and functions of the language. At the start of the school year, the teacher or therapist who uses it begins to listen to the child as he converses normally with others in his environment. The idea is to make a series of "teach/no teach" decisions about the constructions and functions specified in the checklist. Teaching then begins at the lowest point in the sequence at which the child is judged to be having difficulty.

Figure 7.1 contains a flowchart of the analytical procedure. The paragraphs that follow refer to each of the numbered boxes in this diagram.

Box 1. Observation begins by listening only to the child's use of the basic transitive and intransitive clause constructions. A decision is made as to whether or not the child can form them, and the checklist is marked accordingly.

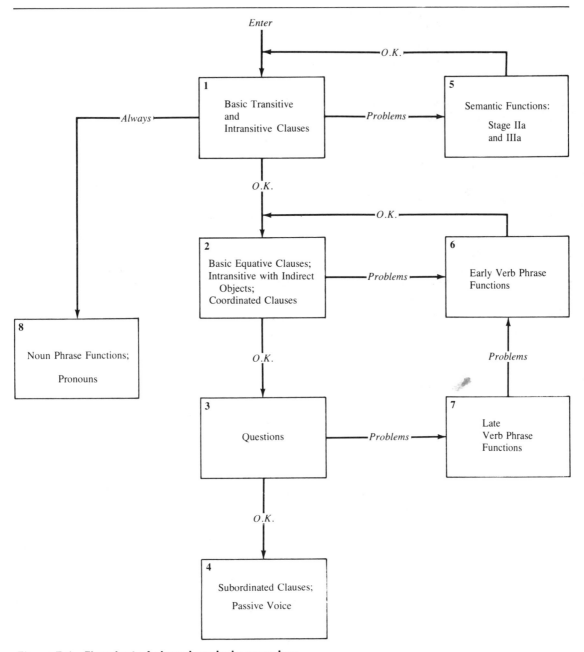

Figure 7.1. Flowchart of clausal analysis procedure.

Box 2. If the decision is made that the child does not need to be taught the basic intransitive and transitive constructions, we shift our attention to listen to the way he forms equative clauses, transitive clauses with indirect objects, and coordinated clauses. Again, a decision is made as to whether or not they must be taught to the child.

Box 3. If the child exhibits no difficulty in using the constructions in Box 2, we again shift our attention and begin to listen to his formation of questions to find out whether or not he is placing tense before the subject. We make a decision as to whether or not we have to teach him to form questions and if so, which ones need to be taught.

Box 4. If the child can form the question construction, we begin to listen to his formation of subordinates and the passive. If we find that he is having no difficulty, the conclusion is that he is probably ready to begin learning to read, and we end the clausal analysis.

If, however, the child appears to be having difficulty at any one of the major checkpoints listed previously, we must branch off to make other observations. This is because difficulty at any one of the four major checkpoints indicates the possibility of difficulty in other places in the hierarchy.

Box 5. If the child needs to be taught the basic intransitive and transitive clause constructions, he may not have the preclausal semantic functions in his repertoire. The chances are that he will be speaking mainly in one or two word utterances. When we find a child who must learn the basic clause constructions, we must also listen closely to decide if we must teach any of the basic semantic functions. If the child is judged to be using most of the semantic functions, we begin to teach the intransitive and transitive clause constructions. If he is not, then we must concentrate on teaching the semantic functions (see Tables 6.2 and 6.6) before beginning to teach the grammar of the intransitive imperative.

Box 6. The child who can form the basic intransitive and transitive constructions may be having difficulty with equatives, transitives with indirect objects, or the coordinated sentence construction (Box 2). If we find any of these to be the case, we direct our attention to his use of the early developing verb phrase functions: the continuum, the modals *may, can,* and *will,* and the dummy DO. Teaching is carried out according to the sequence in Table 6.21 as required.

Box 7. If the child can construct the equative clause, etc., but is not moving tense to the front of the clause in some or all of his questions, we must check to find out whether he has learned the verb phrase functions that carry tense. This will cause us to listen not only to the late developing verb phrase functions (Box 7), but also to at least some of the early developing verb phrase functions (Box 6), such as the dummy DO. Because of the interaction between the verb phrase and the question transformation, careful analysis is a must at this point.

If the analysis leads us as far as the subordinates and the passive (Box 7), there is no branching, and we must teach the transformations with which the child is having difficulty (if any).

Box 8. In any case, if we decide that the child is able to form at least the basic intransitive and transitive clauses, we always observe his use of the various noun phrase functions and their fillers to discover whether or not he is experiencing any difficulty with them. Of course, we must teach whatever of these that must be taught. Table 6.21 provides a useful sequence of instructional objectives for this purpose.

This, then, is the general flow of analysis. It should be clear that these procedures could be short-cutted once the person using the analysis has enough experience. That is, if, on the very first day we meet a child, we find that he is moving tense in some of his questions, we should be able to form the judgment that he has the basic intransitive and transitive clause constructions, and that we do not have to listen to them to find out if he does. In such a case we can immediately begin listening to the subordinate constructions to find out whether or not they have to be taught. That is, entry can actually be made into any point in the system at which the data begin to present themselves despite the fact that formal entry is specified for Box 1. Given the interconnections between the checkpoints in the analytical procedure, analysis can proceed backward as well as forward through the flowchart in Figure 7.1. The first few times you use the checklist, however, it is probably best to stay with the formally stated analytical procedure just to familiarize yourself with the checklist and the process. In any case, never rush an analysis, and do not feel uneasy about repeating a step or changing your mind about early decisions. Always remember that *the only point of the entire enterprise is to discover the next logical construction or function to teach a child.*

The use of the checklist has the same restrictions as the long method of analysis. That is, ellipted utterances must be ignored in making judgments about the child's knowledge of the basic clause type constructions; contractions can never be used as evidence for the existence of the form that is contracted; a single example provides only enough evidence for establishing a hypothesis, i.e., it does not "prove" that a construction or function has or has not been mastered; and so forth. On the other hand, the same freedoms that apply to doing the analysis in its long form also apply to doing it in its short form, e.g., if a child uses constructions that appear late in development, we can assume that a construction or function that appears early in the developmental sequence has been mastered whether examples of it are found or not found.

Obviously, the constraint that a single bit of evidence does not provide for anything more than grounds for a hypothesis that the construction or function may have been mastered is going to cause problems during some analyses. That is, many constructions and functions simply do not appear very often in ordinary conversation. If this idea is true, and if one of these constructions or functions is critical to an assessment, then a way must be found to elicit them from the children who are able to use them. The elicitation devices spelled out at the beginning of this section are very useful and should definitely be tried. It is important to get as much information as you can and to do so as quickly as possible. The analysis is just a beginning, because it tells you what to teach. The actual teaching that must be done is the eventual focus of all of our effort, and the sooner we can get a teaching program started, the better we serve our children.

Examples of the Checklist's Use

Both for the purpose of demonstrating how the checklist works and to provide extra transcripts[2] for practice purposes, three more transcripts are included (pp. 214–22). In this section, the use of the short method will be demonstrated by analyzing transcripts #2, 3, and 4.

---

[2]These transcripts were taken from two sources. Transcript #2 and #3 were made of conversations held with a child who was a subject in the Milwaukee Project (Heber, Garber, Harrington, & Hoffman, 1972), and Rick Heber has kindly made them available to me. Transcript #4 was made by one of my students as part of a class project, as was Transcript #1. My appreciation for the use of these transcripts, from which all identifying names, etc., have been eliminated, is expressed to these students. I have promised to maintain confidentiality in these cases.

A glance at the second transcript tells us that the child is speaking in single-word utterances and is not yet at the stage where she will be forming the basic transitive and intransitive clause types. Therefore, we must analyze preclausal semantic functions (Box 5). Even in this extremely short transcript, we can find examples[3] of the *comment* function (#4, 7, 12, 15, 28, 34, 36, 37) and the *action* function (#1, 8, 9, 10). In addition, there may be an example of the *patient* function (#4?), which alerts us to listen further to find out if she indeed is producing it, and the *location* function (32, 35, 51). In each of the latter three utterances, however, the child's pronunciation was such that the identification of location is largely a guess. In addition, the child seems to express agreement very often (*yeah*), but whether this has any meaning other than that of "sound used in response to question" is open to doubt. That is, in response to the question "Do you know what we're going to do?", the child says "yeah", but then mumbles in response to the adult's question, "What?" This encounter indicates the possibility that the child may simply be giving a stereotyped response to the question intonation, and that the word *yeah* actually has no semantic meaning for her. In addition, there is a lot of repetition of what the adult says that may or may not have meaning (#20–25); this sort of utterance cannot be analyzed.

Transcript #2

Adult	*Child*
I can roll the bear.	1. Roll
You want me to roll the bear?	2. Yeah
	3. Mmm
	4. Bear *(unintelligible)*
Ducks	5. Hmm
Ducks, Sally	6. Hmm
	7. Duck
	8. Pee
You want to go potty?	9. Potty
O.K., let's go potty.	10. Potty
You know what?	11. Yeah
It's all wet.	12. All wet
You know what we're going to have to do?	13. Yeah
What?	14. Hmm
We're going to have to put you on some more.	15. Wet
We'll have to take off your shoes, too.	16. Kay
Your shoes have so many buckles on them.	17. Yeah
Aren't they pretty?	18. Yeah
Hmm? Pretty ducks?	19. Yeah
Can you say *pretty ducks?*	20. Ducks
Can you say *pretty ducks?*	21. Duck
How many ducks?	22. Duck
One . . .	23. Yeah

---

[3]Numbers in parentheses indicate sample items. There may be other instances.

Two . . .	24. Two . . .
Three . . .	25. Two . . .
Four ducks!	26. Mmm
You can't say, "four ducks" yet, can you?	27. *(unintelligible)*
Is that a nice baby?	28. A baby
That's a pretty baby, huh?	29. Baby
Where's the baby's eye?	30. Eye
The baby's nose?	31. Yeah. Nose.
Where's your nose?	32. Haa . . . nose. (Here nose?)
No, that's not the nose!	33. Hair
Hair, that's right.	34. Hair
That's right. Where's Sally's nose?	35. Here nose.
Is that Sally's nose? (laughing)	36. Nose
What's that?	37. Dress
That's a dress, very good.	38. Yeah
Now put down the boy.	39. Duck
Duck!?	40. Yeah
What's this duck got on his head?	41. *(unintelligible)*
A what?	42. *(unintelligible)*
What's on the duck's head?	43. Hair
Hair. What's that?	44. Hair
That's a hat, isn't it?	45. Yeah
Have you got a hat?	46. Yeah
No. You haven't got a hat. I don't wear a hat out there!	47. Hat
The duck has on a hat.	48. Hmm
Is that a duck hat?	49. Hat
Does the baby have on a hat?	50. Yeah
Where?	51. Here

Thus, two semantic functions appear to be clearly identifiable in this transcript, and two more can be hypothesized as present. Further listening would probably reveal more. The teacher's task, when a few more semantic functions have been identified as being present, would be twofold: (*a*) to attempt to teach the semantic functions that the child does not produce; and (*b*) to begin trying to get the child to pair her single-word relational functions with her single-word substantive functions to produce two-word utterances that fill the semantic functions in Stage IIIa.

Transcript 3

The third transcript contains a conversation with the same little girl from whom the previous transcript was taken, but at a much later point in developmental time.

Transcript #3

Adult	*Child*
	1. That's me.
That's you?	2. That my daddy.
Mhmh	3. Me and Jane are there.

Mhmh	4. I talk with Daddy.
	5. The mama daddy
Uh-huh	6. And Daddy's the daddy
Mhmh	7. And Auntie Sue, she (unintelligible), and she came home from (unintelligible, Santa Claus?)
	8. Santa Claus (unintelligible)
	9. Little girl sit on the Santa Claus, see?
Yes.	10. Why?
That little girl is sitting on Santa Claus's knee.	11. Why?
She's talking to him about some toys.	12. About toys?
	13. That little girl got on shoes.
	14. And that girl there, gotta look at toys
	15. I need some toys, Santa . . . ah, Santa Claus
	16. I need a little girl toys.
	17. I gotta /niyz/
What are those?	18. Men
Men	19. Un-huh (affirmative)
	20. Oh. A little girl
	21. And here's one
Uh-huh.	22. That's . . . that's a mama.
	23. That a . . .
	24. That guy's cooky.
	25. That guy's got a cooky something.
Mommy's putting the cookies in the box.	26. That's a girl.
	27. I found something.
	28. Found something
	29. Now. You put on a coat and cloak.
	30. That's it.
	31. I want some of these.
	32. Oh
	33. A firetruck
	34. I ridden on that firetruck.
	35. A no- on that firetruck
That's your fire truck?	36. Uh-huh (affirmative)
	37. I went on a firetruck to a . . . fire.
	38. I said I went outside and help.
Maybe they're going to put out a fire.	39. They gone maybe put out the fire.
	40. There two daddy
	41. That's daddy.
	42. That's Jane.
	43. That's me.
	44. Two of me, Jane
Yeah	45. Uh-huh (affirmative)
Jane and Sally and here Daddy	46. I'd know what my daddy
	47. I finished that.
Hmmm?	48. Finished it
	49. Now, we're gonna look right here.
	50. I got my hat, too.
	51. *(unintelligible)*
	52. That's it.
	53. There's no one in back but me.
Uh-huh	54. I didn't find these.

A man's what?

54. I didn't find these.
55. On there *(unintelligible)*
56. Dogs
57. The . . . the dog gonna bite.
58. But the dog will bite me
59. And I gotta . . .
60. I . . . I got play with that dog.
61. That dog . . . that dog gonna bite Jane's shoe.
62. No, eat it.

You did?
Did the dog bite Jane's shoe?
Oh, he ate Jane's shoe? That's a rough dog.

63. And put that big dog . . .
64. We tied it.
65. I'll put that dog, get the pliers
66. I'm gonna put . . .
67. He won't bite Jane's shoe no more.
68. I'll tell Mom . . . if that dog come
69. Oh.
70. What is that?
71. Huh?
72. Jane new . . .

What is that on there, Sally?

73. A . . . cow
74. Why don't that cow *(unintelligible)*

They look like deer.
They look like deer.

75. Huh?
76. They look like birds.
77. *(unintelligible)*
78. I need someone to be a mama.
79. I could not see that, close up.

You do?
Mhmh

80. I make that close up
81. *(unintelligible)*
82. *(unintelligible)*
83. Oh, watch out! (imperative)
84. I'm gonna play with it, close up.
85. Uh-huh (affirmative)
86. All the doors

Oh, you closed up the doors in your house?

87. That's doors
88. Where that window?
89. That's a more window

Uh-huh
That's the window.

90. Now
91. Uh-huh (affirmative)
92. This one shut right here.

That's the window.

93. I don't wanna read no more.
94. I'll read this.
95. The doctor . . . in there
96. I know . . .
97. What this?
98. Oh, these . . .

What are those?

99. I have a house shoe.

You had your what?
House shoes? Oh.
What is this, Sally?
That's Smokey.

100. House shoes
101. Uh-huh (affirmative)
102. Um . . . Teddy bear
103. Mokey?
104. That Smokey got a mouth?

Process Analysis

Yes	105. And a nose.
	106. A big nose?
See? That's his nose right there.	107. Big nose
	108. A gotta blow my nose.
Here, blow!	109. I need some water.
You do? Here's some.	110. Kay
Look at this.	111. What's this?
	112. Car, and truck
A car and a truck	113. I got two trucks.
Mhmh	114. Uh-huh
	115. Oh, a car!
	116. My daddy bought that . . . that . . . that . . . daddy boughted that . . . that . . .
	117. I want a ride too.
You want to ride?	118. I want a car.

We begin the analysis with transitive and intransitive clauses. Her intransitive clauses have obviously developed (#3, 7, 38), and the data show that we do not have to teach transitive clauses (#4, 16, 27, 28). Therefore, we turn our attention to the constructions in Box #2: equative, transitive with indirect object, and coordinated clauses.

The equative clauses appear to be inconsistently constructed. That is, sometimes she uses the equative predicate (#3, 70) and sometimes she does not (#2, 40). Therefore, we must conclude that we will have to teach it to her. Our attention turns to the verb phrase functions that develop early in the sequence (Box #6). The continuum is present (#49, 66) but the fact that the auxiliary is missing in some places in which it might have been used alerts us to the possibility that she may not yet have developed it (#57, 61), and that we might have to teach it. Note that, in each of these examples, the only information we have is from the use of *gonna* which may not even be a true example of the continuum inflection. The conclusion is that we need some more information on this function, and we may want to try some of the elicitation devices if we do not find examples of the continuum within a fairly short period of time.

We do find an example of the modal *will* (#58) along with several examples of this modal in contracted form. Therefore, we can form the hypothesis that this form is present. Further observation should give us enough information to accept or reject this hypothesis. In addition, there is one example of the modal *could* (#79). Since it is paired with the negative (*could not*) we do not know if this girl controls the form. We do not have much data on the modal function, and it would not be surprising to find that only the *will* form of the modal function actually has developed. Remember that both the equative and the continuum have not yet been clearly shown to have developed. Children will often develop one or two isolated modal forms before they develop either the equative construction, the auxiliary of the continuum, or the rest of the modal fillers.

The only examples of the dummy DO are those in which DO is paired with the negative (#54, 74, 93), or is missing (#104). The hypothesis from this evidence would be that she has not yet developed it to carry tense.

Clearly, the perfective has not yet developed (#14, 34, 39). She probably has, however, developed negation in clauses with auxiliaries (#67, 79) and without auxiliaries (#54, 74, 93). The regular past inflection is present (#48, 116), and a few of the irregulars have their proper form (#28, 38), but not all of them (#116). We would hypothesize that she has not yet developed the regular third singular inflection (#9). If this hypothesis is borne out, we will also find that she has not yet developed the irregular third singular inflections, either.

The picture that emerges is that the equative clause needs to be taught, and that it is necessary for us to find out whether or not she has developed the continuum. If the inflection is present she still may not have the auxiliary. If we find that she has developed the *is,* she may not have developed the other forms of the auxiliary. At any rate, it appears that a little more observation will tell us what we need to know in order to structure the language lesson for tomorrow. That is, we have identified the approximate location in the developmental sequence for this child, and now we must pin down the exact function that we must begin to teach.

As usual, any time a child is beyond the point at which the basic clause types have developed, we check the noun phrase (Box #8) to find out what we can about that construction. Immediately we discover that she is using the determiner$_2$ (#5, 15, 20), but that she has a tendency to use articles where an adult would not (#9, 16). This evidence indicates that we should be sure to include work on the determiner$_2$ in the lessons. She also seems to have developed a loose-knit modifier slot (#20, 89 ?, 107); possibly the determiner$_1$ slot (#86); probably the determiner$_3$ slot (#40, 113); close-knit modifier slot (#16, 25, 100). There are no examples of the post-nominal modifiers or of the limiter, however. The regular plural seems to have developed (#13, 14, 16), but it is inconsistently left off when a determiner$_3$ is used (#40, 113). There is no iformation on the use of irregular plurals, however. The possessive inflection may also have developed (#61), but we do not have much information on which to base a conclusion. There is also no information on the adjective inflections.

The personal pronouns appear to be in good shape. We can find good examples of *I* (#15, 16, 17); *me* (#1, 44, 53); *we* (#49); *you* (#29); *she* (#7), *they* (#39). The hypothesis we could form on the basis of this information is that she has developed all of the personal pronouns; we need more information to confirm or reject it. We can find only *my* among the determiner$_2$ possessive pronouns (#2, 46, 108) and must continue to observe for more information on the other forms. More data on all of these items could be obtained while we were looking for data on the continuum. There is no other information on the other pronouns, and we may have to try to elicit them.

Thus, on the basis of a session that lasted about 15 minutes, we have obtained major information about this child's language development. That is, we will have to begin teaching either the continuum function or the equative clause construction. Most of the personal pronouns which are so necessary in teaching the forms of BE do not have to be taught. Although we need to do more observation on some things, we almost have enough to structure a suitable lesson for tomorrow.

Transcript 4

The last transcript contains a conversation between an adult and a child who is at a somewhat higher point in the developmental sequence than the children in any of the other three transcripts.

It is clear that this child has developed transitive and intransitive clauses (#1, 6, 9, 19); also the equative clause (#5, 26, 29), transitives with indirect objects (#8, 75), and coordinated clauses (#25, 27, 44) all appear to be well-developed. We can find examples of tense being moved in a question clause with an auxiliary (#108) and in a transitive clause with no auxiliary (#43), which leads us to form the hypothesis that questions are

Transcript #4

Adult	*Child*
	1. How come you're pushing that button?
That makes it work. I have to keep the button pushed down.	
	2. But we don't.
So you went swimming on your vacation. What else happened?	3. I got hurt here (points to cut).
What happened? How did that happen?	4. I don't know.
	5. I wasn't there before.
	6. I know how to tie my shoe.
	7. My Mommie . . . I got a shoe tying board.
	8. My Mommie teached me how to tie.
	9. But she went real slow.
Do all your shoes tie or do you have other kinds of shoes?	10. I have other kinds of shoes.
When you were on vacation and you went swimming, did you do anything else?	11. After the man said, "It's time to go," we went home.
	12. At the swimming pool
What man said that?	13. Not until it's dark time.
You must have stayed there really long. When did you leave?	
(Takes out clown.) What could you do with this? Do you know the colors?	14. Orange, red, red hat, red nose.
	15. I know something with a red nose.
What else does it have?	16. Black eyes, white mouth, white hands.
Do you know what this is?	17. What?
It's something you can put money inside.	18. It's a bank.
	19. You put the money in here. (Points to slot.)
What will happen if you shake it? (Takes out miniature toy animals.)	20. The money will fall out.
	21. An elephant.
What are these?	22. Look at the ape.
	23. We saw a movie about an ape.
What was the movie about?	24. They were trying to kill it . . . him.
What happened?	25. The Indians came with bows and arrows and they shot at him.
	26. He was dead.
Have you ever seen any of these other animals?	27. When we was down at Mississippi, we watched TV, and we saw the zoo.
	28. We have some of these, too.
	29. Those are zebras.
	30. The zebras have black stripes.
	31. Our friend has some of these.
He does? What does he do with them?	32. He plays with it.
	33. He lets me play with some, too.
Did you ever see a real elephant?	34. Only on TV.
What do they look like?	35. They're strong.
	36. We saw a baby one, too.
Were the baby ones strong?	37. Only a little
	38. How come this fly keeps getting in my ears?
He'll go away.	39. I wish he would go outside.

What kind of things do you like to play with in the back yard?

What do you like to play?

What else do you play on the outside?
Where is it?

What do you slide on?
How does that make it go?

The real big one?

Did you slide on your stomach?

How did you get to the top of the slide?

What else did you ride at the carnival?
What did they do?

Could you steer it?

You rode a motorcycle?

How did it sound?
Did the cars make sounds?
(Takes out miniature toys.) Do you have trucks at home?
What's that?

Look at that jet. It has a pointed nose. Do you know what that is?

What did it look like?

Have you ever been to an airport?
Where did you go?
You were on an airplane?

40. That's not the back, it's the front.
41. I like the front.
42. I like to play Frisbee.
43. Do you know what?
44. I can climb in that treehouse, and slide down the pole.
45. I have a minibike.
46. Not here we don't.
47. I'm gonna get a swingset.
48. Maybe I'll get a big slide.
49. I'm saving my money.
50. If I had a big slide, like over there, I'd slide down it.
51. I wish it was big and had humps on it.
52. I could go up and down on it.
53. There could be three rows on it and you could go up and down on it.
54. You could get one of those *(unintelligible),* slide down on it, and you put it on the slide and you get on and you slide down.
55. A towel.
56. Fast.
57. But one time my Mommie and Daddy took me to the carnival and I slided on that big slide.
58. Yeah.
59. The real big one, and it had humps on it.
60. No, I went with my Daddy.
61. He holded me on his lap.
62. You just climb up the ladder.
63. On the big slide there is a big ladder.
64. The helicopters.
65. Some of them went up and some of them stayed down.
66. There wasn't a steering thing.
67. On the cars and motorcycles there was.
68. On the carnival.
69. And that thing went around and around.
70. It didn't sound.
71. Uhuh, not even cars.
72. I got big ones.
73. A fire engine.
74. You're supposed to play with it.

75. Uh-huh. When we was down at Mississippi, Uncle John gave me a toy and an airplane.
76. A big airplane.
77. I have it on my chester drawers.
78. No . . . yes. I rode on a plane before.
79. Nowhere, we just stayed.
80. Yeah. I thought, ''Hey Mommie, the clouds are bubbles.''

Do you remember anything else you saw?

You know a pilot can make a plane fly high or low in the sky?

What else?

He can do a lot of things with it.

What would happen?

How do you like the puppy?

Do you have a dog at home?

What did you have for breakfast?

What will you do later today?

Do you stay here all day?

How old are they?

How long were you in Mississippi?

And then what?

What did you make with your Tinker Toys?

Do you make what's in the instructions?

Can you make things on your own? Can you make a house?

What's in there?

I think you can go right now. Bye-bye.

81. I looked out the window and I saw school.

82. He can make it go down here. (Motions.)
83. And he can get up here.
84. Yeah, but what if a strong wind came and made it go Bsshhh crash!
85. It would crash open.
86. I like it.
87. Uhuh, not even a cat.
88. Cookies.
89. They're behind the bar.
90. Animal cookies in a box.
91. I just play.
92. I have to take a nap, but the big boys stay out there.
93. One of them is seven . . . no . . . both of them are seven.
94. About two days.
95. My grandma bought me a toy.
96. Mommie and Daddy bought me a toy.
97. They bought me Tinker Toys.
98. I went to Grandma's and stayed there, but Mommie and Daddy didn't.
99. But I only stayed for one day.
100. We came home.
101. Oh . . . all things.
102. There's instructions in it.
103. I read on it.
104. I look at the pictures.

105. There's no flat things for a house.
106. Tinker Toys . . . real long Tinker Toys.
107. The short ones are orange and the big one is gray.
108. When am I gonna get to go outside and play?
109. Bye-bye!

---

probably well-formed. All information quickly leads us to the point at which we want to investigate this child's subordinates and the passive.

There are only two examples of the passive in the transcript (#3, 74), and both of them are well-formed. We would hypothesize that the child has control over this construction on the basis of these examples; but note that both of them are constructions that could well be interpreted as being examples of other constructions. We are required to hold back from forming any definite conclusions about the passive. The *wh-* object insert is clearly under control (#8, 11, 39), and the adverbial *wh-* insert appears to have developed (#27, 75). The infinitive object insert is present (#8, 24, 108) and probably the gerund in the object as well (#38). We also have examples of the infinitive in the equative complement (#11) and the passive complement (#74). We would hypothesize that the object inserts have developed in this child's speech.

Clearly, this child's language has developed quite far. We do not have any examples, however, of insert clauses in the subject or in restrictive modifier slots. If we do not find them in the near future during natural conversation, we may have to try to elicit them from him. If we find that he is able to form them, we would have no major constructions to teach. At present, however, we still do not know whether or not this is the case.

Finally, we have to check the noun phrase functions. Almost immediately we find examples of the restrictive modifier (#15, 23, 90 ?, 105) and complex nominals (#10), but one complex nominal sounds strange (#77) and we should investigate further. Nevertheless, since they appear to be the last NP functions to develop, such examples would lead us to believe that this child is probably well along in the development of his noun phrase, and that vocabulary development may be the major thing to teach in this construction. Perhaps our first teaching problem would be one of trying to teach him that some nouns have irregular plurals (#8), but even this does not seem to be much of a problem.

In summary, we need more information. We do know, however, that this child has gone through most of the sequence of learning for clausal constructions. We have not yet obtained the information we need to conclude that we do not have to teach him to use inserts in subject slots, or to use insert clauses in restrictive modifier slots; we are fairly sure, however, that the slot itself exists. Therefore, our task is to find a way to discover these things and to teach what he needs to learn (if anything).

Summary

In this chapter two methods of analysis of the level of development of a child's language have been presented. The long method relies on the use of a transcript. In using it, we make an attempt to analyze every construction and function before we specify what has to be taught. In the short method, much greater reliance is made on the developmental sequences, and no transcript is used. Instead, observation first focuses on specific major developmental milestones. When the approximate level of development becomes apparent, intensive observation on specific functions or construction begins. In both the long method and the short method, we focus on only one construction or function at a time until a judgment can be made as to whether the child controls that construction or function, or whether it must be taught in the language program.

The next problem a teacher must contend with is how to teach the constructions or functions he has decided a child must learn. This will be the topic for Chapter 8.

Teaching English as a First Language

Many people have a tendency to think of teaching as the transfer of knowledge from the teacher's head to the head of the learner. This is not a useful view of the instructional process. Its lack of utility stands out sharply in classrooms for retarded children. It is far more useful to think of teaching as being the *guiding of learning*. It is, after all, the learner who must do all of the learning; the teacher can do little more than to help make the process more efficient. Learning always requires activity on the part of the learner. The activity may be physical, cognitive, or both. It is the learner's activity, however, not the teacher's, that determines how much is learned. Given this, then, teaching is a matter of structuring the environment so that the child will engage in activities that cause learning to take place (Dever & Knapczyk, 1977).

The TALK instructional program is one way to structure the learner's environment. It is an instructional program for children whose minimal clausal development has reached Stage IIIb for intransitive and transitive clauses. Children whose development is below this point would profit more from a different method, e.g., those proposed by Kent (1974), or Miller and Yoder (1972, 1974). TALK methodology shares many features with the programs proposed by Crystal et al. (1975), and Lee, Koenigschnecht, and Mulhern (1975), but it differs from each of these programs in a number of ways.

It is entirely possible that many children would benefit by being taught through combinations of two or more of the above methods. Moreover, even with all of this methodology available, there will still be children who need something more and/or different. In these cases, a pure creative act on the part of the teacher may be necessary. When we come right down to it, methodology is the least settled aspect of the teaching process: There is no such thing as "the best method." What works for one child or one group of children will not work for another, and what works for one child at one point in development will not work for the same child at another point. The method to use is the method that works best for the child or the group you are teaching at the moment: TALK drills, another published method, or a technique ideosyncratically derived for a specific child.

The most important aspect of TALK is (and will always be) the method of assessing and pinpointing the child's developmental level (presented in the previous chapters). Knowledge is power for a teacher, and the main thrust of this book is to present the knowledge a teacher needs to discover what the learner must do next. With this knowledge a teacher will not only be able to specify what a learner needs, but also will know whether or not he is making satisfactory progress. Others, including Lee (1974) and Crystal et al. (1975), also believe in this principle. It is a point of view which makes their books extremely valuable resources for the teacher of low-functioning individuals.

TALK: A Method of Applied English Linguistics

The TALK method has a long history in spite of the fact that TALK itself has been around for only a short while. It is squarely in the tradition of applied English linguistics that dates back before the Second World War (Moulton, 1962). It was 1941 when Mortimer Graves first established the Intensive Language Program that eventually became the famed Army School of Foreign Languages (currently located in Monterey, California). Following the war, Charles C. Fries and Robert Lado were foremost among the linguists who turned their attention to the specific problem of the teaching of English to speakers of other languages. Since the late 1940s, books and monographs on the English language and how to teach it as a second language have been profusely published. They are still being written. Several valuable texts for teachers have been published and the interested reader would do well to consult some of the sources noted in the bibliography.

The methods developed by the structural linguists are based on well-established principles that, according to Gatenby (1965), have been in print at least as far back as Montaigne (1533–1592). Due to their common-sense nature, however, these principles have probably formed the basis of most foreign-language learning all the way back to the time when people first made contact with other people who did not speak the same language. In other words, there is truly nothing new under the sun.

The first suggestion that the same principles might deliberately be applied to the teaching of English as a first language was made in a paper presented to the Annual Convention of the National Council of Teachers of English in Milwaukee, in 1968 (Dever, 1968). Since then others have developed first-language teaching methods using these same principles, possibly without realizing that they were doing it. It is interesting how much work has been done independent of the formal discipline of applied English linguistics, i.e., many workers have developed their programs as a result of their work in the discipline of psycholinguistics. Chief among these have been Miller and Yoder (1972, 1974), and Lee and her associates (Lee, 1974; Lee et al., 1975), but there are others. Perhaps the work that is closest in conceptualization to the present text is that done by Crystal et al. (1975).

Surprisingly, many language program developers have not paid much attention to the structure of the English language itself. This is not to say that other programs are not useful; when dealing with children with developmental disabilities, we are duty bound to use what works. The only point is that, historically, most language teaching has not intentionally drawn on the principles of applied English linguistics in spite of the fact that these principles can generate successful teaching techniques in a situation where they are sorely needed.

The Principles of Applied English Linguistics

The principles of applied English linguistics have been stated in many places (e.g., Moulton, 1960; Norris, 1963; Dacanay & Bowen, 1967). These sources make interesting and useful reading for anyone who wishes to teach children with developmental disabilities. Not every principle is immediately applicable to first-language teaching, however. For example, one of the major principles in teaching a second language is that interference from the first language is to be expected while learning the second. Most developmentally disabled children in America will be native speakers of English, however, and they will not experience such interference; we do not have to take it into account when working with them.

Because there are differences between the tasks of teaching English as a first language and teaching it as a second language, we must be concerned mainly with those things that will affect programming for the developmentally disabled child. Therefore, the following list of principles has been edited to fit the instructional problem posed by developmental language disabilities of native speakers of English. The important principles, for our purposes are

1. Language is speech, not writing.
2. Language is for communication.
3. Language is a set of habits that has system.
4. Language is what native speakers say.
5. Teach the language, not about the language.

Let us examine each of these principles in turn in order to understand the effects of each of them on an adequate language program.

Language is Speech, Not Writing

Many native speakers of English, having gone through the American educational system, confuse the written representation of English with the language itself. The "language arts," it seems, turns out largely to be the study of the written word, both as grammar and as literature. In relation to the grammar, we learned rules, such as "The noun past is formed by adding -ed to the end of the word." This rule, of course, refers to the written system, not to the spoken system. It is not at all useful to us in developing programs for children whose spoken language development is at a very low level.

The structural linguists, who developed foreign language instruction, knew very well that languages did not exist solely in their written form. As far back as 1933, for example, Bloomfield had catalogued the world's languages. He showed that there were more than 4,000 languages in use at the time. For one thing, it was clear that very few of these languages had a way of being represented on paper (or any other material, for that matter). For another, it was also clear that even when those languages had writing systems, the spoken language was learned by native speakers long before they learned its written representation. The early applied linguists were convinced from the very beginning that they had to develop methods of instruction that taught people to speak a language even if they never taught them to read and write it (Moulton, 1960).

When we try to teach children with developmental language disabilities, we are in a unique position to understand the instructional ramifications of this principle fully. It is senseless, for example, to try to teach a severely retarded child to read and write English before he learns to speak it.[1]

The first thing we have to do, if we really want to help learners with developmental disabilities to develop communicative competence, is to recognize that writing is simply a representation of speech and turn our attention to teaching the spoken language. Later, when our pupils learn how to use the basic structures of the language, we can begin to concentrate on teaching them to read and write. Note that this is the way a normal child does it, and no matter what labels we manage to give a child, he is still a child and learns to do things the way all other children learn to do them.

Language is for Communication

The only reason to learn a language is because you have something to say to somebody else. The language is only a tool; it is a vehicle to get thoughts from one mind to another, and the thought exists independent of the language. Some would claim that the language shapes the thoughts that you are allowed to have, i.e., that a language is "the spectacles through which we view the world" (Whorf, 1956). I do not think that this is really true. That is, I believe the culture into which we are born forces us to have certain perceptions to which we respond (Olson, 1970; Segal, Campbell, & Herskovits, 1966) and the language used by the people in that culture simply reflects those cultural perceptions. This idea is not particularly new; it is one held by many cultural anthropologists. However there are many people in the field of developmental disabilities who believe that language is thought; they are mistaken. There are many deaf children who can think perfectly well without ever having learned a language (either spoken or signed), and a number of retarded children who use English quite well but who have great difficulty thinking. Such children lead us to believe that language and thought, though interrelated, are also independent systems and can be taught as such. A child who does not know the language used by the people in his environment and who has a thought to communicate is beset with frustration. An illustration of this is the common phenomenon of the disappearance of temper tantrums in deaf children when they first learn how to sign. My opinion of what happens in these cases is that these children simply unlock their thoughts from their bodies, that is, they begin to be able to communicate what they are thinking. Communication has the effect of removing both frustration and the behavioral concomitants to frustration.

---

[1]At least, one would think that this would be the case. But I have been in classroom after classroom in which retarded children were being presented with lessons in reading and writing (some with very elaborate programs) in spite of the fact that they were not yet at the point in development at which they could form transitive clause types. Even more startling is the fact that very often little else is included in the "language program" for many of these children. The only sensical explanation for this that I can develop is that the teachers probably know that this "language instruction" is insufficient, but they lack the conceptual tools with which to structure a more adequate program. Still, they are gamely trying to do something because their children need help.

The point is that the teaching of a language and the teaching of thought must be separated in our conceptualization of the problem. There is no reason why we cannot or should not interrelate and integrate the instructional programs for the two spheres, but we do have to conceptualize them as being separate. What this means for instructional purposes is that we must concentrate on teaching English as a tool for communication; the "things to be communicated" should be taught as separate subjects.

The ultimate goal of language instruction is communicative competence, so that whatever we teach children to say, we teach them to say it the way children normally say it. In other words, we structure our program so that the child can talk about what is important to him at his level of development. I have known many teachers (and worse, language program developers) who insist that children begin to speak or sign in "complete sentences" (whatever that means) from the very beginning of their learning. Such attempts at instruction simply throw the child back on his own devices. A bright child can often rise above such poorly conceived instruction, but a retarded child may well be doomed to failure if we begin this way. It is far better to begin at the child's level of development and advance him through the normal developmental sequence step by step. We help him to progress as he would under normal circumstances. Whatever the level of development, the vocabulary, pronunciation, grammar, and discourse topics should be at the child's level of development and deal with his interests. We might note that this is the basis of the methodology worked out by Miller and Yoder (1972, 1974), Crystal et al. (1975), Lee et al. (1975), and Kent (1974), as well as that used in TALK.

In addition, instruction should be aimed at competence in daily usage. If we try to teach a child to use a grammatical pattern, it must be one which the child can find opportunities to use in his daily life, and we must follow up on it. If we try to teach a child grammatical patterns and do not insist on his using those patterns outside of the formal language instruction, he will not learn to do anything, only parrot the patterns. In relation to TALK, this is a very important point: **We can teach a child a grammatical pattern in lessons, but to teach him how and where to use that pattern we must constantly look for situations outside of the lessons in which we can get the child to use the pattern to talk about his world.** If we concentrate on the real world, the child will find out that the pattern is a useful tool for communication and not just a fun game he plays with the teacher at a specific point in the day.

Language is a Set of Habits that Have a System

By now the fact that English has a system should be abundantly clear. It is not simply an unrelated set of words such as we can find in a dictionary, but rather a set of regularities of behavior we call *rules* that interrelate one with another. The major aspects of that system have been set forth in Chapters 3–5. There are other ways to describe the system. (Lee, 1974, and Crystal et. al., 1975, both use quite different base grammars, for example.) The only reason TALK uses a tagmemic grammar is, as has been said, the fact that it has been found useful.

Most native speakers, even those who have a good command of their language, have little or no awareness of the systemic rules they are following. They speak the language the way they speak it because this is the way they do it. This fact illustrates that the use of a language seems to depend on the learning of a set of habits that will allow speakers and hearers to forget about the system and concentrate on the message that is being transmitted. These habits are unconscious and are built up over a long period of time through practice. We learn a grammatical pattern by using it over and over again, and children normally seem to spend a lot of time just practicing the patterns of language (Weir, 1962).

What does this principle mean for instructional purposes? Since practice is all-important in building habits, we can use drill as a teaching tool. That is, if we set up a situation in which we cause a child to say the same pattern over and over again (all the while changing the vocabulary used in the pattern) we will help him build up his set of habits for that pattern. This method is used not only in TALK, but also in the other programs mentioned previously. The specific set of patterns and the methodology used to get children to drill the patterns varies from program to program, but the idea is the same in all programs that use a form of drill: to build a set of habits so that the child can forget about the grammar and concentrate on the message that he wishes to communicate. The grammatical pattern, given enough repetition, becomes automatic; once learned, it can recede into the background of consciousness. When the pattern has been learned to the point of automatic use in a conversational situation, the true communicative function of language can take its rightful place in the child's life. That is, when he speaks, he can concentrate on *what* he wants to say, not on *how* he has to say it.

Language is What Native Speakers Say

In our country, "language instruction" in the schools typically consists of a combination of the study of "grammar" and "literature." That is, we are taught "rules of grammar" and are exposed to works of literature that are considered suitable. A critique of the literature portion of the language arts curriculum need not concern us here, except to say that it is getting better all the time. The study of grammar in the public schools, in spite of the attempts of people like Paul Roberts and Owen Thomas to change it, has not become appreciably better, however. College students, for example, are still usually convinced that nouns are "persons, places, and things"; that one should never split an infinitive; and that double negatives are strictly forbidden. Getting past these barriers is a formidable task indeed, because Miss Fiddich [Joos's (1961) personification of the typical post-elementary English teacher] has done her work well. Unfortunately, Miss Fiddich's information derives from statements made by eighteenth century grammarians who were convinced of two things:

1. That English-speaking people, even those who are most learned and articulate, speak grammatically incorrect and inaccurate English.
2. That this deplorable situation must be remedied through systematic instruction of "correct" English (C.C. Fries, 1940).

The eighteenth century grammarians were all students of Latin and Greek. They were convinced that these were "perfect" languages. Therefore, English must be made perfect, and the way to do it was to describe it in terms of Latin and Greek. The latter was a little much for most people, but Latin was well-known and perfectly acceptable as a model. Therefore, descriptions of English based on Latin were developed and elaborated upon over the years and taught to school children as a series of prescriptions, e.g., "never split an infinitive" (hence the term *prescriptive grammar*). Even today we find that people study Latin to "improve their knowledge of English." This, of course, is impossible; what happens when we study Latin is that we finally make sense out of the Latin grammar rules that are used to describe English. We may even learn a little Latin on the side. In any event, it is very difficult, for example, to convince students that English does *not* have a future tense because the grammar books that are based on the prescriptivist model say that it *does,* and Miss Fiddich has convinced them that this model is the truth. Latin does have a future tense and this is where the statement comes from. It is also very difficult to convince people that it is perfectly all right to "split an infinitive," i.e., to place an adverb between the marker and the verb. The reason that it is all right is because it is often the case that a meaning difference can result from such an adverbial placement. It makes a difference, for example, to say:

(8.1) He went quickly to find the treasure.

(8.2) He went to quickly find the treasure.

In (8.1) the adverb modifies the head verb in the matrix, whereas in (8.2) it modifies the head verb in the insert. But we were told that such modification is "incorrect." Why? Because in Latin an infinitive is one word, e.g., *cantare* ("to sing"), and therefore it cannot be "split."

We must move away from such muddled thinking about the grammar of the English language if we are to help children with developmental language disabilities. The teaching of English must be based on an adequate description of English, not Latin or any other language. To this end Chapters 3–5 were written for people who are serious about teaching English as a first language.

There is another aspect of this principle that is important. The particular form of the language that is taught must be spoken colloquial English, i.e., the English that is used by the people in the community in which the child is growing up. Matters such as vocabulary, grammar, and pronunciation must take their cues from the people in the child's environment, not from standard written English. Where local usage varies from the grammar presented in Chapters 3–5 (or any other formal grammar you might use), the local usage should prevail. Thus, if the people in certain areas of Texas say "I might could do it," we should teach the children in that area to say the same thing. You will probably find that the description of the language presented in Chapters 3–5 is adequate in most of its statements, because geographical and social dialects tend to vary from this description in only a few particulars. In those cases where there is great variance, you may, in fact, be dealing with a dialect that borders on being a second language. In fact, there are places in the country where the children do have to learn English as a second language. Chief among these would be many of the American Indian children and many of the Spanish speakers along the southwestern border, but there are others as well. Children with developmental language disabilities who are in these situations will first and foremost need to learn their native language as a first language. This task requires a completely different grammar for their programs. It may even require a different statement of the developmental sequence; we just do not know if the sequence for learning clause structures holds true in the learning of other languages. Only research into those areas will provide the information we need.

Teach the Language, Not about the Language

For those of us who have worked with children with developmental disabilities over a period of time, this principle should be self-evident. That is, we cannot teach a child a formal grammar: we must help him develop an intuitive grammar. *We* must have a firm grip on a description of the system of the language we are teaching, or else we will not know when we are doing the right thing. It is senseless to try to teach a child, for example, what "the functions of the verb phrase" are. It is difficult enough to try to teach college students to understand a formal grammar; we would find it simply impossible to teach one to a child with developmental language disabilities.

The instructional implications of this are clear: Our instructional task is to get the children to use the system. *How* this task can be accomplished will vary from program to program. The way it is done in the TALK program is to place the learners in a drill and get them to use a grammatical pattern over and over until it flows easily for them. Then the teacher seeks those situations outside of the drill in which he can cause the child to use the pattern he has been teaching in a situation that is meaningful for the child. Eventually, the habits get built up and the child will "know" the system of language. Like most people, he will more than likely never be able to tell anyone what the formal rules are, but this behavior is irrelevant in terms of communicative competence.

The Goals of a Language Program

In the final analysis, the basic task facing teachers is to help the child attain communicative competence. To do this we must teach him to talk about the things that other people talk about following the same grammatical rules that other people use. We need a good description of the language, therefore, and adequate methods of helping the child to learn the systemic habits that constitute the intuitive grammar. Such habits are developed through usage in situations in which the child needs to communicate a message. Later we can worry about teaching him to read and write; initially, the important thing is to get him to speak (or sign) English.

The TALK Method

The TALK method of teaching English has two components: (*a*) formal lessons, in which the child learns the grammatical patterns of English; and (*b*) an informal transfer component, in which the child learns where and how to use the patterns. The formal component is structured around the TALK drills; the informal component is structured around the child's daily life. The way in which each is carried out will be specified in the sections that follow.

Pattern Drill

Drill sounds terrible when you first run into the term. The negative connotations come from the old days when pupils recited their lessons in unison under the stern eye of a demanding taskmaster who got "letter-perfect" results or else the children got whacked with a ruler or a willow switch. There is none of this in TALK. In fact, experience indicates that children like drill. It can be very comfortable to a young child who has difficulty in understanding all of what is going on around him.

TALK pattern drills have three purposes: (*a*) to focus the child's attention on what it is he is supposed to learn, (*b*) to give him a great deal of practice in using specific patterns so that he can learn to use them easily and naturally; (*c*) to allow the teacher to use the natural ability of a group to instruct its members. If the drill is done well, we have found that children eagerly look forward to participating in it.

The teacher should be careful not to overdo the lesson. Children seem to have a limit on the amount of hard work they can do, and we have found 10–15 minutes to be about the maximum length of time a formal lesson should last for most groups. The teacher will find that allowing the lesson to go much beyond these time limits will cause it to begin to "sag" because the children start to get tired. They have to work hard in TALK lessons, and they will do so willingly. Children *do* have limits, however, and they should not be pushed beyond them because tiredness seems to carry over from day to day. On the occasions when we have made children work too long, lessons for the next several days have not been good ones. It is best, therefore, to hold down the length of the drills.

The drill situation *can* be threatening to a child if we try to demand too much from him, not only in terms of time and effort, but also in terms of conceptual level. Most children who need TALK will make mistakes at the beginning of a new pattern drill. Only gradually will they work out their errors and finally produce what the teacher is trying to get them to produce. The errors do change and eventually drop out with time, however. The satisfying thing to a child seems to be the fact that he makes progress which he, the teacher, and the other children can observe. Children seem to take great pleasure in this learning process. When a child fails to produce the correct pattern immediately, it is not because the child, or the teacher, or TALK has failed. It is because the child must go through a learning sequence. The children appear to recognize this fact instinctively and take pleasure in the learning process itself.

The worst aspect of drill is its possible effects on the teacher. Drill in TALK, even good drill, *can* get boring at times for an adult, especially when difficult patterns seem to take forever for the children to learn. There is some variety in TALK drills, but it is hardly of a challenging nature for an adult native speaker of the language. Teachers already know all there is to know about using the patterns they must teach. Remember that the important thing about drill is the fact that the children seem to like it and that they actually can learn from it. It may sometimes be hard for the teacher to maintain enthusiasm, but it is necessary to do so because of the good which can result from its use. The teacher should take great care to hide any sense of boredom or frustration which he may feel during the drill. These feelings are all too easily communicated to the children, and they can become distracted by them. Distraction can cause a lesson to collapse in ruins.

Actually, the fact that the drill can become so automatic provides a golden opportunity for teachers. So many times we have said to ourselves that we wish we could have noticed something that was pedagogically important, but that we were too "wrapped up" in the material which we were presenting at the time. TALK drills, because they are so automatic, allow the teacher to evaluate what the children are doing during instruction rather than before or after it. This aspect gives the teacher an opportunity to teach prescriptively, which may rarely have been experienced by a teacher before. During the drill, especially during individual responses, the teacher can make note of the "errors" each child is making. He can use these errors as a basis for making decisions on such specifics as which patterns still need work, how well a child is progressing, and what needs to be done outside of the lesson proper in respect to a specific child or children.

Choral Response

Most TALK drills use choral response, i.e., everybody answers in unison. There are two reasons for the emphasis on choral response in TALK: (*a*) It allows all children to get a great deal more practice than does individual drill, i.e., if there are five children in a class, each child can respond five times per unit of time in choral drill. In individual drill each child could respond only once in the same amount of time. The more practice a child gets, the more likely he is to induce the grammatical rules. (*b*) The group response will involve all of the children in the mechanics of the lesson to a greater degree than will individual drill because *the group response itself creates a motivation to learn.* The latter point is extremely important and will be expanded upon in a following section.

Individual Responses

There are four times when the teacher has the option of calling on an individual to respond. The first is during the use of a chain drill in which each child responds individually (see the following). The second time occurs when the teacher wants to test a child to find out how well he is doing with the pattern being taught. To accomplish this, the teacher can single out each of the children toward the end of the lesson (at least once in the final few minutes) and elicit individual responses solely for the purpose of finding out how well each child is handling the pattern being taught. This technique will tell the teacher how much more work must be done with that pattern. The third time an individual drill is used is during those moments when the mind of one child is wandering and his attention must be regained. The danger with this technique is that if it is used too often, the whole lesson could turn into individual drill and the teaching power of the group (see the following) diminishes. Do not use this last method until the group response is well-established. The fourth time an individual drill may be used is to provide a little variety in the drill. As important as choral response is, our teachers have found that a little individual drill once in a while goes a long way toward keeping the lesson "perked up" and moving.

The Conversion Principle

Most TALK pattern drills are structured around the conversion principle. This principle requires that the teacher give the children a stimulus that contains all or most of the information they need to make a response. The children must then take that stimulus and make a change in it so that the response is different from the stimulus in one or more ways. For example, to elicit a question, the teacher would provide a declarative:

(8.3) S: Ask me if that is a dog.
R: Is that a dog?

The shift in word order in this sequence is important; since (8.3) is an equative clause with no auxiliaries, the verb in the stimulus pattern must go in front of the subject in the response pattern in order to become a question. It is the making of the shift which causes the child to work at learning. Mere repetition of the stimulus has not proven to be a good way to teach sentence patterns because children do not have to think at all in order to repeat what the teacher says. There are many different kinds of conversions possible in English, and we try to use them in every lesson. For example, the teacher may want to work on the continuum in the declarative, and to do so he presents stimuli in a question:

(8.4) S: What is John doing?
R: He is holding his nose.

If negation is being taught, the teacher presents a negative truth-value stimulus:

(8.5) S: Is that a chair?
R: No, it is not a chair, it is a desk.

In each case the child is expected to respond with a pattern containing the construction or function being taught.

Typically, in teaching foreign languages, repetition drills are used at least once in awhile. We have found in TALK, however, that low-functioning children cannot be allowed simply to repeat the stimuli, especially in the early stages of the program. The reason for this rule is found in the fact that many low-functioning children will repeat mindlessly for the rest of their lives if we allow them to. Repetition may keep them busy and out of trouble, but the idea behind TALK is not just to keep children busy—it is to get them to learn something. To learn, the children must work at it; using the conversion principle does indeed make them work.

Variant Drills

Not all TALK drills consist of a simple stimulus-response pattern, nor are all drills structured to require strictly choral response. Drill patterns can get very complicated in *dialogue drills,* and *chain drills* provide a variation of choral response that can be very useful.

Dialogues

The term *dialogue* is used in a slightly different manner form that typically seen in TEFL[2] programs. In second-language teaching, it refers to conversations built around a topic of discussion; but in TALK, it refers to a drill sequence in which the children are required to use two or more previously drilled patterns. The patterns in a dialogue are presented in such a way that the drill seems to consist of little ''conversations.'' Responses can be choral, individual, or mixed choral and individual. They can also be structured in a chain drill (see the following). Dialogues are useful (*a*) in reviews, (*b*) as a motivating device, or (*c*) to break up the monotony. More important than anything else, however, is the fact that a dialogue makes the lesson patterns seem more natural than single stimulus-response sequences. What could be more natural, after all, than a conversation?

Dialogue drills can be introduced at any point in the program, even in the very earliest stages of its development. Here is an early dialogue constructed out of some of the lessons on the equative clause:

(8.6) S_1 (Teacher):   Mrs. Jones, ask Johnny what that is.
R_1 (Aide):   Johnny, what is that?
R_2 (Johnny):   It is a hammer.
S_2 (Teacher):   Sally, is that a hammer?
R_3 (Sally):   Yes, it is a hammer.

Although this is a very simple dialogue drill, it is nonetheless a dialogue. It uses only patterns which the children have used before that point in the program. The teacher will find longer, more complicated, and more natural dialogues as the children progress through the lessons. Eventually the drill patterns become very complicated because the semantics of the desired response require a number of stimuli; when this happens, the only drills possible are dialogues. When this point in the program is reached, dialogues will always be specified because they have been found to be the best basic drill patterns to use for the features being taught.

---

[2]Applied linguistics is full of acronyms, e.g., TEFL (Teaching English as a Foreign Language), TESOL (Teaching English to Speakers of Other Languages), ESL (English as a Second Language), and others, among which, of course, is TALK.

Chain Drill

Chain drill is a variant pattern of response in which children both respond to and present stimuli for each other. Rather than using the choral response, which is the mainstay of TALK, the children are allowed first to respond individually and then (if possible) to present the stimulus to the next child in the chain. Stimuli and responses make their way through the class from child to child until all children have had a chance both to respond and to present a stimulus. The following is an example of one kind of a chain drill:

(8.7)	Teacher:	Johnny, ask Sally what that is.
	Johnny:	What is that, Sally?
	Sally:	It is a spoon.
	Teacher:	Sally, ask George if that is a knife.
	Sally:	George, is that a knife?
	George:	No, it is not a knife, it is a spoon.
	Teacher:	George, ask Albert what that is.

There are constraints on the use of the chain drill. In the first place, it is not used unless the children have had practice in the response patterns being used (and in the stimulus pattern as well, if they are to present it to each other). If we try to use a chain to teach a new pattern, we will find that it cannot be done. Chains must involve patterns that the children knew how to construct before they began the day's drill. This rule means that the major uses of the chain drill will be (*a*) for review, (*b*) in testing situations, and (*c*) at those times when everybody simply seems to need a change of pace or just something different.

Secondly, the use of chain drills generally should be held off until the children have become used to the TALK method and structure. It takes a while for the children to come to grips with drill as it is used in TALK, and the teacher should wait for a little while before introducing the first chain drills. Once the children understand how to do it, however, chain drills can be used with greater frequency (especially in review lessons) or as test drills at the end of the lesson. Once again, however, chain drills are not used in situations in which any pattern in the sequence is new to the children.

Other Drills

There are other kinds of drills which the teacher will find in the materials asterisked in the bibliography. In developing TALK, however, we have not had much luck with the other kinds of drills. Overall, the ones mentioned have proven most useful. The teacher should not take this as a dictum, however; let the children be the judge of what works best. We suggest locating one or two of the references on English as a second language and looking through them. The variety of teaching suggestions they contain is pleasantly surprising.

The Group as a Teaching Tool

The importance of the group cannot be overemphasized; it is the major motivational device used in TALK. By causing the children to function as a group, we get the benefit of the ability of a group to instruct its members. The mechanism used by the group is the natural desire children have to emulate other children. If a child wants to do what the other children do (and what child does not?) he will make a good member of a group. The children who are a little behind the rest of the group are in much the same position of the younger brother trying to do what his big brother does, no matter how imperfectly he does it. The little brother seldom is able to participate with the older children in an interactive sense, nor is he able to help make group decisions. But he *is* able to *try* to do what everybody else is doing and to make believe that he is "one of the big kids." In the same way, the slower children in a TALK group try to do what the other children do (with assisting cues from the teacher and the teacher aide) and to follow their lead in the learning. In addition, it appears to be true that the faster or more knowledgeable children in a group have a strong desire to maintain their status, and they, too, keep on working. The net result is motivation of all members of the group.

The motivational features of a group do not constitute the only advantage that group teaching has. It also provides a kind of security blanket for many children. Every one of us does things when we are part of a group that we would not do by ourselves. It is one thing, for example, to sing the national anthem when we are in the stands before the football game starts, and quite another thing to stand up in front of the crowd as an individual and sing it solo. That is, the group provides protection for the individual. When the group is making choral responses it is very comfortable for the child who is not yet responding with the complete pattern. If a child is having difficulty, it does not matter if he makes "mistakes" while responding as part of a group, because he is shielded by the group from standing out like a sore thumb. This technique allows him to make all the "mistakes" that he must make in the language-learning process without being penalized for them. Benefits of this magnitude are hard to come by in the classroom.

Parenthetically, participation in a TALK group can "bring out" the wallflower type of child very nicely. We have seen children, for example, who were extremely shy, who then became nearly extroverted after a period of group functioning. Some children are so withdrawn that they have to be faded into group little by little. But when they become functioning members of the group they begin to bloom and seem to lose much of their former shyness.

We have placed as many as 10 children in a lesson and as few as 1. At this time, 6 or 7 appears to be the maximum number of children for a TALK group. This number allows for activities like grouping around a small table where everybody can handle stimulus objects. This size of group still allows the teacher to retrieve the objects so that the next objects can be brought out. It also allows the teacher to keep track of everybody and what they are doing. Any group larger than 7 tends to begin to get out of hand, and it becomes too easy to lose track of individuals (Miller, 1956). We have also found that less than 4 responding children will usually cause the "group feeling" to disappear, and that this will cause the teaching effectiveness of the TALK drills to drop to a very low level. The only time we have found this not to be true was in a class of blind retarded children in which three would participate effectively.

Everything possible should be done to foster the notion of "group." We have seen several interesting methods. For example, a contest between Group A and Group B as to who does "the best" in the drill is good for the close of the week. Everybody can win in the end, but the idea of "us against them" is a great motivator in our country. Enjoyment of the drill on the part of the teacher and the aide is also good for the involvement of the children. After all, if an adult has fun with this stuff, there must be something to it and it must be good, whatever it is. Aides are invaluable in more ways than one (see the following) and a good aide can make the lesson "swing" if he enjoys the work.

An instructional device useful in groups is turning the attention of the whole group toward a slower child through the idea "Johnny's having trouble with this lesson. Let's all help him learn how to do it." This comment puts the group in the position of having to help one of their classmates and puts peer pressure on the child who needs to learn to do what the other children are doing.

There are many ways to make the group begin to function as a group. Probably the major idea is for the teacher to "think group." Each teacher knows his children and how best to do this. The point is to work as hard as possible toward group unity; both teacher and children must come to "think group"; if unity can be achieved, all children in the group will benefit immeasurably.

Structuring a Group in the Classroom

The most efficient groups are those in which all of the children in the group need to learn exactly the same constructions or functions at the same time. Such cohesiveness is possible only in the very largest schools, i.e., only in schools in which there are a very large number of children can ability grouping be done easily. In most classrooms, however, there will be a range of abilities. Even in those schools in which children are assigned to classrooms on the basis of equivalence of some abilities, most teachers will find that there is variation in terms of language development. The most difficult schools in which to structure language classes are those found in rural areas that have a wide range of students. In these areas there can be little ability grouping of any kind, let alone language ability grouping. Many questions arise in relation to how to go about structuring language classes. There are several things that can be done, and the following is a list of suggestions for the various possibilities that exist.

1. Classrooms in which all children are at about the same point in development are relatively easy to structure. In such cases the teacher can simply begin at about the level of the lowest child in the class and proceed through the sequence of lessons. In these classes, the children who know a little more about the language can actually be of great assistance in getting the program started because they catch on very quickly and pull the rest of the group along. Most classes in these situations can be split into two groups for easy handling, and children can move freely back and forth between groups when numerical balance is needed.

2. In the classrooms in which ability levels split into two distinct groups it is also easy to structure two different language groups for lesson-planning purposes. Each group will pose essentially the same instructional problem that is found in the classroom in which all of the children are at about the same point in development. In any case, no more than six or seven children should be in a single group simply because it is too difficult to handle a larger number. Then, like the situation in which all children are at about the same level, each group can proceed at its own pace.

3. In classrooms in which essentially the situation listed in #2 holds, except for one or two children who are far above or far below the level of the rest of the children, the lucky teacher will be able to find another teacher with whom he can swap children for the language lesson period. That is, if there is one child who is far below the rest of the group in development, it may be possible to find a teacher who has the opposite problem and exchange children for the period of time in which the language lessons are given. This exchange requires a great deal of communication between the teachers, however, because the program does not stop when the drill ends. When the children who change rooms leave the formal lesson and return to their homeroom, their teacher *must* know what is being taught in their lessons so that he can help the child carry the pattern into the rest of the day.

Without a tremendous amount of communication and cooperation between the teachers the program given to the children will not be as effective as it might have been.

4. In classrooms in which there is a great deal of developmental variation and little or no opportunity to swap children, it may not be possible to have formal TALK lessons. Children in these classes may have to be taught individually, which is a less efficient method than group instruction. It requires more time to work individually with five children than it does to place them all in a single group and drill them. Planning should not take up much more time, however. (Even in classrooms in which all children are being given the same lessons at the same time, each child must be assessed and kept track of individually.) The physical act of presenting lessons to five different children would simply mean that there would be five language lessons each day instead of just one. For such situations, methodology of the type developed by Miller and Yoder, or Crystal et al. might be useful. The TALK sequence can be adapted to both of these methodologies. Whatever method to teach the patterns is used, the teacher will still have to try to find the situations during the normal flow of the classroom day in which the child can use his current patterns to carry on the normal affairs of his daily living.

I would also suggest that teachers in situations in which children must be taught individually make a special effort to include the parents in the programming. All teachers should call on the parents to help in the language program, but it is especially important in those situations in which groups cannot be structured. The way one includes parents must be done carefully, though. No teacher should throw technical terms around; we cannot say to a parent who does not understand the tagmemic grammar used throughout this text anything like the following:

(8.8) "We want to get the child to use the continuum function."

There are other ways of communicating the same message without the technical terms. For example, the parent could be told:

(8.9) "We are working on sentences that have the verb ending *-ing* in them. For example, at home you might try to get the child to say, 'He is running,' or 'She is throwing a ball.' Try to get the child to say things like this, but be sure it is natural."

We have found that a couple of examples are usually sufficient to tell parents what is needed. Then, when the child goes home at night, the parents, too, can look for situations in which the construction or function being taught can be used.

Rhythm

The notion of rhythm is very important to TALK, but it is not the kind of rhythm that a drummer would produce. There are three basic rhythms to be aware of.

The first is the kind of rhythm that most of us have in our internal clocks. There are many rhythms during the course of our days; we eat our breakfasts at about the same time each day, go to work at about the same time, etc. In other words, our daily "routine" is a kind of natural life rhythm. TALK uses as many of life's rhythms as possible; the lessons should come at about the same time each day, and the internal structure of the running of the lessons should be about the same each day. The children, in other words, should approximately be able to predict when it is time for the lesson, when all of them will be required to respond as a group, when individuals will be required to respond, when the opening and closing sequences will occur, when the lesson will occur, etc. These events will all contribute to the comfortable life rhythm that most of us thrive on. It seems to be very important to make events predictable so that the children can concentrate on what it is they have to learn without having to cope with a changeable situation each day as well.

The second important rhythm to TALK is the conversational (stimulus-response) rhythm between the teacher and the aide when presenting the basic drill pattern. Many of the things that we want the children to learn occur in the initial part of the response pattern. The conversational rhythm helps cue the children as to when they should begin to respond. This cue makes rhythm itself a teaching device. In spite of the importance of the conversational rhythm, it is always necessary to warn teachers against becoming machines. Conversational rhythm is important, but it should be a conversationally comfortable rhythm—we are a human and our students are humans. The teacher must try to make the stimuli and responses come rhythmically, but not mechanically.

A third important type of rhythm is that which is inherent in the language itself. Each sentence in English has its own melodic features, and breaking up these features can contribute to disaster in a lesson. If a teacher (or the aide) cues the children on each and every word in the pattern separately, for example, the children's response will sound as if they were reading a grocery list. The teacher *must* use the rhythms of American English and *must* present the entire sentence pattern every time, even when first introducing it. Teachers using TALK usually notice the children using the melodic features of a sentence in the learning of a pattern. Adults do the same thing. Most of us have had the experience of learning a song in which we first learned the melody and a few words of a new song, and then little by little we "filled in the blanks" with the rest of the words of the song. Children in TALK often will do the same thing—learn the melody and rhythm of the pattern first and then "fill in the blanks" with words. This is an important illustration of the necessity of consciously using the natural melodies of the language at all times. It is not necessary, however, to overemphasize these melodies; if you do, the response becomes singsong, and you begin to lose contact with the language that you are attempting to teach. Use the melodies that are natural to the language; do not make up new ones.

Teacher Aides

A teacher aide is an integral part of TALK. His major role is that of a model. That is, the children must somehow be informed as to the specific response they are supposed to be making to the stimulus. The best way to ensure that this happens is to have the teacher aide become a "knowledgeable child." He provides a model for making responses. If the aide is busy acting as the third party (see the following), the role changes and the teacher must provide the model. The point is that somebody *must* lead the response so that the children can find out what it is they are supposed to be doing. Given a good model, the children can engage in imitation behavior, i.e., they try to make their responses sound like the model response. Imitation is done *while* the model response is being given; feedback is immediate and efficient in this framework.

A teacher aide is also invaluable for serving as the "third party" required for many responses, e.g.:

(8.10) S: Let's ask Miss Jones if she can run.
       R: Miss Jones, can you run?

It is difficult to get the children to use second person singular pronouns (*you*) without such a third party. When the aide is carrying out this role, the teacher models the appropriate response, as stated previously.

The third function of the aide is to maintain the rhythm of stimulus response which is so important to TALK. Without a conscious effort on the part of the aide, it is very difficult to establish and maintain rhythm; but with the assistance of the aide, it becomes quite easy.

The last, but certainly not the least, important function of the aide is to provide support for the children who have trouble. When a child (or a group) is called on to respond and does not yet know the pattern, the aide must help out. This assistance serves two purposes: (*a*) it keeps the child (or children) from becoming failures in front of everybody, and (*b*) it keeps the rhythm of the lesson itself from flagging. In relation to the last point, one of the most painful things to experience in a TALK drill is silence. The lesson should be kept moving at all times because there is a lot to do in the 10–15 minutes allotted to the TALK lesson. Any break in the lesson is simply a waste of time. The aide has a major role to play in this, i.e., to keep things moving. He must be alert to carry out this function.

What if an aide is not available? This situation presents some problems, but there are many possible solutions. The first thing to try is recruiting an aide from elsewhere in your building. Perhaps the principal would be willing to give 15 minutes of his day (try it, you may be pleasantly surprised to find that most principals enjoy being in the classroom again). If not, try the teacher's room—perhaps there will be someone with a free period to help out. Don't overlook the janitor, either. There are some very sharp janitors in the schools, and most of them enjoy being with the children. We have managed, at times, to use older children from the regular public school classes, volunteers who come in to help out, and we have even found older handicapped children who can function quite nicely as aides. One of the best aides we had was, in fact, a graduate of a special class for retarded children who had been hired by a school as a teacher aide.

Humans make the best aides, but if a person cannot be found, use puppets. We have had some success with puppets, and there are many ways in which they can be used. Make a small puppet theater, for example, and use two puppets—one would be the teacher and the other the teacher aide. Or just one puppet could serve as the aide. Use puppets only as a last resort, however. Humans have always provided us with our best results in the past because their presence ties the language being taught in the lessons to its rightful place in human existence: communication with other people. Best of all choices is an employed aide because he is paid to be there. Do anything to get someone. TALK is one of the few programs in which the paraprofessional has a true teaching function. An aide will be heavily relied upon if he does his job properly.

Format and Feedback

Gold (personal communication) points out that a task analysis requires more than just an analysis of content (what it is that the learner must learn). It requires, in addition, an analysis of process (what it is that the teacher must do to cause learning to take place). A process task analysis has two parts: an analysis of *format* (the behaviors in which the teacher engages), and an analysis of *feedback* (how the teacher lets the learner know when he is doing what he is supposed to be doing). In TALK drills, format and feedback occur simultaneously. It is often difficult to tell where one stops and the other begins. Nevertheless, during TALK drills, the following takes place.

The drill format, as outlined in the preceding sections, is a shaping procedure which uses imitation by the learner of a model provided by the aide. As errors disappear, the model is faded and the children must begin to produce the correct response by themselves. (The model will be reintroduced at any time the learners exhibit problems in producing the response.) Drill patterns are sequenced to form a forward chaining procedure, i.e., each drill depends on the knowledge acquired in previous drills, and new learning is added in steps.

Feedback

Two feedback mechanisms operate in TALK drills. One is external and the other is internal. The internal feedback is provided when the child attempts to do what the aide is doing. If the child's response sounds like the aide's response, he is doing the correct thing. If it does not, he must change his behavior to match that of the aide. This feedback relies heavily on the child's ability to imitate. Note that it may not be possible to specify what it is the child is imitating, especially in the early stages of learning a new pattern. For example, the child may begin by imitating the intonational contour of a pattern; he may begin by imitating the rhythm of the pattern; or he may begin by imitating the last word of the pattern. There are any number of things the child may imitate, and different children may focus on different things at first. Whatever he begins with, however, the child must compare what he says to what the aide says and change his response to match that of the aide's. The external feedback takes two forms: (*a*) verbal correction of errors; and (*b*) no news is good news.

Verbal correction of errors is made in several ways. When a drill pattern is first being introduced, the teacher and the aide always give a few examples of how the drill should sound. The children remain silent during this time. Then the children are told to begin, and in many instances, their responses will not be correct right away. If they have a lot of trouble, the teacher stops them and says, ''Listen to (*name of aide*)'' and goes through the stimulus-response pattern a few more times. The children are then given another opportunity to try the drill. This method continues until the bulk of the group begins to approximate the aide's response. At that point no more interruptions are made, and the drill continues.

It is also possible that most of the group will begin to make the appropriate response within a reasonable amount of time, but that one or two children will continue to make errors. Feedback to these children can be made in several ways. One way, for example, is to engage them in an individual drill and have the aide help the child get through the response a couple of times. When this technique is used, the teacher must be sure not to stop the group drill for any appreciable length of time because the sense of the group will dissipate if he does. If disunity happens too often, the group will be lost as an instructional tool.

For some children, it is just as effective to say to the group, ''John is having trouble with this one. Let's all help him say it the right way.'' The teacher runs through a few stimulus-response patterns with the entire group and then tries an individual drill with the child who is having difficulty just to see how he does. This method has the potential for causing discomfort to some very sensitive children, however, and should be used with caution. Other ways to provide feedback are possible within the group structure. For example, the child who has difficulty might sit next to the aide so that the aide can concentrate on that child. Whatever is used, all correction of errors should be made within the group-drill framework, and they should be made without disturbing the flow of the lesson.

No news is good news is a feedback mechanism that usually operates for most of us in all the things that we do. It happens whenever we are doing what we are supposed to be doing and nobody sees anything extraordinary in the fact that we do it; only when we do something wrong does anyone say something to us. Since TALK is structured as a group activity, anytime a child is singled out of the group for attention by the teacher it may mean that he is not doing something properly, especially if the rhythm of the activity is interrupted, and/or the attention of the group is focused on the individual. As long as the group activity continues, however, any individual in the group can assume that, whatever he is doing, he must be doing it in an acceptable manner.

Reinforcement

Reinforcement is not used as a feedback mechanism in TALK. This is not to say that reinforcement is not used, but that it is not used *as a feedback mechanism*. To do this would require external reinforcers, but these have not been programmed into TALK. That is, the child is never placed into a situation that is so difficult that he requires external reinforcement.[3]

Internal reinforcement is used in TALK, however. That is, participation in the drills is intrinsically reinforcing. To be a member of a group that is making a lot of noise is simply fun for children, and they will work hard *because* they are part of a group. In addition, the learning of the mother tongue is intrinsically reinforcing. Humans have a need to communicate what they are thinking, and the spoken language is the most efficient means of communication we have. The more children learn about its use, the greater the reinforcement that accrues to participation in the drills. This idea, plus the fact that group participation is fun, should be enough to keep most groups going for a long time and to mitigate the need for other kinds of reinforcement. In fact, removal from the group has been found to

---

[3]Some teachers in the experimental groups have tried to use edible reinforcers of one kind or another. Their intent was to make the children work in the lessons. It rarely, if ever, had any positive effect on the lessons, and in fact, they usually have a detrimental effect. That is, some children can make a bit of sweet cereal last for hours; when a child has something in his mouth, he finds it very difficult to make a verbal response. Without verbal responses, TALK is a non-activity. Even when rapidly ingested edibles are used (such as a shot of water from a squirt bottle), the edible can cause more problems than it solves. Other workers have pointed out the other problem: Once we begin to use edibles, it becomes difficult to wean the children from their use (Gold, personal communication; Knapczyk, 1975). They become "hooked" on them. Once this happens, it becomes very difficult to reintroduce the more socially acceptable, intrinsic reinforcers.

The fact that external reinforcers are not used in TALK does not prevent the use of *encouragement* by the teacher. That is, the use of terms such as *good,* or *that's right,* when everything is going well can be comforting and will probably be welcomed by the children. Many teachers view such encouragement as being "positive reinforcement," but this is an incorrect view of the nature of reinforcement. That is, a positive reinforcer is anything that increases the probability that a behavior will be repeated or strengthened when a specific stimulus reoccurs (Bandura, 1969). Randomly inserted expressions of approval do not constitute reinforcers in this sense. Rather, they are encouragement. There is nothing wrong with encouragement, however, and in fact, it can be a very good thing for morale. A good teacher uses it freely.

be a negative reinforcer or a punisher for some children in the experimental programs. Group participation may even have status implications for some children. On the whole, the TALK lesson structure per se provides very useful reinforcement and has proven to be a reliable tool for instruction.

The Lessons

In one sense, a TALK lesson never varies. Vocabulary, materials, objectives, and drill patterns change from lesson to lesson, but each lesson in the program is presented and carried out the same way as every other lesson. In this section, the lesson structure and the conduct of a lesson will be discussed.

The Lesson Plans

All TALK lesson plans follow this format:

Objective

The exit behavior of the child is specified in the objective, i.e., it states what will be taught in the lesson. Required entry behaviors are specified by the objectives of the lesson plans with numbers lower than today's lesson.

Materials

The materials needed for the lesson, if any, are presented in a general way. Special types of words needed for the lesson are sometimes mentioned, but specific required vocabulary is usually not mentioned, because every group will be different and will need different vocabulary items. Some vocabulary items which might be helpful are listed in Appendix C. This list does not exhaust the possibilities, however, and the teacher should not hesitate to add vocabulary items which will be helpful in using the lesson.

One of the things that can be done to help make vocabulary less of a problem is to get together a collection of common objects: eating utensils, a couple of rocks, bottle caps, toy cars, spools, pencils, nails. Anything that is in common use in the children's lives makes excellent vocabulary for TALK drills, and a "junk box" makes objects easier to find. Materials from some of the other commercial "language" programs can be used, if they are available. Some of the latter have excellent pictures that can be used to guide responses in the drills.

Basic Drill Pattern

In the drills, for example, patterns actually used are specified. The teacher presents the stimulus and the children make the response. Sometimes it is necessary for the teacher or aide to respond to something the children say, e.g., when the children ask questions of the teacher or the aide, they should get answers. These places are indicated in the basic drill pattern.

Certain symbols appear over and over in the basic drill patterns. The glossary of terms (Appendix B) contains explanations, and the teacher should make sure he understands the symbols before running the drill for the lesson.

Method

In the method section are special instructions for running the lesson that might be necessary. We have also provided examples of the kinds of things the teacher, the aide, and the children might actually say during the lesson. The possibilities are not limited to the examples; in fact, vocabulary *must* be extended beyond the examples if both teacher and the children are not to be bored to tears.

Things to Look Out For

The last section is a potpourri where comments on the lesson will be made: how it is to be run, the things that might get the lesson into trouble, etc. It can be very helpful to the teacher getting ready to run a drill for the first time, and you should check these notes.

Running a Lesson

Physical Arrangements

It is good to have about the same physical arrangement of the group each time you do a TALK lesson. TALK is built around rhythmic activity, and the same physical arrangement in each lesson will contribute to the daily life rhythm. There are many ways to arrange a group, and the particular arrangement chosen is simply a matter of the teacher's preference and that of the children. Some suggestions are to place the children around a small table; to obtain rug samples from a friendly rug dealer and have the children sit on the floor; or to place the children on chairs in a semicircle. For teachers who like intimate grouping, close seating *does* seem to help the "group feeling," especially with younger children. The actual arrangement, however, is unimportant; sameness, comfort, and the maintenance of "groupedness" *are* important.

The Opening Segment: Get the Group's Attention

It is impossible to get children to learn if they are not attending. A bad start can cause a lesson to disintegrate rapidly, and the best way to have a good lesson is to get it started well. It is not enough simply to have the attention of the individuals within the group. TALK is a group activity program, and the teacher must have the attention of the group as a whole. As part of getting the rhythm of the lesson started, we have found it very helpful to sing a little song. A copy of this song appears in Part IV immediately before the lessons. Sing it with the children whether they can do it or not. This song is an important part of the lesson. Again, it is simply part of the routine, but the routine itself is comforting because it tells the children where they are and what they are doing before the actual lesson begins. It is extremely important that the lesson start right for *all* the children in the group. Anything that will foster total participation from the very beginning of the lesson is to be encouraged.

One teacher used an additional "warmup" *before* the song was sung. She had her children put their heads back and sing, "Ahhhhh . . . " on the same note that the song begins with, and her children loved it. All this teacher was doing was to get the attention of her children and make them start to move their vocal chords. TALK, being an oral program, finds this sort of thing useful, and no teacher should hesitate to use his own touches for getting everything started off on the right foot.

The Lesson Proper: Six Rules to Follow

Maintain Group Unity and Attention

As stated previously, one of the most effective, and therefore one of the most important, aspects of TALK is its ability to use the group as a teaching tool. Children pay attention to each other and attempt to do what the other children are doing. If the group is treated as a group rather than as a collection of individuals, it will respond as a group. However, fractionation of the group, i.e., teacher actions which make any individual the focus of the teacher's attention and exclude the rest of the group (in effect, "shutting them out") will harm the effectiveness of the lesson. It should be noted that it is still possible for the group to remain a group while the teacher is conducting individual drills. This task is done through devices such as "Now let's see if Johnny can do it by himself." This focuses the group's attention on whether or not Johnny will respond correctly. If Johnny fails to do so, the teacher can hold group unity by saying something like "Johnny had a little bit of trouble with that one. Let's all see if we can help him by saying it right a few times." In this way, the group is brought into the action and individual responses become part of group activities.

The major point to be made here is not to say which specific methods will maintain group unity and attention, but rather one of stressing the importance of doing it. When one of the lessons in the developmental phase of TALK has fallen apart, we have often found that group unity was somehow destroyed at some point previous to the breakdown. Different groups require different things to establish and maintain unity, and each teacher should search for the things that will foster group unity and attention.

Once the integrity of the group as a group is established, however, it is difficult to break it up (not that we would ever want to, of course). Children who get together stick together.

Use Choral Drill for the Bulk of the Lesson

Some responses take longer than other responses, but as many responses as the children are capable of making per unit of time should be required of all of them. Choral drill allows each child to respond to each stimulus each time it is given. It is also easier to establish a good conversational rhythm when using choral drill. The rhythm itself serves as the cue for the children to begin responding, as was pointed out earlier. It is important to try to keep the responses from becoming ragged because this raggedness will allow some children to get away with giving only a partial response. The aide can prove to be very helpful here. It is the aide's response to the teacher's stimulus which provides the children with the cue to begin responding, and a good aide will keep the lesson moving.

In addition to the fact that a good conversational rhythm will provide the best cues for responding, the more responses a child can make per unit of time, the more practice he will get. Practice is integral to TALK in that the more responses a child has to make, the more chances he gets to learn the rules for creating new sentences. Be careful, however, not to go *too* fast. It is important for the teacher, the aide, and the children to find a *comfortable* rhythm. Consistency is far more important than pyrotechnics. We have a training film[4] that shows two teachers with totally different teaching styles using TALK. It illustrates very well how adaptable to individual differences among teachers the method really is. You can apply it the way you need to.

Present Stimuli and Require Responses in the Rhythmic and Melodic Patterns of American English

Do not break up the "intonational envelope" of the pattern being taught. We are trying to teach sentence *patterns,* not discrete words. Sentences in English have a beginning, a middle, and an end, and they all fit together into one neat little "intonational package." This "package" has to be maintained for two reasons. First, it serves as a teaching device.

---

[4]Available from Charles E. Merrill, the publisher of this text.

Children seem to learn the melodic contours of the language at a very early age. Babies, for example, use the intonation patterns of their native languages before they begin actually to use sentences in their respective languages. Children in TALK programs are usually quite familiar with American English melodic patterns, and as pointed out previously, will often use them as learning "crutches." We have heard many children in the lessons chiming in with the parts of the pattern they know while leaving out the other parts; they add the other parts with the passage of time. The other parts are all added into the rhythm, with all of the proper vocal inflections, just as many of us do when we learn a song "by ear." The other reason to use American English rhythmic and melodic patterns is this: The end result of TALK is to teach American English, and the patterns used in the lessons should resemble the language as closely as possible. It is absolutely necessary to provide the proper model.

Be Careful of Shortcuts in the Lesson Patterns

It might seem strange to the teacher that some of the required responses consist of elongated responses which would rarely be used in conversation. For example, when first teaching the negative in equative clauses, we use the following pattern:

(8.11) S: Is this a pencil?

R: No, it is not a pencil. It is a paper clip.

We have two reasons for requiring the children to respond this way. As the program develops, features of the language which have been taught in previous lessons will appear later as *parts* of patterns which contain new features. Many aspects of the language will be learned only through continuous use in combinations and recombinations of previous learning with new features. Sentences and parts of sentences rarely occur in isolation in daily living, and the combination and recombination of forms will eventually result in a system of linguistic rules that the child can use. Consider the negative used in the previous example, for instance. Not only will children have to learn to use *not* with *be* ("It is not... "), they will also have to learn to pattern it with transitive and intransitive verbs with no auxiliaries ("He does not go... ") and with auxiliaries ("He has not gone... "), and learn that the determiner$_2$ can also express negation ("He had no money"), etc. In short, the language is extremely complicated, and we have to prepare the child for going on to the next step before we ask him to try to take that step. The second reason for having the child respond with such elongated responses early in the program has to do with ellipsis. As speakers of English conversing with each other, we rarely use "complete" sentences. Rather, we ellipt; that is, we use the linguistic and situational context to carry part of our message. The result is that our sentences would sound very strange if we heard them in isolation. For example, if we heard the following in isolation, we might have difficulty in deciding what the speaker meant:

(8.12a) R: Out.

But if we place it in some context, it makes sense:

(8.12b) S: Where did you go?
R: Out.

Or:

 (8.12c) S: What happened to the batter?
      R: Out.

Or:

 (8.12d) S: I want to come in the house and play.
      R: Out!

All of these responses are ellipted responses and understanding them requires knowledge of the context. Ellipted sentences are perfectly grammatical in American English, but if this is all that a child ever says, we have no way of knowing whether or not he knows the grammar for the corresponding complete utterances. Consequently, we have to make sure that he does, and we can do so only by having the children respond in complete sentence patterns for the features that we are teaching at the moment. Later on, we allow ellipsis and, in fact, we may require it as long as the children have already shown that they can use the complete pattern. The goal of the program is not to make the children sound stilted.

 For example, one lesson uses the following pattern sequence:

 (8.13) S: What is that?
     R: It is a dog.

Later on, when teaching the children to ask the same question used in this response, we allow an ellipted response simply because this is the way Americans talk:

 (8.14) S: Ask Johnny what that is.
     R_1: Johnny, what is that? (This is the pattern being taught.)
     R_2: A dog. (Ellipsis allowed on previously learned pattern.)

Some responses have many different corresponding ellipses, any of which would be allowable in lessons *after* the children have demonstrated that they can make the complete response. For example, the response:

 (8.15a) No, it is not a dog, it is a cat.

could be ellipted in any of the following (and more) ways:

 (8.15b) R_1: No.
      R_2: No, it is not.
      R_3: No, it is a cat.

 There is, then, a general principle guiding the use of the pattern drills: We have to make sure that the children can use the complete pattern; once we know that they can do this, we have to make sure that they sound like American children when they are talking.

 This principle also means that the children will be taught to use features such as contractions. That is, features such as *can't* and *isn't* are part of the spoken language and should be taught. Rarely do these features appear as *cannot* and *is not* in the spoken language. It is interesting to note that the children often seem to go through a stage in which they prefer the uncontracted form, e.g., *is not,* before they use the contraction. In general, teaching of the uncontracted form should always precede teaching of the contracted form and should be continued until the teacher is satisfied that the children have the uncontracted form well in hand. At that point the contracted form can be introduced and used consistently.

Avoid Repetition Drills Whenever Possible

The conversion principle does two things. (*a*) It teaches the interrelated nature of sentence patterns. In Chapters 3–5 we went to great lengths to demonstrate that various sentence patterns are related to each other in many ways. Conversion drills use these relationships, and the children learn them through the drills. (*b*) Conversion requires activity on the part of the learner. Some programs rely on repetition drills somewhat, but we have found that repetition is too easy. The children in the TALK experimental projects were found to have difficulty in making conversions once a pattern of repetition was established. They seemed to learn to repeat patterns with little or no concentration, and once allowed to repeat, it was difficult to stop them from continuing to do so. TALK has a great deal of respect for the ability of all children to work hard at something that is meaningful, and, in fact, TALK *requires* them to work hard at learning the language. One way of causing the children to work at learning is to use the conversion prinicple. This is not to say that repetition should never be used, but that it should be used with great care and *only* when no conversion is possible.

Close the Lesson Visibly and Audibly

It is important to mark the end of the lesson in a definite way. TALK can be very noisy at times, the excitement generated can carry over into the next activity. There are several things which can be done here. One way of quieting the group down is to save the individual drills (which are used as test situations to see if the children can use the features being taught in the lesson's frame) for the end of the lesson. This technique begins to close down the choral drill and starts a "quieting down" phase. After a few more choral drills, the teacher can have the children settle down, pick up their mats or chairs, or whatever, and put them away quietly. This method will allow the teacher to begin the next teaching activity which follows the TALK lesson with a minimum of strain. Other closing devices are readily available. The important thing is to quiet the lesson down so that it does not interfere with the next activity of the day.

Recycling the Lessons

TALK lessons cannot be thought of as independent of one another. However, drill is of a nature such that the teacher can get very tired of presenting the same lesson day after day to children who do not catch on very quickly. Therefore, if a lesson is not responded to completely by all children in the first few days of presentation, you should go on to the next lesson for a couple of days, and then return to the first lesson again. Do not continue working on any one lesson for a very long period of time—the children usually have many things to learn, and any one particular lesson may not be giving each child everything he needs. It may be necessary to go through several subsequent lessons before returning to the point where the children began to have difficulty. This method is called *recycling,* and some especially slow groups may have to go through a number of cycles over a period of a year or two (or more in some cases). When recycling, skip the lessons that teach contructions or functions that the group already knows, even if they are next in the sequence. Do not go too far in a cycle. It would be going too far, for example, to get into questions before the children can handle declarative active transitive clauses. As a general rule, the sequence in Table 6.21, p. 174, should serve very well as a guide to how far you can go.

The teacher may also want to do a lesson, occasionally, that has successfully been learned by the children before. Returning to a known lesson can be a good motivational device for those days when nothing has gone right. It is a way to demonstrate to the children who are having problems that they *can* do something after all.

Breaking Patterns

The pattern will be broken if you introduce elements which are not supposed to be in the pattern being taught. For example, if the pattern for the day is the equative with the third person singular subject, e.g.:

(8.16) S: Is this a (*noun*)?
R: Yes, it is a (*noun*).

sudden introduction of a third person plural subject before the children are familiar with it could wreck the drill because it requires a change in the verb:

(8.17) S: Are these (*nouns*)?
R: Yes, they are (*nouns*).

The above change is unpredictable from the point of view of the specified drill objective, and it can cause the drill to fall apart. The teacher must carefully consider the materials to be used in the lesson (pictures, objects, flannel board materials, etc.) *before each lesson* to make sure that the pattern will not be broken when they are used. The point is, the teacher must make sure that nothing unpredictable happens in any lesson.

The TALK Program in the Rest of the Day

TALK Cannot Stop with the End of the Lesson

The use of the language is continuous. It occurs in all situations in the school and at home during all portions of the day. The children in the experimental programs have been found to be able to drill satisfactorily for a *maximum* of about 15 minutes. After this (and sometimes sooner) they begin to get very tired. Beyond the formal lesson, however, TALK *can and should permeate the day*. If the day's lesson has been on questions, for example, it is a simple matter to find many situations during the day where the teacher can tell a child, e.g., "Johnny, ask Billy if (*pattern*)." The teacher will find that there are innumerable situations during the day in which he will be able to get the children to use past and current patterns in real life situations. TALK, as has been stated, is concerned with teaching the language. Since the language is used in all social situations, TALK can be extended infinitely.

Using the patterns outside the formal lesson period will assist the children in generalizing what they have learned in the lesson to real life situations. The formal TALK lesson cannot teach a child how to use English; it can only teach him what the patterns are. Real life situations are needed for teaching how and where to use the patterns which are being taught in the formal lessons. The drill is artificial and the children know this. If TALK is to work at all, therefore, the teacher *must* become alert to those situations in which the lesson pattern for the day can be used to communicate facets of daily living. For example, if the lesson for the day is on the *yes/no* question using modals, it is rather easy to find a situation in which the child wants or needs something, and you can say:

(8.18) S: Go ask (*aide*) if you can have a pencil.
R: (*Aide*), can I have a pencil?

Such a situation is real life and must be used as much as possible.

It is because much of the actual teaching is done outside of the formal drill that it is better for a classroom teacher to use TALK, and not a speech or language therapist. The teacher is with the child for much longer periods of time and has more access to the situations outside of the formal drill where so much learning must take place. Speech and language therapy personnel do not ordinarily have the continual contact with the children that is necessary to bring the patterns into daily living. I would, therefore, urge therapists to become resource persons to teachers who would find TALK useful. The knowledgeable therapist can function more effectively as a resource person to 10 teachers than as a twice-a-week visiting teacher of children. The resource role has a much greater instructional payoff for the therapist than does the direct instruction role.

We have also encountered a very real problem when teaching a form of signed English to deaf children. Some educators in the deaf community (both deaf and hearing) prefer Amerslan and will resist the use of pedagogical sign (see Moores, 1974, for complete definitions). They may not provide the followup that is necessary to demonstrate to the children that the pedagogical forms of sign can be useful communication systems. If there is no cooperation from other persons in the child's life outside of the classroom, the teaching of English in its signed form may not be possible. Hearing children do not run into this problem, since the parents, the lady at the checkout counter in the supermarket, and the kids next door all use the language being taught in school, and they all assist in the followup.

The Structure of TALK Lesson Plans: Writing New Lessons

Part IV contains a number of lesson plans, but they are far from being complete. Not every construction or function listed in Chapters 3–5 has a lesson plan, nor was there an attempt to make the teaching program exhaustive. There are three reasons why these are not included.

1. It is simply impossible to include lessons for everything in a program of this nature, and some choices had to be made. If lessons had been written for everything that could be taught, the program would have become so unwieldy as to be not useful. Anyone who tried to teach from a program that included everything would get so bogged down in specifics that they would lose the thread that runs through the lesson sequence. As it is, at any point in the program it is relatively easy to see where you have been and where you are going in terms of the instructional sequences.

2. It is our good fortune that most low-functioning children in this country are native speakers of English. They are in constant contact with other speakers of the language, and they will receive training in English outside of the pattern drills. This training occurs in two ways: (*a*) by receiving the natural instruction that adults always give to children; and

(*b*) by being given formal instruction in other instructional areas that include instruction in the language. The determiner$_3$, for example, is a major preoccupation in beginning arithmetic instruction, and determiner$_3$ lessons in TALK would simply have been redundant.

3. The functions and constructions receiving the most attention in TALK are those which were hypothesized in Chapter 2 of the text to be the most important to the development of the language. They will provide the conceptual matrix within which the learning that must take place outside the drills will occur.

In summary, the lessons constitute more of a framework for what can be done than they are a specification of what has to be done. They provide enough basics for a teacher who needs time to work through the underlying concepts, and enough flexibility for the accomplished teacher to be as creative as possible. There will always come a time, however, when a good teacher will need to write a lesson for a function or a construction that has not been included in the program. For those times it is necessary to know how the TALK lesson plans were written so that you can go through the same process and build your own lessons. The following is a mini-manual on how to write TALK-type lesson plans.

There are three steps to writing a plan. These are sequenced, i.e., to write a plan you first do Step 1, then Step 2, and finally, Step 3.

Step 1. Decide precisely which construction or function must be taught. In accomplishing this step it is very important to be specific. It is one thing, for example, to decide that you want to teach "adjectives," and quite another to decide that you have to teach the loose-knit modifier function. The former involves vocabulary building that can be carried out within *either* an existing loose-knit modifier slot *or* the complement slot in the equative clause. A decision as to what you actually need to teach is absolutely critical before you do anything else. Once you have specified the construction or function to be taught, however, the rest of the task becomes nearly mechanical.

Step 2. Choose a pattern that exemplifies the specific construction or function that you wish to teach. Because the construction or function that you wish to teach is a generalization, there will always be a number of different ways it can be expressed in behavior. Suppose, for example, that you decide to teach the restrictive modifier function in the noun phrase. Any one of the following three patterns might be used:

(8.19a) Subject: (the noun + restrictive modifier) - Predicate - Direct Object
The *man in the hall* found the box.

(8.19b) Subject-Predicate-Direct Object: (the *noun + restrictive modifier*)
John threw the *ball with the stripe*.

(8.19c) Subject-Predicate-Indirect Object: (the *noun + restrictive modifier*)-Direct Object
John gave the *man on the corner* the money.

In the above three examples, the first contains the restrictive modifier in the subject, the second has it in the direct object, and the third has it in the indirect object. There might be very good reasons for choosing any one of the three patterns. Examples (8.19a) and

(8.19c) both develop later than (8.19b). If, however, you are setting out specifically to teach the restrictive modifier in the subject slot, (8.19b) would be the pattern to choose. Note that these three patterns do not exhaust the possibilities. In all three, for example, we have used only prepositional phrases. We would introduce a completely different set of patterns if we were to use insert clauses to fill the restrictive modifier function. There are many different possible patterns that could exemplify the same concept and there would be reasons for using any one or all of them.

Suppose, for example, we must develop a lesson plan to introduce the restrictive modifier for the first time. We would choose the pattern with the noun phrase in the direct object because it is the slot in which the restrictive modifier develops at the earliest time. We would also probably choose to use prepositional phrases as fillers of the slot, not only because insert clauses develop at a later point in time, but also because, of all the possible restrictive modifier fillers, prepositional phrases seem to be the most common. Thus, we might develop the following patterns:

(8.20) Subject-Predicate-Direct Object: (the *noun* + *restrictive modifier*)
John wants the *doggy in the window.*
Wilbert likes the *smell from the garden.*
Mary is eating the *hamburger from the kitchen.*
Mother feeds the *fish in the tank.*

Step 3. Choose a stimulus pattern that will elicit the target pattern naturally. This step is very important. The idea is to set up a drill in which it is normal for the children to use the pattern you wish them to learn. In addition, the drill must provide all of the information required for the children to use in creating the pattern. In the case of the restrictive modifier function, it would probably be necessary to supply the information in several steps: That is, we have to supply the information that (*a*) the restrictive modifier responds to the question *which noun,* and (*b*) the restrictive modifier slot is to be filled by a prepositional phrase. The following drill pattern does just this:

(8.21) S_1: Where is (*noun phrase*)?
R_1: It is (*prepositional phrase*).
S_2: Does (*name*) (*verb phrase*) (*noun*)?

R_2: Yes $\left\{\begin{array}{l} \text{he} \\ \text{she} \end{array}\right.$ does.
R_2: Yes, $\left\{\begin{array}{l} \text{he} \\ \text{she} \end{array}\right\}$ does.
S_3: Which (*noun*) does (*name*) (*verb phrase*)?
R_3: Name (*verb phrase*) the (*noun* + *restrictive modifier*).

Example 8.21 is now a pattern that you could use in a drill. It would take forms such as the following:

(8.22) S_1: Where is the doggy?
R_1: In the window.
S_2: Does John want the doggy?
R_2: Yes, he does.
S_3: Which doggy does he want?
R_3: John wants the doggy in the window.

Note how the final stimulus pattern elicits the restrictive modifier. Since the restrictive modifier responds to the question *which (noun)?*, we have used this characteristic specifically to elicit the pattern we have chosen, i.e., S_3 specifies that we want to hear a restrictive modifier.

At this point, now we can begin to choose materials that can be used in a drill. We might choose pictures, objects, flannel board materials, or anything else that could be useful in structuring the drill. Now that we have a useful drill pattern, it should be relatively easy to make the choice. One choice would be to use pictures which show both a person and an object, the name of which could be used in a restrictive modifier slot. Others might have different ideas which would be equally valid. So long as they do the job, specifics can vary.

The previous lesson is designed to teach a relatively little-used function. We might have chosen any other pattern to construct, and many of them would have been simpler. Question patterns, for example, require only one stimulus for the most part:

(8.23) S: Ask me if *declarative clause).*
(For example), Ask me if this is a pencil.
R: Is that a pencil?

At this point, it would probably be instructive for the reader to look over some of the drills in Part IV. All of them have been constructed using the three-step process just described. First the construction or function to be taught was chosen, then a pattern that exemplified that function or construction was chosen, and finally a stimulus pattern to elicit that pattern was chosen. Only then were the materials chosen and the lesson plan completed. Anyone can do the same thing and in fact, all teachers are encouraged to do so when the need arises.

Limitations of the Use of TALK

TALK is a group learning activity. We have found that it works best in a situation where children are exposed to other children who are doing the same learning, and where they can see the effects of that learning on other children. The group is more important than the individual in TALK, because the group brings subtle pressures to bear on the individual which make him *want* to learn. All children want to do what the other children can do, and this desire to "be like the others" makes them work very hard to learn something. TALK uses this need extensively through the use of the choral drill. It seems to work very well this way, but it also places a very serious limitation on who can participate in TALK lessons: if a child is so disruptive behaviorally that he cannot function as a member of a group, TALK probably will not do him or the other children much good. We have found it best to exclude all children who are extremely disruptive from the group until they can participate actively. Not only do they not learn very much, they also prevent the others from learning. Therefore, any teacher who wants to give TALK lessons to a child who is too hyperactive to function as part of the group is advised to find another way to present the child with the lesson. Perhaps teaching could be done on an individual basis outside of the regular TALK sessions so that the child can be integrated into the group at a later point. Where group participation has been used as a reinforcer for acceptable behavior, we have often seen the "behavior problems" abate somewhat. It seems that many children really want to become part of a group that is having a good time. The fact that TALK uses the group as a teaching tool also limits its use in those situations in which there are not enough children to form a group. Suggestions have been made to help out in these instances (see previous section).

The third limitation has to do with what the children know. If a teacher has a group that is functioning at or below Stage IIIa, they are probably not yet ready for TALK. For these children, we suggest that the teacher turn to another program, such as Miller and Yoder's *Syntax Teaching Program* (1972, 1974). When they have gone through this or a similar program, they will be at Stage IIIa and will be ready for TALK.

The Place of TALK in the Classroom

TALK or some other program designed to teach English to children who need to learn it has a place in the classroom, but how much of a place? Part of the answer to this question lies in the problem of how much your children will need to use a language. If you believe that there is no need for a child to use a language or that your children know all they need to know, then there is no place for TALK or any similar program in that child's day. If, however, you believe that because he has things to communicate, a child's day involves the use of a language from the time he gets up in the morning until the time he goes to bed at night (and sometimes in the middle of the night as well), then the importance of a language teaching program for language-handicapped children will be apparent to you.

The formal TALK lessons should not constitute the entire teaching day, however. Any child whose language development is so far behind that of his peers that he requires lessons in how to speak his native language is sure to require instruction in many other matters as well. A language, as was said previously, is simply a tool that is used to communicate the other things he has learned or is learning. It is not the only thing that must be learned. Because the formal TALK lessons are structured, there may be a temptation to use it more than it should be used. Resist it; there is too much else to do. You may end up taking time away from something equally as valuable.

Summary

This chapter has presented a rationale for and an example of the way in which applied English linguistics can be adapted to the teaching of English as a first language. The method developed is called the TALK Program. This program has found use in a number of different situations, including the teaching of English to retarded children, hard-of-hearing children, and deaf children (in the latter group, the language taught must be a form of pedagogical sign; Moores, 1974). TALK does not pretend to be the only way in which English can be taught as a first language, but it has been used in classrooms for these children for a number of years now. It provides the teacher with one more tool in carrying out the job. For some children it has been shown to be a good tool, and for others, problems have been found. It does not work very well at all for children whose transitive and intransitive clauses are below Stage IIIa, for example. Also, because it involves group activity as a major teaching device, individual instruction is difficult to carry out using TALK lessons. In these cases, other programs for accomplishing the same thing have been suggested. The important thing is, and will be, the teacher's assessment of the developmental status of the child: where he is and what he would ordinarily learn next. Given this knowledge, a teacher should be able to devise a way to teach a child the next construction or function if TALK proves to be not useful in a situation.

TALK is structured within five principles of applied English linguistics. It concentrates on teaching the form of the language that is spoken by most people and adapts to local usage wherever necessary. It teaches sentence patterns of the language by trying to develop habits through drill, but this is only part of the program. After the children begin to develop the patterns being taught in the drills, we try to get them to use those patterns in their ordinary day-to-day life situations to communicate their thoughts to other people. In all of our teaching, a conscious attempt is made to get the children to use the language; but we seldom, if ever, verbalize any "rules" to them. That is, the learning of the grammar is induced. The job of TALK is to make that induction as easy as possible for the child by concentrating on just one construction or function at a time.

PART 4

The Lessons

CONTENTS

The Lessons

5.3   To drill the modal *may* in the sense of granting permission, in both affirmative and negative patterns.
5.4   To drill the simple future with *going to*.
5.5   To drill the simple future using adverbials of time.
5.6   To drill the adverbial of time without specifying it in the stimulus.
5.7   To drill the simple future with the adverbial of manner.
5.8   To drill the contrast between *before* and *after*.
5.9   To drill the contrast between *during,* and *before* and *after*.
5.10   To drill the modal *will* using adverbs of time.
5.11   To drill the negative with the modal *will*.

Section 6. The Dummy DO and Coordinates   **356**

Lesson   Objective

6.1   To drill the negative and affirmative declaratives using the dummy DO in the nonpast tense with *I, you, we,* or *they* as the subject.
6.2   To drill the contrast between negative and affirmative in the statements using the dummy DO in the past tense.
6.3   To drill the affirmative and negative emphatic DO in the present tense.
6.4   To drill the third singular form of the dummy DO (*does*) in the negative and affirmative.
6.5   To drill conjoined imperative clauses using *and*.
6.6   To drill conjoined active, declarative clauses in the simple present tense, using the conjunction *and*.
6.7   To drill conjoined active, declarative sentences with the continuum, using *and*.
6.8   To drill the response to questions conjoined by *or*.
6.9   To drill questions conjoined by *or*.

Section 7. Early Questions: *Yes/No* and *Wh-* Replacements; Tags   **372**

Lesson   Objective

7.1   To drill the *yes/no* equative question.
7.2   To drill *wh-* subject replacements in transitive and intransitive clauses.
7.3   To drill *wh-* complement replacements in equative questions.
7.4   To drill *wh-* replacement for the possessive pronoun in the determiner$_2$.
7.5   To drill *yes/no* questions involving movement of the continuum auxiliary.
7.6   To drill *yes/no* questions involving movement of the auxiliary in the continuum in clauses with *BE going to*.
7.7   To drill *wh-* object replacements in transitive questions with an auxiliary in the verb phrase.
7.8   To drill the *wh-* replacement of the adverbial complement in the equative clause.
7.9   To drill *yes/no* questions in intransitive and transitive clauses with no auxiliaries.
7.10   To drill *wh-* object replacements in transitive questions with no auxiliaries.
7.11   To drill the *wh-* replacement for adjectives.
7.12   To drill *yes/no* questions for clauses with the modal *will*.
7.13   To drill the *wh-* replacement for the adverbial of time in intransitive and transitive clauses.
7.14   To drill the *wh-* replacement for the adverbial of manner.
7.15   To drill the *yes/no* question using the modal *can*.
7.16   To drill the *yes/no* question using the modal *may*, with both affirmative and negative responses.
7.17   To drill the negative tag using the equative clause with BE.
7.18   To drill the affirmative tag in the equative clause.
7.19   To drill tag questions using transitive and intransitive verbs and the dummy DO.
7.20   To drill the tag question with the modals *can* and *will* and *must*.
7.21   To drill the pattern "*Why* (CLAUSE)?"

The Lessons

How to Use the TALK Lesson Plans

In working out the lesson plans for TALK, we have tried to be as thorough as possible. At first glance, it may look as though we have done all of the preparation work for the teacher, but nothing could be further from the truth. Successful drills require that the teacher know what will happen at each and every step along the way during the drill; nothing should be left to chance. Therefore, at the risk of appearing overprotective (and maybe even overbearing), the following list of things to do before and during all lessons is presented.

1. Read over the lesson plan before you try to use it, so that you will understand what has to be done in the lesson. Pay particular attention to the basic drill pattern which is to be used and try to see how it fits into the flow of the other lessons. The developmental continuity of the lessons is a very important feature of TALK, and the teacher should try to become familiar with the way each lesson fits in with all of the other lessons. The Contents lists all the objectives for the lessons in one place, and you should make it a habit to refer to this table often.

2. Be sure that both you and your aide know the pattern you will be working with before you begin the lesson. If you present the wrong pattern, you run the risk of wasting a whole lesson. You may change the lesson pattern if you wish, but if you change the pattern in any way without communicating to your aide what those changes are, you run the risk of creating confusion. To help out in understanding the basic drill pattern, a few examples of what it could sound like have been included in each lesson. You should not think of these examples as being limiting. They indicate only some of the possibilities for the lesson. You *must* extend (or change) the list greatly in each lesson.

If you use the lesson exactly the way it is specified, note that, in each pattern, there are certain substitutions which can be made. Which substitutions are possible are specified in the basic drill pattern. The major parts of each pattern as they are stated are invariant, however. For example, the following is one pattern that might be used in one of the lessons:

S: Ask me if that is a *(noun)*.

The changeable part of this pattern is the *(noun)*, and a number of different nouns could be used. Note what happens if the demonstrative *these* is substituted for *that* in the stimulus, however: (*a*) the verb must change from singular to plural, and (*b*) the semantic referent of the demonstrative pronoun changes, i.e., *that* refers to something physically apart from the speaker while *these* refers to something physically close to the speaker. Accordingly, the teacher who changes *that* to *these* requires the children to make two changes that they may not be ready for at that particular time. In lessons where this problem has occurred, we have seen the rhythm fall apart, and sometimes the entire lesson has broken down to the point where it was unable to be salvaged. The point is that you must realize that any seemingly minor change in the stimulus of the drill is likely to require structural changes in the children's responses that they may not be able to make. There is no reason for you not to make changes, but you must be able to specify what effects on the children's response any changes will have *before* you make adjustments in the basic drill pattern.

3. Know exactly what materials you will need before the lesson begins, and arrange them so that you can reach them easily and quickly. It is difficult to pull things out of a shopping bag and keep a good tempo going while doing so, for example. Much better results have been obtained by laying out the objects (puppets, flannel board materials, etc.) beforehand. You might want to pull a small table beside you for this purpose.

It might also be worthwhile for you to put the vocabulary you will use in pencil on the same page that contains the basic drill pattern, especially if you are not going to be using any objects in the lesson. It is inevitable that you will fumble for a word once in a while, and it is better for the rhythm of the lesson if you have something to which you can refer when you get into this position.

4. If the children take a long time to catch on to a particular pattern, don't be afraid to break the monotony by going on to the next lesson for a couple of days, or to drop back to a lesson the children have already done successfully. Keep recycling back through the lessons until the children have mastered them. In general, do not consider a lesson completed until all (or almost all) of your children have shown that they can do it successfully, even if you leave it for another lesson. You can always return to an incomplete lesson. Remember there may always be some children in a group who will have to recycle all the way back through the lesson again before they finally catch on.

5. Do not let the fact that the lessons have numbers "throw you" in relation to time. You cannot expect three lessons to be done in 3 days unless your children do not need TALK. In fact, we have had to spend as much as 2 weeks or more on one lesson before it began to filter through to some low-functioning children. In this time we recycled back and forth through the lessons in an attempt to keep things from becoming boring for the teacher, and the perseverance paid off.

6. It is very important to try to work out dialogue drills as quickly as possible. As soon as your children can handle it, take two patterns from a section and put them together in a single drill. The lessons in each section are arranged in such a way that this task should be relatively easy in most cases. In the early sections, dialogue drills are specified for you. Remember that the primary function of any language is conversation, and that conversation rarely consists of a single stimulus-response exchange. The more you can get several basic drill patterns into a single drill, the more natural and less forced the drill becomes.

7. There are many drills which combine two or more drills into a single pattern. In some of these drills the mixing of functions or fillers of a function may be too much for the children to handle. For example, in the case of some of the pronouns, first, second, and third person pronouns are mixed right from their introduction. It may be necessary to break lessons like these down into several different drills, each concentrating on only a single filler, until the children can handle each filler separately. Then, once they are able to do so, the basic drill pattern can be drilled as it is stated. Do not hesitate to do anything that will help your children learn, and if a pattern contains too much, simply break it down to a form that can be handled.

8. Above all, remember that you can teach a child a pattern in the drill, but to teach him how and where to use that pattern in his daily life you must help him to carry that pattern over into the real world. As you get used to the pattern for each drill, you will find innumerable places during the child's day in which the pattern can be put to use. If you try to get the child to use the pattern in those places, whether it is in the lunchline or in an arithmetic lesson, he will find that the language lessons have a connection to reality. If you do not carry the patterns out of the drills and into the child's real world, however, you will be doing nothing more than teaching him to parrot meaningless forms. Without a conscious attempt on your part to make the connection between the drill and daily living, there will be little or no transfer from TALK to conversation. Your work will have been all for nothing then, and you will have wasted both your time and that of your children, which you cannot afford to do.

Language Song

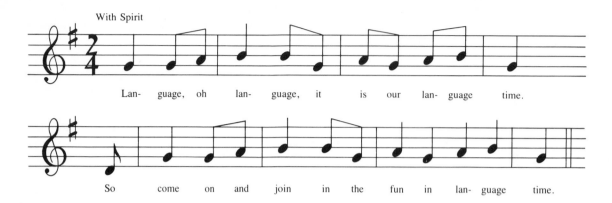

With Spirit

Lan- guage, oh lan- guage, it is our lan- guage time.

So come on and join in the fun in lan- guage time.

Checklist for a
TALK Lesson

1. Do you know and understand the pattern for today's drill? _____
2. Do you see how it fits in with all of the other lessons? _____
3. Do you have all of the necessary objects and materials for today's lesson? _____
4. Are they readily available for use during the lesson? _____
5. Will any of your objects or materials cause the pattern for today's drill to be changed (even "slightly")? _____
6. Do you have a list of vocabulary items ready? _____
7. Will any of these words cause the pattern to change? _____

Terms and Symbols Used in TALK Lessons

When one of the following terms appears in a pattern, choose an appropriate item or construction from the class indicated and insert it into the pattern at the point indicated.

adjective: refers to class of items that can fill the loose-knit modifier slot in the noun phrase, e.g., *red, big, rough*

adverbial: refers to the optional slot in the clause construction that can be filled by:

> *adverbial*$_{time}$: *now, then,* or any other word or construction that responds to the question *when*
>
> *adverbial*$_{place}$: *here, there,* or any other word or construction that responds to the question *where*
>
> *adverbial*$_{manner}$: *in this fashion, quickly,* or any other word or construction that responds to the question *how*

AUX: shorthand notation used to refer to all auxiliaries in the verb phrase:

MODALS, HAVE, BE.

BE: shorthand notation used to refer to all of the following forms:

am	was
are	were
is	be

CLAUSE: refers to any construction that fills the following definitions:

$$\pm \text{ subject} + \text{predicate} \pm \text{indirect object} \pm \left\{ \begin{array}{l} \text{complement} \\ \text{direct object} \end{array} \right\}$$

complement: refers to the obligatory slot in the equative clause that can be filled by a proper name, an adjective phrase, a pronoun, a noun phrase, or an *adverbial*$_{place}$ (see CLAUSE)

DO: shorthand notation used to refer to the following forms:

do   does   did

HAVE: shorthand notation used to refer to the following forms:

have   has   had

name: proper name of any person, e.g., *Johnny, Mrs. Jones*

NEG: refers to any of the forms of the negative that are attached to the function that carries tense in the verb phrase

noun: refers to the class of items that can fill the head function in the noun phrase, e.g., *snow, chair, pipe.* The variant, *nouns,* refers to the noun inflected for plurality.

object: refers to an obligatory slot in the transitive clause. It can be filled by proper nouns, pronouns, or noun phrases. Most objects will be direct objects, but indirect objects can also appear in the patterns (see CLAUSE).

pronoun: refers to any one of the following classes of items:
personal pronouns:

I	we	me	us
you	you	you	you
he, she, it	they	him, her, it	them

determiner$_2$ possessive pronouns:

my	our
your	your
his, her, its	their

noun substitute possessive pronouns:

mine	ours
yours	yours
his, hers, its	theirs

ROLE: refers to the name for stereotypic job roles played by people, e.g., nurse, teacher, mailcarrier

subject: refers to the obligatory slot in the clause that can be filled by proper names, pronouns, or noun phrases (see CLAUSE).

thing: refers to any object in common use that can be used as a physical prompt for a vocabulary item, often a noun, e.g., *block, pencil,* pictures of objects.

verb: refers to the class of items that can fill the head function in the verb phrase, e.g., *run, see.* The following variants also appear:

> *verb* -ing: verb inflected for present participle
> *verb* -ed: verb inflected for past tense
> *verb* -en: verb inflected for past participle

YES/NO QUESTION: refers to any *yes/no* question in the language that fits the sense of the drill pattern.

Symbols

(   ) : Items in parentheses are those with many possible fillers, e.g., *(noun), (verb).*

$\left\{\ \right\}$: Items in brackets indicate that there are two or more items or classes of items that are mutually substitutable. Italics indicate classes of items, e.g., *adjective,* while a lack of italics indicates a specific item, e.g., me, not.

S: Designates stimulus pattern. When more than one appears, subscripts indicate order of appearance in the drill, e.g., S_1, S_2.

R: Designates response pattern. Subscripts indicate order in the drill, e.g., R_1, R_2.

R_1 or R_2: Designates mutually substitutable response pattern: Either may be used at the teacher's discretion.

GROUP: Designates subgroup in a TALK class.

item$_1$ or $_2$: Designates that choice of items is possible for this slot.

$\pm$: Designates optional slot in the pattern, e.g., $\pm$ *(object)*.

item   *item*: Indicates that one but only one of the two items must appear in
    (one but not both)   the pattern.

The Basic Intransitive and Transitive Clauses

In the first section of lesson plans we will concentrate on doing two things. The first is to introduce the children to the notion of drill: what it is and how it is done. The second is to develop the basic intransitive and transitive clause patterns.

The lessons begin by introducing the intransitive imperative pattern, because this pattern requires only the predicate for it to be fully formed. Once the children begin to drill smoothly, clausal functions will be added, one at a time, using the following sequence:

1. intransitive imperatives

2. transitive imperatives

3. intransitive declaratives

4. transitive declaratives

Note how this sequence allows us to take the simple predicate with which we begin the lessons and add first an object, then a subject, and finally, to put them all together in a single pattern.

Two other units will be introduced in this section as well. The first is the adverbial modifier in the form of the adverbial of place, and the second is the negative. Thus, by the time the children finish the drills in this section, they will be saying things such as:

Andrew eats at home.
Johnny sees a dog there.
Mary can't eat a table.

Rationale

The very first task in the TALK program is to teach the children how to drill. For some children this will not be easy, and it may take some time to accomplish; the act of sitting down in a group and taking part in a highly structured activity in unison may be quite foreign to many of them. It may take you a couple of weeks to teach a group to listen to the aide, take their cues from him, and to respond in unison or as individuals when and only when they are called on to do so. To assist this learning, we will need drills that are as simple as possible grammatically.

We get the required simplicity by beginning the drills with the intransitive imperative. It is the first construction to reach Stage IV, and it does so because of its simplicity. For one thing, the intransitive imperative clause requires only the predicate to be expressed, and for another, the verb phrase that fills the predicate requires only the head function to be expressed (tense does not appear in the imperative verb phrase). A more simple clause pattern is not possible in English.

Beginning with the intransitive imperative and adding one clausal function at a time gives us certain instructional advantages. For one thing, we will follow the natural sequence of clausal acquisition that all children seem to go through, and one lesson flows into another. We also are able to help smooth out the learning of "how to drill" by beginning with the imperative and having the children give commands to each other. This technique gives them some action early in the program; they say something and something happens as a result of their having said it. The drills are then fun to do right from the beginning. Life does not consist of always giving commands, however, and the children will need to move on to the declaratives as soon as possible. Declaratives will help them to learn to talk about the things they need to talk about by teaching them the most often used conversational patterns in the language.

The Lessons

The vocabulary in the first section of lesson plans is to be kept simple. All subject functions will be filled by either names of people or the pronouns *he* or *she*. All verb phrases are to be filled using only the head function, which will be filled by a single verb, or by a two-word verb that acts like a single word (*stand up, sit down*). The only exception to this will be made when we add the negative to the verb phrase; this exception will consist only of the forms *can't* or *don't*. All objects will also be simple. At the most they will consist of a determiner$_2$ filled by the articles *a* or *the,* and a noun. The adverbials will all be adverbials of place, filled either by the word *there,* or a simple prepositional phrase using *in* or *on* and a noun phrase. Such simplicity is necessary. There will be plenty of opportunity to develop complexity in future sections. For now, the important thing is to get the clausal functions firmly established so that they can be used as matrices within which that complexity can be taught.

The lesson plans in this section may prove to be easy for some groups and quite difficult for some others. You should go through the lessons as quickly as your children are able. As soon as one lesson is going smoothly, move on to the next. As soon as you can, begin to mix patterns from one lesson in with those from another. Lessons 1.6 and 1.13 are formally structured as dialogues. If your children can handle lessons in which the patterns from two or more drills can be mixed, however, do not wait until you get to the formal dialogues to begin doing so. Conversely, if your children have trouble mixing more than one pattern into a drill, break the drill down into smaller units, drill those units separately until the children can handle each part, and then bring the parts together in a single drill (see Note 4, Lesson 1.5). Remember that any time your children begin to have trouble with a drill, they are telling you that they have something to learn. You must do some thinking at that point and find out what it is that is giving them difficulty. If a pattern is too complex, you must break it down into smaller steps that they can handle more easily.

Finally, remember to look for situations outside of the drill where you can get your children to use the patterns they are learning in the drill. The drill exists simply to teach the children the patterns. Teaching them how and where to use the patterns requires you to be in the real world, where these patterns are used to communicate an idea.

LESSON 1.1

Objectives: 1. To teach the children how to drill.

  2. To drill the intransitive imperative clause pattern.

Materials: None needed.

Basic Drill Pattern:

S: Tell me to (*verb*).
R: (*Verb*)!

Method: The children order the teacher to do something and the teacher does it.

Examples:

Teacher:	(demonstrates drill with aide)
Teacher:	Tell me to stand up.
Aide and children:	Stand up!
Teacher:	Tell me to sit down.
Aide and children:	Sit down!
Teacher:	Tell me to look up.
Aide and children:	Look up!
Teacher:	Tell me to wave.
Aide and children:	Wave!

Things to Look Out For:

1. The children will find this drill to be a lot of fun if their commands get results. If the teacher tells the children to give a command, and if they do give it, they deserve to see it carried out. Do what the children tell you to do when they tell you to do it.

2. Be careful to choose vocabulary that will allow you to carry out the commands without having to use up a lot of time doing it. There are a large number of intransitive verbs that can be used in this lesson. Some examples are *wave, wiggle, blink,* and *scratch,* as well as all of the words that indicate animal noises: *meow, bark, moo,* and *grunt.*

3. Note that there are also a number of intransitive verbs with particles that can be used in this lesson: *stand up, sit down, look around, look up,* and *look down.* There are also a number of others that could be used if the situation presents itself, especially outside of the lesson proper: *come in, go out, get out,* and *lie down.* It would be very difficult to use the latter group of verbs in a TALK lesson without destroying the rhythm of the lesson because the actions take too much time to accomplish. They should be avoided unless a puppet (we call ours Otto) is used to serve as the object of the commands. In this case the stimulus will change slightly:

S: Tell Otto (or: him) to lie down.
R: Lie down!

4. You may be pleasantly surprised to find that your children can do this pattern almost as soon as it is introduced. If they can, do not feel any hesitation about going on to the next lesson immediately, i.e., you can add the vocative as soon as the children can handle it. In fact, you should go on to drill transitive imperatives and the declarative patterns as soon as possible. The idea is to help the children become functional, not to drag our feet. If they do not need to go slowly, no purpose is served in doing so.

LESSON 1.2

Objective: To drill the intransitive imperative clause pattern expressing the topic as a vocative.

Materials: You may or may not choose to use a puppet to carry out the commands.

Basic Drill Pattern:
S: Tell (*name*) to (*verb*).
R: (*Verb*), (*name*)!

Method: The children order the aide, a puppet, the teacher, or each other to do something.

Examples:

Teacher:	(demonstrates drill with aide)
Teacher:	Everybody, tell Johnny to stand up.
Aide and children:	Stand up, Johnny!
Teacher:	Tell Johnny to sit down.
Aide and children:	Sit down, Johnny!
Teacher:	Tell Sally to smile.
Aide and children:	Smile, Sally!

Things to Look Out For:

1. This pattern is exactly the one as found in Lesson 1.1, except that the vocative has been added to it. The same notes apply, and the teacher should take a look at them again.

2. It may be possible for your children to address two people at a time, e.g., Johnny and Sally. Before terminating this lesson, try to get them to do it. Do not be upset if they cannot, however, and do not push too hard if it does not come easily for them.

3. See Note 4, Lesson 1.1.

LESSON 1.3

Objective: To drill the imperative using transitive verbs.

Materials: Refer to body parts (head, hand, etc.) for this lesson.

**Basic Drill
Pattern:** S: Tell *(name)* to *(verb)* a *(noun)*.
R: *(Name)*, *(verb)* a *(noun)*!

Method: The children can order the aide, a puppet, the teacher, or each other to act upon something.

Examples: Teacher: (demonstrates drill with aide)

Teacher: Tell Otto to touch a nose.
Aide and children: Otto, touch a nose!
Teacher: Tell him to rub a head.
Aide and children: Otto, rub a head!
Teacher: Tell him to feel a cheek.
Aide and children: Otto, feel a cheek!

**Things to
Look Out For:** 1. Note that it is possible for the vocative to appear either at the *end* of the response or at the beginning. You may want to play with this response for the sake of variety once the children appear to be responding well, e.g.,

R: Rub an elbow, Otto!

2. Very young children seem to find vocabulary referring to body parts the easiest to handle. You may find that your children can handle the vocabulary for small objects (a truck, a bottle cap, a stone, a tin can, etc.). Providing this vocabulary presents no problem for the children, you may use it freely.

3. It would be easy for the teacher to slip a possessive pronoun into this pattern, but doing this could cause problems if the children must learn both possessive pronouns *and* transitive verbs. We try to hold down the number of things to be learned in each lesson in order to keep the child's task as simple as possible. Therefore, we have specified that indefinite articles be used to mark the nouns instead of the possessors. Since this article develops early, your children should have no trouble using it. If some children experience difficulty with the article, keep drilling until it comes smoothly.

4. See Note 4, Lesson 1.1.

LESSON 1.4

Objective: To drill the imperative with the negative *don't*.

Materials: Use actions or imagined actions of the children.

Basic Drill Pattern:
S: Tell (*name*) not to (*verb*) ± (*object*).
R: (*Name*), don't (*verb*) ± (*object*)!

Method:

Examples:

Teacher:	(demonstrates drill with aide)
Teacher:	Tell Sue not to smile.
Aide and children:	Sue, don't smile!
Teacher:	Tell Mary not to fall down.
Aide and children:	Mary, don't fall down!
Teacher:	Tell Joe not to touch Tom.
Aide and children:	Joe, don't touch Tom!

Note: 1. For the first time in the program, a negative appears in the basic drill pattern. *Don't* is a form that appears very early and should give the children little or no trouble. If it does give them trouble, however, drop back to the patterns used in Lessons 1.1 to 1.3 and interject the pattern for this lesson once in awhile.

2. The object is optional for this lesson. You may use either transitive verbs with an object, or intransitive verbs without an object. See Note 3, Lesson 1.1.

3. You may have trouble finding vocabulary for the predicate in this lesson. It might be fun to treat the lesson as a big game, and have the children say things like

R: Don't kiss an elephant!
R: Don't eat the chair!
etc.

LESSON 1.5

Objective: To drill the imperative with an adverbial.

Materials: Assorted small objects, some of which can be put in or on other things or places.

Basic Drill Pattern:
S: Tell (*name*) to (*verb*) ± (*object*) (*adverbial*$_{place}$).
R: (*Name*), (*verb*) ± (*object*) (*adverbial*$_{place}$)!

Method:

Examples:

Teacher:	(demonstrates drill with aide)
Teacher:	Everybody, tell Sally to put a pencil on the desk.
Aide and children:	Sally, put a pencil on the desk!
Teacher:	Everybody, tell Jack to put the ball in the cup.
Aide and children:	Jack, put the ball in the cup!
Teacher:	Everybody, tell Mary to hold the block there.
Aide and children:	Mary, hold the block there!

Things to Look Out For:

1. Although there are a number of possible adverbials of place, we will begin with only the three used in the examples: $\begin{Bmatrix} \text{In} \\ \text{On} \end{Bmatrix}$ (*article*) (*noun*); and *there*. Others will be introduced at a later point in the program.

2. Adverbials of place are easy in relation to adverbials of time and manner, and for this reason we have introduced them early in the program. They will be introduced again later, and if your children have trouble with them now, terminate this lesson and go on to the next.

3. See Note 2, Lesson 1.1.

4. It is not necessary to restrict the verbs in this drill, i.e., you may use either transitives or intransitives. If switching back and forth causes problems for your children (and it should not), split the lesson into two parts, one drilling intransitives and the other drilling transitives. Drill each separately until the drills go smoothly, and then begin to mix the two patterns.

LESSON 1.6

Objectives: 1. Review.

        2. To teach the children and teacher how to use the dialogue drill.

Materials: Use the same materials that you used in Lessons 1.1–1.5.

**Basic Drill
Pattern:** S$_1$: Tell (*name*) to (*verb*) ± (*object*) ± (*adverbial*).
R$_1$: (*Name*), (*verb*) ± (*object*) ± (*adverbial*)!
S$_2$: Tell him not to (*verb*) ± (*object*) ± (*adverbial*).
R$_2$: Don't (*verb*) ± (*object*) ± (*adverbial*)!

Method: The method is a simple combination of all of the drills used in previous lessons. You may add objects, adverbials, or the negative as you choose. The drill should be connected from S–R couplet to S–R couplet, however.

Examples:

Teacher:	(demonstrates drill with aide)
Teacher:	Tell Johnny to stand up.
Aide and children:	Johnny, stand up!
Teacher:	Tell him to sit down.
Aide and children:	Sit down!
Teacher:	Tell him to hold a nose.
Aide and children:	Hold a nose!
Teacher:	Tell him not to let go.
Aide and children:	Don't let go!

**Things to
Look Out For:** 1. See Note 4, Lesson 1.1.

        2. See Note 3, Lesson 1.4.

        3. Note how the negative becomes easier to insert when there is some connected dialogue going on.

LESSON 1.7

Objective: To drill the declarative using intransitive verbs.

Materials: Common tools (or pictures of them), such as a knife, a fork, a saw, or other common objects which require intransitive verbs to describe their use, such as a pencil, a cup, etc.

Basic Drill Pattern:

S: What does (*name*) do with this?

R: $\begin{Bmatrix} He \\ She \end{Bmatrix}$ (*verbs*).

Method: Teacher holds up object so that all the children can see it and presents stimulus.

Examples:

Teacher:	(demonstrates drill with aide)
Teacher:	(Holds up fork.) What does Johnny do with this?
Aide and children:	He eats.
Teacher:	(Holds up hearing aid.) What does Frankie do with this?
Aide and children:	He hears.
Teacher:	(Holds up cup.) What does Jeff do with this?
Aide and children:	He drinks.

Things to Look Out For:

1. The stimulus pattern specifies that the pronouns *he* or *she* will be used to fill the subject function. For children who need this lesson, it may be too soon to introduce them. If your children experience difficulty with them, switch immediately to using proper names:

R: Johnny eats.
R: Frankie writes.
R: Jeff drinks.

2. Be sure to use intransitive verbs referring to action that the children know about, e.g., *sit, walk, drink, eat, cut, saw, read, write*.

3. If the children seem to be able to do this pattern easily, go directly to Lesson 1.8, which simply adds adverbials of place to the same pattern.

4. You may find that your children do not use the third person singular verb inflection with the proper noun subject. Do not worry about it. It is typical for very young children to say things like

R: Johnny swim.
R: Mary swim.

This is of no concern at this time because the inflection will be drilled later in the program.

LESSON 1.8

Objective: To drill the declarative pattern with intransitive verbs and adverbials of place.

Materials: Use the same type of materials that were used in Lesson 1.7. You may also use actions that the children do every day.

Basic Drill Pattern:

S: Where does $\begin{Bmatrix} ROLE \\ name \end{Bmatrix}$ (verb)?

R: $\begin{Bmatrix} Name \\ ROLE \\ He \\ She \end{Bmatrix}$ (verbs) (adverbial$_{place}$).

Method: If you use pictures of people playing roles, hold them up and give the person in the picture a name or a role title, e.g., *John, Mr. Jones, the nurse*. Ask the children where that person carries out his role. If you use actions of the children for vocabulary, no materials are needed.

Examples:

Teacher:	(demonstrates drill with aide)
Teacher:	Everybody, where does the nurse work?
Aide and children:	She works in the hospital.
Teacher:	Where does Mother cook?
Aide and children:	She cooks in the kitchen.
Teacher:	Where does Johnny play?
Aide and children:	He plays in the playground.

Things to Look Out For:

1. The kinds of adverbials to use in this lesson are those that specify where something happens, e.g., *in school, in the classroom, on the sidewalk, here, there*. Again, limit the prepositions to *in, on, here* and *there*. See Note 2, Lesson 1.5.

2. Review all notes for Lesson 1.7.

LESSON 1.9

Objective: To drill the intransitive declarative with a negative.

Materials: No concrete materials are needed for this lesson. Use actions that the children cannot do (and that they know they cannot do) or that they will not do.

Basic Drill
Pattern: S: Can (*name*) (*verb*)?
R_1: No, (*name*) can't (*verb*).
or:
R_2: *Yes,* $\left\{ \begin{array}{c} he \\ she \end{array} \right\}$ *(verbs).*

Method: Simply quiz the children about possible or impossible actions following the basic drill pattern. Treat the drill as a game (see Lesson 1.4) by asking the group if one child can carry out an action. Try to get the child named to shake his head "yes" or "no" to give the group the cue to respond.

Examples:

Teacher:	(demonstrates drill with aide)
Teacher:	Everybody, can Johnny fly?
Aide and children:	No, he can't fly.
Teacher:	Can Ralph drive?
Aide and children:	No, he can't drive.
Teacher:	Can Sally wink?
Aide and children:	Yes, she winks.

Things to
Look Out For: 1. Be careful to choose actions carefully. It is rather easy to threaten a child by saying aloud that he *can't* do something. This whole drill should be couched in the spirit of mischievous fun. Otherwise some child may get hurt feelings.

2. Note that the negative used is *can't*. This word should not present too much difficulty, however, because young children usually seem to learn it as a negative form at a very early age. You cannot expect your children to use *can,* however, if they are functioning at such a level as to need lessons in basic declarative clause patterns. The contrast between *can* and *can't* requires the child to understand both the negative and modals. Many children will not be ready for such a contrast at this point.

3. See Note 1, Lesson 1.7.

4. See Note 4, Lesson 1.7.

LESSON 1.10

Objective: To drill the declarative using the transitive verbs *see, hear, feel*.

Materials: Pictures of familiar objects, animals, and possibly, of people in familiar roles, such as a nurse or police officer. Real objects may also be used for this drill, as well as objects that can be heard or felt.

Basic Drill Pattern:

S: What does (*name*) $\left\{ \begin{array}{l} \text{see} \\ \text{hear} \\ \text{feel} \end{array} \right\}$?

R: $\left\{ \begin{array}{l} \text{He} \\ \text{She} \end{array} \right\}$ $\left\{ \begin{array}{l} \text{sees} \\ \text{hears} \\ \text{feels} \end{array} \right\}$ (*object*).

Method: The teacher holds pictures of objects in the view of everybody and asks what one of the children sees; or he may make a noise with an object and ask what a child hears; or he may touch a child with an object and ask what the child feels. If pictures are used, ask what a child sees.

Examples:

Teacher:	(demonstrates drill with aide)
Teacher:	What does Johnny see?
Aide and children:	He sees a ball.
Teacher:	What does Mary hear?
Aide and children:	She hears a bell.
Teacher:	What does Maxie feel?
Aide and children:	He feels a rock.

Things to Look Out For:

1. You can extend this drill in many ways. For example, a shopping bag full of small objects can be a grab bag: A child reaches into the bag, pulls out an object, holds it up, and the teacher asks

S: What does (*name*) $\left\{ \begin{array}{l} \text{have} \\ \text{hold} \end{array} \right\}$?

Note that in all patterns for this chapter, the stimulus pattern specifies all vocabulary for the child before we ask him to use it in the response. It is all right to be creative and vary the basic drill pattern somewhat, but be careful not to make it a guessing game. This is all too easy when using a stimulus like

S: What does (*name*) do?

The possible responses to this stimulus are infinite, and it should be avoided.

2. See Note 1, Lesson 1.7.

3. See Note 4, Lesson 1.7.

4. If the children handle this pattern easily, go directly to Lesson 1.11 and begin adding adverbials of place.

LESSON 1.11

Objective: To drill the transitive declarative using an adverbial of place.

Materials: No concrete materials required. Use actions from the daily lives of the children.

Basic Drill Pattern: S: Where does *(name)* *(verb)* *(object)?*
R: *(Name)* *(verbs)* *(object)* *(adverbial* place*).*

Method: Quiz the children about their daily actions following the basic drill pattern.

Example:

Teacher:	(demonstrates drill with aide)
Teacher:	Everybody, where does Johnny use the soap?
Aide and children:	He uses the soap in the bathroom.
Teacher:	Where does Sally wash the dishes?
Aide and children:	She washes the dishes in the sink.
Teacher:	Where does Herman feed the fish?
Aide and children:	He feeds the fish in the fish tank.

Things to Look Out For:

1. Choose vocabulary carefully. The teacher who has the children do a number of chores regularly will find it easy to do this lesson. See Note 2, Lesson 1.5.

2. One adverbial that can be used throughout this lesson is the phrase *over there* accompanied by a pointing gesture. There is nothing wrong with using this adverbial throughout the lesson, although we suggest using prepositional phrases, too. The goal of the lesson is to teach the children to pattern the adverbial of place, not to teach specific vocabulary. Some low-functioning children may well be limited to pointing accompanied by this phrase.

3. See Note 1, Lesson 1.7.

4. See Note 1, Lesson 1.8.

LESSON 1.12

Objective: To drill the declarative negative pattern using a transitive verb.

Materials: No concrete materials are required for this lesson. Use actions that the children do not do.

Basic Drill Pattern:

S: Can *(name) (verb) (object)?*

R: No, $\begin{Bmatrix} \text{he} \\ \text{she} \end{Bmatrix}$ can't *(verb) (object)*.

Method: Quiz the children about actions they will not or cannot do, following the basic drill pattern.

Examples:

Teacher:	(demonstrates drill with aide)
Teacher:	Everybody, can Johnny wiggle his hair?
Aide and children:	No, he can't wiggle his hair.
Teacher:	Can Janey build a city?
Aide and children:	No, she can't build a city.
Teacher:	Can Ludwig wear a dress?
Aide and children:	No, he can't wear a dress.

Things to Look Out For:

1. See Note 1, Lesson 1.7.

2. See Note 1, Lesson 1.9.

3. See Note 2, Lesson 1.9.

LESSON 1.13

Objective: To review the declaratives in a dialogue drill.

Materials: Materials similar to those used in the rest of Chapter 1.

Basic Drill
Pattern: S_1: What does *(name)* do with this?

R_1: $\left\{\begin{array}{c} \text{He} \\ \text{She} \end{array}\right\}$ *(verbs)*.

S_2: Where does *(name) (verb)?*

R_2: $\left\{\begin{array}{c} \text{He} \\ \text{She} \end{array}\right\}$ *(verbs) (adverbial*$_{\text{place}}$*)*.

S_3: What does *(name) (verb)?*

R_3: $\left\{\begin{array}{c} \text{He} \\ \text{She} \end{array}\right\}$ *(verbs) (object)*.

S_4: Does *(name) (verb) (object) (adverbial*$_{\text{place}}$*)?*

R_4: Yes, $\left\{\begin{array}{c} \text{he} \\ \text{she} \end{array}\right\}$ *(verbs) (object) (adverbial*$_{\text{place}}$*)*.

S_5: Can *(name) (verb) (object)?*

R_5: No, $\left\{\begin{array}{c} \text{he} \\ \text{she} \end{array}\right\}$ can't *(verb) (object)*.

Method: Combine some or all of the above patterns in a connected flow.

Examples:

Teacher:	(demonstrates drill with aide)
Teacher:	Everybody, what does Johnny do with this?
Aide and children:	He eats.
Teacher:	Where does Johnny eat?
Aide and children:	He eats at the table.
Teacher:	What does Johnny eat?
Aide and children:	He eats food.
Teacher:	Does Johnny eat food at a table?
Aide and children:	Yes, he eats food at a table.
Teacher:	Can Johnny eat the table?
Aide and children:	No, he can't eat the table.

Things to
Look Out For: 1. Note that there are not many verbs that can be both transitive and intransitive, and that you may not be able to develop a full dialogue each time you try. If a verb does not fit all the patterns, break the dialogue where it is necessary and change verbs. You probably will want to change the name of the child at the same time.

2. Review all notes for each basic drill pattern in Section 1.

SECTION 2

The Continuum, Equative, and Subject Pronouns

The drills in Section 2 assume that the children now have control over the basic clausal functions in intransitive and transitive clauses. In the lessons that follow, we will begin to drill some of the complexities of the verb phrase.

The specific verb phrase function that will be introduced in this section is the continuum. The lessons for this function begin with the third singular subject and the *is* form of the BE auxiliary. Once the children can respond smoothly with the continuum, *is* will also be introduced into the head of the verb phrase in the equative clause. Once the children are able to handle *is*, the other present tense forms of BE (*am, are*) will be introduced. Again, they will first be drilled as auxiliaries in the continuum function, and then as fillers of the head in the verb phrase of the equative clause. While these forms are being drilled, we will also use the negative.

In addition to these verb forms, the following personal pronouns will also be introduced into the drills in this section: *I, we, you, they* and *it*.

Rationale

Once the basic clausal functions of the intransitive and transitive clauses reach Stage IV status, children have a matrix within which they can learn the complexities of the verb and noun phrases. The first verb phrase function to appear is the continuum with the third singular present tense auxiliary. The equative predicate with *is* appears soon after, and then the other present tense forms of BE make their appearance, first in the continuum, and then in the equative predicate. It is this sequence that is followed here.

Before any of the other forms of BE can appear, certain personal pronouns must develop. It is impossible to use *am* or *are* in any sensical way without having the subjective personal pronouns *I, we, you* and *they* available to indicate that these forms are required. Therefore, in order to introduce *am* and *are,* we must first make sure that the children know these pronouns. To assist in their acquisition, we will use the intransitive and transitive clause patterns that were drilled in Section 1. As long as we are working on pronouns, we will also introduce *it* to fill out the subjective personal pronoun paradigm.

Since the negative is attached to whatever carries tense, we will include negation with the drills on the continuum and the equative. Before the drills in this section are completed, it may even be possible for some children to begin contracting the negative to BE. We will try it even though it may not work out too well for some children this early in the program.

The Lessons

Some of the drills in this section are actually several drills rolled up into one. Lesson 2.7, for example, specifies a single basic drill pattern for all of the pronouns included in the drill. It may prove to be necessary to break this drill (and some of the others) down into a number of subdrills in which each form specified in the basic drill pattern is drilled separately. Other drills have just the opposite problem: They may be too specific. Lesson 2.3, for example, has no variants at all. Some groups may get bored by this drill, and in those instances it will be necessary to go on rather quickly.

One way or another, some of the drills in this section are likely to be too wide in their specifications, and some are likely to be too narrow. In either case it will be necessary for the teacher to make adjustments. If such adjustments do prove to be necessary, the children will let you know what they are: They will have problems in shifting from one form of the basic drill pattern to another, or they will whip right through the pattern too easily. Listen to them and make the adjustments as necessary.

Most of the drills in this section will probably prove to be at just about the right degree of complexity, however, and you should find that the children are making regular progress as they go through them; do not forget to take the function or construction they are learning at the moment (and have been learning in the recent past) out of the drills and into the children's daily lives. Move on as quickly as the children's ability will allow, and as slowly as they require. As usual, wherever it is possible, mix drill patterns from one lesson in with the patterns from another lesson or lessons. Lessons 2.6 and 2.13 were written to help you do this, but you should not wait for these lessons to begin if the children are capable of handling more than one pattern in a drill.

LESSON 2.1

Objective: To drill the present tense continuum with the third person singular present auxiliary.

Materials: Use pictures, pairs of objects, or pantomimed actions by the children themselves. All actions used must be clearly recognized and named by the children.

Basic Drill Pattern:

S: What is $\left\{\begin{array}{l} \text{he} \\ \text{she} \\ \text{the } noun \end{array}\right\}$ doing?

R: $\left\{\begin{array}{l} \text{He} \\ \text{She} \\ \text{It} \end{array}\right\}$ is (verb -ing) ± (object)

Method: Tell the children to *Do this,* and then do something (e.g., smile, wave) that can be used as the topic of the children's reponse. Pictures of people or animals engaged in actions that the children recognize can be used.

Examples:

Teacher:	(demonstrates drill with aide)
Teacher:	What is the dog doing?
Aide and children:	It is eating.
Teacher:	What is the lady doing?
Aide and children:	She is swatting flies.
Teacher:	What is the man doing?
Aide and children:	He is digging.
Teacher:	What is the airplane doing?
Aide and children:	It is flying.

Things to Look Out For:

1. Rhythm is going to be very important in the drills on the continuum and the equative. In this drill, for example, the tendency of naive children is to respond as follows:

R: She eating.
R: He holding ball.

The rhythm of the response we want to hear is different, i.e., there is an extra "beat":

R: She is eating.
R: He is holding a ball.

Children will need to feel this extra beat before they begin to put in the auxiliary. In spite of its importance to this pattern, however, it would be a serious mistake to dwell so heavily on rhythm that the melody of the response is lost. You will have to tread that fine line between making the auxiliary clear and destroying the language. Be careful.

2. Note the introduction of the pronoun *it*. You should not experience any difficulty using it.

3. Be very careful when using pictures or performing actions to elicit responses from the children. It is very easy to be obscure, and the children should not have to guess at what word they are supposed to use. You may want to take a few moments before the lesson begins to demonstrate actions or pictures and the vocabulary that goes with them.

LESSON 2.2

Objective: To drill the negative in the continuum.

Materials: Use the same kinds of materials suggested for Lesson 2.1.

Basic Drill Pattern:

S_1: Is $\begin{Bmatrix} \text{the } noun \\ pronoun \\ name \end{Bmatrix}$ (*verb* -ing) ± (*object*)?

R_1: $\begin{Bmatrix} \text{Yes} \\ \text{No} \end{Bmatrix}$, (*pronoun*) $\begin{Bmatrix} \text{is} \\ \text{is not} \end{Bmatrix}$ (*verb* -ing) ± (*object*).

S_2: (If R_1 is negative): What is (*pronoun*) doing?

R_2: (*Pronoun*) is (*verb* -ing) ± (*object*).

Method: Do this lesson the same way you did Lesson 2.1. Use S_2 and R_2 only when R_1 is a negative response. The (*pronoun*) in the pattern can be *he, she, it* just as in Lesson 2.1.

Examples:

Teacher:	(demonstrates drill with aide)
Teacher:	Sue, do this (demonstrates). Is she patting the desk?
Aide and children:	No, she is not patting the desk.
Teacher:	What is she doing?
Aide and children:	She is shaking a finger.
Teacher:	Is she running?
Aide and children:	No, she is not running.
Teacher:	What is she doing?
Aide and children:	She is sitting.
Teacher:	Is she listening to us?
Aide and children:	Yes, she is listening to us.

Things to Look Out For:

1. See Notes 1 and 3, Lesson 2.1.

2. The examples show how one child (or the aide) can be used as the topic of something approaching connected discourse. This technique is very good to use because such a drill contains text of a much higher order than those with simple S–R patterns. Nevertheless, it is not necessary to do it the way the examples suggest, i.e., you can use a different child or picture for each response. At this point in the program, the major task is to present the continuum function, and many children at this level may not be able to handle this much connected discourse yet.

3. For some groups it might be best to stick with pictures of people in action. It is easy to get into drill patterns that require the determiner₂ possessive pronoun:

S: Is she holding *her* foot?

This stimulus would be fine for children who can handle the possessive, but it can be disruptive to children who cannot. The rule to follow is this: Try it; if it causes no problems, continue. If it causes problems, stick with the pictures and actions not requiring the possessive. Lessons on the possessive pronouns appear later in the program if they need to be taught.

4. Be sure to include affirmative responses in the drill. A drill with all negative responses in it is not only boring, it is unreal and requires useless work on the part of the children.

The Continuum, Equative, and Subject Pronouns   **289**

LESSON 2.3

Objective: To drill the equative clause pattern with the third person singular subject.

Materials: Only things known to the children. With very young or very low-functioning children we have found it best to begin with body parts, especially parts of the head. Once you start getting responses, you can work down and out to the trunk, limbs, and extremities before going on to clothing and objects in the room. Many groups will be able to respond to pictures.

Basic Drill Pattern:
S: What is that?
R: It is a (*noun*).

Method: Hold up objects or point to body parts, articles of clothing, etc., and ask questions following the basic drill pattern.

Examples:

Teacher:	(demonstrates drill with aide)
Teacher:	Everybody, what is that?
Aide and children:	It is a nose.
Teacher:	Everybody, what is that?
Aide and children:	It is a chin.
Teacher:	What is that?
Aide and children:	It is a cheek.

Things to Look Out For:

1. When using the demonstrative adjective *that,* it is important to recognize that it refers to things relatively remote from the speaker and/or listener (the children will be taught to distinguish between *this* and *that,* as well as *these* and *those* at a later point). Use *that* only when you are pointing to or holding up something that is about an arm's length or more away from you.

2. It is also possible to use familiar classroom objects or flannel board materials as stimulus objects. Just be sure that all vocabulary items are within the knowledge of the children.

3. It may take a while to get the children to respond with the full pattern in this lesson, especially if your children are very young and/or very low functioning. To inject a little variety, go on to Lesson 2.4 within a few days from the time you begin to drill this lesson. You can also return to Lessons 2.1 and 2.2 if you like. Come back to this one as long as you need to.

4. Some of the children, especially if they are well along in their learning, may want to respond with the contraction, *it's.* Do not allow this response. Use of the contraction sets up a rhythm in the response that can allow a slower child to continue saying "It a (*noun*)." Once *all* of the children can use the full form, we will require them to contract because that is the way we do it in conversation. For now, however, it is forbidden.

LESSON 2.4

Objective: To drill the equative clause pattern in the negative.

Materials: The same type of materials that you used in Lesson 2.3 can be used in this lesson.

Basic Drill
Pattern: S: Is that a (*noun*)?

R: $\begin{Bmatrix} \text{Yes} \\ \text{No} \end{Bmatrix}$, it $\begin{Bmatrix} \text{is} \\ \text{is not} \end{Bmatrix}$ a (*noun*).

Method: Introduce the drill with the aide and run choral drills using familiar objects as stimuli.

Examples:

Teacher:	(demonstrates drill with aide)
Teacher:	Everybody, is that a shirt?
Aide and children:	No, it is not a shirt.
Teacher:	Is that a shoe?
Aide and children:	No, it is not a shoe.
Teacher:	Is that a foot?
Aide and children:	Yes, it is a foot.

Things to
Look Out For:

1. Remember that in this lesson, the children are not asked to name the things you point to. Rather, they must simply negate or affirm the stimulus pattern. If, however, they volunteer additional information following the negation, e.g., "No, it is not a face, it is an arm," they are simply indicating that they are ahead of you. This response does no harm, and you can accept it when offered (as long as it does not hurt the rhythm of the drill).

2. After drilling this lesson and the previous ones, you *may* feel that your children may have learned enough about *is* to begin contracting. You may change the response of the basic drill pattern *if* you feel that the children can handle it, but be alert for problems. You may find, for example, that some children actually resist contracting and may even fall back to deleting the *is,* i.e., "That a dog." If they begin to do this, stop contracting immediately; these children are telling you that they do not yet have control over *is.* Simple resistance is another matter. When you begin introducing contractions, you will be, in effect, introducing a completely new lesson, and it can take time for some children to learn it; you should have no trouble telling whether or not there is a problem.

LESSON 2.5

Objective: To drill the equative clause pattern contrasting affirmative and negative responses.

Materials: The same materials as used in Lesson 2.3 are to be used in this lesson. Again, new materials may be added at your option, but they should be objects which are familiar to most of the children.

Basic Drill Pattern:
S: Is that a ($noun_1$)?
R_1: No, it is not a ($noun_1$), it is a ($noun_2$).
or
R_2: Yes, it is a ($noun_1$).

Method: Hold up or point to the objects you are using and present the stimulus.

Examples:

Teacher:	(demonstrates drill with aide)
Teacher:	Is that a leg?
Aide and children:	No, it is not a leg, it is a chin.
Teacher:	Is that a face?
Aide and children:	Yes, it is a face.
Teacher:	Is that a finger?
Aide and children:	Yes, it is a finger.
Teacher:	Is that a book?
Aide and children:	No, it is not a book, it is a pencil.

Things to Look Out For:

1. Many of the children will want to respond "No, it is a ($noun_2$)." While this is a perfectly good response in the adult grammar, it does not tell us whether or not the child can put together the two responses as specified. Do not allow such a response at this time. Later it will be acceptable, but only after everyone has demonstrated his ability to give the full response for this lesson.

2. If the children have difficulty joining the two responses, review Lessons 2.1, 2.2, 2.3, and 2.4 in a brief dialogue drill (see Lesson 2.6) and try again. Use the aide for demonstrating the desired response as often as necessary. Do not stay too long on this lesson, however.

3. If the children are getting proficient in using this drill pattern, allow them to ellipt R_2:
   S: Is that a ($noun_1$)?
   R_2: Yes, it is.

4. See Note 2, Lesson 2.4.

LESSON 2.6

Objective: To review the response patterns for Lesson 2.3–2.5 in a dialogue.

Materials: Use the same materials used in Lessons 2.3–2.5. Do not introduce any new materials.

Basic Drill Pattern:
S_1: What is that?
R_1: It is a (*noun₁*).
S_2: (Different object)   Is that a (*noun₂*)?
R_2: Yes, it is a (*noun₂*).
S_3: Is that a (*noun₁*)?
R_3: No, it is not a (*noun₁*).
S_4: What is it then?
R_4: It is a (*noun₂*).
S_5: Say the whole thing. Is it a (*noun₁*)?
R_5: No, it is not a (*noun₁*), it is a (*noun₂*).

Method: Contrast two objects, represented by (*noun₁*) and (*noun₂*).

Examples:

Teacher:	(demonstrates drill with aide)
Teacher:	What is that?
Aide and children:	It is a dog.
Teacher:	Is that a cat?
Aide and children:	Yes, it is a cat.
Teacher:	(Points to cat.) Is that a dog?
Aide and children:	No, it is not a dog.
Teacher:	What is it, then?
Aide and children:	It is a cat.
Teacher:	Say the whole thing. Is it a dog?
Aide and children:	No, it is not a dog, it is a cat.

Things to Look Out For:

1. If any of the children seem to be having trouble with this drill, it should be quite easy for you to identify where they are having problems and to drop back to a previous lesson to drill the specific pattern required.

2. The teacher should feel free to make up other drills to elicit any of the above response patterns. Be careful, though, that any drills you make up are possible in American English. Do not make up drills for features that will come later.

4. See Note 2, Lesson 2.4.

5. See Note 3, Lesson 2.5.

LESSON 2.7

Objective: To drill the subjective personal pronouns *I, you, we, they* in intransitive and transitive clause patterns.

Materials: Use ordinary objects from the "junk box." You can also use current or remembered actions from the teacher's, aide's, and children's daily lives as long as they pose no conceptual or vocabulary problems for the children.

Basic Drill Pattern:
S: Who *(verbs)* ± *(object)* ± *(adverbial*$_{place}$*)*?
R: *(Pronoun) (verb)* ± *(object)* ± *(adverbial*$_{place}$*)*.

Method: The method varies with the pronoun to be elicited. For all pronouns, current and remembered actions involving contrasts between what the teacher and the children do in school can be used as topics.

Examples:

Teacher:	(demonstrates drill with aide)
Teacher:	Who teaches school?
Aide and children:	You teach school.
Teacher:	Who plays in the playground?
Aide and children:	We play in the playground.
Teacher:	Who has red pants?
Johnny:	I have red pants.

Things to Look Out For:

1. To contrast *I* and *you,* you can distribute a number of objects to the children and yourself. Ask the children who has which object. You can also talk about classroom duties, etc.

2. The children may have difficulty handling all of the pronouns at first. If this is the case, break the lesson down and work on each pronoun separately.

3. When drilling the first person singular pronoun (*I*), you *must* use individual drills. There is no other way to elicit this pronoun. For this reason, when drilling this pronoun, each child will make fewer responses per unit of drill than he ordinarily would make, and it may take longer to complete the drill (it may not, too).

4. Feel free to invent other drills to elicit these pronouns if you feel you need to.

5. See Note 3, Lesson 2.2.

LESSON 2.8

Objective: To drill the continuum auxiliaries, *am* and *are,* in contrast to *is.*

Materials: Actions (real or pantomimed), or pictures of people or animals in action can be used.

Basic Drill Pattern:

S: Who is *(verb -ing)* ± *(object)* ± *(adverbial)?*

R: *(Pronoun)* $\left\{\begin{array}{c} \text{is} \\ \text{am} \\ \text{are} \end{array}\right\}$ *(verb -ing)* ± *(object)* ± *(adverbial).*

Method: Question the children about actions that people are carrying out. You may wish to engage in an action and instruct a child or more than one child to mimic that action; then present the stimulus.

Examples:

Teacher:	(demonstrates drill with aide)
Teacher:	Who is digging a hole?
Aide and children:	He is digging a hole.
Teacher:	Who is talking to the teacher?
Aide and children:	We are talking to the teacher.
Teacher:	Who is talking to children?
Aide and children:	You are talking to children.
Teacher:	Who is playing on the playground?
Aide and children:	(pointing) They are playing on the playground.
Teacher:	Johnny, who is wearing brown shoes?
Johnny:	I am wearing brown shoes.

Things to Look Out For:

1. Again, *they* and *I* will cause some problems that may or may not be easily solved. If there is another group of children in the room which is not in the TALK lesson, it could be used as the topic of the *they* responses. Otherwise, you are limited to chance sightings of people or pictures. *I* requires individual responses. Given the number of possible variations on this drill, however, it should be relatively easy to slip in several individual responses for this purpose during each day's drill.

2. Remember that the objective of this lesson is to elicit and contrast *am, are,* and *is,* not to teach pronouns. If the children are still having problems with pronouns, you will have to return to Lesson 2.7 and drill them. Do not try to use this lesson to teach pronouns.

3. Also remember that introducing *am* and *are* all at the same time is likely to cause problems for many children. It may prove to be the case that you have to introduce first one and then the other before you can contrast them in the same drill. In fact, to ease the group into the *am* and *are* portion of the lessons, it may be necessary to go back and drill *is* first. The *is* part of this lesson is actually Lesson 2.1, and you should turn back and review that lesson before you begin.

LESSON 2.9

Objective: To drill affirmative and negative responses with the continuum.

Materials: Use the same materials found helpful in previous drills in this section.

Basic Drill Pattern:

S_1: $\left\{\begin{array}{l}\text{Am}\\\text{Are}\\\text{Is}\end{array}\right\}$ $\left\{\begin{array}{l}\textit{pronoun}\\\text{that }\textit{noun}\\\text{the }\textit{nouns}\end{array}\right\}$ (*verb*$_1$ -ing) $\pm$ (*object*) $\pm$ (*adverbial*$_{\text{place}}$)?

R_1: Yes, (*pronoun*) $\left\{\begin{array}{l}\text{am}\\\text{is}\\\text{are}\end{array}\right\}$.

or:

R_2: No, (*pronoun*) $\left\{\begin{array}{l}\text{am}\\\text{is}\\\text{are}\end{array}\right\}$ not (*verb*$_1$ -ing) $\pm$ (*object*) $\pm$ (*adverbial*$_{\text{place}}$).

S_2: (If R_1 is negative): What $\left\{\begin{array}{l}\text{am}\\\text{is}\\\text{are}\end{array}\right\}$ (*pronoun*) doing $\pm$ then?

R_3: (*Pronoun*) $\left\{\begin{array}{l}\text{am}\\\text{is}\\\text{are}\end{array}\right\}$ (*verb*$_2$ -ing) $\pm$ (*object*) $\pm$ (*adverbial*$_{\text{place}}$).

Method: Hold up pictures or refer to actions currently being carried out by the children, the teacher, or the aide.

Examples:

Teacher:	(demonstrates drill with aide)
Teacher:	Is that man wearing a hat?
Aide and children:	Yes, he is.
Teacher:	(Touches scarf.) Am I wearing a hat?
Aide and children:	No, you are not wearing a hat.
Teacher:	What am I wearing, then?
Aide and children:	You are wearing a scarf.
Teacher:	Are you sitting in chairs?
Aide and children:	Yes, we are.

Things to Look Out For:

1. Note that R_1 in the basic drill pattern calls only for a pronoun. You can try to elicit "that (*noun*)" if you wish. This filler of the determiner$_2$ appears early for many children, and it might not cause any problem at all for your children:

R_1: No, that monkey is not eating an orange.

Do not try to elicit the contrast between *this* and *that* at this point, however. It may be necessary for some groups to leave the basic drill pattern the way it is and have *that* appear only in the stimulus. See Note 1, Lesson 2.3.

2. Note also that we are suggesting the possibility of an elipted response when the response is in the affirmative. If some of your children do not yet produce the full affirmative pattern (as in Lesson 2.8), continue to require the following:

R$_1$: Yes, *(pronoun)* $\begin{Bmatrix} \text{am} \\ \text{is} \\ \text{are} \end{Bmatrix}$ *(verb$_1$ -ing)* $\pm$ *(object)* $\pm$ *(adverbial$_{\text{place}}$)*.

In other words, do not go to the ellipted pattern until your children are ready for it. Once they are ready, however, do not hesitate to use it.

LESSON 2.10

Objective: To drill the equative clause in the affirmative, using an adjective to fill the complement function.

Materials: Objects, flannel board materials, or the children themselves.

Basic Drill Pattern:

S: $\left\{ \begin{array}{l} \text{Is} \\ \text{Am} \\ \text{Are} \end{array} \right\}$ $\left\{ \begin{array}{l} \text{that } noun \\ \text{the } noun\text{(s)} \\ pronoun \end{array} \right\}$ (*adjective*)?

R: $\left\{ \begin{array}{l} \text{Yes} \\ \text{No} \end{array} \right\}$, (*pronoun*) $\left\{ \begin{array}{l} \text{is} \\ \text{am} \\ \text{are} \end{array} \right\}$ ± NEG (*adjective*).

Method: While pointing to or holding up materials, ask the children about the various characteristics (color, size, shape, etc.) of each object. It might be easier to have pairs of objects so that you can use polar adjectives such as *big* and *small, long* and *short.*

Examples:

Teacher:	(demonstrates drill with aide)
Teacher:	Everybody, is the ball round?
Aide and children:	Yes, the ball is round.
Teacher:	Are the birds blue?
Aide and children:	Yes, the birds are blue.
Teacher:	Is that line long? (contrasted with "short" line)
Aide and children:	Yes, it is long.
Teacher:	Am I small?
Aide and children:	No, you are not small.

Things to Look Out For:

1. When you are working with contrasts, be certain that the children understand what the contrasts are. For example, *long* and *short* are contrasts, but they are relative contrasts. A mile is very short to the pilot of a jet, but long to someone on foot, and very long to a turtle. Whenever you are going to use relative contrasts such as these, introduce them to the children before you begin the drill just to make sure that they see the contrast. If they do not understand the contrast, do not use it in the drill at first. You may introduce contrasts which you would like to teach *after* the children begin to get the pattern working correctly; this method has been used in the past with some success. Do not forget, however, that the basic goal of TALK is to teach sentence patterns, not vocabulary.

2. You may want to rely mainly on the cognitive characteristics of *color, size,* and *shape* (e.g., *red, big, square*) and, additionally, restrict shape to *round* and square. These things will become important in another lesson that uses the words *color, size,* and *shape* in the basic drill pattern.

3. We have known teachers who stopped using TALK when they got to this lesson because the children did not know their colors and the teachers could see no point in going on. The only thing to be said in response to this problem is that it should make no difference whether or not the children know certain adjectives. The lessons with adjectival complements are not designed to teach cognitive skills (such as knowing which colors are which), but rather to teach the adjective filler of the complement function in the equative clause pattern. Even if your children can contrast only two things, like *fat* and *skinny,*

yellow and *blue* (two of the three primary colors), or *big* and *little,* they can learn to use the drills with adjectival complements. Do not let extraneous things distract you from the task at hand. The specific vocabulary you use is relatively unimportant; if your children do not know their colors, use something else. There are many things to teach handicapped children during the day, and teaching the clause patterns of English is only one of those things. Cognitive discrimination may be quite another teaching task for a group of children.

LESSON 2.11

Objective: To drill the equative clause in the negative, using an adjective complement.

Materials: Use the same materials as in Lesson 2.10: flannel board materials, colored objects, etc.

Basic Drill Pattern:

S: $\left\{ \begin{matrix} \text{Am} \\ \text{Is} \\ \text{Are} \end{matrix} \right\}$ $\left\{ \begin{matrix} pronoun \\ \text{the } noun \\ \text{that } noun \end{matrix} \right\}$ *(adjective₁)?*

R₁: No, $\left\{ \begin{matrix} pronoun \\ \text{the } noun \\ \text{that } noun \end{matrix} \right\}$ $\left\{ \begin{matrix} \text{am} \\ \text{is} \\ \text{are} \end{matrix} \right\}$ not *(adjective₁),* it is *(adjective₂).*

or:

R₂: Yes, $\left\{ \begin{matrix} pronoun \\ \text{the } noun \\ \text{that } noun \end{matrix} \right\}$ $\left\{ \begin{matrix} \text{am} \\ \text{is} \\ \text{are} \end{matrix} \right\}$ *(adjective₁).*

Method: Introduce the drill with the aide just as in all TALK drills and follow the basic drill pattern with the children. Negate the truth value of the stimulus in order to elicit the negative response.

Examples:

Teacher:	(demonstrates drill with aide)
Teacher:	Everybody, is the ball blue?
Aide and children:	No, the ball is not blue, it is yellow.
Teacher:	Is the shirt white?
Aide and children:	Yes, the shirt is white.
Teacher:	Is the circle square?
Aide and children:	No, the circle is not square, it is round.
Teacher:	Am I fat?
Aide and children:	No, you are not fat, you are skinny.
Teacher:	Is Johnny short?
Aide and children:	Yes, he is short.

Things to Look Out For:

1. Review all notes for Lesson 2.5.

2. See Note 2, Lesson 2.9.

3. Review all notes for Lesson 2.10.

LESSON 2.12

Objective: To drill the equative clause with an adverbial complement.

Materials: Use vocabulary that refers to objects in the room: clothing and jewelry being worn by you, the aide and the children, and possibly places in the school such as the principal's office and the playground.

Basic Drill Pattern:

S: $\begin{Bmatrix} \text{Is} \\ \text{Am} \\ \text{Are} \end{Bmatrix} \begin{Bmatrix} \text{the } \textit{noun} \\ \text{that } \textit{noun} \\ \textit{pronoun} \end{Bmatrix}$ (*adverbial*$_{\text{place}}$)?

R: $\begin{Bmatrix} \text{Yes} \\ \text{No} \end{Bmatrix}$, (*pronoun*) $\begin{Bmatrix} \text{is} \\ \text{am} \\ \text{are} \end{Bmatrix}$ ± NEG (*adverbial*$_{\text{place}}$).

Method: Ask the children about the location of objects, people or places.

Examples:

Teacher:	(demonstrates drill with aide)
Teacher:	Is that clock on the wall?
Aide and children:	Yes, it is on the wall.
Teacher:	Is that shoe on Johnny?
Aide and children:	No, it is not on Johnny.
Teacher:	Am I on the playground?
Aide and children:	No, you are not on the playground.
Teacher:	Are you here?
Aide and children:	Yes, we are here.

Things to Look Out For:

1. Ease the children into the drill by starting off with only affirmative responses. When they begin to respond well, introduce the negative responses. At this point, such responses should not pose much of a problem, since the only thing that is different from the previous drills in this lesson is the fact that the adverbial is now being used to fill the complement function.

2. Review Lesson 2.11, since this is the same drill except for the adverbial complement.

LESSON 2.13

Objective: To drill the equative pattern with the contracted negative in contrast to the affirmative pattern.

Materials: Use the same materials that you have been using in the previous drills on the equative.

Basic Drill Pattern:

$$S: \begin{Bmatrix} Am \\ Are \\ Is \end{Bmatrix} \begin{Bmatrix} \text{the } \textit{noun} \\ \text{that } \textit{noun} \\ \textit{pronoun} \end{Bmatrix} \begin{Bmatrix} \text{a } \textit{noun} \\ \textit{adjective} \\ \textit{adverbial}_{\text{place}} \end{Bmatrix} ?$$

$$R_1: \text{Yes, } (\textit{pronoun}) \begin{Bmatrix} am \\ are \\ is \end{Bmatrix} \begin{Bmatrix} \text{a } \textit{noun} \\ \text{adjective} \\ \text{adverbial}_{\text{place}} \end{Bmatrix} .$$

$$R_2: \begin{Bmatrix} Yes \\ No \end{Bmatrix} (\textit{pronoun}) \begin{Bmatrix} am \\ are \\ is \end{Bmatrix} \pm NEG \begin{Bmatrix} \text{a } \textit{noun} \\ \text{adjective} \\ \text{adverbial}_{\text{place}} \end{Bmatrix} .$$

Method: Require the children to contract the negative to BE. Other than this, Lesson 2.13 is the same as several previous drills.

Examples:

Teacher:	(demonstrates drill with aide)
Teacher:	Everybody, is the circle round?
Aide and children:	Yes, it is round.
Teacher:	Is the circle square?
Aide and children:	No, it isn't square.
Teacher:	Am I a child?
Aide and children:	No, you aren't a child.
Teacher:	Are you children?
Aide and children:	Yes, we are.

Things to Look Out For:

1. Since the basic element to be taught in this drill is the contraction of the negative to BE, you should try to elicit negative responses about half the time. Always finish up a dialogue sequence with an affirmative, however.

2. You may find that your children are not yet ready to contract. Do not be overzealous if this is true. It is easy to return to this lesson at a later time.

3. Note that the basic drill pattern now specifies that the following all be varied: (a) the forms of the predicate; (b) the pronoun subjects; and (c) the filler of the complement. Review the notes throughout the chapter for possible trouble spots. When you find problems, return to the lesson that teaches the feature involved and drill that lesson again.

4. Note, too, that am does not have a contraction. That is, in English there is no form like *amn't that is analogous to isn't and aren't.

LESSON 2.14

Objective: To make a game of reviewing patterns contained in previous lessons.

Materials: Familiar classroom objects. It is possible to use objects in this drill which you have not yet used; but again, do not introduce any objects which the children are not able to name. The prime goal of the TALK drills, as we said before, is not to teach vocabulary, but rather, to teach sentence patterns.

Basic Drill Patterns: All basic drill patterns from Lessons 2.3 to 2.13.

Method: Tell the children they are going to play a game of naming classroom objects, and that the teacher and aide will ask them questions. The teacher then points to an object and says ''Aide, ask Johnny (or 'everybody')... '' (Insert one of the stimuli from the basic drill patterns of this section.)

The aide asks the question and a child or the group tries to answer using the pattern learned in the previous drills. Because the aide is asking the questions, the teacher must stand ready to help a child who needs it. When the group responds chorally, the teacher may have to help lead the response just as the aide did when the teacher was providing the stimulus questions. Mix up the stimuli and create an atmosphere of a little competition. It might even be possible to divide up the group into competing teams to see ''who can answer the loudest.''

Examples:

Teacher:	Miss Jones, ask everybody what that is.
Aide:	Everybody, what is that?
Teacher and children:	It is a pencil.
Teacher:	Miss Jones, ask Johnny if that is a pencil.
Aide:	Johnny, is that a pencil?
Johnny (and teacher if necessary):	No, it is not a pencil, it is a book.
Teacher:	Miss Jones, ask Sally if she is wearing a shoe.
Aide:	Sally, are you wearing a shoe?
Sally:	Yes, I am.

Things to Look Out For: 1. This is not a dialogue drill, and the patterns need not follow any specific sequence.

2. It is probably not possible for the children to ask each other the stimulus questions at this point in lesson sequence because they have not yet been drilled on the asking of questions. There may be some children, however, who can ask a good question. It can do no harm for these children to do the asking, *providing* their being singled out to ''act as teacher'' does not cause hard feelings among the children who cannot ask a good question. It may be safer to allow the aide to do all of the question-asking at this point in the lessons, but the choice is yours.

3. Do not forget, with the aide asking the questions, the teacher must be ready to take on the aide's role.

4. There is no reason why the teacher cannot make up his own games. All work and no play... (etc.) It is quite all right to use any game that helps get the basic drill pattern across to the children. Feel free to experiment. As in most aspects of TALK, there is a primary rule here: If it works, use it!

5. Review all notes in this section for the lessons on the equative.

SECTION 3

Indirect Objects, More Pronouns, Noun Plurals, and Loose-Knit Modifiers

In Section 3 we will present drills on the last transitive clause: the transitive clause with an indirect object. In conjunction with this pattern, we will also introduce the objective forms of the personal pronouns: *us, him, her,* and *them,* along with the forms *you* and *it* that are used in both the objective and subjective positions. The nondefinite pronoun *one* will also be introduced for the first time in this section.

In Section 3 we also begin to drill some of the complexities of the noun phrase. Specifically, the concept of plurality will be introduced in the form of the regular noun plural inflection. In addition, the adjective, which has previously appeared only as a filler of the complement function in the equative, will now be introduced into the noun phrase as a filler of the loose-knit modifier function.

Rationale

In Sections 2 and 3 the intransitive, transitive, and equative clause patterns were drilled. The indirect object tends to develop at about the time the equative clause develops, and it is now time to teach the children to use it. As we prepare to teach it, we must note that, very often, a personal pronoun fills the indirect object function. We have already drilled all of the subjective forms of the personal pronouns, and at this point we will begin to drill the objective forms by using them as fillers of the indirect object function. The entire personal pronoun paradigm will be complete by the time this job has been done.

Plurality is not a new concept in the lessons. The pronoun *we*, for example, appeared as a filler of the subject slot for the continuum and equative drills. Now we will drill the rule for inflecting the "regular" nouns for plurality. We will not drill "irregular" plurals in TALK, however, because they are so varied that they preclude the induction of a generalized rule for forming them. The "irregulars" will have to be taught individually, outside of the drill.

Adjectives are also not new to the TALK drills. They appeared as fillers of the complement function in equative clauses in Section 2. The loose-knit modifier function in the noun phrase seems to develop at a relatively early point, and in this section we will begin to use adjectives to fill this function. In doing so, the drills will be structured in such a way as to illustrate the connection between the equative complement and the loose-knit modifier.

The Lessons

Other than the transitive with an indirect object pattern and the addition of the loose-knit modifier function in the noun phrase, the drills in this section are largely repetitions or variations of drills that have appeared previously. Consequently, there are a number of suggestions to the effect that the notes from previous sections should be reviewed. It might be a good idea to do this prior to beginning the drills in this section.

Lessons 3.10, 3.11, and 3.12 are formally structured as review lessons for all the Section 3 lessons (except for the drills on transitives with indirect objects). Once you have gone beyond the first two lessons, you should make an attempt to progress as quickly as possible to these review lessons. You will find, as pointed out previously, that there are not many "new" drill patterns in this section. As a consequence, it should be a little easier to get to the point at which you can begin using dialogues than it was in the first two sections. One of the instructional problems we face is that of enabling the children to engage in connected conversations. Single stimulus-response unit drills switch topics rapidly and do not facilitate this learning. It is far better for us to try to maintain a single topic longer, as would be done in a conversation. An attempt to show how this task can be accomplished has been made in the construction of the dialogue drills. As always, the teacher should feel free to make up his own connected dialogue drills using the basic drill patterns from the immediately preceding lessons. There should also be no problem in introducing patterns from either Section 1 or 2 into any connected dialogue drill in order to provide "setups" to drill patterns which are currently being taught.

Again, as always, make a serious attempt to get the children to use the drill patterns outside of the drills. Without this, there is no connection to real life, and consequently, little transfer.

LESSON 3.1

Objective: To drill the transitive imperative clause with an indirect object.

Materials: Use a number of objects which can be picked up easily. A puppet might be helpful for this lesson.

Basic Drill Pattern: S: Tell $\left\{ \begin{array}{c} name_1 \\ pronoun \end{array} \right\}$ to *(verb) (name₂) (object)*.

R: *(Name₁), (verb) (name₂) (object)*!

Method: The children can order the aide, a puppet, you, or another child to do something to somebody.

Examples:

Teacher:	(demonstrates drill with aide)
Teacher:	Tell Otto to give Johnny the block.
Aide and children:	Otto, give Johnny the block!
Teacher:	Tell him to give Sally a smile.
Aide and children:	Otto, give Sally a smile!
Teacher:	Tell Johnny to hand Albert the block.
Aide and children:	Johnny, hand Albert the block!

Things to Look Out For: 1. It may be more natural for your children to place the vocative at the *end* of the response:

R: Show Maxine a truck, Otto!

You may allow them to do so, if you wish.

2. You may also add any adverbials of location which fit the sense of the command and the capabilities of the children, e.g.,

R: Show Alice the block on the left, Otto!
R: Mrs. Jones, give Arnold the marble from the table!

3. Although we have used the puppet in the examples, you should not think of your lesson as having to use one. The children can carry out commands, too, as can you and/or your aide.

4. Note that a proper noun is being used as the indirect object. This is a setup for the pronouns that follow in the rest of the chapter.

5. Note also that the examples show the objective form of the pronoun in the stimulus. It is best for the children to hear it before they are required to produce it:

Teacher: Tell Otto to hand Sally the block.
Teacher: Tell *him* to hand Johnny the ball.

The pronoun can only be used when the person or puppet being directed to carry out the command was the *(name₁)* of the previous response. Of course, *her, him,* and *me* may be used:

Teacher: Tell me to give Johnny a pat.

6. In using the pattern with the indirect object, we need verbs which semantically involve action between one person and another: *give, show, tell, hand* (an object), *play* (a song), *ask, call* (a name), *catch, crack* (a nut), *cook,* etc. Verbs with only one person involved in the action are never used in this pattern, e.g., *ride:* we never say things like "Ride us a horse." Use any verb your children can handle, but be careful to choose only verbs that can take indirect objects.

LESSON 3.2

Objective: To drill the object forms of the singular personal pronouns as indirect objects.

Materials: Use objects that can be picked up easily. You may wish to use a puppet to carry out the commands, but you, your aide, or any of the children can also serve in this role.

**Basic Drill
Pattern:** S: Ask $(name_1)$ to *(verb)* $\begin{Bmatrix} pronoun \\ name_2 \end{Bmatrix}$ a *(noun)*.

R: $(Name_2)$, *(verb)* $\begin{Bmatrix} me \\ us \\ him \\ her \end{Bmatrix}$ a *(noun)*, please.

Method: Follow the specified basic drill pattern in the same manner as you did in Lesson 3.1.

Examples:

Teacher:	(demonstrates drill with aide)
Teacher:	Everybody, ask Otto to show you a pencil.
Aide and children:	Otto, show us a pencil, please.
Teacher:	Ask Otto to give Johnny a rock.
Aide and children:	Otto, give him a rock, please.
Teacher:	Ask Otto to blow Sally a kiss.
Aide and children:	Otto, blow her a kiss, please.

**Things to
Look Out For:** 1. In this drill you are having the children make a request ("Ask Otto... " rather than "Tell Otto... "). Hence, you can rightfully expect them to say *please*. As a variant response, you could allow the *please* to appear following the vocative, if you wish:

R: Otto, please tell Melvin the color.

2. In drilling the objective forms of the pronouns, it is not absolutely necessary to use the clause with indirect objects as the drill pattern *ad nauseam*. For variety, you can go back through the program and pick out any previous drill that uses transitive verbs. It should be easy for you to plug pronouns into the object slots of most patterns used thus far.

3. Again, any time the response uses the first person singular pronoun *(me)*, you must use an individual drill. Hold off introducing it until the children feel comfortable with the pattern as a group.

4. See Note 6, Lesson 3.1.

5. As in the lessons on the subjective pronouns, you may find that introduction of all four of the pronouns at once is just too much. If this is the case, simply break this drill down into four separate drills, one for each form.

LESSON 3.3

Objective: To drill the third person plural objective pronoun as an indirect object.

Materials: Use materials similar to those used in the other lessons in this section.

Basic Drill Pattern: S: Tell me to show $\begin{Bmatrix} \text{GROUP}_1 \\ \text{GROUP}_2 \end{Bmatrix}$ (*object*).

R: Show them (*object*).

Method: Divide the children into two groups and give them titles (*Group 1* and *Group 2*, *Tigers* and *Lions*, etc.). The children direct their responses to you.

Examples:

Teacher:	(demonstrates drill with aide)
Teacher:	Group$_1$, tell me to show Group$_2$ the penny.
Aide and Group$_1$:	Show them the penny!
Teacher:	Group$_2$, tell me to show Group$_1$ some pencils.
Aide and Group$_2$:	Show them some pencils!
Teacher:	Group$_1$, tell me to show Group$_2$ some pennies.
Aide and Group$_1$:	Show them some pennies!

Things to Look Out For:

1. The only thing that keeps this drill from being a repetition drill is the conversion from the group's name to *them*.

2. This may be a very dull drill, and some groups will catch on very quickly (of course, some will not, too). Do not beat your class to death with it.

3. You should be able to introduce a dialogue drill for review purposes at this point. Use all of the patterns drilled in Lessons 3.1–3.3, and switch back and forth between the directions:

S: $\begin{Bmatrix} \text{Everybody} \\ Name_1 \\ \text{GROUP}_{1\ or\ 2} \end{Bmatrix}$, tell me to show $\begin{Bmatrix} \text{you} \\ \text{them} \\ name_2 \end{Bmatrix}$ (*object*).

R: Show $\begin{Bmatrix} \text{me} \\ \text{us} \\ \text{them} \\ name_2 \end{Bmatrix}$ (*object*).

This drill can be done with the children sitting in two groups.

4. See Note 5, Lesson 3.2.

LESSON 3.4

Objective: To drill the continuum in clauses with an indirect object.

Materials: Use objects, pictures, etc., that will elicit transitive verbs that can take an indirect object, but which can also pattern without it, such as *show, give, hand, make*.

Basic Drill Pattern:

S: $\begin{Bmatrix} \text{Everybody} \\ Name \end{Bmatrix}$, (verb) $\begin{Bmatrix} name \\ pronoun_1 \end{Bmatrix}$ (object). What $\begin{Bmatrix} is \\ are \end{Bmatrix}$ (pronoun₂) doing?

R: (Pronoun₂) $\begin{Bmatrix} is \\ are \end{Bmatrix}$ (verb -ing) (pronoun₁) (object).

Method: Have the children do things for you and for each other, either in fact or in pantomime, and follow the basic drill pattern.

Examples:

Teacher:	(demonstrates drill with aide)
Teacher:	Johnny, show us a circle. What is he doing?
Aide and children:	He is showing us a circle.
Teacher:	Alice, hand me a truck. What is she doing?
Aide and children:	She is handing you a truck.
Teacher:	Martha, show us a foot. What is she doing?
Aide and children:	She is showing us a foot.
Teacher:	Everybody, show me a nose. What are you doing?
Aide and children:	We are showing you a nose.

Things to Look Out For:

1. This lesson also works quite well in individual drill once the children have caught on to it.

Teacher:	Johnny, show us a hand. What are you doing?
Johnny:	I am showing you a hand.
or:	
Teacher:	Everybody, show Johnny the clock. Johnny, what are they doing?
Johnny:	They are showing me the clock.

Once again, however, because this drill can only be done with individual drill, you should not use it until the pattern is being produced smoothly.

2. See Note 5, Lesson 3.2.

LESSON 3.5

Objective: To drill the plural subject with the *are* form of BE.

Materials: Use flannel board cutouts in pairs, pictures of two or more objects, or pairs of objects that you can handle easily as pairs.

**Basic Drill
Pattern:** S: Are the (*noun*pl) (*adjective*)?
R₁: Yes, the (*noun*pl) are (*adjective*).
or:
R₂: No, the (*noun*pl) are not (*adjective*).

Method: Use pictures, objects, or flannel board materials as stimuli, just as you did for the equative clause lessons in Section 2.

Examples: Teacher: (demonstrates drill with aide)

Teacher: Are the cats fluffy?
Aide and children: Yes, the cats are fluffy.
Teacher: Are the dogs green?
Aide and children: No, the dogs are not green.
Teacher: Are the pencils thin?
Aide and children: Yes, the pencils are thin.

**Things to
Look Out For:**   1. Use any regular nouns in this pattern. Your major problem will be in the choice of items used as stimuli in the drill. If your children know all about plurals before you begin, they will not have any trouble no matter what stimuli you choose. But if they still must learn (and these are the children who need this drill), choosing objects with irregular plurals (*knives, oxen,* etc.) will throw a distracting element into the drill. The teaching of irregular plurals is probably not a matter for TALK lessons. There are so many of them, and they are so varied in their formation, that they are probably best taught informally. Once the regular plural rules are learned, however, it should be a simple matter to introduce the irregulars one at a time.

2. One good way to tell if your children are actually learning is to look for new kinds of "mistakes" they might begin to make. The plural illustrates this very well. If children do not have the rule for the regular plural, they often have some of the irregulars present in their correct form. As soon as they learn the rule for the regular plural, however, they begin to apply it to the irregulars as well. Thus, if your children begin suddenly to produce forms like *two mans* during or after this lesson has been introduced, they have probably learned the rule you were teaching. If they are already doing this, by the way, you probably do not have to drill them on plurality because they are demonstrating that they already know the regular plural rules.

3. You may wish to separate words that end in /s, z, š, ž, č, ǰ/ and drill them separately. These are words like *brush, fox, package, glass, dress, vase, watch, bush, box, dish, branch, rose, nose, hose, orange, peach,* and *fence.* These words require an extra syllable in the plural (*peaches*). Do not separate them from the other plurals unless you find that you have to make an extraordinary effort to teach them, however.

4. Do not use words like *ice, grass,* or *sand.* These are mass nouns and have no plurals. Some words, like *fish,* are made plural as *fishes* in some dialects and *fish* in others. If the plural is irregular (*fish*) in your area, do not use it. If it is regular, go ahead.

5. Once the children begin to respond well to this pattern, you can return to the dialogue drills for the equative in Section 2 and add the plural/singular contrast as another variation.

6. Review all notes on the equatives in Lessons 2.3–2.13.

LESSON 3.6

Objective: To drill the loose-knit modifier in the noun phrase.

Materials: Use the same materials that you used in the previous lesson. New materials may be used if they are familiar to the children, but be sure that all materials used can somehow be characterized with an adjective that is within the grasp of the children.

Basic Drill Pattern:

S_1: $\left\{ \begin{array}{c} \text{Is} \\ \text{Are} \end{array} \right\}$ $\left\{ \begin{array}{c} \text{that} \\ \text{those} \end{array} \right\}$ $\left\{ \begin{array}{c} \text{a } noun \\ nouns \end{array} \right\}$?

R_1: Yes, $\left\{ \begin{array}{c} \text{they} \\ \text{it} \end{array} \right\}$ $\left\{ \begin{array}{c} \text{are} \\ \text{is} \end{array} \right\}$ $\left\{ \begin{array}{c} nouns \\ \text{a } noun \end{array} \right\}$.

S_2: $\left\{ \begin{array}{c} \text{Is} \\ \text{Are} \end{array} \right\}$ $\left\{ \begin{array}{c} \text{it} \\ \text{they} \end{array} \right\}$ *(adjective)*?

R_2: Yes, $\left\{ \begin{array}{c} \text{it} \\ \text{they} \end{array} \right\}$ $\left\{ \begin{array}{c} \text{is} \\ \text{are} \end{array} \right\}$ *(adjective)*.

S_3: *What kind of* $\left\{ \begin{array}{c} noun \\ nouns \end{array} \right\}$ $\left\{ \begin{array}{c} \text{is} \\ \text{are} \end{array} \right\}$ $\left\{ \begin{array}{c} \text{it} \\ \text{they} \end{array} \right\}$ $\pm$ *then?*

R_3: $\left\{ \begin{array}{c} \text{It} \\ \text{They} \end{array} \right\}$ $\left\{ \begin{array}{c} \text{is} \\ \text{are} \end{array} \right\}$ *(adjective)* $\left\{ \begin{array}{c} noun \\ nouns \end{array} \right\}$.

Method: This drill is a dialogue drill. The children should be quite familiar with dialogue drills by now and should have little or no trouble with it. Only R_3 is new.

Examples:

Teacher:	(demonstrates drill with aide)
Teacher:	Everybody, is that a circle?
Aide and children:	Yes, it is a circle.
Teacher:	Is it round?
Aide and children:	Yes, it is round.
Teacher:	What kind of circle is it then?
Aide and children:	It is a round circle.
Teacher:	Is that a bird?
Aide and children:	Yes, it is a bird.
Teacher:	Is the bird blue?
Aide and children:	Yes, it is blue.
Teacher:	What kind of bird is it then?
Aide and children:	It is a blue bird.

Things to Look Out For:

1. The dialogue is a very useful device for this lesson, because we want to be able to get across the nature of adjectives, i.e., that they *describe* things. By eliciting the adjective (which has been only used to fill the equative complement thus far) with the question *what kind of (noun) is it,* we are able to make the point quite well.

2. All of the patterns, except R_3, have been used by the children before. There should be no problem with them at this point, but if there is, simply run a fast drill using the lesson which drilled the specific pattern that still gives trouble.

3. Review the notes on the equative in Section 2.

LESSON 3.7

Objective: To drill the contrast between negative and affirmative in the equative clause using a prenominal adjective.

Materials: Any materials which have been used successfully before.

Basic Drill Pattern:

S: Is $\left\{ \begin{array}{l} \text{this} \\ \text{that} \end{array} \right\}$ *(noun)* *(adjective)*?

R₁: Yes, the *(noun)* is an *(adjective)* *(noun)*.

or:

R₁: No, the *(noun)* is not an *(adjective)* *(noun)*.

Method: Follow the basic drill pattern as in previous lessons, using pictures or real objects.

Examples:

Teacher:	(demonstrates drill with aide)
Teacher:	Everybody, is this bird green?
Aide and children:	No, the bird is not a green bird.
Teacher:	Is this box empty?
Aide and children:	Yes, the box is an empty box.

Things to Look Out For:

1. The pattern used in this lesson is actually a "set-up" pattern for Lesson 3.8. It is a variation of the lessons which have been done previously and probably sounds a little stilted while you are speaking it. However, because it does lead into the next drill, in which a nondefinite pronoun is substituted for a noun, it *is* important. You should be just as careful in getting the children to respond to this drill as you have been with all of the others.

2. Note the suggestion in the stimulus pattern that both *this* and *that* be used. Again, it is best to have the children hear such contrasts before being asked to use them. *This* should be used to indicate anything close to you, while *that* would refer to anything remote, such as the clock on the wall. The *this/that/these/those* distinctions will be drilled in Section 4.

LESSON 3.8

Objective: To drill the nondefinite pronoun with an adjective modifier.

Materials: Use the material which can take adjectives that you have used before, such as *full, bright,* the various colors, etc.

Basic Drill Pattern:

S_1: Is $\begin{Bmatrix} \text{this} \\ \text{that} \end{Bmatrix}$ (noun) the *(adjective) (noun)?*

R_1: Yes, the (noun) is the *(adjective)* one.

S_2: What kind of (noun) is it then?

R_2: It is an *(adjective)* one.

Method: Introduce this drill with the aide, just as all TALK drills are introduced. Point to or hold up one of a pair of objects in the case of adjectives, such as those that identify colors, or use just one object in the case of adjectives, such as *empty,* or *bright.*

Examples:

Teacher:	(demonstrates drill with aide)
Teacher:	Everybody, is this glass an empty glass?
Aide and Children:	Yes, the glass is an empty one.
Teacher:	Then what kind of glass is it?
Aide and Children:	It is an empty one.
Teacher:	Is this bird a blue bird?
Aide and Children:	Yes, the bird is a blue one.
Teacher:	Then what kind of bird is it?
Aide and Children:	It is a blue one.

Things to Look Out For:

1. Review the notes from previous lessons on the equative.

2. See Note 2, Lesson 3.7.

3. The pronoun *one* is one of the "all-purpose" words in English. For nouns we have *thing,* for verbs we have DO, and for pronouns we have *one.* It can refer to nearly anything, and as such, it is an important word in the language. It has no contrast for gender (e.g., *he, she, it*), and it is pluralized with the regular inflection (*They are blue ones*).

LESSON 3.9

Objective: To drill the loose-knit modifier using the words *color, size,* and *shape* as stimuli. This drill is optional and may be omitted if the children are not ready for it.

Materials: The same materials as have been used in previous lessons in Section 3. Do not introduce *any* unfamiliar materials at this point.

Basic Drill
Pattern: S: Tell me what $\begin{Bmatrix} \text{color} \\ \text{size} \\ \text{shape} \end{Bmatrix}$ $\begin{Bmatrix} \text{this} \\ \text{that} \end{Bmatrix}$ *(noun)* is.

R: It is an *(adjective)* $\begin{Bmatrix} \text{one} \\ \text{noun} \end{Bmatrix}$.

Method: Just as in all TALK lessons, introduce the pattern with the aide and run the drills according to the basic drill pattern, eliciting responses that refer to the objects used.

Examples:

Teacher:	(demonstrates patterns with aide)
Teacher:	Everybody, tell me what color that ball is.
Aide and children:	It is a red ball.
Teacher:	Tell me what size that pencil is.
Aide and children:	It is a big pencil.
Teacher:	Tell me what shape this box is.
Aide and children:	It is a square box.
Teacher:	Tell me what color that shirt is.
Aide and children:	It is a white shirt.
Teacher:	Tell me what size that bird is.
Aide and children:	It is a small bird.
Teacher:	Tell me what shape this circle is.
Aide and children:	It is a round circle.

Things to
Look Out For: 1. For the first time in the lessons, we have a primary concern with teaching some vocabulary: the words *color, size,* and *shape.* Many children will know the first; the second two may take a little time. In spite of the fact that vocabulary enters into this lesson as an objective, the main objective is still the grammar: We are using the question word *what* as the eliciting stimulus for the adjective (*what color, what size,* and *what shape*). With semantic and syntactical learning converging in one pattern drill, it may take awhile to get the drill going.

2. Size and shape sometimes begin to merge as concepts. For example, do *fat* and *thin* refer to size or shape? You may also wish to introduce the words *length, width,* and *height* into the drill. If you do, be careful; use only the words *big* and *small* in reference to size in the first few drills using this pattern, and do not use words like *long,* or *thick,* until the children can handle the vocabulary given (*color, size,* and *shape*) in the first few drills. For many retarded children, however, especially young ones, you will not wish to deviate from the stated objectives.

3. It is possible to get yourself into a real trap with some adjectives in this drill. For example, it is usually very easy for the following to be elicited:

Teacher:	Tell me what shape that circle is.

Aide and children:	It is a round circle.
Teacher:	Tell me what shape that box is.
Aide and children:	It is a square box.

But when you use a triangle as a stimulus, watch what happens to the adjective:

| Teacher: | Tell me what shape that pyramid is. |
| Aide and children: | It is a triangular pyramid. |

The latter adjective is beyond many, if not most, of the children who need TALK. We have seen lessons that fell apart completely when things like this were called for in the response. Be sure you know what adjectives will be required for the response before you begin!

LESSON 3.10

Objective: To review the basic drill patterns for loose-knit modifiers.

Materials: All the materials which have been used in Section 3. Again, new materials may be added, but only if they are familiar to the children. All materials used must have identifying characteristics expressible as adjectives, just as has been true of all of the materials used in the lessons for adjectives.

Basic Drill Pattern:

S_1: What is that?
R_1: It is a *(noun)*.
S_2: Is the *(noun)* *(adjective$_1$)*?
R_2: No, it is not *(adjective$_1$)*, it is *(adjective$_2$)*.
S_3: What kind of *(noun)* is it then?
R_3: It is an *(adjective$_2$)* *(noun)*.
S_4: Is the *(noun)* *(adjective$_3$)*?
R_4: No, it is not *(adjective$_3$)*, it is *(adjective$_4$)*.

S_5: Tell me what $\left\{ \begin{array}{c} \text{color} \\ \text{size} \\ \text{shape} \end{array} \right\}$ the *(noun)* is then.

R_5: It is an *(adjective$_4$)* *(one)*.

Method: In the entire dialogue sequence, just one object is to be used until the next sequence begins. Introduce this dialogue just as you introduce all TALK drills and then run the drill just as you have run all drills in Section 3.

Examples:

Teacher:	(demonstrates drill with aide)
Teacher:	What is that?
Aide and children:	It is a pencil.
Teacher:	Is the pencil square?
Aide and children:	No, it is not square, it is round.
Teacher:	What kind of pencil is it then?
Aide and children:	It is a round pencil.
Teacher:	Is the pencil thin?
Aide and children:	No, it is not thin, it is fat.
Teacher:	Tell me what shape the pencil is then.
Aide and children:	It is a fat one.

(Teacher begins again with a new object)

Things to Look Out For: 1. The dialogue sequence is not the only possible sequence you can use. Lesson 3.11 provides an alternate dialogue, and you may wish to make up your own combination of any of the basic drill patterns in Sections 1 through 3 to make a longer dialogue sequence. The only thing to watch out for is to make the dialogue sequence "fit together" so that it sounds like it might be a conversation. The reason for having dialogue drills in the first place is to make the lesson basic drill patterns sound natural, and any dialogue that you make up should fit into logical sequence.

2. Review all of the notes for previous lessons in Sections 2 and 3.

LESSON 3.11

Objective: To review all the syntactic concepts drilled in Section 3 in an alternate dialogue drill.

Materials: All the materials used in Section 3, as well as any new materials the teacher would like to use, which (a) have characteristics specified by an adjective; (b) are familiar to the children.

Basic Drill
Pattern: S: What is that?

R_1: It is a (noun).

S_2: Is the (noun) (adjective₁)?

R_2: No, the (noun) $\begin{Bmatrix} \text{is not} \\ \text{isn't} \end{Bmatrix}$ (adjective₁).

S_3: Is the (noun) an (adjective₂) (noun)?

R_3: Yes, it is an (adjective₂) (noun).

S_4: What kind of (noun) is it then?

R_4: It is an (adjective₂) one.

Method: The teacher introduces this drill with the aide just as it is done in all TALK drills and runs the drill according to the basic drill pattern.

Examples:

Teacher:	(introduces drill with aide)
Teacher:	Everybody, what is that?
Aide and children:	It is a box.
Teacher:	Is the box empty?
Aide and children:	No, the box is not empty.
Teacher:	Is the box a full box?
Aide and children:	Yes, it is a full box.
Teacher:	What kind of box is it then?
Aide and children:	It is a full one.
Teacher:	What is that?
Aide and children:	It is a circle.
Teacher:	Is the circle green?
Aide and children:	No, the circle is not green.
Teacher:	Is the circle an orange circle?
Aide and children:	Yes, it is an orange circle.
Teacher:	What kind of circle is it then?
Aide and children:	It is an orange one.

Things to
Look Out For: 1. Again, the dialogue is simply one of many which could be used. It contains all the major concepts drilled in this section and many of the equative clause patterns from Section 2. It does not contain all of the basic drill patterns of these sections. You are free to make up additional dialogue drills if you feel they are needed.

2. (*Adjective₁*) and (*adjective₂*) in the patterns refer to "true" and "false" adjectives. See the examples for how this is used.

3. If the children are ready for it, any possible contraction, negative or non-negative, may be used.

Indirect Objects, More Pronouns, Noun Plurals, and Loose-Knit Modifiers **317**

LESSON 3.12

Objective: To make a game out of drilling the basic drill patterns found in previous lessons.

Materials: All new materials. Perhaps objects in the room would be good to use for this lesson, such as doorknobs, walls, or desks.

Basic Drill Pattern: Use whatever individual drills you feel the children need work with, or use a dialogue drill sequence as you prefer.

Method: There is no real reason to be motionless for this lesson. Feel free to move around the room and point to things in the environment. The children have been functioning in the drills long enough to understand what is expected of them by this time, and they should be able to follow the lesson in spite of the fact that the teacher is moving around. This technique may not work for some groups, however, and the teacher is the best judge of what to do.

Like the game in Section 2, tell the aide to ask the question; some of the children may also be able to ask them. Elicit choral drill by telling the questioner to ask "everybody," and elicit individual drills by naming a specific child to make the response.

You may wish to divide the children up into teams to "see who can answer the best" (or "loudest," etc.). Do not be afraid to introduce a little competitiveness in the classroom—children like it.

Examples:

Teacher:	(demonstrates drill with aide)
Teacher:	Aide, ask everybody if that doorknob is round.
Aide:	Everybody, is that doorknob round?
Teacher and children:	Yes, the doorknob is round.
Teacher:	Ask Team$_1$ if that chalkboard is white.
Aide:	Team$_1$: Is that chalkboard white?
Teacher and Team$_1$:	No, the chalkboard is not white, it's black (or green, etc.).
Teacher:	Ask Team$_2$ if that desk is brown.
Aide:	Team$_2$, is that desk brown?
Teacher and Team$_2$:	Yes, that desk is brown.

Things to Look Out For:

1. If you are moving about the room, you will have to know exactly what you are going to say before you begin. Be sure that you have the patterns "down pat" so that you do not introduce any extraneous elements into the running of the lesson.

2. Use all of the patterns found in Section 3. The examples do not show all of these, but you should be familiar enough with TALK by now to be able to fill in the patterns in the right way.

3. If your children cannot drill well with you in motion, return to your original materials and a stationary position.

SECTION 4

The Determiner₂, Possession, Past Time, and Location Adverbials

Section 4 begins by drilling the functions of the determiner₂. The first lessons drill the contrasts between the demonstrative pronouns (*this/that/these/those*). Following these drills, there are drills on the possessive pronouns (*my, your, our,* etc.) and the genitive inflection (*'s*). Once the drills on the determiner₂ are completed, the possessive pronouns that fill clausal functions (*yours, hers, mine*) will be drilled. Next come lessons on past time that provide drill for both (*a*) the regular past tense inflection for transitive and intransitive verbs, and (*b*) the past tense forms of BE. The latter includes both the auxiliary of the continuum and the predicate of the equative clause. Finally, the section ends with drills on some of the prepositions that are used in phrases that fill adverbials of place.

Rationale

Section 4 is a kind of "loose-ends" set of lesson plans. Many of the concepts in this section have appeared before, either in stimulus patterns, or as an isolated form in the response patterns. Some demonstrative pronouns, for example, have been used in the stimulus since Section 1, and adverbials using *in, on,* and *under* also appeared in Section 1. We will take these concepts now and extend them.

The class of determiner₂ fillers that express possession have not previously been drilled, but this is the only remaining filler class of this determiner. "Possession" as a concept appears early in development for most children, however. Therefore, we will now drill both the pronominal fillers of the determiner$_2$ and the genitive inflection that appears on nouns. When this task is completed, all filler classes of the determiner$_2$ will have been drilled. The alert teacher will notice there are still many nondefinite articles that have not been and will not be drilled in the lessons. The determiner$_2$ slot and its filler classes will now be available for vocabulary development, however, and you will want to continue to pay attention to this function outside of the drills long after the lessons on it have been completed.

Insertion of the lessons for the nominal possessive pronouns at this point is an attempt to capitalize on whatever conceptual momentum can be built up during the drills on the determiner$_2$ possessive. Because possession develops at an early point, the nominals should be in approximately the correct place in the sequence. These pronouns are quite different from the determiner$_2$ possessives, however, because they fill functions on the clause level, not on the phrase level (see Chapter 4). As a consequence, they have to be drilled separately.

Past time appears at about the time that the equatives and the continuum are being learned. Indeed, the equative and the continuum are not completely learned until they can be used in their past tense forms. In order to introduce past time into the drills, we will first concentrate on drilling the regular past tense inflection that appears on intransitive and transitive verbs, and then go on to drill past time with the continuum and finally the equative.

The last thing to be drilled in this chapter will be adverbials of place using a number of different pronouns. The drills begin by concentrating on three prepositions that have appeared before: *in, on,* and *under*. Very quickly, however, other prepositions are introduced.

The Lessons

Many of the lessons in this section may have been overreduced in terms of their specificity. There are five lessons on the demonstrative pronouns, for example, where two could conceivably have been written (as was done, for example, with the lessons for the personal pronouns). Many teachers will find that they can very rapidly progress through the lessons to the drills that combine all four of the demonstratives, while other teachers will find that they have to go through the lessons one at a time, steadily and slowly, because it takes their children a long time to catch on. However, when doing the lessons in this section, whatever the speed of the group, go through the single stimulus-response drills as quickly as you can. This strategy enables you to mix the patterns being drilled all in one lesson (especially in Lessons 4.1 to 4.11). There are complicated concepts to be learned in these drills, however, and these concepts are important enough to the language to take whatever time is needed.

The lessons on the prepositions at the end of the section provide a very special problem. Many of these words may prove to be just too much to learn for most children who are at this point in development. If you find your group getting mired down in some of these prepositions, do not hesitate to drop them from the lessons and return to them several months or a year later. The prepositions in Lessons 4.16 to 4.19 have been grouped in Section 4 as much for organizational purposes as they have for learning purposes. Keep this in mind and it should be no problem for you to drop the ones that give your children too much trouble and return to them when you think they are more ready for them.

LESSON 4.1

Objective: To drill the contrast between *this* and *that*.

Materials: The only materials you should need for this lesson are the children themselves and the things near them that they can touch. The vocabulary for the lesson is made up of body parts, chairs, tables, floor, clothing, etc.

Basic Drill Pattern:

S: Everybody, do this. What is $\begin{Bmatrix} \text{this} \\ \text{that} \end{Bmatrix} \begin{Bmatrix} \text{I am} \\ \text{you are} \end{Bmatrix}$ *verb* -ing)?

R: $\begin{Bmatrix} \text{This} \\ \text{That} \end{Bmatrix}$ is a (*noun*).

Method: This is a lesson in which everybody is in motion. The teacher tells the children to touch something in some way while she does the same thing and then drills the pattern. During the entire lesson *this* and *that* should be contrasted with each other continuously.

Examples:

Teacher:	(demonstrates drill with aide)
Teacher:	Everybody, do this. (Touches nose.) What is that you are touching?
Aide and children:	This is a nose.
Teacher:	Everybody, do this. (Touches chin.) What is that you are touching?
Aide and children:	This is a chin.
Teacher:	What is this I am touching?
Aide and children:	That is a chin.

Things to Look Out For:

1. Do not do anything that the children cannot do as well. The contrast between *this* and *that* in this lesson is based on *identical* actions by teacher and children. All things touched must be identifiable as *this* by the children. If they have to reach too far, it might become identifiable as *that*. Keep "the things touched" close to the body.

2. You are not limited to the word *touch*. For example:

   S: What is that you're patting?
   S: What is that you're rubbing?
   S: What is that you're feeling?
   S: What is that you're wiping?

   All verbs used, however, must refer to present, ongoing actions. Therefore, all verbs used will be inflected with the present progressive *-ing: holding, pushing,* etc.

3. All "things touched" must be singular. Do not have the children touch both ears at once, for example. This question would call for the plurals, *are, these,* and *those.* Plural words belong in the next lesson.

4. You may contract *is* and *are.* If the children are ready, they may contract *is* in the appropriate places.

5. As soon as the children begin to get the contrast between *this* and *that,* move to Lesson 4.2 and then on into the dialogues (4.2 and 4.4) as soon as possible.

LESSON 4.2

Objective: To drill the contrast between *these* and *those*.

Materials: Use the same materials as in Lesson 4.1, except that all objects touched will now be in the plural.

Basic Drill Pattern: S_1: Everybody, do this. (Teacher demonstrates.) What are $\left\{\begin{array}{l}\text{these}\\\text{those}\end{array}\right\}$ $\left\{\begin{array}{l}\text{I am}\\\text{you are}\end{array}\right\}$ (*verb* -ing)?

R_1: $\left\{\begin{array}{l}\text{These}\\\text{Those}\end{array}\right\}$ are (*noun*$_{pl}$).

Method: Same as for Lesson 4.1. Again, there should be a continuous contrast between *these* and *those*.

Examples:

Teacher:	(demonstrates drill with aide)
Teacher:	Everybody, do this. (Touches ears.) What are those you are touching?
Aide and children:	These are ears.
Teacher:	What are these I am touching?
Aide and children:	Those are ears, too.
Teacher:	Everybody, do this. (Touches shoes.) What are those you are touching?
Aide and children:	These are shoes.
Teacher:	What are these I am touching?
Aide and children:	Those are shoes, too.

Things to Look Out For:

1. See notes on Lesson 4.1.

2. All things touched must be plural so that *these* and *those* will make sense.

3. Again, as soon as the lesson begins to run smoothly, go on to Lesson 4.3, in which all four demonstratives are contrasted.

LESSON 4.3.

Objectives: To drill the contrast between *this, that, these,* and *those* in a dialogue.

Materials: Combine all materials that you used in Lessons 4.1 and 4.2.

Basic Drill Pattern: S_1: Everybody, do this. (Teacher demonstrates.) What is $\begin{Bmatrix} \text{this} \\ \text{that} \end{Bmatrix}$ $\begin{Bmatrix} \text{I am} \\ \text{you are} \end{Bmatrix}$ (*verb* -ing)?

R_1: $\begin{Bmatrix} \text{This} \\ \text{That} \end{Bmatrix}$ is a (*noun*).

S_2: Do this. (Demonstrates.) What are $\begin{Bmatrix} \text{these} \\ \text{those} \end{Bmatrix}$ $\begin{Bmatrix} \text{I am} \\ \text{you are} \end{Bmatrix}$ (*verb* -ing)?

R_2: $\begin{Bmatrix} \text{These} \\ \text{Those} \end{Bmatrix}$ are (*noun*$_{\text{pl}}$).

Method: This lesson is simply a combination of Lessons 4.1 and 4.2. Do the same things that you did in those lessons, except that singular and plural are to be included in the same lesson.

Examples:

Teacher:	(demonstrates drill with aide)
Teacher:	Everybody, do this. (Rubs knee.) What is that you are rubbing?
Aide and children:	This is a knee.
Teacher:	What is this I am rubbing?
Aide and children:	That is a knee.
Teacher:	Do this. (Waves hands.) What are those you are waving?
Aide and children:	These are hands.
Teacher:	What are these I am waving?
Aide and children:	Those are hands, too.

Things to Look Out For: 1. See all notes under Lessons 4.1 and 4.2.

2. While you do not always have to touch something singular one time and something plural the next, try to balance singular and plural so that you get approximately equal numbers of both in the lesson.

3. If your children experience difficulty with all of these contrasts, drop back to Lesson 4.1 or 4.2 for awhile, and then return to this lesson.

LESSON 4.4

Objective: To integrate the demonstrative into the patterns drilled in previous basic drill patterns with a dialogue.

Materials: Use the same materials you used in Lessons 4.1–4.3.

Basic Drill Pattern: *Note:* Singular/plural and *this/that* or *these/those* contrasts do not appear in the following sequence because of the visual clutter which could result if they were all put in. Consider each singular pattern as having a plural counterpart. Vary all contrasts made in Lessons 4.1–4.3.

S_1: Everybody, do this. What is that you're (*verb* -ing)?
R_1: This is a (*noun*).
S_2: Is that (*noun*) (*adjective*$_1$)?
R_2: No, this (*noun*) is not (*adjective*$_1$).
S_3: Is that (*noun*) (*adjective*$_2$)?
R_3: Yes, this (*noun*) is (*adjective*$_2$).
S_4: What kind of (*noun*) is it, then?
R_4: This is an (*adjective*$_2$) one.
S_5: What are these I am (*verb* -ing)?

(Pattern repeats for each new object or objects that the teacher touches.)

Method: 1. There is nothing new in this drill because it has all been done before in previous lessons.
2. In R_4, at your option, the children may respond:

   R_4: This is an (*adjective*$_2$) (*noun*).

Example:

Teacher:	(demonstrates drill with aide)
Teacher:	Everybody, do this. What is that you're touching?
Aide and children:	This is a tooth.
Teacher:	Is that tooth orange?
Aide and children:	No, this tooth is not orange.
Teacher:	Is that tooth white?
Aide and children:	Yes, this tooth is white.
Teacher:	What kind of tooth is it, then?
Aide and children:	This is a white one.
Teacher:	What is this I am touching?
Aide and children:	That is a tooth, too.
Teacher:	Is this tooth purple?
Aide and children:	No, that tooth is not purple.
Teacher:	Is this tooth white?
Aide and children:	Yes, that tooth is white.
Teacher:	What kind of tooth is it, then?
Aide and children:	That is a white tooth.

Things to Look Out For: 1. The form of the dialogue you use is relatively unimportant and the form above is not the only one possible. The only important thing about this dialogue is the fact that the demonstratives are being used in patterns other than the one in which they were taught. You are free to make up a different dialogue if you wish; look back over Sections 1, 2, and 3 for ideas. The only thing you must maintain is the relative nearness/farness distinction necessary to *this* and *that* contrasts.

2. Review all notes for Lessons 4.1–4.3.

LESSON 4.5

Objective: To drill the contrast between *this, that, these,* and *those* without having a contrast present in the stimulus.

Materials: Use the same material which you have been using in Lessons 4.1–4.4.

Basic Drill Pattern:

S_1: Everybody, do this. (Demonstrates.) What are you (*verb* -ing)?

R_1: $\left\{ \begin{matrix} \text{This} \\ \text{These} \end{matrix} \right\}$ $\left\{ \begin{matrix} \text{is} \\ \text{are} \end{matrix} \right\}$ $\left\{ \begin{matrix} \text{a } noun_{\text{sg}} \\ noun_{\text{pl}} \end{matrix} \right\}$.

S_2: What am I (*verb* -ing)?

R_2: $\left\{ \begin{matrix} \text{That} \\ \text{Those} \end{matrix} \right\}$ $\left\{ \begin{matrix} \text{is} \\ \text{are} \end{matrix} \right\}$ $\left\{ \begin{matrix} \text{a } noun_{\text{sg}} \\ noun_{\text{pl}} \end{matrix} \right\}$.

Method: Use the same method used in Lessons 4.1–4.4. If you wish, in this drill you can also call on specific children to be the only ones to touch things.

Examples:

Teacher:	(demonstrates drill with aide)
Teacher:	Everybody, do this. What are you touching?
Aide and children:	This is a nose.
Teacher:	What am I touching?
Aide and children:	That is a nose, too.
Teacher:	Johnny, do this. Everybody, what is Johnny touching?
Aide and children (except Johnny):	That is a nose.
Teacher:	Johnny, what are you touching?
Johnny:	This is a nose.

Things to Look Out For:

1. By now the children should understand the *this/that/these/those* distinctions. This drill was written simply to demonstrate the fact that they do not have to occur in contrast to one another. Since any one of the four forms may occur alone (and usually do), it is probably best to demonstrate this principle.

2. You should feel free to make up games within which the drill may be run. One child, for example, may be designated to go around the room touching things for the following pattern:

S_1: What is he touching?
R_1: That is a wall.
S_2: Johnny, what are you touching?
R(Johnny): This is a wall.

The children can take turns at going around the room. Lots of games are possible in this and any other drill in TALK and *should* be used at any time the teacher feels a need for variety.

3. Note that we have not exhausted the possibilities for drill with the demonstratives. If you feel it is necessary to do so, you can drill the children on a pattern in which *this* and *these* refer to something common to the entire group, *including* the teacher and aide:

S_1: What are these we are (*verb* -ing)?

R_1: These are (*noun*$_{pl}$).

S_2: What $\begin{Bmatrix} \text{is} \\ \text{are} \end{Bmatrix} \begin{Bmatrix} \text{that} \\ \text{those} \end{Bmatrix}$ we are (*verb* -ing)?

R_2: $\begin{Bmatrix} \text{That} \\ \text{Those} \end{Bmatrix} \begin{Bmatrix} \text{is} \\ \text{are} \end{Bmatrix} \begin{Bmatrix} \text{a } noun_{sg} \\ noun_{pl} \end{Bmatrix}$.

By now, however, it may be that you are getting tired of the demonstrative and would like to move on to something different. The above drill(s) are not required. You may do them or not, or come back to them at a later time.

4. Review all notes for Lessons 4.1–4.4.

LESSON 4.6

Objective: To drill the possessive inflection.

Materials: You may use any materials which can be used to indicate possession, e.g., the children and their body parts and clothing, or pictures of people holding objects.

Basic Drill Pattern:

S: Whose $\left\{\begin{array}{l} noun \\ nouns \end{array}\right\} \left\{\begin{array}{l} is \\ are \end{array}\right\} \left\{\begin{array}{l} this \\ these \end{array}\right\}$?

R: (*Pronoun*) $\left\{\begin{array}{l} is \\ are \end{array}\right\} \left\{\begin{array}{l} the\ noun \\ name \end{array}\right\}$'s.

Method: Simply ask the children who owns various things. The possessive noun may be either a proper noun (name) or a common noun.

Examples:

Teacher:	(demonstrates drill with aide)
Teacher:	Everybody, whose bone is this?
Aide and children:	It is the dog's.
Teacher:	Whose shoes are these?
Aide and children:	They are Johnny's.
Teacher:	Whose hoof is this?
Aide and children:	It is the horse's.
Teacher:	Whose fishing poles are these?
Aide and children:	They are the boys'.
Teacher:	Whose desks are these?
Aide and children:	They are the children's.

Things to Look Out For:

1. One of our teachers popped M&M's into open mouths following a response to: "Whose candy is this!" The children liked it quite a lot, but you should realize that this can cause the rhythm of the drill to be quite slow. For teaching purposes we have found that edible reinforcers are not usually necessary, but this could make a good Friday afternoon drill, or possibly a good drill for a holiday party.

2. If you use body parts and articles of clothing, do not let the child who is the demonstrator respond. He will have to say "It is mine" if you do, and this response does not fit the pattern. Do not use your own body parts or articles of clothing, either, because these call for the response, "It is yours." See Lessons 4.7 and 4.8 for these pronouns.

3. In any of the lessons on possessives, you can play a game in which you act confused, as if you do not know who owns what. Let the children correct you. You would probably want to wait until they start to get fairly good control over a pattern before you introduce the game, but other than this there are no restrictions. It makes a nice break for those days when everyone needs one.

LESSON 4.7

Objective: To drill the noun substitute possessive pronoun in the singular *his, hers,* and *yours.*

Materials: Use materials similar to those you used in Lesson 4.6.

Basic Drill Pattern:

S: Here is $\left\{ \begin{array}{l} \text{my} \\ \textit{name's} \end{array} \right\}$ *(noun).* Whose *(noun)* is it?

R: It is $\left\{ \begin{array}{l} \text{his} \\ \text{hers} \\ \text{yours} \end{array} \right\}$. (Children point to appropriate person.)

Method: Use an approach similar to that used in Lesson 4.6.

Examples:

Teacher:	(demonstrates drill with aide)
Teacher:	Everybody, here is my shoe. Whose shoe is it?
Aide and children:	It is yours.
Teacher:	Here is Johnny's shirt. Whose shirt is it?
Aide and children:	It is his.
Teacher:	Here is Sally's sock. Whose sock is it?
Aide and children:	It is hers.
Teacher:	Here is the boy's leg. Whose leg is it?
Aide and children:	It is his.
Teacher:	Here is the cow's calf. Whose calf is it?
Aide and children:	It is hers.

Things to Look Out For:

1. The children may want to use inflections at first, but the aide's response will take them in the required direction.

2. See Note 4 for Lesson 4.6.

3. An alternate basic drill pattern, if you want one, might be:

S: Is this $\left\{ \begin{array}{l} \textit{pronoun} \\ \textit{name's} \end{array} \right\}$ *(noun)?*

R_1: Yes, it is $\left\{ \begin{array}{l} \text{his} \\ \text{her} \\ \text{yours} \end{array} \right\}$.

or:

R_2: No, it isn't $\left\{ \begin{array}{l} \text{his} \\ \text{hers} \\ \text{yours} \end{array} \right\}$, it is $\left\{ \begin{array}{l} \textit{name's} \\ \textit{pronoun} \end{array} \right\}$.

Examples:

Teacher:	Is this Johnny's shoe?
Aide and children:	Yes, it is his.
Teacher:	Is this my arm?
Aide and children:	No, it isn't yours, it is Nancy's.
Teacher:	Is this Charlie's nose?
Aide and children:	No, it isn't his, it is yours.

Do not use the contracted form of the negative R_2 if the children are not ready for it.

LESSON 4.8

Objective: To drill the noun substitute plural possessive pronouns *ours*, *yours*, and *theirs*.

Materials: Use materials similar to those in Lessons 4.6–4.7.

Basic Drill Pattern:

$$\text{S: GROUP}_{1or2}, \text{ whose } \left\{ \begin{matrix} \text{is} \\ \text{are} \end{matrix} \right\} \left\{ \begin{matrix} \text{this} \\ \text{these} \end{matrix} \right\} ?$$

$$\text{R: } \left\{ \begin{matrix} \text{It} \\ \text{They} \end{matrix} \right\} \left\{ \begin{matrix} \text{is} \\ \text{are} \end{matrix} \right\} \left\{ \begin{matrix} \text{ours} \\ \text{theirs} \\ \text{yours} \end{matrix} \right\} .$$

Method: Divide the children into two groups and designate some objects to be possessed in common by each group. Ask questions of each group in turn. The group responds with a pointing gesture and the appropriate pattern.

Examples:

Teacher	(demonstrates drill with aide)
Teacher:	Group $_1$, whose is this?
Aide and Group $_1$:	It is ours.
Teacher:	Group $_2$, whose is this?
Aide and Group $_2$:	It is theirs.
Teacher:	Group $_1$, whose are these?
Aide and Group $_1$:	They are theirs.

Things to Look Out For:

1. An alternate drill pattern for this lesson might be:

$$\text{S: GROUP}_{1or2} \left\{ \begin{matrix} \text{is} \\ \text{are} \end{matrix} \right\} \left\{ \begin{matrix} \text{this} \\ \text{these} \end{matrix} \right\} \left\{ \begin{matrix} \text{yours} \\ \text{ours} \\ \text{theirs} \end{matrix} \right\} ?$$

$$\text{R: No, } \left\{ \begin{matrix} \text{it} \\ \text{they} \end{matrix} \right\} \left\{ \begin{matrix} \text{is} \\ \text{are} \end{matrix} \right\} \left\{ \begin{matrix} \text{yours} \\ \text{ours} \\ \text{theirs} \end{matrix} \right\} .$$

Use of this drill pattern requires that you violate the truth value of the stimulus so that the children can respond in the negative.

Example:

Teacher:	Group $_1$, is this yours?
Aide and Group $_1$:	No, it is theirs.
Teacher:	Group $_2$, are these yours?
Aide and Group $_2$:	No, they are yours.

2. Dividing the children into groups may force you to have groups of fewer than four responding children. Try it anyway, and if it doesn't work very well see if you can talk about the class next door as having possessions versus your students having possessions. There is really no easy way to do this drill. If you have only six children in your group, however, it may still work out as the drill is specified, especially if you have your groups

face each other while they are responding. If the lesson is very difficult, try mixing it in with other lessons so that you do it every other day or so. This technique may help you to keep up the tempo of the lesson.

3. In the demonstration with the aide, you can drill the concept of plurality by using yourself and the aide as one group, and the children as the other. You do not have to say *Group*$_1$ or *Group*$_2$ when you are demonstrating the drill.

4. To elicit *It is yours* simply provide a pile of things which are to be "possessed" by you and the aide in common, and use them as you would use the objects possessed by Group$_1$ and Group$_2$.

5. See Note 4 for Lesson 4.6.

LESSON 4.9

Objective: To drill the first person singular noun substitute possessive pronoun *mine*.

Materials: Use the same type of materials that you used in Lessons 4.6 and 4.7.

**Basic Drill
Pattern:** S: *(Name)*, is this your *(noun)*?
R_1: Yes, it is mine.
or:

R_2: It is not mine, it is $\begin{Bmatrix} \text{his} \\ \text{hers} \\ \text{yours} \\ \textit{name's} \end{Bmatrix}$.

Method: Use an approach similar to that used in Lessons 4.6 and 4.7.

Examples:

Teacher:	(demonstrates drill with aide)
Teacher:	Johnny, is this your shoe?
Johnny (with aide):	It is not mine, it is yours.
Teacher:	Sally, is this your nose?
Sally (with aide):	It is not mine, it is his.
Teacher:	Melvin, is this your head?
Melvin (with aide):	Yes, it is mine.

**Things to
Look Out For:** 1. In this lesson, as in any lesson involving the first person singular pronouns, there is no choral drill possible. You can, however, do Lesson 4.6 as an alternate drill, this time allowing the child used as a demonstrator to respond. See Note 3 for Lesson 4.6; you can elicit *mine* using the basic drill pattern for Lesson 4.6 if it is easier for you. You can also insert the drill pattern above into Lesson 4.6 and get a little dialogue going:

S_1: Whose *(subject)* $\begin{Bmatrix} \text{is} \\ \text{are} \end{Bmatrix}$ $\begin{Bmatrix} \text{this} \\ \text{these} \end{Bmatrix}$?

R_1: $\begin{Bmatrix} \text{It} \\ \text{They} \end{Bmatrix}$ $\begin{Bmatrix} \text{is} \\ \text{are} \end{Bmatrix}$ $\begin{Bmatrix} \text{the } \textit{noun's} \\ \textit{name's} \\ \textit{pronoun} \end{Bmatrix}$.

S_2: (Name), is this your *(noun)*?
R_2: Yes, it is mine.
or:
R_3: No, it is not mine, it is *(pronoun)*.

All this drill pattern does is to put together the basic drill patterns for Lessons 4.6 and 4.9. As usual, this strategy is to be encouraged, and you should try others on your own.
2. See Note 4 for Lesson 4.6.

LESSON 4.10

Objective: To drill the determiner$_2$ singular possessive pronouns fillers *your*, *his*, *her*, and *its*.

Materials: Use materials similar to those used in Lessons 4.6–4.9.

Basic Drill Pattern:

S$_1$: Whose (*noun$_1$*) is this?
R$_1$: It's (*name's*) (*noun$_1$*).
S$_2$: Whose (*noun$_2$*) is this?

R$_2$: That is $\begin{Bmatrix} \text{his} \\ \text{her} \\ \text{your} \end{Bmatrix}$ (*noun$_2$*), too.

Method: Do this drill just as you did the other drills for possessives.

Examples:

Teacher:	(demonstrates drill with aide)
Teacher:	Whose nose is this?
Aide and children:	It is Janey's nose.
Teacher:	Whose sock is this?
Aide and children:	That is her sock, too.
Teacher:	Whose shoe is this?
Aide and children:	It is Johnny's shoe.
Teacher:	Whose chair is this?
Aide and children:	That is his chair, too.

Things to Look Out For:

1. Remember, you are now drilling determiner$_2$ fillers. The children may have a tendency to respond with the noun substitutes because they have been drilling them for quite awhile now. There is a distinction, however, and you want to make sure that your children can make it.

2. You can use this basic drill pattern to drill *my* by simply calling for a negative response as specified in Lesson 4.9. For this reason we are not writing a separate lesson for *my*. Wait until most of the children can handle Lesson 4.10 fairly well, then intersperse individual drills:

Teacher:	Johnny, is this your sock?
Johnny:	It is not my sock, it is Sally's.

See notes for Lesson 4.9.

4. See Note 4 for Lesson 4.6.

LESSON 4.11

Objective: To drill the determiner$_2$ plural possessive pronouns *our, your,* and *their*.

Materials: Use materials similar to those you have been using in the other lessons for possessives in this section.

Basic Drill Pattern:

S: Whose $\begin{Bmatrix} noun \\ nouns \end{Bmatrix} \begin{Bmatrix} is \\ are \end{Bmatrix} \begin{Bmatrix} this \\ these \end{Bmatrix}$?

R: $\begin{Bmatrix} It \\ They \end{Bmatrix} \begin{Bmatrix} is \\ are \end{Bmatrix} \begin{Bmatrix} our \\ their \\ your \end{Bmatrix} \begin{Bmatrix} noun \\ nouns \end{Bmatrix}$.

Method: Form two groups of children and use yourself and the aide as a third group for eliciting *your,* just as in Lesson 4.8.

Examples:

Teacher:	(demonstrates drill with aide)
Teacher:	Group $_1$, whose ball is this?
Aide and Group $_1$:	It is our ball.
Teacher:	Group $_1$, whose pencil is this?
Aide and Group $_1$:	It is their pencil.
Teacher:	Group $_1$, whose blocks are these?
Aide and Group $_1$:	They are your blocks.
Teacher:	Group $_2$, whose chairs are these?
Aide and Group $_2$:	They are their chairs.
Teacher:	Group $_2$, whose shoes are these?
Aide and Group $_2$:	They are our shoes.

Things to Look Out For:

1. See Note 2 for Lesson 4.8.

2. You may use a basic drill pattern similar to that used in Lesson 4.8 if you wish, instead of or in addition to this pattern. See Note 1 for Lesson 4.8.

3. You should have no trouble working up a dialogue drill for review purposes at this point.

4. See Note 4 for Lesson 4.8.

LESSON 4.12

Objective: To drill the past tense inflection on regular verb stems.

Materials: Use actions by yourself and the children, pictures of people or things in action, or a puppet that can be made to do things.

Basic Drill Pattern: S_1: $\left\{\begin{array}{l} Name \\ Everybody \end{array}\right\}$, do this. (Indicate action.) What $\left\{\begin{array}{l} is \\ are \end{array}\right\}$ (*pronoun*) doing?

R_1: (*Pronoun*) $\left\{\begin{array}{l} is \\ are \end{array}\right\}$ (*verb* -ing) ± (*object*).

S_2: O.K., now stop. What did (*pronoun*) do?

R_2: (*Pronoun*) (*verb* -ed) ± (*object*).

Method: Note that there are two responses in this drill. The first is made while the action is going on, and the second is made after it has stopped.

Examples:

Teacher:	(demonstrates drill with aide)
Teacher:	Everybody, do this. What are you doing?
Aide and children:	We are touching our noses.
Teacher:	O.K., now stop. What did you do?
Aide and children:	We touched our noses.
Teacher:	Johnny, do this. What is he doing?
Aide and children:	He is patting his knees.
Teacher:	O.K., now stop. What did he do?
Aide and children:	He patted his knee.
Teacher:	Everybody, do this. What are you doing?
Aide and children:	We are waving.
Teacher:	O.K., now stop. What did you do?
Aide and children:	We waved.

Things to Look Out For:

1. This lesson uses only regular verbs. Remember, the regular verbs are those which are inflected for past by adding /-t, -d, or ɨd/.

2. Remember that if any of your children regularly use these endings on the irregulars, they are telling you that they know the rules for the regular past inflections and do not need to drill them.

3. If you use pictures of people or things in action, you will have to change the basic drill pattern slightly. If you show pictures, for example, it could go like this:

Teacher:	Here is a man who delivers milk. What is he doing?
Aide and children:	He is delivering milk.
Teacher:	Now he is all through. What did he do?
Aide and children:	He delivered the milk.

If you use a puppet, it might go like this:

Teacher:	Otto can wave a flag. What is he doing?
Aide and children:	He is waving a flag.
Teacher:	Now he has stopped. What did he do?
Aide and children:	He waved a flag.

The Determiner₂, Possession, Past Time, and Location Adverbials   335

LESSON 4.13

Objective: To drill the past tense of the auxiliary in the continuum.

Materials: Use materials similar to those used in the Lesson 4.12.

Basic Drill Pattern:

S: $\begin{Bmatrix} Name \\ Everybody \end{Bmatrix}$, do this. (Indicate action) Now stop. What $\begin{Bmatrix} was \\ were \end{Bmatrix}$ (*pronoun*) doing?

R: (*Pronoun*) $\begin{Bmatrix} was \\ were \end{Bmatrix}$ (*verb* -ing) ± (*object*).

Method: Use an approach similar to those used in Lesson 4.12. If you use pictures or a puppet, you can use the same variations suggested for Lesson 4.12.

Examples:

Teacher:	(demonstrates drill with aide)
Teacher:	Johnny, do this. O.K., now stop. What was he doing?
Aide and children:	He was waving his hand.
Teacher:	Look at this girl eating her breakfast. Now she is all through. What was she doing?
Aide and children:	She was eating her breakfast.

Things to Look Out For:

1. Notice that even though some verbs are irregular in the simple past, this fact has no bearing on the form of the past continuum. It is quite regular, and your choice of verbs is wide open.

2. The past continuum is the same thing as the present continuum except for the fact that the auxiliary BE is inflected for tense. This is the first time that the concept of inflecting the auxiliary appears in the program, but the children should have little difficulty with it by now. It will come up again and again when we get to the modals and the other tense-carriers such as *have*.

3. Review the notes for Lesson 4.12.

LESSON 4.14

Objective: To drill the past tense forms of the equative BE.

Materials: Use pictures or objects which can be held in one hand.

Basic Drill Pattern:

S_1: See $\begin{Bmatrix} \text{this} \\ \text{these} \end{Bmatrix}$ $\begin{Bmatrix} noun \\ nouns \end{Bmatrix}$? (Hide the object.) What $\begin{Bmatrix} \text{was} \\ \text{were} \end{Bmatrix}$ $\begin{Bmatrix} \text{it} \\ \text{they} \end{Bmatrix}$?

R_1: $\begin{Bmatrix} \text{It} \\ \text{They} \end{Bmatrix}$ $\begin{Bmatrix} \text{was} \\ \text{were} \end{Bmatrix}$ $\begin{Bmatrix} a\ noun \\ nouns \end{Bmatrix}$.

S_2: What $\begin{Bmatrix} \text{color} \\ \text{size} \\ \text{shape} \end{Bmatrix}$ $\begin{Bmatrix} \text{was} \\ \text{were} \end{Bmatrix}$ $\begin{Bmatrix} \text{it} \\ \text{they} \end{Bmatrix}$?

R_2: $\begin{Bmatrix} \text{It} \\ \text{They} \end{Bmatrix}$ $\begin{Bmatrix} \text{was} \\ \text{were} \end{Bmatrix}$ (*adjective*).

Method: Show the picture or object, then hide it someplace—behind your back, etc. Then present the stimulus following the basic drill pattern.

Examples:

Teacher:	(demonstrates drill with aide)
Teacher:	See this? What was it?
Aide and children:	It was a ball.
Teacher:	What color was it?
Aide and children:	It was red.
Teacher:	See these? What were they?
Aide and children:	They were blocks.
Teacher:	What size were they?
Aide and children:	They were small.

Things to Look Out For:

1. You can make a real game out of this drill.

2. Be sure that whatever you use can be hidden. It is also possible to use something like slides or filmstrips in this drill, because they can be removed easily and quickly.

3. For S_2 and R_2 you could also use the following:

S_2: $\begin{Bmatrix} \text{Was} \\ \text{Were} \end{Bmatrix}$ $\begin{Bmatrix} \text{it} \\ \text{they} \end{Bmatrix}$ (*adjective$_1$*)?

R_2: Yes, $\begin{Bmatrix} \text{it} \\ \text{they} \end{Bmatrix}$ $\begin{Bmatrix} \text{was} \\ \text{were} \end{Bmatrix}$.

or:

R_2: No, $\begin{Bmatrix} \text{it} \\ \text{they} \end{Bmatrix}$ $\begin{Bmatrix} \text{was} \\ \text{were} \end{Bmatrix}$ not (*adjective$_1$*), $\begin{Bmatrix} \text{it} \\ \text{they} \end{Bmatrix}$ $\begin{Bmatrix} \text{was} \\ \text{were} \end{Bmatrix}$ (*adjective$_2$*).

4. The lessons on the present tense forms of BE in Section 2 provide many suggestions for other possible drill patterns. Feel free to adapt them.

5. If varying singular and plural causes any problems, break the drill down into two separate drills, one for singular and one for plural, and recombine them when the children can handle both.

LESSON 4.15

Objective: To drill the prepositions *in, on,* and *under.*

Materials: At least two objects, one of which is able to contain the other (to express *in*).

**Basic Drill
Pattern:**   S: Where is the ($noun_1$)?

$$R: \text{It is } \begin{Bmatrix} \text{in} \\ \text{on} \\ \text{under} \end{Bmatrix} \text{ the } (noun_2).$$

Method: The teacher demonstrates positions of the two objects and asks the children questions following the basic drill pattern.

Examples:

Teacher:	(demonstrates drill with aide)
Teacher:	Everybody, where is the ball?
Aide and children:	It is in the can.
Teacher:	Where is the ball now?
Aide and children:	It is under the can.
Teacher:	Where is the ball now?
Aide and children:	It is on the can.

**Things to
Look Out For:**   1. These are probably the easiest three prepositions to teach. Your children may know them already; if they do, don't spend a great deal of time drilling them.

2. One teacher we know had a great deal of success with boxes that washing machines and refrigerators come in. She had the children go in, out, and around them, asked them where the floor and rug were and placed various objects on top of them. For the prepositions in this lesson and those such as *between* (Lesson 4.16), she used two boxes, etc., and used the basic drill pattern:

S: Where are you now?

$$R: \begin{Bmatrix} I \\ we \end{Bmatrix} \begin{Bmatrix} am \\ are \end{Bmatrix} \begin{Bmatrix} \text{in} \\ \text{on} \\ \text{in front of} \\ \text{behind} \end{Bmatrix} \text{ the boxes.}$$

You may find this kind of thing to be a great deal of fun when you do dialogues with all of the prepositions. Varying the basic drill pattern in this way presents no problems. Use your imagination!

LESSON 4.16

Objective: To drill the prepositions *beside, between,* and *behind.*

Materials: Use the same type of materials which you used in Lesson 4.15.

Basic Drill Pattern:

S: Where is the (*noun$_1$*)?

R: It is $\begin{Bmatrix} \text{beside} \\ \text{between} \\ \text{behind} \end{Bmatrix}$ the (*noun$_2$*).

Method: Use the same method as in Lesson 4.15. You may vary the basic drill pattern as outlined in Note 2 for Lesson 4.15 if you wish. You will need a pair of at least one of the objects (to drill *between*).

Examples:

Teacher:	(demonstrates drill with aide)
Teacher:	Everybody, where is the marble?
Aide and children:	It is beside the box(es).
Teacher:	Where is the marble now?
Aide and children:	It is between the boxes.
Teacher:	Where is the marble now?
Aide and children:	It is behind the box(es).

Things to Look Out For:

1. A dialogue is possible at this point. See Note 2 for Lesson 4.15.

2. You may vary from singular to plural using the prepositions *beside* and *behind,* but you must use only the plural (e.g., *boxes*) for between.

3. The prepositions are getting a little more difficult now, and you should not be surprised if this drill takes a little more time than the first one did. If these prepositions prove to be too much for your children, do not be afraid to move on to something else and come back to them at a later time.

LESSON 4.17

Objective: To drill the prepositions *to, from, into, through,* and *out of.*

Materials: Use the same type of materials you used in Lessons 4.15 and 4.16. A variety of materials might be helpful for this drill if you use several different verbs.

Basic Drill Pattern:

S: Where did I *(verb)* ± *(object)*?

R: You *(verb -ed)* ± *(object)* $\begin{Bmatrix} to \\ from \\ into \\ out\ of \\ through \end{Bmatrix}$ the *(noun₂)*.

Method: The prepositions in this lesson all involve motion in some way. The teacher makes the appropriate motion *before* asking the question.

Examples:

Teacher:	(demonstrates drill with aide)
Teacher:	Everybody, where did I push the block?
Aide and children:	You pushed the block to the cup.
Teacher:	Now where did I push the block?
Aide and children:	You pushed the block from the cup.
Teacher:	Now where did I put the block?
Aide and children:	You put the block into the cup.
Teacher:	Now what did I dump the block out of?
Aide and children:	You dumped the block out of the cup.
Teacher:	Now where did I slide the block?
Aide and children:	You slid the block through the hole.

Things to Look Out For:

1. Notice the sequencing of the prepositions in these examples. If *from* is drilled after *out of*, we would probably want to say *away from* rather than simply *from*. By sequencing it immediately after *to*, however, we get a much more natural response from the children. It would do no harm to drill the children on *away from* (e.g., "You take the block away from the cup"), but it seems best to make sure that *from* is established before you do.

Note that there are many other combinations possible: *up to, over to,* etc. You may also wish to drill these, but if you do, try to use motions appropriate to them. *Up to,* for example, requires a height differential. ("You bring the ball up to the cup.")

2. You should be mixing in occasional prepositions from the previous lessons, e.g.,

Teacher:	Where did I sit?
Aide and children:	You sat in a chair.

3. Note the use of the past tense in this drill. You should have no problems with those that are inflected regularly. If the irregulars give your children a problem, do not use them. The prepositions are enough for them to have to concentrate on.

4. Conceptually, the prepositions in this lesson are really difficult. You may find that you must come back to them at a later time.

LESSON 4.18

Objective: To drill the prepositions *at* and *with*.

Materials: Pictures of people and animals doing things; the other children in the room or people in the school can also be used.

Basic Drill Pattern:

S: Where $\begin{Bmatrix} is \\ are \end{Bmatrix}$ $\begin{Bmatrix} name \\ the\ noun_1 \end{Bmatrix}$?

R: $\begin{Bmatrix} Pronoun \\ The\ noun_1 \end{Bmatrix}$ $\begin{Bmatrix} is \\ are \end{Bmatrix}$ $\begin{Bmatrix} at \\ with \end{Bmatrix}$ the $(noun_2)$.

Method: Show the pictures to the children and ask the question.

Examples:

Teacher:	(demonstrates drill with aide)
Teacher:	Everybody, where is the daddy in this picture?
Aide and children:	He is at the factory.
Teacher:	And where is the boy in this picture?
Aide and children:	He is with the girl.
Teacher:	And where are the cats in this picture?
Aide and children:	They are at the mouse hole.
Teacher:	And where is the girl in this picture?
Aide and children:	She is with her friends.

Things to Look Out For:

1. In addition, you can also talk about people everybody knows, e.g.,

   S: Where is the principal?
   R: He is at the office.

2. Make a dialogue using all of the prepositions drilled so far.

LESSON 4.19

Objective: To provide some alternate basic drill patterns for some of the prepositions drilled in Section 4.

Materials: Use the same kind of materials you have been using where appropriate.

Basic Drill Patterns:

S: Did you ever see a $(noun_1)$ $(verb)$ $\pm$ $(object)$ $(adverbial)$?

R: Yes, $\left\{ \begin{array}{c} \text{I} \\ \text{we} \end{array} \right\}$ saw a $(noun_1)$ $(verb)$ $\pm$ $(object)$ $(adverbial)$.

Example: Did you ever see a dog in a house?
Yes, I saw a dog in a house.

S: Can you $(verb)$ the $(noun_1)$ $\pm$ $(adverbial)$?
R: Yes. There—I $(verb$ -ed$)$ the $(noun_1)$ $\pm$ $(adverbial)$.

Example: Can you put the ball into the cup?
Yes. There—I put the ball into the cup.

S: Is the $(noun)$ $(adverbial_1)$?
R: Yes, the $(noun)$ is $(adverbial_1)$.
or:
R: No, the $(noun)$ is $(adverbial)$.

Example: Is the ball in the cup?
No, the ball is out of the cup.

Method: The basic reason for including this lesson is to develop a few different illustrative drill patterns for the same prepositions we have been drilling. Actually, virtually any drill pattern used in the program thus far can be used because adverbials are optional in any clause pattern. You should feel free to make up your own drills.

Thing to Look Out For: 1. You may find yourself having a little difficulty if any pattern you make up requires the children to use rules they are not yet familiar with. The modals, for example, will not be drilled until later on in the program, and the children might have some difficulty making the response, "Yes, I can $(verb)$ $\pm$ $(object)$ $(adverbial)$."

Modals (*May, Can, Will*), Future Time, and More Adverbials

At this point a new verb phrase function will be introduced: the modal. To do this, only three modal fillers will be used: *may, can,* and *will.* These will be used only in their present tense forms. In order to teach modals, the concept ''future time'' will be introduced for the first time in the program, along with the adverbials of time. Finally, the adverbial of manner will be drilled.

After the continuum develops, the modals begin to appear regularly. The first forms used consistently to fill this function are the present tense forms, *may, can* and *will.* The *must* form appears later, and the *shall* form rarely appears at all, except in certain dialects. Past tense forms of all the modals also appear much later, so we will restrict the modal lessons in this section to just the three already mentioned.

   The first two modals are relatively easy to work into the sequence at this point, but the third (*will*) presents us with the problem of future time reference. This problem has not been given any attention in the program thus far, and before we try to introduce *will,* we will have to do some work on the concept of future time. To start this, we will use the device of *is going to.* It is possible to bring up some strong objections to the introduction of this device so early in the program on the grounds that it requires the use of an infinitive insert too early. However, children regularly use *gonna* at an early time, and it appears to have little or nothing to do with the infinitive at first. When we begin to use it in the drills, we will not require the children to produce *is going to* if they are not ready; *gonna* will be quite acceptable for our purposes. Remember that we wish to elicit statements about the future, not to drill the infinitive. The main task is to set the stage for the use of *will* and the adverbials of time.

The adverbials of time assist us in making time switches easily. To talk about events that have happened in the past, that will happen in the future, or that are happening now, we need rapid and smooth shifts in grammatical structures of the verb phrase. Time adverbials can be very useful in conversation. The adverbial of manner will also be drilled in this section. It is logical to have these drills follow the adverbials of time because adverbials of manner are less frequently used, yet the momentum to drill adverbials should be present.

The Lessons

The lessons on the first two modal fillers (*may* and *can*) should not cause many instructional problems, and you are likely to find that these lessons go quietly and smoothly. The lessons on future time, however, may give some children trouble, largely because it is far more difficult to think about the "things that will be" than it is to conceive of the "things that were." Yesterday's present is today's past, but the future does not exist yet. In terms of the grammar there is not much to learn about future, but in terms of conceptual load, future time can be very difficult for some children. For this reason we try to load the drills on future time with signals: not only will we use grammatical signals like *is going to* and *will,* but we will also use adverbials of time. All of these are in the lessons on the future through deliberate choice, and if you invent any new drill patterns for "future time," you should make a conscious attempt to include as many signals as possible.

As part of the adverbial of time group of lessons, drills using the prepositions *before, during* and *after* are included. Note that they refer to time not in absolute terms, but in relation to another time ("I make my bed before I eat my breakfast"). These prepositions may be too much for children in the early stages of development. Try them, though, and you may be pleasantly surprised at the results. These lessons come at the end of the section and are optional. They should be drilled at some point, however, and if you find that you need to skip them, be sure to come back to them later.

LESSON 5.1

Objective: To drill the modal *can* with the meaning of "ability to do something."

Materials: Use the experience of the children and talk about actions that they know can or cannot be carried out.

Basic Drill
Pattern: S: Can *(subject) (verb)* ± *(object)* ± *(adverbial)?*

R: $\left\{ \begin{array}{c} \text{Yes} \\ \text{No} \end{array} \right\}$, *(subject)* $\left\{ \begin{array}{c} \text{can} \\ \text{cannot} \end{array} \right\}$ *(verb)* ± *(object)* ± *(adverbial)*.

Method: Ask the children questions about things they know they, the aide, or you can or cannot do.

Examples:	Teacher:	(demonstrates drill with aide)
	Teacher:	Everybody, can you see the blackboard?
	Aide and children:	Yes, we can see the blackboard.
	Teacher:	Can I go in the teacher's lounge?
	Aide and children:	Yes, you can go in the teacher's lounge.
	Teacher:	Can you fly an airplane?
	Aide and children:	No, we cannot fly an airplane.

Things to
Look Out For: 1. *Can,* in this lesson, is being used in the sense of "ability to do something." It will be used in the sense of "permission" in Lesson 5.2. Do not mix the two senses in this lesson.

2. When you begin the drill, do not introduce the negative until it begins to go fairly smoothly. When you do begin using the negative, *do not* use *can't.* This form often develops as a simple alternative negative form before the modal itself develops, and the intent of this drill is to teach the children to negate the modal. *Cannot* is best for this purpose.

3. An alternate drill for this lesson might be the following:

S: Which *(noun)* can *(subject) (verb),* the *(adjective₁)* one or the *(adjective₂)* one?
R: *(Subject)* can *(verb)* the *(adjective₁ or ₂)* one.

Examples:	Teacher:	Which pencil can you see, the long one or the short one?
	Aide and children:	We can see the long one.

To run this drill you will need pairs of objects or pictures that are contrasted along some salient dimension. Show both, then hide one and ask about the object or picture still in view.

4. In addition, any of the drill patterns for Lessons 5.1–5.3 are adaptable to any use of the modals *may* and *can.* Feel free to adapt or make up different drills.

LESSON 5.2

Objective: To drill the modal *can* in the sense of "granting permission."

Materials: Use objects or the experiences of the children.

Basic Drill
Pattern: S: Can *(subject)* *(verb)* ± *(object)* ± *(adverbial)*?

R: $\begin{Bmatrix} Yes \\ No \end{Bmatrix}$ *(subject)* $\begin{Bmatrix} can \\ cannot \end{Bmatrix}$ *(verb)* ± *(object)* ± *(adverbial)*.

Method: Use only actions that the children are capable of carrying out. Allow all actions for which permission has been granted to be carried out. The aide should probably signal *yes* or *no* with a nod or a shake of the head before the children's response begins.

Examples:

Teacher:	(demonstrates drill with aide)
Teacher:	Everybody, can Johnny touch his nose?
Aide and children:	Yes, he can touch his nose.
Teacher:	Can Melvin stamp his foot?
Aide and children:	No, he cannot stamp his foot.
Teacher:	Can he wiggle his little finger?
Aide and children:	Yes, he can wiggle his little finger.

Things to
Look Out For:

1. Think about this. When a child is *not* granted permission to do something, you may wish to immediately allow him to do something else. It is too easy to read nonpermission as punishment or rejection, even in a game-like situation such as this particular drill.

2. You might like to divide your children into teams for this drill and let each team grant the other permission to do things.

3. See Notes 2 and 4 for Lesson 5.1.

4. A good game for this drill is Giant Steps.[1]

"Johnny you can take two giant steps."
"Can I?"

" $\begin{Bmatrix} Yes \\ No \end{Bmatrix}$, you $\begin{Bmatrix} can \\ cannot \end{Bmatrix}$." (If negative): "You can take two baby steps."

Most people learned this game using the modal *may*. If using *can* in its place presents you with a problem, wait for the lesson on *may* to play this game.

5. Contract the negative when you feel the children are ready for it.

---

[1]Also known as Mother, may I?, depending on where you were brought up.

LESSON 5.3

Objective: To drill the modal *may* in the sense of granting permission, in both affirmative and negative patterns.

Materials: No materials are required for this drill.

Basic Drill Pattern:

S$_1$: Ask us if (*subject*) may (*verb*) ± (*object*).

S$_2$: May (*subject*) (*verb*) ± (*object*)?

R: $\left\{ \begin{matrix} \text{Yes} \\ \text{No} \end{matrix} \right\}$, (*pronoun*) $\left\{ \begin{matrix} \text{may} \\ \text{may not} \end{matrix} \right\}$ (*verb*) ± (*object*).

Method: The teacher addresses the aide and tells him to ask for permission to do something. The teacher and the children either grant or deny the permission. The teacher should indicate *yes* or *no* with a nod or a shake of the head before the children begin their response.

Examples:

Teacher:	(demonstrates drill with aide)
Teacher:	Mr. Jones, ask us if you may stand up.
Mr. Jones:	May I stand up?
Children and teacher:	Yes, you may stand up.
Teacher:	Ask us if you may sit down.
Mr. Jones:	May I sit down?
Children and teacher:	Yes, you may sit down.
Teacher:	Ask us if you may put your hand on your head.
Mr. Jones:	May I put my hand on my head?
Children and teacher:	No, you may not put your hand on your head.

Things to Look Out For:

1. The teacher must lead the response in this drill since the aide is acting as "third party."

2. You can also easily make this drill into a version of the game Giant Steps. Do not *require* the children to ask questions yet, however (but you can *allow* them to do so if they are able). Perhaps dividing the class into two groups, one to take giant steps, one to do the "granting of permission" is possible.

3. There is no reason why you should not be able to use *may* and *can* in the same drill. You should also be able to do a dialogue drill for review purposes now. When you mix them in the same drill, however, use *can* meaning "is able to," and reserve *may* for granting permission.

4. For this drill, the class takes the role of "complete authority," who dispenses permission at whim. These whims, however, will have to be guided by the teacher so that everyone will say the same thing at once. Nods or shakes of the head (to indicate negation) are adequate cues.

5. See Notes 2 and 4, Lesson 5.1.

LESSON 5.4

Objective: To drill the simple future with *going to*.

Materials: Any objects that can be picked up, moved, or used in pantomime. You may use a hand puppet for this drill if you wish.

Basic Drill Pattern:

S: (*Name*) will (*verb*) ± (*object*). What is (*pronoun*) going to do?

R: (*Pronoun*) is going to (*verb*) ± (*object*).

Method: From your assortment of objects, indicate that something will happen to one of them. Then have a child, the aide, yourself, or the puppet do what is indicated.

Examples:

Teacher:	(demonstrates drill with aide)
Teacher:	Everybody, Otto will wave his flag. What is he going to do?
Aide and children:	He is going to wave his flag.
Teacher:	Now he will pick up the pencil. What is he going to do?
Aide and children:	He is going to pick up his pencil.
Teacher:	Now he will drop the pencil. What is he going to do?
Aide and children:	He is going to drop the pencil.

Things to Look Out For:

1. Note that you can get a little dialogue quite easily by following up the basic drill pattern response with the stimulus.

"What did he do?"

This technique will allow you to vary future and past in the same drill. Give the children enough time to get used to using the future before you start mixing in the past, though.

2. From many children you will get the following response:

(*Subject*) gonna (*verb*) ± (*object*).

Do not spend a lot of time trying to elicit the auxiliary of the continuum in this pattern. If you get it, fine, but if you do not, do not worry about it. Remember that what we are really looking for is statements about future time, not the grammatical construction of object infinitive inserts. A child who says "(*Subject*) gonna (*verb*)" is giving us everything we need at this time.

LESSON 5.5

Objective: To drill the simple future using adverbials of time.

Materials: None needed, but you can use materials similar to those used in Lesson 5.4 if you wish.

Basic Drill Pattern: S: When $\left\{\begin{array}{l}\text{am}\\\text{is}\\\text{are}\end{array}\right\}$ (*subject*) going to (*verb*) $\pm$ (*object*)? (*adverbial*~time~)?

R: Yes, (*subject*) $\left\{\begin{array}{l}\text{am}\\\text{is}\\\text{are}\end{array}\right\}$ going to (*verb*) $\pm$ (*object*) (*adverbial* of time).

Method: Ask the children questions about their daily lives as they usually occur. You can ask about things that the entire group does, or things that individuals do.

Examples:

Teacher:	(demonstrates drill with aide)
Teacher:	Everybody, when are you going to eat lunch? At lunchtime?
Aide and children:	Yes, we are going to eat lunch at lunchtime.
Teacher:	When are you going to play? At recess?
Aide and children:	Yes, we are going to play at recess.
Teacher:	When are you going to sleep? Tonight?
Aide and children:	Yes, we are going to sleep tonight.
Teacher:	When is Johnny going to have a birthday? Tomorrow?
Aide and children:	Yes, he is going to have a birthday tomorrow.

Things to Look Out For:

1. You may also elicit negative responses if you wish.

2. Remember that adverbials of time always answer the question *when*. Note that you need not choose only adverbs. There are many prepositional phrases which function like adverbs:

> He woke at 8 o'clock.
> He woke in the morning.

Adverbs are parts of speech, while prepositional phrases are constructions. Hence the use of the term *adverbial* (meaning "adverb-like"), instead of *adverbs*. For the time being, you should probably stick with the prepositions *at (time)*, and *in (period of time)*. You may find that your children have difficulty handling the prepositional phrases at this time. If so, stick with the simple adverb fillers, because the main objective of this lesson is, again, to drill statements of future time, not prepositional phrases.

3. See Note 2, Lesson 5.4.

4. *Am* is to be used only in individual drills, of course. Remember the kinds of problems you can get into with the first person singular pronoun *I*. (See Sections 2 and 3.)

LESSON 5.6

Objective: To drill the adverbial of time without specifying it in the stimulus.

Materials: You may wish to use the same materials you used in Lesson 5.4, or you may wish to use no materials at all, as in Lesson 5.5.

Basic Drill Pattern:

S: (*Name*), when $\begin{Bmatrix} \text{am} \\ \text{is} \\ \text{are} \end{Bmatrix}$ (*subject*) going to (*verb*) ± (*object*)?

R: (*Subject*) $\begin{Bmatrix} \text{am} \\ \text{is} \\ \text{are} \end{Bmatrix}$ going to (*verb*) ± (*object*) (*adverbial*$_{\text{time}}$).

Method: If you use a puppet, ask the children "When is Otto going to . . . ?" If you use the children, name them first.

Examples:

Teacher:	(demonstrates drill with aide)
Teacher:	Everybody, when is Otto going to eat lunch?
Aide and children:	He is going to eat lunch at lunchtime.
Teacher:	When is he going to sleep?
Aide and children:	He is going to sleep tonight.
Teacher:	When will Otto eat breakfast?
Aide and children:	He is going to eat breakfast in the morning.

Things to Look Out For:

1. Be sure you choose your adverbials carefully. An adverb of time always answers the question *when*. Also, be pretty specific about the types of actions you choose. In Lesson 5.5 you supplied the adverbials, but now the children will have to do it. Choose actions that follow the rhythms of life—waking, sleeping, eating, going to school, vacations. This will make the drill much less of a guessing game for the children. It may be quite difficult for low-functioning children to do this drill; if it is too frustrating for them you may want to pass it by.

2. See Note 2, Lesson 5.4.

3. See Note 2, Lesson 5.5.

4. See Note 4, Lesson 5.5.

LESSON 5.7

Objective: To drill the simple future with the adverbial of manner.

Materials: Use materials similar to those used in Lessons 5.4–5.6. It is possible to use pictures of people doing things.

Basic Drill Pattern:
S: How is (*subject*) going to (*verb*) ± (*object*)? (*adverbial*_{manner})?

R₁: Yes, (*subject*) is going to (*verb*) ± (*object*) (*adverbial*_{manner}).
or:
R₂: No, (*subject*) is not going to (*verb*) ± (*object*) (*adverbial*_{manner}).

Method: Use actions of the puppet; or, holding up pictures, elicit the responses.

Examples:

Teacher:	(demonstrates drill with aide)
Teacher:	Everybody, how is Otto going to sweep the table? Carefully?
Aide and children:	Yes, Otto is going to sweep the table carefully.
Teacher:	How is Otto going to pick up the pencil? Quickly?
Aide and children:	Yes, Otto is going to pick up the pencil quickly.
Teacher:	How is Otto going to sleep? Quietly?
Aide and children:	Yes, Otto is going to sleep quietly.

Things to Look Out For:

1. Adverbials of manner pattern like adverbials of time. Semantically, however, they answer the question *how*. Again, pick your adverbials carefully, choosing them from the children's daily lives. Note that just as in Lesson 5.5, you need not always use an adverb because many prepositional phrases function just like adverbs of manner. For example:

He rode carefully/with care.
He rode swiftly/with speed.
He rode spiritedly/with great spirit.

Any of these choices fill adverbial of manner slots, along with many other words and phrases. Like the adverbs of time, however, you may have to use only true adverbs in this drill. See Note 2, Lesson 5.5.

2. Again, do not elicit negative responses until the affirmative responses come smoothly.

3. It will be rather easy for you to make up several dialogues at this point. Simply combine the basic drill patterns involving future and/or past time.

LESSON 5.8

Objective: To drill the contrast between *before* and *after*.

Materials: You may wish to use pictures, objects, or the experiences of the children. Pictures and objects, if used, should relate to the rhythmic events in the daily lives of the children: eating, sleeping, brushing teeth.

Basic Drill Pattern:

S: $\left\{ \begin{array}{l} \text{Does} \\ \text{Did} \end{array} \right\}$ *(subject) (verb)* ± *(object),* before *(event)* or after *(event)*?

R: *(Subject) (verb)* ± *(object)* $\left\{ \begin{array}{l} \text{before} \\ \text{after} \end{array} \right\}$ *(event).*

Method: Question the children about events in their lives which occur regularly, possibly using pictures or objects as referents.

Examples:

Teacher:	(demonstrates drill with aide)
Teacher:	Everybody, does the boy eat breakfast before school or after school?
Aide and children:	He eats breakfast before school.
Teacher:	Did he ride the bus before breakfast or after breakfast?
Aide and children:	He rode the bus after breakfast.
Teacher:	Does he brush his teeth before bedtime or after bedtime?
Aide and children:	He brushes his teeth before bedtime.

Things to Look Out For:

1. Your vocabulary for the "events" in this lesson must be chosen very carefully. One of the common fillers of *before* and *after* adverbials is a clause. Compare the following utterances:

> He rides the bus after breakfast.
> He rides the bus after he eats breakfast.

The second example contains two clauses, whereas the first contains only one clause with a prepositional phrase. We will not drill subordination until much later in the program, and you should avoid responses like the second.

2. You should not have any trouble mixing tenses in the stimulus. If you do have trouble, however, restrict the stimulus DO to the *does* form.

LESSON 5.9

Objective: To drill the contrast between *during*, and *before* and *after*.

Materials: Use materials similar to those used in Lesson 5.8.

Basic Drill Pattern:

S: $\begin{Bmatrix} \text{Does} \\ \text{Did} \end{Bmatrix}$ *(subject)* *(verb)* $\pm$ *(object)* $\begin{Bmatrix} \text{before} \\ \text{during} \\ \text{after} \end{Bmatrix}$ *(event)* or $\begin{Bmatrix} \text{before} \\ \text{during} \\ \text{after} \end{Bmatrix}$ *(event)*?

R: *(Subject)* *(verb)* $\pm$ *(object)* $\begin{Bmatrix} \text{before} \\ \text{during} \\ \text{after} \end{Bmatrix}$ *(event)*.

Method: Drill this pattern in a manner similar to Lesson 5.8, presenting a choice between *during* and either of the other two prepositions.

Examples:

Teacher:	(demonstrates drill with aide)
Teacher:	Does the bus come during or after school?
Aide and children:	The bus comes after school.
Teacher:	Do we eat during or after lunchtime?
Aide and children:	We eat during lunchtime.
Teacher:	Do we sleep during or before nighttime?
Aide and children:	We sleep during nighttime.

Things to Look Out For:

1. See Note 1 for Lesson 5.8.

2. You may mix *before, during,* and *after* freely, but you should use *during* quite a bit, since it is new to the program.

3. This lesson is the same as Lesson 5.8 except for the addition of *during*. For many children this word may prove to be too much at this time. If so, drop it and return at a later point.

LESSON 5.10

Objective: To drill the modal *will* using adverbs of time.

Materials: All you need for this lesson is the daily experience of the children.

Basic Drill
Pattern: S: When will (*subject*) (*verb*) ± (*object*)?
               R: (*Subject*) will (*verb*) ± (*object*) (*adverb*$_{time}$).

Method: Ask the children questions about their daily lives.

Examples: Teacher: (demonstrates drill with aide)

Teacher: Everybody, when will you sleep?
Aide and children: We will sleep tonight.
Teacher: When will you eat lunch?
Aide and children: We will eat lunch at lunchtime.
Teacher: When will Johnny wake up?
Aide and children: He will wake up in the morning.

Things to
Look Out For: 1. The adverbs of time are being used to tie the modal *will* to future time. As we will see in Lesson 5.11, there are uses of *will* which might be confused with uses of *can* if the time element is not first established firmly.

2. Eventually, you will have to allow contraction of *will* to the subject: *he'll, she'll, it'll, Johnny'll,* etc. No lesson will be written for this contraction.

3. Note that this is approximately the same drill as that found in Lesson 5.6, except for the use of the modal instead of *is going to*. Review all notes for Lessons 5.4, 5.5 and 5.6.

LESSON 5.11

Objective: To drill the negative with the modal *will*.

Materials: Assorted objects, flannel board materials, etc., that will allow you to carry out the required actions.

Basic Drill Pattern: S: Will *(subject)* *(verb)* $\pm$ *(object)* $\pm$ *(adverbial of time)*?

R: $\left\{ \begin{array}{c} \text{Yes} \\ \text{No} \end{array} \right\}$, *(subject)* $\left\{ \begin{array}{c} \text{will} \\ \text{will not} \end{array} \right\}$ *(verb)* $\pm$ *(object)* $\pm$ *(adverbial$_{time}$)*.

Method: Ask the children if various actions will occur. You could do things like show the objects and then hide them before asking the question. The children should be able to predict easily from the situation whether the response should be affirmative or negative.

Examples:

Teacher:	(demonstrates drill with aide)
Teacher:	Everybody, will Johnny see a ball?
Aide and children:	Yes, he will see a ball.
Teacher:	Will Sally touch a table?
Aide and children:	No, Sally will not touch a table.
Teacher:	Will Melvin hear a noise?
Aide and children:	Yes, Melvin will hear a noise.
Teacher:	Will Harry find a million dollars?
Aide and children:	No, Harry will not find a million dollars.
Teacher:	Will we get up tomorrow morning?
Aide and children:	Yes, we will get up tomorrow morning.
Teacher:	Will I go home tonight?
Aide and children:	Yes, you will go home tonight.

Things to Look Out For:

1. This drill is nearly unlimited in the possible actions. For example:

   S: Will the bird fly?
   S: Will the mailbox run?
   S: Will she come out?

2. The aide may have to cue the children on some responses as to affirmation or negation. Cues can be given with a shake of the head, but it would be better if the children know whether a response should be affirmative or negative through their own experience.

3. See Note 2 for Lesson 5.10. The same comment applies to contracting the negative.

4. See Note 3 for Lesson 5.10.

5. After all the children have been using the basic drill pattern well for awhile, they will have to learn to ellipt:

   S: Will Johnny see the circle?
   R: Yes, he will.

6. See Notes 2 and 4 for Lesson 5.1.

SECTION 6

The Dummy DO and Coordinates

Two major concepts will be drilled in this section. One is the use of the dummy DO in its role as carrier of tense and person markings in declaratives, and the other is the coordination of clauses. In drilling the dummy DO, we will concentrate on emphatic statements and negatives. In drilling coordinates, we will use only the conjunctions *and, but* and *or*.

Rationale

In terms of developmental sequences, the dummy DO develops at about the same time as the modals *may, can,* and *will*. Since we have now drilled these modals, the time is right to introduce the dummy DO. DO is one of those words in English that are devoid of lexical meaning, i.e., it exists only to carry tense and person markings for intransitive and transitive clauses under certain conditions; it is also the all-purpose verb substitute. In conversation we use it mostly in the asking of questions, which will be drilled in Section 7. In order to begin getting ready for the drills on questions, therefore, we will introduce the dummy in declaratives, first in its use as an "emphasis-giver," and then as it is found in negation.

For the first time in the program we are also about to place two clauses together in the same sentence. The first of the multiple-clause constructions to appear is the coordinated clause construction, and it first appears at about the time that the dummy DO shows up. This place in the program is natural for this construction, therefore.

Note that coordinates can become very complex in terms of the relationships that can be expressed between clauses by conjunctions. There are many conjunctions in the language, but we will introduce only three: *and, but,* and *or.* This limit will hold down the semantic complexity and still allow us to teach the grammar.

The Lessons

Note that the dummy DO appeared in one of the lessons in the last section. In this section it will now be drilled in all of its forms *do, does, did,* but only in terms of its emphatic use and in negation. Some of the emphatic responses may begin to sound a little awkward after you have been drilling them for several days. If this happens, change lessons and come back later if you need to. Also, as usual, move as swiftly as you can toward combining basic drill patterns in dialogue drills.

The lessons on the coordinates drill only the use of *and, but,* and *or.* The first two develop quite early, but the third (*or*) usually does not develop until a little later. If your children have an inordinate amount of difficulty with *or,* drop it and come back to it at a later time, perhaps after the first few lessons on questions. Note that we take great care in introducing this conjunction; that is, the first lesson drilling *or* (Lesson 6.8) allows it to appear only in the stimulus, and the children are not required to use it until after they have been listening and responding to it for awhile.

The lessons on the coordinates also have a number of alternate drills specified in the "Things to Look Out For" sections. You may use as many or as few of these as you choose; as usual you can make up your own drills if that is your preference and/or need.

LESSON 6.1

Objective: To drill the negative and affirmative declaratives using the dummy DO in the nonpast tense with *I, you, we,* or *they* as the subject.

Materials: Use materials ordinarily found in the classroom. You can also use the children themselves as the material for the drills.

Basic Drill Pattern:

S: Do $\begin{Bmatrix} \text{I} \\ \text{we} \\ \text{you} \\ \text{they} \end{Bmatrix}$ (verb) ± (object) ± (adverbial)?

R: $\begin{Bmatrix} \text{Yes} \\ \text{No} \end{Bmatrix}$, $\begin{Bmatrix} \text{I} \\ \text{we} \\ \text{you} \\ \text{they} \end{Bmatrix}$ $\begin{Bmatrix} \text{do} \\ \text{do not} \end{Bmatrix}$ (verb) ± (object) ± (adverbial).

Method: Ask the children questions about the objects, sounds, etc., in their ordinary environment.

Examples:

Teacher:	(demonstrates drill with aide)
Teacher:	Everybody, do you see a blackboard?
Aide and children:	Yes, we do see a blackboard.
Teacher:	Do I hear a bird?
Aide and children:	No, you do not hear a bird.
Teacher:	Do you wear shoes?
Aide and children:	Yes, we do wear shoes.
Teacher:	Do we eat our lunch in the morning?
Aide and children:	No, we do not eat our lunch in the morning.

Things to Look Out For:

1. Do not vary from the stimulus question word *do.* This rule requires avoidance of the third person singular subject, e.g.,

   Does the girl run fast?
   Does the rain fall?

2. Adverbials will inject a little variety, e.g.,

   Do you sit quietly?
   Do you sit in your chairs?
   Do you wear coats in the wintertime?

LESSON 6.2

Objective: To drill the contrast between negative and affirmative in the statements using the dummy DO in the past tense.

Materials: Use events out of the daily lives of the children for your materials, e.g., school, sleep.

Basic Drill Pattern:

S: Did (*subject*) (*verb*) $\pm$ (*object*) $\pm$ (*adverbial*$_{time}$)?

R: $\left\{ \begin{array}{c} \text{Yes} \\ \text{No} \end{array} \right\}$, (*subject*) $\left\{ \begin{array}{c} \text{did} \\ \text{did not} \end{array} \right\}$ (*verb*) $\pm$ (*object*) $\pm$ (*adverbial*$_{time}$).

Method: Use a method similar to that used in Lesson 6.1.

Examples:

Teacher:	(demonstrates drill with aide)
Teacher:	Everybody, did you come to school this morning?
Aide and children:	Yes, we did come to school this morning.
Teacher:	Did you wear your overcoats today?
Aide and children:	No, we did not wear our overcoats today.
Teacher:	Did you see the accident this morning?
Aide and children:	Yes, we did see the accident this morning.

Things to Look Out For: 1. We are assuming that all special-class and ghetto teachers are sensitive to issues such as some children not getting breakfast in the morning. Use stimuli that can only get the choral response you are trying to drill.

LESSON 6.3

Objective: To drill the affirmative and negative emphatic DO in the present tense.

Materials: Use materials similar to those used in Lessons 6.1 and 6.2.

**Basic Drill
Pattern:** S_1: Does everybody (*verb*) ± (*object*) ± (*adverbial*)?

R_1: $\left\{ \begin{array}{c} \text{Yes} \\ \text{No} \end{array} \right\}$, $\left\{ \begin{array}{c} \text{we} \\ \text{they} \end{array} \right\}$ $\left\{ \begin{array}{c} \text{do} \\ \text{do not} \end{array} \right\}$.

S_2: I don't believe you. $\left\{ \begin{array}{c} \text{Do} \\ \text{Does} \end{array} \right\}$ $\left\{ \begin{array}{c} \text{you} \\ \text{they} \end{array} \right\}$ really?

R_2: No, $\left\{ \begin{array}{c} \text{we} \\ \text{they} \end{array} \right\}$ $\left\{ \begin{array}{c} \text{do} \\ \text{do not} \end{array} \right\}$ (*verb*) ± (*object*) ± (*adverbial*).

Method: Use the same general approach used in Lessons 6.1 and 6.2, varying tense and "truth value" of the stimulus to get positive and negative, and past and present responses. In making R_2, the response containing the emphatic, stress is placed on the DO.

Examples:

Teacher:	(demonstrates drill with aide)
Teacher:	Does everybody here wear shoes?
Aide and children:	Yes, we do.
Teacher:	I don't believe you. Do you really?
Aide and children:	Yes, we *do* wear shoes.
Teacher:	Did the children come to school this morning?
Aide and children:	Yes, they did.
Teacher:	I don't believe you. Did they really?
Aide and children:	Yes, they *did* come to school this morning.
Teacher:	Did the fourth graders go to sleep just now?
Aide and children:	No, they did not.
Teacher:	I don't believe you. They really didn't?
Aide and children:	No, they *did not* go to sleep just now.

**Things to
Look Out For:** 1. In S_2, when eliciting the negative, it sounds more natural in the author's dialect to say "You really didn't?" rather than "Didn't you really?" although the latter is closer to the specified drill pattern for the affirmative. You may use either one.

2. Note that we have put *do* in lowercase italic letters in the examples of R_2 to indicate that it should receive the emphasis in the children's response.

LESSON 6.4

Objective: To drill the third singular form of the dummy DO (*does*) in the negative and affirmative.

Materials: Use materials similar to those used in the previous lessons of Section 6.

Basic Drill
Pattern: S_1: Does (*name*) (*verb*) ± (*object*) ± (*adverbial*)?

R_1: $\left\{ \begin{array}{l} \text{Yes} \\ \text{No} \end{array} \right\}$ (*pronoun*) $\left\{ \begin{array}{l} \text{does} \\ \text{does not} \end{array} \right\}$ (*verb*) ± (*object*) ± (*adverbial*).

S_2: $\left\{ \begin{array}{l} \text{Does} \\ \text{Doesn't} \end{array} \right\}$ (*pronoun*) really?

R_2: $\left\{ \begin{array}{l} \text{Yes} \\ \text{No} \end{array} \right\}$, (*pronoun*) $\left\{ \begin{array}{l} \text{does} \\ \text{does not} \end{array} \right\}$.

Method: Ask children questions about things that are visible to them, or about events out of their daily lives.

Examples:

Teacher:	(demonstrates drill with aide)
Teacher:	Everybody, does Johnny wear black shoes?
Aide and children:	Yes, he does wear black shoes.
Teacher:	Does he really?
Aide and children:	Yes, he does.
Teacher:	Does Sally go barefoot in the snow?
Aide and children:	No, she does not go barefoot in the snow.
Teacher:	Doesn't she really?
Aide and children:	No, she does not.

Things to Look Out For: 1. Be very careful to choose situations in which you know the children will be able to respond with the "correct" response. If you ask if "Sally has purple eyes," for example, the children may know that she doesn't, but they may not be able to tell you what color they really are.

2. You should be able to work out dialogues in which all of the basic drill patterns involving the dummy DO are combined for drill and review purposes at this point.

LESSON 6.5

Objective: To drill conjoined imperative clauses using *and*.

Materials: Actions by the children are good for this drill. You can also involve objects from your box of things, especially small objects that can be passed from person to person with a minimum of fuss.

Basic Drill
Pattern:
S_1: Can (*name*) (*verb$_1$*) ± (*object*)?
R_1: Yes, he can.
S_2: Can (*pronoun*) (*verb$_2$*) ± (*object*)?
R_2: Yes, he can.
S_3: Tell (*pronoun*) to do both of them.
R_3: (*Name*), (*verb$_1$*) ± (*object*) and (*verb$_2$*) ± (*object*).

Method: Select two actions that can logically be done simultaneously or successively and have the children instruct one of the children, you, or the aide, to do these things.

Examples:

Teacher:	(demonstrates drill with aide)
Teacher:	Can Johnny touch his nose?
Aide and children:	Yes, he can.
Teacher:	Can he smile?
Aide and children:	Yes, he can.
Teacher:	Tell him to do both, then.
Aide and children:	Johnny, touch your nose and smile.
Teacher:	Can Francine give Albert a truck?
Aide and children:	Yes, she can.
Teacher:	Can she give me a ball?
Aide and children:	Yes, she can.
Teacher:	Tell her to do both, then.
Aide and children:	Francine, give Albert a truck and give (teacher) a ball.

Things to
Look Out For: 1. It is probable that children who cannot conjoin clauses can conjoin noun or adjective phrases.

> Mary and Johnny are wearing black shoes.
> The ball is red and blue.

If not, you may need to drill them in these things before you drill Lesson 6.5. This can be done as follows:

> To conjoin objects, use the basic drill pattern for Lesson 6.5, but use the same intransitive verb in both S_1 and S_2 with different objects:

> S_1: Can Marilyn find a ball?
> S_2: Can Marilyn find a truck?
> S_3: Tell her to do both, then.
> R_3: Marilyn, find a ball and a truck.

To conjoin subjects, return to any of the basic drill patterns using declarative clauses, present two of them using the same verb, but two different subjects:

S₁: Is the ball red?
R₁: Yes, it is red.
S₂: Is the block red?
R₂: Yes, the block is red.
S₃: What color are the ball and the block, then?
R₃: The ball and the block are red.

2. If your children can already conjoin some clauses, do not ignore Lessons 6.5–6.7. It may be that they can conjoin some clauses but not others. You should try at least one lesson for each basic drill pattern just to make sure that they can do all the forms of conjoining that are drilled.

3. You may find that your children are conjoining strings of subjects, objects, or complements:

Mary, and Billy, and Johnny and Harry, and everybody came to school today.
I saw a dog and a cat and a house and a tree.

In adult speech and writing we usually delete all but one *and* and we may, under some circumstances, delete all *ands*. However, stringing out conjunctions is a common thing for children to do until some time after they begin to read. It is not cause for concern at this point.

4. You may want to look back at Section 1 and refresh your memory on imperative drills. Any two imperatives can be conjoined. Some examples are

(With some hats): Tell Johnny to pick one and wear it.
To Johnny: Tell him to wave his hands and shake his head for us slowly.
(With a person in the hall): Tell him to come in and visit.
(With marbles on the desk): Tell Johnny to pick a blue one and hold it.
(With a box): Tell Johnny to put it on the desk and open it.

Many of these situations would be good outside the drill proper.

5. You do not need to drill this item, but you may find yourself stringing out more than two imperative clauses, outside the drill, e.g.,

Put on your coats, stand by the door, and wait for me.

Note that we will often delete all but the last conjunction. You may want to test the children on their ability to do this before and after Lesson 6.5 has been drilled.

6. Remember, too, that equative verbs can be conjoined. In drilling imperatives, however, we must use the tenseless form of the equative, which has not been drilled in the program thus far:

Look nice and be polite.

Such imperatives should be introduced in this lesson, but because the *be* form has not appeared before, you may run into the problems typically encountered when introducing something new. If this is the case, wait until the children are able to handle transitives and intransitives in the basic drill pattern of this lesson easily before introducing the equatives into it.

LESSON 6.6

Objective: To drill conjoined active, declarative clauses in the simple present tense, using the conjunction *and*.

Materials: You should be able to use the experience of the children in this drill, but you may want to use pictures or small objects that can represent the nouns used in the drill.

Basic Drill Pattern:

S_1: $\begin{Bmatrix} \text{Do} \\ \text{Does} \\ \text{Did} \end{Bmatrix}$ (*subject*$_1$) (*verb*$_1$) $\pm$ (*object*)?

R_1: Yes, (*pronoun*) $\begin{Bmatrix} \text{do} \\ \text{does} \\ \text{did} \end{Bmatrix}$.

S_2: $\begin{Bmatrix} \text{Do} \\ \text{Does} \\ \text{Did} \end{Bmatrix}$ (*subject*$_2$) (*verb*$_2$) $\pm$ (*object*)?

R_2: Yes, (*pronoun*) $\begin{Bmatrix} \text{do} \\ \text{does} \\ \text{did} \end{Bmatrix}$.

S_3: What $\begin{Bmatrix} \text{do} \\ \text{did} \end{Bmatrix}$ they do, then?

R_3: (*Subject*$_1$) (*verb*$_1$) $\pm$ (*object*), and (*subject*$_2$) (*verb*$_2$) $\pm$ (*object*).

Method: If you use pictures, hold up the first picture for S_1, the second for S_2, and both together for S_3. If you do not use pictures, ask questions about activities which the children know are typical for the person, animal, or thing to do.

Examples:

Teacher:	(demonstrates drill with aide)
Teacher:	Do birds fly?
Aide and children:	Yes, they do.
Teacher:	Do fish swim?
Aide and children:	Yes, they do.
Teacher:	What do they do, then?
Aide and children:	Birds fly and fish swim.
Teacher:	Does the mechanic fix cars?
Aide and children:	Yes, he does.
Teacher:	Does the doctor help sick people?
Aide and children:	Yes, he does.
Teacher:	What do they do, then?
Aide and children:	The mechanic fixes cars and the doctor helps sick people.

Things to Look Out For: 1. S_3 of the basic drill pattern may not be comfortable for some people. For those who wish to use an alternate stimulus pattern the following is perfectly acceptable:

S_3: What $\begin{Bmatrix} \text{do} \\ \text{did} \end{Bmatrix}$ (*subject*$_1$) and (*subject*$_2$) do, then?

Example:

What do birds and fish do, then?

2. After the children begin responding well, you may wish to introduce an alternate basic drill pattern using a contrary-to-fact statement to elicit the conjunction *but*. The following would be an appropriate sequence:

S_1: $\begin{Bmatrix} \text{Does} \\ \text{Do} \\ \text{Did} \end{Bmatrix}$ (*subject*$_1$) (*verb*$_1$) $\pm$ (*object*)?

R_1: Yes, (*pronoun*) $\begin{Bmatrix} \text{does} \\ \text{do} \\ \text{did} \end{Bmatrix}$.

S_2: $\begin{Bmatrix} \text{Does} \\ \text{Do} \\ \text{Did} \end{Bmatrix}$ (*subject*$_2$) (*verb*$_1$) $\pm$ (*object*)?

R_2: No, (*pronoun*) $\begin{Bmatrix} \text{does} \\ \text{do} \\ \text{did} \end{Bmatrix}$ not.

S_3: $\begin{Bmatrix} \text{Do} \\ \text{Did} \end{Bmatrix}$ (*subject*$_1$) and (*subject*$_2$) (*verb*$_1$) $\pm$ (*object*), then?

R_3: No, (*subject*$_1$) (*verb*$_1$) $\pm$ (*object*), but (*subject*$_2$)   does   not $\pm$ (*verb*$_1$) $\pm$ (*object*).

Examples:

S_1: Do children play games?
R_1: Yes, they do.
S_2: Do rocks play games?
R_2: No, they do not.
S_3: Do children and rocks play games, then?
R_3: No, children play games but rocks do not $\pm$ (play games).

This basic drill pattern requires that S_2 contain a contrary-to-fact statement so that it will receive a negative response. The contrary-to-fact statement should contrast in some obvious way with the declarative in S_1.

3. Both of these basic drill patterns can be used for conjoining equative clauses, such as:

S_1: Be (*subject*$_1$) (*complement*$_1$)?
R_1: Yes, (*pronoun*) BE.
S_2: BE (*subject*$_2$) $\begin{Bmatrix} complement_1 \\ complement_2 \end{Bmatrix}$?
R_2: $\begin{Bmatrix} \text{Yes} \\ \text{No} \end{Bmatrix}$, (*pronoun*) BE $\pm$ NEG.
S_3: What BE (*subject*$_1$) and (*subject*$_2$), then?
R_3: (*Subject*$_1$) BE (*complement*$_1$), $\begin{Bmatrix} \text{and} \\ \text{but} \end{Bmatrix}$ (*subject*$_2$) BE $\pm$ NEG (*complement*$_2$).

Examples:

R_3: Johnny is a boy, and Sally is a girl.
R_3: Johnny is a boy, but Sally is not.
R_3: Houses are big, and pebbles are small.
R_3: Houses are big, and pebbles are not.

4. In any of these drills, the negative can be contracted if the children are sufficiently familiar with DO and BE: *don't, doesn't, isn't, aren't.*

LESSON 6.7

Objective: To drill conjoined active declarative sentences with the continuum, using *and*.

Materials: Pictures of people, animals, or things in various activities.

**Basic Drill
Pattern:** S_1: BE (*subject₁*) (*verb₁* -ing) $\pm$ (*object*)?
R_1: Yes, (*pronoun*) BE.
S_2: BE (*subject₂*) (*verb₂* -ing) $\pm$ (*object*)?
R_2: Yes, (*pronoun*) BE.
S_3: What BE they doing, then?
R_3: (*Subject₁*) BE (*verb₁* -ing) $\pm$ (*object*), and (*subject₂*) BE (*verb₂* -ing) $\pm$ (*object*).

Method: Hold up the first picture for S_1, the second for S_2, then both together for S_3.

Examples: Teacher: (demonstrates drill with aide)
(Teacher has pictures of a monkey and a cat)
Teacher: Is the monkey eating a banana?
Aide and children: Yes, it is.
Teacher: Is the cat licking its paw?
Aide and children: Yes, it is.
Teacher: What are they doing, then?
Aide and children: The monkey is eating a banana, and the cat is licking its paw.
(Teacher has pictures of a woman and a man)
Teacher: Is the woman riding in a boat?
Aide and children: Yes, she is.
Teacher: Is the man swimming?
Aide and children: Yes, he is.
Teacher: What are they doing, then?
Aide and children: The woman is riding in a boat, and the man is swimming.

**Things to
Look Out For:** 1. See Note 1 for Lesson 6.6. If S_3 does not "feel right" to you, you may use:
     S_3: What BE (*subject₁*) and (*subject₂*) doing, then?

2. See Notes 1 and 2, Lesson 6.5.

3. Once the children appear to be handling this drill well, you should do some drilling of the ellipted negative form. The following basic drill pattern can be used to do this:
     S_1: BE (*subject₁*) (*verb₁* -ing) $\pm$ (*object*)?
     R_1: Yes, (*pronoun*) BE.
     S_2: BE (*subject₂*) (*verb₁* -ing) $\pm$ (*object*)?
     R_2: No, (*pronoun*) BE + NEG.
     S_3: What BE they doing, then?
     R_3: (*Subject₁*) BE (*verb₁* -ing) $\pm$ (*object*), and (*subject₂*) BE + NEG.
This basic drill pattern can use either *and* or *but*.

     S_1: Is the duck swimming on the water?
     R_1: Yes, he is.
     S_2: Is the bumblebee swimming on the water?

R$_2$: No, he is not.

S$_3$: What are they doing, then?

R$_3$: The duck is swimming on the water, $\left\{\begin{array}{c} \text{and} \\ \text{but} \end{array}\right\}$ the bumblebee is not.

Contract NEG to BE if the children are ready to do so.

4. Another way to drill *but* is to use the main basic drill pattern, substituting a tag question for the *yes/no* question specified in S$_2$, and introducing this question with *but:*

S$_1$: BE (*subject*$_1$) (*verb*$_1$ -ing) ± (*object*)?

    R$_1$: Yes, (*pronoun*) BE.

S$_2$: But (*subject*$_2$) BE (*verb*$_2$ -ing) ± (*object*), BE + NEG (*pronoun*)?

R$_2$: Yes, (*pronoun*) BE.

S$_3$: What are they doing, then?

R$_3$: (*Subject*$_1$) BE (*verb*$_1$ -ing) ± (*object*), but (*subject*$_2$) BE (*verb*$_2$ -ing) ± (*object*).

Examples:

S$_1$: Is Johnny wearing red socks?

R$_1$: Yes, he is.

S$_2$: But Marvin is wearing blue socks, isn't he?

R$_2$: Yes, he is.

S$_3$: What are they wearing, then?

R$_3$: Johnny is wearing red socks, but Marvin is wearing blue socks.

Note that S$_2$ should be surprising or noteworthy *because of the contrast* with S$_1$.

5. Any of the above R$_3$ responses can be found in day-to-day situations. Look for them and use them.

    Johnny is doing his work but Ralph is looking at the ceiling.

LESSON 6.8

Objective: To drill the response to questions conjoined by *or*.

Materials: Pairs of objects or flannel board materials that differ along a dimension that can be labeled with an adjective referring to color, size, shape, weight, mass, etc.; or alternately, simply choose different objects from your junk box that can be named.

**Basic Drill
Pattern:** S_1: Here is a *(thing$_1$)* and a *(thing$_2$)*. Tell *(name)* to pick one and show it.
R_1: Pick one and show it, *(name)*.

S_2: Did *(pronoun)* pick the $\left\{ \begin{array}{l} adjective_1 \text{ one} \\ noun_1 \end{array} \right\}$ or $\left\{ \begin{array}{l} adjective_2 \text{ one} \\ noun_2 \end{array} \right\}$?

R_2: *(Pronoun)* picked the (proper response).

Method: Simply show the children two objects with S_1 and then drop the objects into a hat, box, or some other container and present S_2. If flannel boards materials are used, the child doing the choosing might be able to use a pointer to choose with.

Examples:

Teacher:	(demonstrates drill with aide)
Teacher:	Here is a red marble, and here is a blue marble. (Drops marbles into hat.) Let's tell Johnny to pick one and show it.
Aide and children:	Johnny, pick one and show it.
Teacher:	Did he pick the red one or the blue one?
Aide and children:	He picked the red one.
Teacher:	Here is a big car and a little car. Tell me to pick one and show it.
Aide and children:	Pick one and show it, Mr. Jones.
Teacher:	Did I pick the big one or the little one?
Aide and children:	You picked the big one.

**Things to
Look Out For:** 1. You may not have to spend a very long time on this drill pattern. Actually, it is a "set-up" for the children's production of *or*, and the only reason for its existence is to make sure that the children understand that *or* implies a choice.

2. If flannel board materials are used, the last part of S_1, rather than being "Pick one and show it," might sound better if you say "Tell *(name)* to point to one." This action will cause no problems with R_2 in this drill.

3. If the children string out subjects or complements with *or*, it simply indicates that they are learning to use it. See Note 3, Lesson 6.5.

4. Note that S_1 uses the indefinite article *a*, while S_2 and R_2 use the definite article *the*. Labeling in S_1 requires the indefinite article, but the *or* choice requires the definite article.

5. You can change S_2 as follows:

   S_2: Which one did *(pronoun)* pick?

This strategy allows you to specify something other than adjectives. The basic drill pattern would then have examples like this:

S_1: Here is a car and a horse. Tell me to pick one and show it.
R_1: Pick one and show it, teacher.
S_2: Did I pick the car or the horse?
R_2: You picked the car.

This would be a good alternate drill for this concept.

LESSON 6.9

Objective: To drill clauses conjoined by *or*.

Materials: Use the same materials you used in Lesson 6.8. Flannal board materials may prove awkward to use in this drill.

Basic Drill
Pattern:
S_1: Here BE a (*thing$_1$*) and a (*thing$_2$*). Should I pick one up?
R_1: Yes.
S_2: Which one should I pick?
R_2: It does not matter.
S_3: Tell me to pick one.
R_3: Pick the (*thing$_1$*) or pick the (*thing$_2$*).
R_4: (Appropriate response.)

Method: The teacher tells the children to instruct him as to what to do.

Examples:

Teacher:	(demonstrates drill with aide)
Teacher:	Here is a round button, and here is a square button.
Aide and children:	Yes.
Teacher:	Which one should I pick?
Aide and children:	It does not matter.
Teacher:	Tell me to pick one.
Aide and children:	Pick the round button or pick the square button.
Teacher:	I pick the square one. (holds up)

Things to
Look Out For:

1. As soon as this drill starts to move smoothly, let the children take turns picking an object:

   S_3: Tell Johnny to pick one.

2. See Notes 3 and 4, Lesson 6.8.

3. Note that the examples show the children asking for an "(adjective) one." You can also use nouns with no modifiers:

   R_3: Pick the car or the truck.

4. Do not forget to build a dialogue drill using as many of the patterns in Lessons 6.5–6.9 as possible.

5. Another basic drill pattern that could be used here is one that has the children ask a question in R_4 form. Since questions have not yet been drilled in the program, you may find that your children cannot use it. If they can, however, it might make a nice change.

Basic Drill
Pattern:
S_1: Here BE a (*thing$_1$*) and a (*thing$_2$*). Tell (*name*) to pick one and hide it.
R_1: Pick one and hide it, (*name*).
S_2: Did (*pronoun*) pick the (*thing$_1$*)?
R_2: We don't know.
S_3: Did (*pronoun*) pick the (*thing$_2$*)?
R_3: We don't know.
S_4: Ask (*name*) which one (*pronoun*) picked.

R$_4$: (*Name*), did you pick the (*thing$_1$*) or the (*thing$_2$*)?
R$_5$: Appropriate response.

Examples:

Teacher:	(demonstrates drill with aide)
Teacher:	Here is a round button and here is a square button. Tell Johnny to pick one and hide it.
Aide and children:	Pick one and hide it, Johnny.
Teacher:	Did he pick the round one?
Aide and children:	We don't know.
Teacher:	Did he pick the square one?
Aide and children:	We don't know.
Teacher:	Ask Johnny which one he picked.
Aide and children:	Johnny, did you pick the round one or the square one?
Johnny:	The square one.

SECTION 7

Early Questions: *Yes/No* and *Wh-* Replacements; Tags

Section 7 concentrates on drilling the placement of tense before the subject in some of the questions that appear early in development. Included in the section are drills on *yes/no* questions, *wh-* questions, and tag questions. The drills are further subdivided in terms of the major types of questions, i.e., (*a*) equatives with no auxiliaries; (*b*) all clauses with auxiliaries, and (*c*) intransitive and transitive clauses with no auxiliaries that require the use of the dummy DO.

Throughout the section, *yes/no* questions are intermixed with *wh-* questions. The section begins with the equative *yes/no* question, then drills subject, object, and some noun phrase *wh-* replacements, and moves on to drill the more complicated constructions that involve auxiliaries and the dummy DO. Following this sequence, tag questions will be drilled, and finally the section ends with a lesson drilling the *why* replacement of a *because* coordinate clause.

Rationale

By this point in the program the children should be well-acquainted with the obligatory clausal functions and those functions in the verb phrase that develop early. They have also had experience with using the dummy DO to carry tense and person markers. In other words, they now have the concepts that will allow them to move on and learn how (*a*) to place tense in front of the subject to form questions, and (*b*) to make *wh-* replacements.

In terms of the construction of the question patterns, the drills in this section are relatively uncomplicated. The *yes/no* questions deal simply with tense placement, and most *wh-* replacements are those for the subject, object, and adverbial functions. There are a couple of drills for *wh-* replacement of the possessor filler of the determiner₂ function and the loose-knit modifier functions of the noun phrase, but these should pose no special problems for the children at this point. The one lesson that may present a problem is the final lesson, which drills the *why* replacement for a coordinated *because* clause. Coordination is not a new concept, however, and the lesson was included in the section.

Two groups of questions will not be drilled: (*a*) those involving late-developing verb phrase functions, i.e., the passive, perfective, and past tense modals; and (*b*) *yes/no* negative questions such as the following:

Can't you do that?
Won't supper ever come?

The first group of questions will not be drilled because these functions develop late. The functions per se will be drilled in Section 9, and question drills should be given along with the declarative drills at that time. The second group that will not be drilled involves patterns which are seldom used; when they are used they tend to be "conversation-makers." It is very difficult to structure sensible drills for use in choral response for these patterns, and they are probably best taught *in situ* on an individual basis.

The Lessons

Most of the lessons in this section are pretty straight-forward and should present little or no special difficulty. The fact that all of the patterns being made into questions have been drilled as declaratives before should make it easy for you to structure dialogue drills. In Lesson 7.1, for example, the equative question with no auxiliaries is drilled. It should be a simple matter to return to the earlier sections that drilled the equative declarative for dialogue drills; just get the children to ask the questions in those drills.

The tag questions do present a problem, however. Although tag questions are a major construction in English, their use is rather limited. Legitimate concerns as to how important they are to a language program can be raised; for now, their importance to the children will be left up to the teacher. The lessons were included for those teachers who feel that their children must learn tag questions; you can leave them out if you cannot justify the time spent on them. Remember, too, that you can always come back to them at a later time.

The single lesson on *why* may pose problems for many children, since *because* coordinated clauses have not been drilled. On the other hand, this pattern may prove to be quite easy at this point in the program. If it seems to slow you down too much, do not hesitate to drop it and return to it at a later time. Remember that the major objective of this section is to teach your children to place tense before the subject in the question construction, not to drive them beyond their abilities. Specific constructions that present too many problems can always be returned to later.

LESSON 7.1

Objective: To drill the *yes/no* equative question.

Materials: Use the same type of materials you used to elicit equative declaratives.

**Basic Drill
Pattern:**
S: Ask me if (*subject*) BE (*complement*).
R$_1$: BE (*subject*) (*complement*)?
R$_2$: (appropriate reply)

Method: The basic method used in this and all lessons dealing with asking questions will be to say

to the children "Ask (*name*) $\begin{Bmatrix} \text{if} \\ \text{where} \\ \text{what} \\ \text{etc.} \end{Bmatrix}$ .... " This question-eliciting device has been

found to be quite effective. Remember that all questions asked by the children must be answered by somebody.

Examples:

Teacher:	(demonstrates drill with aide)
Teacher:	Everybody, ask me if those are circles.
Aide and children:	Are those circles?
Teacher:	Yes, they are.
Teacher:	Ask me if that is a dog.
Aide and children:	Is that a dog?
Teacher:	Yes, it is.
Teacher:	Everybody, ask me if that circle is red.
Aide and children:	Is that circle red?
Teacher:	Yes, it is.
Teacher:	Ask me if that pencil is long.
Aide and children:	Is that pencil long?
Teacher:	No, it is not.

**Things to
Look Out For:**
1. Notice the ellipted response by the person responding. You will probably want your children to ask each other questions, either individually or in chain drills. Allow them to ellipt their responses, too. Some teachers will have one or two children who have not yet learned the full declarative response. For these children it will be necessary to drill the lessons involving the full responses again anyway, and you might allow them to ellipt their responses in the question drills. Do not forget that there are *many* things for some children to learn, and that it may take more than one cycle through the lessons for some of them to "put it all together."

In making negative responses you may wish to supply the correct response, as presented in the examples, or you may wish to have the children supply it:

R$_2$: No, it isn't. What is it, Johnny?
R$_{Johnny}$: It is a spoon.

This technique would be especially useful if there were one or two children in the group who have not yet learned to make the full declarative response.

2. Remember that the reason for asking a question is to get a bit of information quickly and efficiently. If the children's questions are not answered, you take away their reason for asking them.

3. It is possible to direct the question to the aide, but if you do, you must remember to lead the children's response yourself. In this case the stimulus varies slightly:

     S: Let's ask Miss Jones if . . . .

4. Once again, do not contract BE until your children can handle the contraction.

5. You can develop a good dialogue by using the dialogues from the declarative equative patterns (see Sections 2 and 3). It is easy to have the children ask the questions in these dialogues.

6. The basic drill pattern is completely flexible. In the (*subject*) slot you can use noun phrases, pronouns, or demonstratives; in the predicate you can use any form of BE that your children are comfortable with; in the complement slot you can use nominal, adjectival, or adverbial fillers. Be creative. The basic drill pattern does not specify variants such as plurality, but they may be used, of course. Your children should be quite familiar with them by now. You should also use past tense, e.g., showing an object and hiding it before presenting the stimulus.

     R: Was that circle blue?
     R: Were those pencils long?

7. Your response to the question does not have to be a simple *yes* or *no* after you have drilled this pattern awhile. After the drill gets started, you might wish to introduce dissimilar objects and get this kind of an exchange:

     R: Were those circles red?
     R(teacher): One was, but the other was not.

Eventually the children will have to make complex responses using conjunctions, subordinators, etc., and introductions to some of them now would help lay some initial groundwork.

8. Be careful not to slip into the drill continuums disguised as equatives. That is, the following are *not* equatives:

     R: Am I smiling?
     R: Are you running?

LESSON 7.2

Objective: To drill *wh-* subject replacements in transitive and intransitive clauses.

Materials: Use pictures of people in action, the actions of the children, or daily activities of the children, teacher, and aide that everyone knows about.

Basic Drill Pattern:
S: $\left\{\begin{array}{l}\text{Ask}\\\text{Let's ask}\end{array}\right\}$ *(name)* $\left\{\begin{array}{l}\text{who}\\\text{what}\end{array}\right\}$ *(verbs)* $\pm$ *(object)*.

R$_1$: *(Name)*, $\left\{\begin{array}{l}\text{who}\\\text{what}\end{array}\right\}$ *(verbs)* $\pm$ *(object)*?

R$_2$: (Appropriate reply.)

Method: The teacher directs the children to ask him, the aide, or each other who or what carries out the activities chosen for vocabulary.

Examples:

Teacher:	(demonstrates drill with aide)
Teacher:	Let's ask Mr. Jones who cleans the blackboard this week.
Teacher and children:	Mr. Jones, who cleans the blackboard this week?
Aide:	Johnny does.
Teacher:	Let's ask Mr. Jones what carries that machinery.
Teacher and children:	Mr. Jones, what carries that machinery?
Aide:	The truck carries it.

Things to Look Out For:

1. This drill should not occupy much time, since there is relatively little that is new in it. Because the *wh-* replacement is of the subject, there is no tense movement involved.

2. You can vary present and past tense freely. Also, use any auxiliaries that the children are comfortable with. Because there is no tense movement, the verb phrase will maintain its declarative order:

R$_1$: Who is tapping his foot?
R$_1$: Who was singing loudly?
R$_1$: What can hold flowers?
R$_1$: What will write on blackboards?

This fact means that you are not limited to a single verb in the predicate. You may use any degree of verb phrase complexity that your children can handle in declaratives.

LESSON 7.3

Objective: To drill *wh-* complement replacements in equative questions.

Materials: Two types of materials should be used: those which can be referred to as *who* and those which can be referred to as *what*. Pictures of persons, the children themselves, the aide, etc., are good for the former; distinctive parts of costumes (hats, etc.) and/or ordinary objects known to the children are good for the latter.

Basic Drill Pattern:

S: Ask *(name)* $\begin{Bmatrix} \text{who} \\ \text{what} \end{Bmatrix}$ *(subject)* BE.

R_1: $\begin{Bmatrix} \text{Who} \\ \text{What} \end{Bmatrix}$ BE *(subject)*?

R_2: (Appropriate reply.)

Method: Have the children ask you, the aide, and each other the questions.

Examples:

Teacher:	(demonstrates drill with aide)
Teacher:	Ask me who he is.
Aide and children:	Who is he?
Teacher:	He is Johnny.
Teacher:	Let's ask Mr. Jones who that is.
Teacher and children:	Mr. Jones, who is that?
Aide:	She is the nurse.
Teacher:	Johnny, ask Melvin what that is.
Johnny:	Melvin, what is that?
Melvin:	It is a spoon.

Things to Look Out For:

1. As in Lesson 7.1, note the complete flexibility of the pattern. You should feel free to vary the fillers of the subject and predicate as much as the children are capable of handling. In order to do so, you may want to change the basic drill pattern slightly. For example, if you introduce the past tense into the drill, you will have to carry out some action that will elicit past tense, such as those used in the lessons of Section 4 (review this section for ideas). Remember that, in this lesson, you are drilling complement replacement and tense movement, and anything that can be used from previous lessons to teach the *wh-* question is fair game.

2. Review all notes for Lesson 7.1.

LESSON 7.4

Objective: To drill *wh-* replacement for the possessive pronoun in the determiner$_2$.

Materials: You can use the children themselves for this lesson, and no special materials are needed.

Basic Drill Pattern:

S: Ask $\left\{\begin{array}{l}\text{me} \\ \text{(name)}\end{array}\right\}$ whose (*noun* sg. or pl.) $\left\{\begin{array}{l}\text{this} \\ \text{these}\end{array}\right\}$ $\left\{\begin{array}{l}\text{is} \\ \text{are}\end{array}\right\}$.

R$_1$: Whose (*noun* sg. or pl.) $\left\{\begin{array}{l}\text{is} \\ \text{are}\end{array}\right\}$ $\left\{\begin{array}{l}\text{that} \\ \text{those}\end{array}\right\}$?

R$_2$: (Appropriate reply.)

Method: Have the children ask you, the aide, or each other questions about articles of clothing or body parts.

Examples:

Teacher:	(demonstrates drill with aide)
Teacher:	Ask Mr. Jones whose shoe this is.
Teacher and children:	Mr. Jones, whose shoe is that?
Aide:	It is Johnny's.
Teacher:	Ask Sally whose hands these are.
Aide and children:	Sally, whose hands are those?
Sally:	They are mine.

Things to Look Out For:

1. Note that the drill involves the possessive filler for the determiner$_2$. The person who gives R$_2$ will use the nominal possessive pronoun, however. If any children are still having problems with the nominal, they can benefit from making this response. Note that R$_2$ can also use the *-s* inflection.

LESSON 7.5

Objective: To drill *yes/no* questions involving movement of the continuum auxiliary.

Materials: Use pictures of people in action, or use pantomimed actions, as you prefer.

**Basic Drill
Patterns:** S: Let's ask (*name*) if the (*subject*) BE (*verb* -ing) ± (*object*).
R$_1$: (*Name*) BE (*subject*) (*verb* -ing) ± (*object*)?
R$_2$: (Appropriate reply.)

Method: Show the pictures or pantomime the actions and tell the children to ask you, the aide, and each other if the respondent knows what is or was happening. Present tense requires demonstrations to be concurrent with the stimulus; past requires demonstration to occur prior to the stimulus.

Examples:

Teacher:	(demonstrates drill with aide)
Teacher:	Everybody, let's ask Mr. Jones if the boy is playing baseball.
Teacher and children:	Mr. Jones, is the boy playing baseball?
Mr. Jones:	Yes, he is.
Teacher:	Let's ask Mr. Jones if the girl was making a sand castle.
Teacher and children:	Mr. Jones, was the girl making a sand castle?
Mr. Jones:	No, she was riding a bicycle.

**Things to
Look Out For:** 1. See all notes for Lesson 7.1.

LESSON 7.6

Objective: To drill *yes/no* questions involving movement of the auxiliary in the continuum in clauses with *BE going to*.

Materials: Use pictures and/or pantomime much as you did in Lesson 7.5; you could also use no materials at all and rely on the experiences of the children.

Basic Drill Pattern:
S: Let's ask *(name)* if *(subject)* BE going to *(verb)* ± *(object)*.
R₁: *(Name)* BE *(subject)* going to *(verb)* ± *(object)*?
R₂: (Appropriate response.)

Method: Drill this pattern in much the same manner as you drilled the one for Lesson 7.6.

Examples:

Teacher:	(demonstrates drill with aide)
Teacher:	Everybody, let's ask Mr. Jones if the ball is going to bounce.
Teacher and children:	Mr. Jones, is the ball going to bounce?
Mr. Jones:	Yes, it is.
Teacher:	Let's ask Mr. Jones if it was going to rain yesterday.
Teacher and children:	Mr. Jones, was it going to rain yesterday?
Mr. Jones:	No, it wasn't.
Teacher:	Let's ask Mr. Jones if he was going to sing this morning.
Teacher and children:	Mr. Jones, were you going to sing this morning?
Mr. Jones:	Yes, but I had to go out and I couldn't.

Things to Look Out For:

1. See Notes 1–7 for Lesson 7.1.

2. Note that the past tense of the auxiliary does not necessarily involve simple past time, but, rather may involve time that is relative to another time:

R: Were you going to school after breakfast this morning?

If your children have trouble with such a complicated time relationship, stay with the present tense of the auxiliary and the simple future:

R: Are you going to ride the bus this afternoon?

LESSON 7.7

Objective: To drill *wh-* object replacements in transitive questions with an auxiliary in the verb phrase.

Materials: Use actions that the children are carrying out, or pictures of people, animals, or objects (such as machinery) in action.

Basic Drill Pattern:

S: $\left\{\begin{array}{l}\text{Ask}\\\text{Let's ask}\end{array}\right\}$ *(name)* $\left\{\begin{array}{l}\text{who}\\\text{what}\end{array}\right\}$ *(subject)* BE *(verb* -ing).

R₁: *(Name),* $\left\{\begin{array}{l}\text{who}\\\text{what}\end{array}\right\}$ BE *(subject) (verb* -ing)?

R₂: (Appropriate reply.)

Method: If you use pictures, ask the children about the actions being carried out in the pictures. If you use actions of the children, first get the action going by saying something like "Do this," and then ask the group about the action being carried out.

Examples:

Teacher:	(demonstrates drill with aide)
Teacher:	Johnny, do this (demonstrates). Everybody, ask me what Johnny is waving.
Aide and children:	What is Johnny waving?
Teacher:	He is waving his hand. Do this. (Demonstrates.) Ask me what you are touching.
Aide and children:	What are we touching?
Teacher:	You are touching your noses. Everybody, look there. (Points.) What are you looking at?
Aide and children:	We are looking at the clock.

Things to Look Out For:

1. Because we are drilling tense movement using auxiliaries, you must not allow dummy DO questions. These will be drilled later.

2. Vary tense freely:

   R: What was Johnny touching?
   R: What were we looking at?

3. Note, too, that you are limited to transitive clauses because intransitives have no objects. Since we are drilling object replacements, only transitives are possible.

LESSON 7.8

Objective: To drill the *wh-* replacement of the adverbial complement in the equative clause.

Materials: Objects in the room or objects or places outside of the room.

Basic Drill Pattern:

S: $\left\{ \begin{matrix} \text{Ask} \\ \text{Let's ask} \end{matrix} \right\}$ (*name*) where (*subject*) BE.

R₁: (*Name*), where BE (*subject*)?

R₂: (aide): (Appropriate reply.)

Method: The teacher leads the children in asking the aide the location of various places or objects.

Examples:

Teacher:	(demonstrates drill with aide)
Teacher:	Everybody, let's ask Mr. Jones where the light switch is.
Teacher and children:	Mr. Jones, where is the light switch?
Aide:	It is on that wall.
Teacher:	Let's ask Mr. Jones where the windows are.
Teacher and children:	Mr. Jones, where are the windows?
Aide:	They are over there.
Teacher:	Let's ask Mr. Jones where lunch was.
Teacher and children:	Mr. Jones, where was lunch?
Aide:	It was in the cafeteria.

Things to Look Out For:

1. You may use modified nouns if you wish:

S: Ask (*aide*) where the (*adjective*) (*noun*) is.

Any variations in the noun phrase that the children can handle are allowed. The verb phrase, however, is to be filled by the equative BE with no auxiliaries.

LESSON 7.9

Objective: To drill *yes/no* questions in intransitive and transitive clauses with no auxiliaries.

Materials: You can use pictures, flannel board materials, objects from the junk box, or you can rely on the experiences of the children.

Basic Drill
Pattern: S: Let's ask (*name*) if (*subject*) (*verbs*) ± (*object*).
R$_1$: (*Name*), DO (*subject*) (*verb*) ± (*object*)?
R$_2$: (Appropriate response.)

Method: Have the children address the questions to the aide or to each other. Use the "Let's ask" device.

Examples:

Teacher:	(demonstrates drill with aide)
Teacher:	Let's ask Mr. Jones if he sees the floor.
Teacher and children:	Mr. Jones, do you see the floor?
Mr. Jones:	Yes, I do.
Teacher:	Let's all ask Mr. Jones if he heard a bird.
Teacher and children:	Mr. Jones, did you hear a bird?
Mr. Jones:	Yes, I did.
Teacher and children:	Let's ask Mr. Jones if he wears sneakers.
Mr. Jones:	No, I never wear sneakers.

Things to
Look Out For: 1. Responses should be factual—as a result of their factual nature, they may be complicated grammatically, but there is nothing wrong with this.

2. As a past tense variant, it might be possible to use the following variation:

    S: Let's ask Mr. Jones if he ever saw a rattlesnake.
    R: Mr. Jones, did you ever see a rattlesnake?

The adverb *ever* expresses a complex time relationship that your children may or may not be able to handle. There is no harm in trying it, though.

3. A set of examples that you can use for an alternate drill could be

    R: Do birds fly?
    R: Did Johnny jump over the school?

This type of sentence can be used for making games out of the drill. It has been found useful.

LESSON 7.10

Objective: To drill *wh-* object replacements in transitive questions with no auxiliaries.

Materials: Use materials similar to those suggested for Lesson 7.3.

Basic Drill Pattern:

S: $\left\{ \begin{array}{l} \text{Ask} \\ \text{Let's ask} \end{array} \right\}$ *(name)* $\left\{ \begin{array}{l} \text{who} \\ \text{what} \end{array} \right\}$ *(subject)* $\left\{ \begin{array}{l} \textit{verbs} \\ \textit{verbed} \end{array} \right\}$.

R₁: *(Name)*, $\left\{ \begin{array}{l} \text{who} \\ \text{what} \end{array} \right\}$ DO *(subject)* *(verb)*.

R₂: (Appropriate reply.)

Method Varying present and past, drill this pattern in the same manner as was done for Lesson 7.3.

Examples:

Teacher:	(demonstrates drill with aide)
Teacher:	Everybody, ask me what this man delivers.
Aide and children:	What does that man deliver?
Teacher:	He delivers mail.
Teacher:	Ask me what this man fixes.
Aide and children:	What does that man fix?
Teacher:	He fixes cars.

Things to Look Out For:

1. Only transitive verbs can be used in this drill because no object replacement is possible if you use intransitives.

LESSON 7.11

Objective: To drill the *wh-* replacement for adjectives.

Materials: Pairs of objects, flannel board materials, or pairs of pictures in which two different actions are being carried out.

Basic Drill Pattern:

S: Let's ask (*name*) which (*noun* $_{\text{sg. or pl.}}$) (*verb*) $\pm \left\{ \begin{array}{l} object \\ complement \end{array} \right\}$.

R$_1$: (*Name*), which (*noun* $_{\text{sg. or pl.}}$) (*verb*) $\pm \left\{ \begin{array}{l} object \\ complement \end{array} \right\}$?

R$_2$: (Appropriate response.)

Method: Place the materials so that the children can give the proper response to the questions. One way to do it is to place the choices at opposite ends of the flannel board so that the pointing responses required can be read accurately as to whether they are correct or incorrect. If pairs of objects are used, hold up one in each hand. The children can also hold pairs of objects, if you have enough to go around.

Examples:

Teacher:	(demonstrates drill with aide)
Teacher:	Everybody, let's ask Mr. Jones which pencil is the long one.
Teacher and children:	Mr. Jones, which is the long pencil?
Aide:	This is the long pencil.
Teacher:	Let's ask Mr. Jones which circle is the red one.
Teacher and children:	Mr. Jones, which is the red circle?
Aide:	That one is red.
Teacher:	Let's ask Mr. Jones which man delivers mail.
Teacher and children:	Mr. Jones, which man delivers mail?
Aide:	(Holds up picture) This one.

Things to Look Out For:

1. Watch your materials. you may use more than two of any set of materials if you wish, of course, but at least one of them must be distinguishable from the others along some dimension which can be identified.

2. Note that since the basic drill pattern uses a subject replacement, there is no tense movement, and any one of the basic clause patterns can be used.

3. Also note that the fact that using the subject replacement means that this drill is very close to being a repetition drill. An alternate drill to accomplish the same objective could be the following:

S$_1$: Let's ask (*name*) which (*noun*) (*subject*) (*verb*).

R$_1$: (*Name*), which (*noun*) does (*subject*) (*verb*)?

R$_2$: (Appropriate reply.)

Examples:

S$_1$: Let's ask Johnny which dog he likes.

R$_1$: Johnny, which dog do you like?

R$_2$: The big one.

This drill puts the *wh-* replacement into the object, but note that the dummy DO must be used. Using DO will probably cause no problems at this point in the program, and you can try it if you wish.

LESSON 7.12

Objective: To drill *yes/no* questions for clauses with the modal *will*.

Materials: No materials are required for this drill.

Basic Drill Pattern:

S: Let's ask (*name*) if (*subject*) will (*verb*) ± $\left\{\begin{array}{l}\textit{object} \\ \textit{complement}\end{array}\right\}$.

R₁: (*Name*), will (*subject*) (*verb*) ± $\left\{\begin{array}{l}\textit{object} \\ \textit{complement}\end{array}\right\}$?

R₂: (Appropriate response.)

Method: Tell the children to ask the aide or the other children whether specific actions will occur. The actions may be carried out by you, by the aide, or by the children. The children may also ask questions of each other.

Examples:

Teacher:	(demonstrates drill with aide)
Teacher:	Everybody, let's ask Mr. Jones if he will stand up.
Teacher and children:	Mr. Jones, will you stand up?
Mr. Jones:	O.K., I will. (Stands up.)
Teacher:	Let's ask Mr. Jones if he will sit down now.
Teacher and children:	Mr. Jones, will you sit down now?
Mr. Jones:	O.K., I will. (Sits.)
Teacher:	Let's ask Johnny if he will touch his nose.
Teacher and children:	Johnny, will you touch your nose?
Johnny:	No, I won't.
Teacher:	Let's ask Sally if Alice will be a Brownie.
Teacher and children:	Sally, will Alice be a Brownie?
Sally:	Yes, she will.

Things to Look Out For:

1. Any accompanying motor response is alright as far as the pattern is concerned, but for the sake of the rhythm it is probably best if you do not let the children run all over the room.

2. Note that this lesson can be either a polite command, as in most of the examples, or a request for information:

S: Let's ask Mr. Jones if lunch will be at 12 o'clock.

S: Let's ask Johnny if he will get out of bed tomorrow morning.

3. You can vary transitive, intransitive, and equative clauses as long as your children can handle it. Provision for this variation has been made in the basic drill pattern. If your children have difficulty with the equative pattern at first, make up a separate lesson to drill only the equative. After they are comfortable with it, you will be able to mix it in.

LESSON 7.13

Objective: To drill the *wh-* replacement for the adverbial of time in intransitive and transitive clauses.

Materials: No particular materials are needed for this lesson, since events occurring in a time dimension will be used as topics.

**Basic Drill
Pattern:** S: Ask (*name*) when (*subject*) (*verb*) ± $\begin{Bmatrix} object \\ complement \end{Bmatrix}$.

R₁: (*Name*), when $\begin{Bmatrix} DO \\ will \end{Bmatrix}$ (*subject*) (*verb*) ± $\begin{Bmatrix} object \\ complement \end{Bmatrix}$?

R₂: (Appropriate response.)

Method: Have the children ask you, your aide, or each other the question.

Examples:

Teacher:	(demonstrates drill with aide)
Teacher:	Everybody, let's ask Mr. Jones when we will eat.
Teacher and children:	Mr. Jones, when will we eat?
Aide:	At lunchtime.
Teacher:	Ask me when I go to bed.
Aide and children:	When do you go to bed?
Teacher:	At night.
Teacher:	Let's ask Johnny when he comes to school.
Teacher, aide and children:	Johnny, when do you come to school?
Johnny:	In the morning.

**Things to
Look Out For:** 1. Note that several time relationships are expressed in this question:

   R₁: When will we go home?
   R₁: When did the dog come here?

Mixing present, past, and future times should not cause any problems. If it does, do one at a time until the children can handle each; then mix them.

2. Note, too, that there is a parallel question:

   R: At what time (*verb phrase*)?
   example: At what time do we go home?

You may or may not wish to drill this pattern. It is used only rarely and such a drill may use up too much time. If your class already knows a lot about questions, however, it may be a good variation.

3. See Note 3, Lesson 7.12.

LESSON 7.14

Objective: To drill the *wh-* replacement for the adverbial of manner.

Materials: Pantomimed actions, events in the immediate past or future, or normal daily routine activities can be used as topics. No concrete materials are needed.

Basic Drill Pattern:
S: Ask (*name*) how (*subject*) (*verb*) ± (*object*).
R_1: (*Name*), how DO (*subject*) (*verb*) ± (*object*).
R_2: (Appropriate response.)

Method: Have the children ask questions of all present.

Examples:

Teacher:	(demonstrates drill with aide)
Teacher:	Everybody, let's ask Mr. Jones how he brushes his teeth.
Teacher and children:	Mr. Jones, how do you brush your teeth?
Aide:	This way. (Pantomimes.)
Teacher:	Let's ask Mr. Jones how you kiss a porcupine.
Teacher and children:	Mr. Jones, how do you kiss a porcupine?
Aide:	Very carefully.
Teacher:	Let's ask Johnny how he eats his lunch.
Teacher and children:	Johnny, how will you eat your lunch?
Johnny:	This way. (Pantomimes.)

Things to Look Out For:

1. Note the alternate parallel form using *in what manner*:

    R: In what manner (*verb phrase*)?

See Note 2 for Lesson 7.13.

2. Also observe that the form *how* can elicit words such as adverbial intensifiers:

    R_1: How quickly can you run?
    R_2: Very quickly; not so quickly; etc.

At this point you might be able to insert these variations easily, and you could try such a drill. If it proves too difficult, however, discontinue it and try it again later.

3. Equative clauses are impossible with this pattern, i.e., we do not say things like:

    R: *He is tall quietly.

LESSON 7.15

Objective: To drill the *yes/no* question using the modal, *can*.

Materials: No materials required.

Basic Drill Pattern:

S: Let's ask (*name*) if (*subject*) can (*verb*) $\pm$ $\left\{ \begin{array}{l} object \\ complement \end{array} \right\}$.

R$_1$: (*Name*), can (*subject*) (*verb*) $\pm$ $\left\{ \begin{array}{l} object \\ complement \end{array} \right\}$?

R$_2$: (Appropriate response.)

Method: Tell the children to ask you, the aide, or the other children the question.

Examples:

Teacher:	(demonstrates drill with aide)
Teacher:	Everybody, let's ask Mr. Jones if he can swim.
Teacher and children:	Mr. Jones, can you swim?
Aide:	Yes, I can.
Teacher:	Let's ask Johnny if he can run.
Teacher and children:	Johnny, can you run?
Johnny:	Yes, I can.
Teacher:	Let's ask Sally if she can fly like a bird.
Teacher and children:	Sally, can you fly like a bird?
Sally:	No, I can't.
Teacher:	Let's ask Mr. Jones if he can be a fish.
Teacher and children:	Mr. Jones, can you be a fish?
Aide:	No, I can't.

Things to Look Out For:

1. The aide should lead the children, of course, when you have them ask you the questions.

2. Notice that this pattern requests information. When used with the first person singular (*I*), or the first person plural (*we*) it can also be a request for permission to do something.

R: Can I touch my nose?
R: Can we stamp our feet?
R: Can I fly to the moon?

Both uses should be drilled. Note, however, that the "permission" usage is quite similar to the pattern drilled in Lesson 7.16 (*may I*). Because both patterns requesting permission to do something are in common usage, it is probably best to drill them both. The difference between them lies in the degree of formality. When drilling the "request for permission" with *can,* you may want to allow the children to give permission to each other; but in Lesson 7.16, you will probably want to structure a more formal situation. See notes for Lesson 7.16.

3. This particular drill can also be a good contrary-to-fact "fun" drill. The sillier you make the question, the more fun the children can have with it:

S: Can you smoke a dog?
S: Can you hear a star?
S: Can you carry a house?

When you do this, however, mix the silly questions with "straight" questions, e.g.,

S: Can you eat a sandwich?

Too much silliness wears thin, even for children.

LESSON 7.16

Objective: To drill the *yes/no* question using the modal *may*, with both affirmative and negative responses.

Materials: You need few, if any, materials for this lesson. You can get by with ordinary objects in the room—desks, chairs, etc.

Basic Drill Pattern: S: Ask me if you may (*verb*) ± (*object*).

R: May $\begin{Bmatrix} I \\ we \end{Bmatrix}$ (*verb*) ± (*object*)?

R: (Appropriate response.)

Method: You may structure this as a formal drill or as a game situation, e.g. Giant Steps.[1]

Examples:

Teacher:	(demonstrates drill with aide)
Teacher:	Everybody, ask me if you may stamp your foot.
Aide and children:	May we stamp our feet?
Teacher:	Yes, once.
Teacher:	Ask me if you may raise your arms.
Aide and children:	May we raise our arms?
Teacher:	No, you may not. you may raise one arm.

Things to Look Out For:

1. Because of the similarity of the patterns in Lessons 7.15 and 7.16, both in pattern and meaning, you may be able to go directly to a game situation. You could play Giant Steps; you could divide your class into teams; or you could have one child granting permission to the class or individuals touching various objects around the room, etc. There is no reason to stay indoors, either.

2. See Note 2 for Lesson 7.15.

---

[1] Also known as Mother May I?

LESSON 7.17

Objective: To drill the negative tag using the equative clause with BE.

Materials: No special materials are needed, since you can use the experience of the children in this drill. You may use objects that are familiar to the children, if you wish.

Basic Drill Pattern:

S₁: BE (*subject*) (*complement*)?
R₁: Yes, (*pronoun*) BE.
S₂: You know that, don't you?
R₂: Yes, $\left\{ \begin{matrix} we \\ I \end{matrix} \right\}$ do.
S₃: Ask me if (*subject*) BE (*complement*), then.
R₃: (*Subject*) BE (*complement*), BE + NEG (*pronoun*)?
R₄: (Appropriate response.)

Method: Drill the children on matters that are true following the basic drill pattern.

Examples:

Teacher:	(demonstrates drill with aide)
Teacher:	Is Billy here?
Aide and children:	Yes, he is.
Teacher:	You know that, don't you?
Aide and children:	Yes, we do.
Teacher:	Ask me if Billy is here, then.
Aide and children:	Billy is here, isn't he?
Teacher:	Yes, he is.
Teacher:	Is Mr. Principal a man?
Aide and children:	Yes, he is.
Teacher:	You know that, don't you?
Aide and children:	Yes, we do.
Teacher:	Ask me if Mr. Principal is a man.
Aide and children:	Mr. Principal is a man, isn't he?
Teacher:	Yes, he is.

Things to Look Out For:

1. Note how this drill sequence sets up the idea of the children asking a question about something they already know to be true. Do not set up situations that are false; this will be done in Lesson 7.18.

2. Any equative clause can be tagged. For example:

Those blocks are red, aren't they?
That was a bird, wasn't it?
The iguanas were in the tank, weren't they?
I will be hungry, won't I?

3. If the children do not have the contraction under control yet, they may have difficulty with the tag because it almost always appears in its contracted form. This situation causes a problem when the BE form being used is *am* because it does not get contracted.

*I am big, amn't I?

In fact, *ain't* developed just because of this fact. If *am* is used in a tag, we must shift the pronoun and negative:

I am big, am I not?

Because "acceptable" responses have to be so sophisticated, you may wish not to drill tags with *am*.

LESSON 7.18

Objective: To drill the affirmative tag in the equative clause.

Materials: Use the same type of materials that could be used in Lesson 7.17.

Basic Drill Pattern:

S₁: BE (*subject*) (*complement*)?
R₁: No, (*pronoun*) BE + NEG.
S₂: You know that, don't you?
R₂: Yes, we do.
S₃: Ask me if (*subject*) BE (*complement*), then.
R₃: (*Subject*) BE + NEG (*complement*), BE (*pronoun*)?
R₄: (Appropriate response.)

Method: Drill the children on matters that are patently false, following the basic drill pattern.

Examples:

Teacher:	(demonstrates drill with aide)
Teacher:	Are we on the moon?
Aide and children:	No, we aren't.
Teacher:	You know that, don't you?
Aide and children:	Yes, we do.
Teacher:	Ask me if we are on the moon, then.
Aide and children:	We are not on the moon, are we?
Teacher:	No, we aren't.

Things to Look Out For:

1. You must be careful to choose situations that are clearly contrary to fact.

2. You can mix Lessons 7.17 and 7.18 in a single drill once the children begin to catch on.

3. Note notes for Lesson 7.17, especially Note 2.

4. Observe that the negative contraction to BE is optional in the declarative part of the question in this drill.

5. Once the children start to do Lesson 7.18 well, you should do the same drill (and Lesson 7.17 as well) using BE (*verb* -ing). This drill can be done as follows:

S₁: BE (*subject*) (*verb* -ing) ± (*object*)?
R₁: $\left\{ \begin{array}{c} \text{Yes} \\ \text{No} \end{array} \right\}$, (*pronoun*) BE ± NEG.
S₂: You know that, don't you?
R₂: Yes, we do.
S₃: Ask me if (*subject*) BE (*verb* -ing) ± (*object*), then.
R₃: (*Subject*) BE ± NEG (*verb* -ing), BE ± NEG
  (one but not both)
R₄: (Appropriate response.)

Examples: Johnny isn't playing ball, is he?
Franky is sitting down, isn't he?

This is the same drill as found in the basic drill patterns of 7.17 and 7.18, except for the fact that BE is used as an auxiliary instead of as the main verb. Note that R₃ specifies both tags. Only one NEG is optional; the other must appear.

LESSON 7.19

Objective: To drill tag questions using transitive and intransitive verbs and the dummy DO.

Materials: Use the same types of materials used in Lessons 7.18 and 7.19.

Basic Drill Pattern:

S_1: DO (*subject*) (*verb*) ± (*object*)?

R_1: $\left\{ \begin{array}{c} \text{Yes} \\ \text{No} \end{array} \right\}$ (*pronoun*) DO ± NEG.

S_2: You know that, don't you?

R_2: Yes, we do.

S_3: Ask me if (*subject*) (*verb*) ± (*object*), then.

R_3: (*Subject*) ± (<u>DO + NEG</u>) (*verb*) ± (*object*) DO ± <u>NEG</u> (*pronoun*)?

            |⎯⎯⎯ (one but not both) ⎯⎯⎯|

R_4: (Appropriate response.)

Method: Drill the children about obviously true or false situations following the basic drill pattern.

Examples:

Teacher:	(demonstrates drill with aide)
Teacher:	Does Johnny wear shoes?
Aide and children:	Yes, he does.
Teacher:	You know that, don't you?
Aide and children:	Yes, we do.
Teacher:	Ask me if Johnny wears shoes, then.
Aide and children:	Johnny wears shoes, doesn't he?
Teacher:	Yes; he does.
Teacher:	Do turtles fly?
Aide and children:	No, they don't.
Teacher:	You know that, don't you?
Aide and children:	Yes, we do.
Teacher:	Ask me if turtles fly, then.
Aide and children:	Turtles don't fly, do they?
Teacher:	No, they don't.

Things to Look Out For:

1. Lesson 7.19 is actually two drills. R_3 in the basic drill pattern has optional DO and DO + NEG stated. Compare this statement with the two corresponding responses by the children in the examples. If DO appears in the declarative part of the question, the NEG must accompany it and the tag is affirmative; if it *does not* appear in the declarative, the DO that appears in the tag *must* have the NEG.

2. Begin with either affirmative or negative tags in one drill, switch to the opposite in a different drill, and then combine the two in a third drill. This sequence may be spread out over more than one lesson so that drill may be carried out for affirmative tags before switching to negative tags, and later both may be combined. Let your children's ability guide the speed at which you go.

3. See Note 2, Lesson 7.17.

LESSON 7.20

Objectives: To drill the tag question with the modals *can, will,* and *must.*

Materials: Use the same type of materials used in Lessons 7.17–7.19.

Basic Drill Pattern:

S_1: $\left\{\begin{array}{l}\text{Can}\\\text{Will}\\\text{Must}\end{array}\right\}$ *(subject) (verb)* ± *(object)*?

R_1: $\left\{\begin{array}{l}\text{Yes}\\\text{No}\end{array}\right\}$, *(pronoun)* $\left\{\begin{array}{l}\text{can}\\\text{will}\\\text{must}\end{array}\right\}$ ± NEG.

S_2: You know that, don't you?

R_2: Yes, we do.

S_3: Ask me if *(subject)* $\left\{\begin{array}{l}\text{can}\\\text{will}\\\text{must}\end{array}\right\}$ *(verb)* ± *(object)*, then.

R_3: *(Subject)* $\left\{\begin{array}{l}\text{can}\\\text{will}\\\text{must}\end{array}\right\}$ ± NEG *(verb)* ± *(object)*, $\left\{\begin{array}{l}\text{can}\\\text{will}\\\text{must}\end{array}\right\}$ ± NEG *(pronoun)*?

(one but not both)

R_4: (Appropriate response.)

Method: Drill the children about obviously true or false situations following the basic drill pattern.

Examples:

Teacher:	(demonstrates drill with aide)
Teacher:	Can Johnny see his hands?
Aide and children:	Yes, he can.
Teacher:	You know that, don't you?
Aide and children:	Yes, we do.
Teacher:	Ask me if Johnny can see his hands, then.
Aide and children:	Johnny can see his hands, can't he?
Teacher:	Yes, he can.
Teacher:	Will the sky fall today?
Aide and children:	No, it won't.
Teacher:	You know that, don't you?
Aide and children:	Yes, we do.
Teacher:	Ask me if the sky will fall, then.
Aide and children:	The sky won't fall, will it?
Teacher:	No, it won't.

Things to Look Out For: 1. Your children may be ready to try the past tense forms of *can* (*could*), *will* (*would*), *shall* (*should*), and *may* (*might*). Try it: If it works, continue; if it doesn't work, stop. Do not contract the past modals at first, however. Remember that children produce the full construction before they contract. In addition, negation of *might* results in *mightn't,* a form that again is seldom used today. Do not push too hard if your children have difficulty with the past forms, because these forms will be drilled later in the program.

LESSON 7.21

Objective: To drill the pattern "*Why* (CLAUSE)?"

Materials: Again, no materials are needed for this drill. Use experiences out of daily lives of the children.

**Basic Drill
Pattern:**
S: Ask (*name*) why (CLAUSE).
R₁: (*Name*), why (CLAUSE)?
R₂: Because (*appropriate response*).

R_1: (*Name*), why (CLAUSE)?
R_2: Because (*appropriate response*).

Method: Have the children ask you, the aide, and each other questions, just as in the other drills in Section 7.

Examples:

Teacher:	(demonstrates drill with aide)
Teacher:	Everybody, let's ask Mr. Jones why people eat food.
Teacher and children:	Mr. Jones, why do people eat food?
Aide:	Because they get hungry.
Teacher:	Ask me why birds fly.
Aide and children:	Why do birds fly?
Teacher:	Because they have wings.

**Things to
Look Out For:**

1. You can easily use the negative in this drill:

S: Why can't people fly?
R: Because they don't have wings.

2. *Why* replaces a coordinated clause in a sentence. This replacement makes the response to the question different from all of the other responses to questions in this section. In Section 6, coordinates were drilled, but those drills concerned only *and, but,* and *or.* You may wish to drill both questions and responses using this drill. If you do drill responses because the children need to work at them, remember to include both clauses in the response:

$S_{teacher}$: Why can't people fly?
$R_{children}$: People can't fly because they don't have wings.

You should be able to get the children both to ask the questions and make the responses before you are through.

SECTION 8

Subordinates: Object and Adverbial Inserts

In this section we begin to drill the placing of insert clauses into the object and adverbial slots of matrix clauses. We will present drills for both infinitive and *wh-* inserts.

The section begins with five lessons on the infinitive as a direct object filler, and one on the infinitive as an equative complement filler. Then it moves on to drill the *wh-* inserts, first as a filler of the direct object slot, and then as an adverbial filler. Both *wh-* declaratives and clauses with *wh-* replacements will be used as inserts in these drills. The section ends with drills for restrictive modifier *wh-* inserts. In these drills, the restrictive modifier will appear only in the complement or direct object functions of the matrix clause.

Rationale

It is very interesting that children often begin placing rudimentary infinitive and *wh-* inserts into object and adverbial slots of matrix clauses before they complete the learning of the verb phrase. At this point in the program we will take advantage of this fact to introduce subordination in its simplest terms: inserts as object, complement, and adverbial fillers.

Subordination is one of the four transformations with which we must be concerned. We have already drilled some coordinates and questions, and the fourth transformation, the passive, appears very late in development. Section 8 is the proper place in the program for the object and adverbial subordinates.

The infinitives appear to have a slight edge over *wh-* inserts in terms of sequence of appearance, so they are being drilled first in the section. Because children seem to have a "false infinitive" (using *gonna, wanna,* etc.) at an early time, the drills on the infinitive will be set up in Lesson 8.1 with a drill using *going to;* only after this seems to be going smoothly will the children be required to use a "true" infinitive. This task will be done by requiring the use of the infinitive subject. The next three lessons all present variants of Lesson 8.2.

Once the infinitive drills are going along well, the *wh-* insert will be introduced. By the time it appears in the program, the concept of subordination should be well on its way, and the children will be able to concentrate on the complexities of *wh-* insertion.

The Lessons

All of the drills in this section are made up of dialogue drills. Without dialogues, a great deal of imagination would be required of the children in putting two clauses together. In the dialogue, however, we can take the time to give the children all the information they need in as natural a setting as possible. Structuring the drills this way, however, means that your job will be more complicated. You will be required to do more in the way of memorizing the basic drill patterns, for example, because they are much longer than they have been to this point in the program. It will also probably take you longer to structure the vocabulary, because you will have to make sure that no part of the basic drill pattern breaks down for the specific vocabulary you have chosen. The result should be worth the effort, however.

One other problem you might run into could be that of dialect, especially for the drills on the *wh-* inserts. You should be very careful to note how people in the child's home environment use the *wh-* words in subordinates. For example, the objective in Lesson 8.12 is to drill *while;* there are many dialects, however, that use the word *when* to express the same semantic relationships. In these circumstances, the local usage should take precedence for low-functioning children.

LESSON 8.1

Objective: To drill infinitive subordinate clauses as fillers of the direct object slot.

Materials: Pictures of people about to do something, preferably holding objects that can be used in the action; you can also use actions that the children engage in during their daily routine that involve tools, e.g., erasers, trays, etc.

Basic Drill Pattern:
S_1: DO (*subject*) have a (*noun*) $\pm$ (*adverb*$_{place}$)?
R_1: Yes, (*pronoun*) DO.
S_2: What is (*subject*) going to do with it $\pm$ (*adverb*$_{time}$)?
R_2: (*Subject*) is going to (*verb*) $\pm$ (*object*).

Method: Hold the picture up at S_1 and present the drill pattern.

Examples:

Teacher:	(demonstrates drill with aide)
Teacher:	Does this man have a lawn mower?
Aide and children:	Yes, he does.
Teacher:	What is he going to do with it?
Aide and children:	He is going to mow the grass.
Teacher:	Does this boy have a bicycle?
Aide and children:	Yes, he does.
Teacher:	What is he going to do with it?
Aide and children:	He is going to ride it.
Teacher:	Do I have an eraser here?
Aide and children:	Yes, you do.
Teacher:	What is Johnny going to do with it this afternoon?
Aide and children:	He is going to erase the blackboard.

Things to Look Out For:

1. Note that *going to* has appeared in previous drills. It should pose few problems for the children; it was deliberately chosen as an "introducer" to the infinitives because of the fact that it has been used before.

2. In your vocabulary, be careful not to talk about objects with multipurpose or unknown usages. It would be easy to allow this drill to slip into a guessing game. You may want to go over the vocabulary with the children before beginning the drill itself.

3. As the children begin to demonstrate competence with the basic drill pattern, you can increase its scope by changing the pattern slightly to include a few more verbs in the dominant clause:

S_1: Does this (*noun*$_1$) have a (*noun*$_2$)?
R_1: No, it doesn't.
S_2: What am I forgetting to do?
R_2: You are forgetting to (*verb*) $\pm$ (*object*).

Examples:

Hold jar in one hand, cap in the other.
S_1: Does this jar have a cap?
S_1: No, it doesn't.

S$_2$: What am I forgetting to do?

R$_2$: You are forgetting to put on the cap.

Another verb that will fit this pattern is *trying*.

S$_1$: What is (*subject*) (*verb*$_1$ -ing)?

R$_1$: (*Subject*) is (*verb*$_1$ ing) ± (*object*).

S$_2$: What is (*subject*) trying to do?

R$_2$: (*Subject*) is trying to (*verb*$_2$) ± (*object*).

Examples:

R$_1$: He is holding a kite.

R$_4$: He is trying to fly the kite.

4. Although it may not immediately be apparent, Lessons 8.1–8.6 are all the same lesson, i.e., they all drill the infinitive clause as a direct object. There are a number of different matrix verbs that take infinitive clauses as direct objects, and they fit into several different patterns. You may wish to treat the basic drill patterns in Lessons 8.1–8.7 as being alternative drills rather than as being separate drills. You may wish to combine two or more in the same lesson—in fact, there are many ways in which this could be done, e.g., choose a single topic and then use that topic with two or more of the basic or alternate drill patterns.

LESSON 8.2

Objective: To drill infinitives as object fillers with the subject of the infinitive being expressed.

Materials: Children's knowledge of the daily routine.

Basic Drill Pattern:

S_1: (*Name*), will you (*verb*) ± (*object*) (*adverb* $_{future\ time}$)?

R_1: (*Name*): Yes, I will.

S_2: What did I $\begin{Bmatrix} tell \\ ask \end{Bmatrix}$ (*name*) to do?

R_2: You $\begin{Bmatrix} told \\ asked \end{Bmatrix}$ (*name*) to (*verb*) ± (*object*).

S_3: What did (*name*) promise?

R_3: $\begin{Bmatrix} He \\ She \end{Bmatrix}$ promised to do it.

S_4: Do you think $\begin{Bmatrix} he \\ she \end{Bmatrix}$ will?

R_4: We think so, because $\begin{Bmatrix} he \\ she \end{Bmatrix}$ promised to.

Method: Select some activity that everyone knows will happen that day and where one person is usually selected to assist, such as serving milk or cookies, going to the cafeteria, etc. In S_1, ask one person if he will be that assistant or leader.

Examples:

Teacher:	(demonstrates drill with aide)
Teacher:	Sally, will you pass out the milk today?
Sally:	Yes, I will.
Teacher:	What did I ask her to do?
Aide and children:	You asked her to pass out the milk.
Teacher:	What did Sally promise?
Aide and children:	She promised to do it.
Teacher:	Do you think she will?
Aide and children:	We think so, because she promised to.
Teacher:	Johnny, will you lead the class to the cafeteria at lunchtime?
Johnny:	Yes, I will.
Teacher:	What did I ask him to do?
Aide and children:	You asked him to lead the class to the cafeteria.
Teacher:	What did Johnny promise?
Aide and children:	He promised to do it.
Teacher:	Do you think he will?
Aide and children:	We think so because he promised to.

Things to Look Out For:

1. This basic drill pattern can be modified somewhat:

    S_1: (*Name*), (*verb*) ± (*object*), ± please.

    R_1: (Appropriate response.)

    S_2: Did (*name*) hear me?

    R_2: Yes, (*pronoun*) did.

S_3: What did I tell (*pronoun*) to do?

R_3: You told (*pronoun*) to (*verb*) ± (*object*).

S_4: Why do you think (*pronoun*) did it?

R_4: Because (*pronoun*) heard you tell him to.

Examples:

S_1:	Johnny, touch your nose, please.
R_1(Johnny):	O.K.
S_2:	Did Johnny hear me?
R_2:	Yes, he did.
S_3:	What did I tell him to do?
R_3:	You told him to touch his nose.
S_4:	Why do you think he did it?
R_4:	Because he heard you tell him to.

2. Both of these basic drill patterns spin out the objective infinitive clauses well and include ellipses. Note especially the ellipses in R_4 in the alternate pattern in Note 1 of this lesson:

R_5: (He did it) because he heard you (to) tell him to (do it).

The parts in parentheses are the ellipted parts of the sentence. Most of them depend on the existence of the dialogue for their ability to be ellipted and still make sense.

3. You can weave negatives into this pattern when the child addressed cannot hear or promise:

S_4: Why don't you think $\left\{ \begin{matrix} he \\ she \end{matrix} \right\}$ will?

S_4: Why do you think $\left\{ \begin{matrix} he \\ she \end{matrix} \right\}$ didn't do it?

4. Another matrix verb in this class is *use*. It is easy to use it with much the same results.

S_1: What BE this?

R_1: It BE (*noun*).

S_2: What do you use it for?

R_2: You use it to (*verb*) ± (*object*).

Examples:

S_1: What is this?

R_1: It is a pencil.

S_2: What do you use it for?

R_2: You use it to write.

Note that you do not get the same deletions, however.

5. Still another basic drill pattern which can be used to reach this objective is the following:

S_1: DO (*subject$_1$*) (*verb$_1$*) ± (*object*) ± (*adverb*)?

R_1: Yes, (*pronoun*) DO.

S_2: Can (*subject$_2$*) (*verb$_2$*) ± (*object$_2$*)?

R_2: Yes, (*subject$_2$*) DO.

S_3: Tell me why (*subject*) (*verb$_1$*) ± (*object$_1$*), then.

R_3: (*Subject*) (*verb$_1$*) (*object$_1$*) to (*verb$_2$*) ± (*object$_2$*).

Method: Present an action which can cause or modify another action such as "wearing overshoes" and "keeping feet dry," "eating too many green apples" and "making a person sick," etc. These actions must clearly be causal, i.e., the first must lead to the second.

Examples:

Teacher:	(demonstrates drill with aide)
Teacher:	Do you wear overshoes when it rains?
Aide and children:	Yes, we do.
Teacher:	Can they keep your feet dry?
Aide and children:	Yes, they can.
Teacher:	Tell me why you wear overshoes, then.
Aide and children:	We wear overshoes to keep our feet dry.
Teacher:	Does the barber have hair clippers in his barbershop?
Aide and children:	Yes, he does.
Teacher:	Can he cut people's hair with them?
Aide and children:	Yes, he can.
Teacher:	Tell me why he has hair clippers, then.
Aide and children:	He has hair clippers to cut people's hair.

6. See Note 4, Lesson 8.1.

LESSON 8.3

Objective: To drill infinitive clauses as (objects) of matrix verbs that express internal states.

Materials: Objects or pictures of things which cannot function because parts are gone or in the wrong place, such as a bicycle with the wheels off.

Basic Drill
Pattern: S_1: Can we (*verb₁*) this (*object*)?
R_1: No, we cannot.
S_2: Why can't we?
R_2: Because (*subject*) BE ± not (*complement*).
S_3: Should we (*verb₂*) (*object*) first?

R_3: Yes, we $\left\{\begin{array}{l}\text{want}\\ \text{need}\\ \text{ought}\end{array}\right\}$ to (*verb₂*) (*object*) first.

S_4: Why do we $\left\{\begin{array}{l}\text{want}\\ \text{need}\end{array}\right\}$ to (*verb₂*) (*object*)?

R_4: To (*verb₁*) it.

Method: Present the picture or object and ask about that which is necessary to make the object function. Then ask how we use the object.

Examples:

Teacher:	(demonstrates drill with aide)
Teacher:	Can we ride this bicycle?
Aide and children:	No, we cannot.
Teacher:	Why can't we?
Aide and children:	Because the wheels are not on (it).
Teacher:	Should we put them on first?
Aide and children:	Yes, we ought to put them on.
Teacher:	Why do we need to put them on?
Aide and children:	To ride it.
Teacher:	Can we sit on this chair?
Aide and children:	No, we cannot.
Teacher:	Why can't we?
Aide and children:	Because the legs are broken off.
Teacher:	Should we fix them first?
Aide and children:	Yes, we ought to fix them.
Teacher:	Why do we need to fix them?
Aide and children:	To sit on it.

Things to
Look Out For: 1. For this drill, choose objects that are clearly nonfunctional due to disassembly, disorganization, or because the parts are obviously missing.

2. For parts that are missing and whose whereabouts are unknown, you may want to use the following as an alternate drill pattern. (It will also drill *try to* and the past tense of modals, and for this reason may be an inappropriate drill for many groups.)

S_1: Can we (*verb₁*) this (*object₁*)?

R_1: No, we cannot.

S_2: $\begin{Bmatrix} \text{Will} \\ \text{Would} \end{Bmatrix}$ (verb$_2$ -ing) (object$_2$) help?

R_2: Yes, it would.

S_3: What could we try to do, then?

R_3: We could try to (verb$_2$) (object$_2$).

Example: (A car with the wheels gone, whereabouts unknown.)

Teacher:	Can we drive this car?
Aide and children:	No, we cannot.
Teacher:	Would finding some wheels help?
Aide and children:	Yes, it would.
Teacher:	What could we try to do, then?
Aide and children:	We could try to find some wheels.

Note the use of *would* and *could* in this drill pattern. Your children may not know these words. (They are not drilled until Section 5.) If they do not, these words will cause problems in the drill. Do not use them unless your children can already handle them.

3. See Note 4, Lesson 8.1.

LESSON 8.4

Objective: To drill infinitive clauses as objects of the verbs *wanting, liking,* or *desiring.*

Materials: Pictures of people or animals in situations where they obviously want to do something, such as a man sitting in bed and yawning, a boy holding his glass toward someone with a carton of milk, or a dog carrying his food dish in his teeth and approaching his master.

Basic Drill Pattern:
S_1: BE *(subject) (verb$_1$* -ing) $\pm$ *(object$_1$)*?
R_1: Yes, *(pronoun)* BE.
S_2: Does that mean *(pronoun)* BE *(adjective)*?
R_2: Yes, it does.
S_3: What DO *(subject)* want $\pm$ to do, then?
R_3: *(Pronoun)* want(s) to *(verb$_2$)* $\pm$ *(object$_2$)*.

Method: Present the picture, indicate the feature of the picture that signifies that the picture's subject wants to do something and use it in the drill pattern.

Examples:

Teacher:	(demonstrates drill with aide)
Teacher:	Is the dog carrying his dish?
Aide and children:	Yes, he is.
Teacher:	Does that mean he is hungry?
Aide and children:	Yes, it does.
Teacher:	What does he want to do, then?
Aide and children:	He wants to eat.
Teacher:	Is the man yawning?
Aide and children:	Yes, he is.
Teacher:	Does that mean he is sleepy?
Aide and children:	Yes, it does.
Teacher:	What does he want to do, then?
Aide and children:	He wants to sleep.

Things to Look Out For:

1. You may need to go through some magazines to find pictures that will serve well in this drill. Select pictures in which a person or animal is doing something that is an obvious signal that he wants something else, such as a dog scratching on the door to signal that he wants to go in.

2. This drill pattern may not be sufficient for all actions. If so, you may expand it for those cases, using this alternate:

S_1: BE *(subject) (verb$_1$)* $\pm$ *(object$_1$)*?
R_1: Yes, *(pronoun)* BE.

S_2: Does *(verb$_1$* -ing) $\pm$ *(object$_1$)* mean that *(pronoun)* $\begin{Bmatrix} \text{want} \\ \text{like} \\ \text{need} \\ \text{hate} \\ \text{hope} \end{Bmatrix}$ to *(verb$_2$)* $\pm$ *(object$_2$)*?

R_2: Yes, it does.

$$S_3: \text{ What DO } (pronoun) \begin{Bmatrix} \text{want} \\ \text{like} \\ \text{need} \\ \text{hate} \\ \text{hope} \end{Bmatrix} \pm (\text{to do}), \text{ then?}$$

$$R_3: (Pronoun) \begin{Bmatrix} \text{want} \\ \text{like} \\ \text{need} \\ \text{hate} \\ \text{hope} \end{Bmatrix} \text{ to } (verb_2) \pm (object_2).$$

Example:

Teacher:	Is the woman making a shopping list?
Aide and children:	Yes, she is.
Teacher:	Does making a shopping list mean that she needs to go to the store?
Aide and children:	Yes, it does.
Teacher:	What does she need to do, then?
Aide and children:	She needs to go to the store.

3. In selecting vocabulary for the basic drill pattern (for S_2), many actions (being thirsty, hungry, or sleepy) will convert (in R_3) to wanting *to drink, to eat,* and *to sleep.* If you cannot find a good adjective complement to represent the action in a specific case, then use the alternate drill shown in Note 2.

4. Gerunds may often be substituted for the simple infinitives in this drill, especially when the infinitives take a direct object, such as "He likes eating (ice cream, steak, etc.)," "He hates playing hockey," etc. If you wish to drill gerunds, this would be a good basic drill pattern to use. Be sure that they will work with each matrix verb you are going to use before you begin, though, i.e., you cannot pattern a gerund with *want,* as in *"He wants flying airplanes."

5. Pictures may also be selected which include features that indicate that the subject is "trying to do something" with a greater or lesser degree of success. For the past tense, use a picture of a subject who "forgot" or "failed" to do something. You may prepare and drill these alternates in the same type of drill pattern if you wish.

6. See Note 4, Lesson 8.1. Note 5 above should demonstrate the relationships in these lessons.

LESSON 8.5

Objective: To drill infinitive clauses as objects of matrix verbs expressing being required to or "being allowed to."

Materials: A puppet whose actions can be discussed with no threat to the children. Use the common knowledge of the children or imagined situations that are easily conceivable.

Basic Drill Pattern:

S_1: Otto $\left\{\begin{array}{l}\text{wants}\\\text{hates}\end{array}\right\}$ to (*verb$_1$*) (*object$_1$*), doesn't he?

R_1: Yes, he does.

S_2: But I $\left\{\begin{array}{l}\text{want}\\\text{told}\end{array}\right\}$ (*pronoun*) to (*verb$_2$*) (*object$_2$*) (*adverb$_{\text{time}}$*).

$\pm$ (So), what does he $\left\{\begin{array}{l}\text{have}\\\text{get}\end{array}\right\}$ to do $\pm$ (then)?

R_2: He $\left\{\begin{array}{l}\text{has}\\\text{gets}\end{array}\right\}$ to (*verb$_2$*) (*object$_2$*) $\pm$ (*adverb$_{\text{time}}$*).

Method: Introduce the drill with the aide and follow the basic drill pattern with the children as you have done in all TALK lessons.

Examples:

Teacher:	(demonstrates drill with aide)
Teacher:	Otto wants to stay up all night, doesn't he?
Aide and children:	Yes, he does.
Teacher:	But I want him to go to bed early. What does he have to do, then?
Aide and children:	He has to go to bed early.
Teacher:	Otto hates to eat his spinach doesn't he?
Aide and children:	Yes, he does.
Teacher:	But I told him he can leave it this time. So, what does he get to do?
Aide and children:	He gets to leave his spinach.

Things to Look Out For:

1. Note the change that occurs if *must* is used in S_2:

S_2: What must he do, then?

R_2: He must leave his spinach.

If you wish to drill the modal *must,* you can use this basic drill pattern.

2. The material in S_1 and S_2, when modified, can yield a sentence like, "Otto wants to stay up all night, but I told him to go to bed now." This modification is similar to the way in which *but* was drilled in Section 6.

3. Note that the thought expressed in "I told him to go to bed now" is contrary to that in the direct object in the clause "Otto wants to stay up all night." Such considerations are used to set the context for the contrast between having to do something and being required to do something; or between getting to do something and being allowed to do something. Note, too, how using the (*adverb$_{\text{time}}$*), e.g., *now, this time, next time, today, tomorrow,* etc., specifies that the action in this clause is going to alter the intention of the actor in the first clause.

4. Reflexives may be used as alternates, e.g., *himself, herself*, and verbs, such as *promised,* may be used instead of *told* in S$_2$.

Example:

Teacher:	Otto wants me to let him leave his spinach, doesn't he?
Aide and children:	Yes, he does.
Teacher:	But I promised myself to make him eat it this time. What do I have to do (to him), then?
Aide and children:	You have to make him eat it.
Teacher:	Why do I have to make him eat it?
Aide and children:	Because you promised yourself to.

Drills for the reflexives do not appear in the program, and if you wish to drill them, you might be able to use this as a drill pattern.

LESSON 8.6

Objective: To drill both the gerund and infinitives in the complement slot of the declarative equative clause.

Materials: Common knowledge of the children.

Basic Drill Pattern:

S_1: Do you like (*verb* -ing) ± (*object*)?

R_1: $\left\{ \begin{array}{c} \text{Yes} \\ \text{No} \end{array} \right\}$, we do ± NEG.

S_2: It is (*adjective*), isn't it?

R_2: Yes, it is.

S_3: What is (*adjective*) ± (to do), ± (then)?

R_3: (*Verb* -ing) ± (*object*) is (*adjective*).

S_4: Is it really?

R_4: Yes, it is (*adjective*) $\left\{ \begin{array}{c} \text{to } verb \\ verb \text{ -ing} \end{array} \right\}$ ± (*object*).

Method: Select some activity that is liked or disliked and use it in the drill pattern.

Examples:

Teacher:	(demonstrates drill with aide)
Teacher:	Do you like eating ice cream?
Aide and children:	Yes, we do.
Teacher:	It is fun, isn't it?
Aide and children:	Yes, it is.
Teacher:	What is fun, then?
Aide and children:	Eating ice cream is fun.
Teacher:	Is it really?
Aide and children:	Yes, it is fun to eat ice cream.
Teacher:	Do you like making new friends?
Aide and children:	Yes, we do.
Teacher:	It is good, isn't it?
Aide and children:	Yes, it is.
Teacher:	What is good to do, then?
Aide and children:	Making new friends is good.
Teacher:	Is it really?
Aide and children:	Yes, it is good to make new friends.

Things to Look Out For:

1. Notice how the gerund form substitutes for the infinitive in the subject of the equative pattern (R_3).

2. In selecting adjectives for this drill, you need to choose those which can be considered "judgmental," such as *fun, good, scratchy, prickly,* or *healthy.* etc. Adjectives such as *red, cold,* or *fancy* seldom relate to liking or disliking an activity.

3. You may use a third person, such as Otto, for "dislikes" in order to elicit a negative response in R_1. For this, use an optional *but* to begin S_2. For example:

Teacher:	Does Otto like eating spinach?

Aide and children: No, he does not.
Teacher: But it is healthy, isn't it?

In this case, a reorganization of the material in S_1 and S_2 can produce the sentence, "Otto does not like eating, but it is healthy."

4. R_4 indicates that either an infinitive or a gerund can be used. It would probably be best to use the alternate forms in separate drills, i.e., use the R_4 infinitive in one lesson, and the R_4 gerund alternate on another day in a separate lesson. If you try to mix them, the drill could turn into a guessing game for the children.

LESSON 8.7

Objective: To drill declarative *wh-* insert clauses in the direct object slot with matrix verbs *said, told,* etc.

Materials: No materials are needed, but you might like to use a puppet as the "third party."

**Basic Drill
Pattern:** S_1: Ask (*name*) if (CLAUSE).
R_2: (*Name*), (YES/NO QUESTION)?
R_2: (*Name*): (Appropriate response in clausal form.)
S_2: Everybody, tell $\left\{ \begin{matrix} \text{me} \\ \text{Otto} \end{matrix} \right\}$ what (*name*) $\left\{ \begin{matrix} \text{said} \\ \text{told us} \end{matrix} \right\}$.
R_3: (*Pronoun*) $\left\{ \begin{matrix} \text{said} \\ \text{told us} \end{matrix} \right\}$ that (CLAUSE).

Method: You may have the children ask any *yes/no* question; require R_2 to be a full clause (no ellipsis). R_3 then becomes a matter of reporting what that clause was.

Examples:

Teacher:	(demonstrates drill with aide)
Teacher:	Ask Mr. Jones if he ever flies airplanes.
Teacher and children:	Mr. Jones, do you ever fly airplanes?
Aide:	No, I never fly airplanes.
Teacher:	Everybody, tell Otto what Mr. Jones said.
Aide and children:	Otto, Mr. Jones said that he never flies airplanes.
Teacher:	Ask Johnny if he ever eats mashed potatoes.
Aide and children:	Johnny, do you ever eat mashed potatoes?
Johnny:	Yes, I sometimes eat mashed potatoes.
Aide and children:	Otto, Johnny told us that he sometimes eats mashed potatoes.

**Things to
Look Out For:**   1. This, like most subordinate clause drills, would be a repetition drill if it were not for very small changes. In this drill the change is from first person subject in R_2 to third person subject in R_3, and its accompanying change in the verb.

LESSON 8.8

Objective: To drill *wh-* replacement clauses as subject, direct object, and complement inserts.

Materials: Use a puppet to act as "third party." You will also want objects, flannel board materials, or pictures with people or animals in recognizable common activities.

Basic Drill
Pattern: S_1: Is this (*complement*)?
   R_1: Yes, it is.
   S_2: Do we know $\begin{Bmatrix} \text{who} \\ \text{what} \end{Bmatrix}$ (CLAUSE)?
   R_2: Yes, we do.
   S_3: Does Otto know that?
   R_3: No, he does not.
   S_4: What doesn't Otto know?
   R_4: He does not know $\begin{Bmatrix} \text{who} \\ \text{what} \end{Bmatrix}$ (CLAUSE).

Method: Choose an object from the materials and show it with S_1. In S_2 ask about some aspect of it. Require information that would follow logically from a *wh-* question, such as who or what did something, who or what something *verbed,* who or what something is, or who or what is something. You ask if Otto knows these things, but it turns out that Otto never knows anything in this drill.

Examples:

Teacher:	(demonstrates drill with aide)
Teacher:	Is this some mail?
Aide and children:	Yes, it is.
Teacher:	Do we know who delivers it?
Aide and children:	Yes, we do.
Teacher:	Does Otto know that?
Aide and children:	No, he does not.
Teacher:	What doesn't Otto know?
Aide and children:	Otto does not know who delivers it.
Teacher:	Is this a fork?
Aide and children:	Yes, it is.
Teacher:	Do we know what we use it for?
Aide and children:	Yes, we do.
Teacher:	Does Otto know that?
Aide and children:	No, he does not.
Teacher:	What doesn't Otto know?
Aide and children:	He does not know what we use it for.
Teacher:	Is this a radio?
Aide and children:	Yes, it is.
Teacher:	Do we know what sound it makes?
Aide and children:	Yes, we do.
Teacher:	Does Otto know that?
Aide and children:	No, he does not.
Teacher:	What doesn't Otto know?
Aide and children:	He does not know what sound it makes.
Teacher:	Is this an umbrella?

Aide and children:	Yes, it is.
Teacher:	Do we know what it is?
Aide and children:	Yes, we do.
Teacher:	Does Otto know?
Aide and children:	No, he does not.
Teacher:	What doesn't Otto know?
Aide and children:	He does not know what it is.
Teacher:	Is this a school bus?
Aide and children:	Yes, it is.
Teacher:	Do we know who rides in it?
Aide and children:	Yes, we do.
Teacher:	Does Otto know it?
Aide and children:	No, he does not.
Teacher:	What doesn't Otto know?
Aide and children:	Otto does not know who rides in it.
Teacher:	Is this a zither?
Aide and children:	Yes, it is.
Teacher:	Do we know what it does?
Aide and children:	Yes, we do.
Teacher:	Does Otto know that?
Aide and children:	No, he does not.
Teacher:	What doesn't Otto know?
Aide and children:	He does not know what it does.

Things to Look Out For:

1. Notice how the basic drill pattern leaves the choice of the subordinate clause open. Many different clauses fit this paradigm, and only a few could be specified. Consequently, there are more examples than usual. The thread running through all of them is the *wh-* replacement. Since the children have already drilled *wh-* questions, this should pose no problems for them.

2. Note, too, that many different *wh-* replacements could be made in the same clause:

(of a spoon)

Do we know what it does?
Do we know who uses it?
Do we know what we use it for?
Do we know what it is?

Thus, using just the spoon, a whole set of drills could be started by using S_1–R_1 initially, and then returning to S_2 for each subsequent *wh-* (CLAUSE).

3. There are several different verbs that can be used in the matrix clause (S_2) other than *know*. Some of these are verbs dealing with sensations (*see, hear, feel*) or other internal processes (*understand, wonder*). There are a number of internal processes over which we exercise no active control (*look, listen*) which *cannot* be used here, however. Once the children begin to respond well to the patterns with *know,* begin to use some of the other verbs in the matrix.

4. Adverbial replacements should be drilled separately from subject and object replacements. The following three lessons (8.9–8.13) drill the adverbial *wh-* replacements.

5. The basic drill pattern in this lesson can be used to drill adverbials simply by using *when, where,* or *how* in S_2 and R_4. (Note that *why* also fits here.)

LESSON 8.9

Objective: To drill *wh-* replacement clauses as adverbial of time inserts.

Materials: Use daily activities as topics of the drills.

Basic Drill Pattern:

S_1: DO (CLAUSE$_1$)?

R_1: Yes, $\begin{Bmatrix} name \\ pronoun \end{Bmatrix}$ DO.

S_2: DO (CLAUSE$_2$)?

R_2: Yes, $\begin{Bmatrix} name \\ pronoun \end{Bmatrix}$ DO.

S_3: BE (*subject*) (*verb* -ing) $\pm$ (*object*) (*adverbial* $_{time}$)?

R_3: No, (*pronoun*) BE + NEG.

S_4: Tell me when (*subject*) (*verb*) $\pm$ (*object*) $\pm$ then.

R_4: (*Subject*) (*verb*) $\pm$ (*object*) when (CLAUSE$_1$)

Method: Select two actions that have a causal relationship or that can reasonably be expected to co-occur. Some examples are coming to school and riding the school bus; the fire alarm ringing and going outside for a fire drill, etc. Present the more general or causal action as the first clause, the resulting action as the second; have the children subordinate the second clause in the adverb slot.

Examples:

Teacher:	(demonstrates drill with aide)
Teacher:	Do you come to school?
Aide and children:	Yes, we do.
Teacher:	Do you ride the school bus?
Aide and children:	Yes, we do.
Teacher:	Are you riding the school bus right now?
Aide and children:	No, we are not.
Teacher:	Tell me when you ride the school bus.
Aide and children:	We ride the school bus when we come to school.
Teacher:	Did the fire alarm ring yesterday?
Aide and children:	Yes, it did.
Teacher:	Are we going outside for a fire drill now?
Aide and children:	No, we are not.
Teacher:	Tell me when we went outside for a fire drill, then.
Aide and children:	We went outside for a fire drill when the fire alarm rang yesterday.
Teacher:	Does it rain?
Aide and children:	Yes, it does.
Teacher:	Do you get wet?
Aide and children:	Yes, we do.
Teacher:	Are you getting wet now?
Aide and children:	No, we are not.
Teacher:	Tell me when you get wet.
Aide and children:	We get wet when it rains.

Things to
Look Out For: 1. You must choose vocabulary very carefully for this drill. Use actions and/or events in which there is (*a*) a causal relationship, or (*b*) a reasonable expectation that the two actions or events occur together. If the association is too remote, the drill will not work.

Examples of causality can be found in many daily events: going outside and a fire drill; raining and getting wet; taking a bath and getting clean. Note that the subordinate clauses formed with these events and actions use *when,* e.g., "We went outside when the fire drill started." The same events can also be used in a *because* clause, e.g., "We went outside because the fire drill started." This means that you can also run the basic drill pattern in this lesson as a *because* drill simply by substituting *why* for *when* in S_4. See also Note 4 for Lesson 8.8:

S_4: Tell me why (*pronoun*) (*verb$_2$*) $\pm$ (*object*).

R_4: (*Pronoun*) (*verb$_2$*) $\pm$ (*object*) because (*pronoun*) (*verb$_1$*) $\pm$ (*object*).

Examples of events occurring together are sleeping and snoring; shaving and looking in the mirror, etc. One of these will be more general and the other more specific, e.g., "coming to school" is more general than "riding on the school bus." The more general event or action becomes the matrix clause. Either could be too general or too specific for the two events to be reasonably expected to occur together. The naming of a specific TV show may be too specific to occur with "watching television" because there are so many programs to watch on TV, and the specific show is only one of them. (For your children, however, these two events may occur together all the time and thus it would be all right to use them—but you must *know* that they do.) On the other hand, when men shave they *usually* look in the mirror, and these events can be reasonably considered to occur together.

LESSON 8.10

Objective: To drill *wh-* replacement clauses as adverbial of place inserts.

Materials: Known events in the children's lives that occur in specific, known places.

Basic Drill Pattern:
S_1: When (CLAUSE$_1$), DO (CLAUSE$_2$)?
R_1: Yes, *(subject)* DO.
S_2: DO (CLAUSE$_3$) *(adverbial$_{place}$)*?
R_2: NO, *(subject)* DO + NEG.
S_3: Where DO (CLAUSE$_3$)?
R_3: (CLAUSE$_3$) where (CLAUSE$_2$).

Method: Select two events that physically occur in the same place to be (CLAUSE$_1$) and (CLAUSE$_3$). (CLAUSE$_2$) is used to indicate where this place is. The *(adverbial$_{place}$)* in S_2 indicates the wrong place for (CLAUSE$_3$) to occur.

Examples:

Teacher:	(demonstrates drill with aide)
Teacher:	When we buy food, do we pay the lady at the cash register?
Aide and children:	Yes, we do.
Teacher:	Do they put the food in a bag where the meat is?
Aide and children:	No, they do not.
Teacher:	Where do they put the food in the bag?
Aide and children:	They put the food in the bag where the cash register is.
Teacher:	When you eat lunch, do you sit at the table?
Aide and children:	Yes, we do.
Teacher:	Do you eat dessert out on the playground?
Aide and children:	No, we don't.
Teacher:	Where do you eat your dessert?
Aide and children:	We eat dessert where we eat lunch.
Teacher:	Do mothers cook supper?
Aide and children:	Yes, they do.
Teacher:	Do they make coffee outside?
Aide and children:	No, they do not.
Teacher:	Where do they make coffee?
Aide and children:	They make coffee where they cook supper.

Things to Look Out For:

1. The events for the first and last clauses in the drill must be those which are ordinarily carried out in the same physical place. Choose events that logically occur together, e.g., sewing clothes and sewing buttons; mowing the grass and raking it; putting on shoes and putting on socks; etc.

2. The basic drill pattern for Lesson 8.9 can be adapted to drill the adverbial of place with just a couple of minor changes:

S_1: DO (CLAUSE$_1$)?
R_1: Yes, $\left\{ \begin{array}{c} name \\ pronoun \end{array} \right\}$ DO.
S_2: DO (CLAUSE$_2$)?

R_2: Yes, $\left\{ \begin{array}{c} name \\ pronoun \end{array} \right\}$ DO.

S_3: DO (CLAUSE$_2$) where (CLAUSE$_3$)?

R_3: No, (*subject*) DO + NEG.

S_4: Tell me where (CLAUSE$_2$) $\pm$ then.

R_4: (CLAUSE$_2$) where (CLAUSE$_1$).

Example:

Teacher:	Do people cut their grass?
Aide and children:	Yes, they do.
Teacher:	Do they rake their grass?
Aide and children:	Yes, they do.
Teacher:	Do they rake their grass where the street is?
Aide and children:	No, they do not.
Teacher:	Tell me where they rake their grass.
Aide and children:	They rake their grass where they cut it.

LESSON 8.11

Objective: To drill *wh-* replacement clauses as adverbial of manner inserts.

Materials: From your junk box, assemble a set of tools and utensils, e.g., spoon, hammer, flashlight.

Basic Drill
Pattern: S_1: Does Otto know what this is?
R_1: Yes, he does.
S_2: How does he *(verb)* with it?
R_3: He doesn't know how he *(verb*s) with it.
S_3: We'd better tell him.
R_3: We *(verb)* ± *(object)* with it like this. (demonstrate)

Method: As in Lesson 8.9, the puppet does not know anything, and the children have to tell or show him.

Examples:

Teacher:	(demonstrates drill with aide)
Teacher:	(Holds up spoon.) Does Otto know what this is?
Aide and children:	Yes, he does.
Teacher:	How does he eat with it?
Aide and children:	He doesn't know how he eats with it.
Teacher:	We'd better show him.
Aide and children:	We eat with it like this. (demonstrate)
Teacher:	(Holds up picture of drill press.) Does Otto know what this is?
Aide and children:	Yes, he does.
Teacher:	How does he drill holes with it?
Aide and children:	He doesn't know how he drills holes with it.
Teacher:	I'd better tell him. You drill holes in it by pushing this button and pulling this handle.

Things to
Look Out For: 1. When you are eliciting R_3, you can have children respond individually, or in chorus, or you can tell the puppet how to *(verb)* with it yourself; since R_3 is not a critical pattern, it doesn't matter how you handle it.

2. The matrix verb in R_2 does not always have to be *know*. You can use verbs like *understand*, or *see*. See Note 3, Lesson 8.9.

LESSON 8.12

Objective: To drill *wh-* replacement clauses as adverbial inserts using *while*.

Materials: Use pantomime. You may also use pictures of people and things that are doing more than one thing, e.g., *walking* and *eating an ice cream cone*.

Basic Drill
Pattern:
S_1: BE (*subject*) (*verb$_1$* -ing) ± (*object$_1$*)?
R_1: Yes, (*subject*) BE.
S_2: BE (*subject*) (*verb$_2$* -ing) ± (*object$_2$*), too?
R_2: Yes, (*subject*) BE.
S_3: BE (*subject*) doing both at the same time?
R_3: Yes, (*subject*) BE.
S_4: What BE (*subject*) doing while (*pronoun*) (*verb$_1$*) ± (*object*)?
R_4: (*Subject*) BE (*verb$_2$* -ing) ± (*object$_2$*) while (*pronoun*) (verb) ± (*object$_1$*).

Method: Hold up the picture as you present S_1 and continue to present it through R_4.

Examples:

Teacher:	(demonstrates drill with aide)
Teacher:	Am I touching my nose?
Aide and children:	Yes, you are.
Teacher:	Am I pulling my ear?
Aide and children:	Yes, you are.
Teacher:	Am I doing both at the same time?
Aide and children:	Yes, you are.
Teacher:	Then what am I doing while I touch my nose?
Aide and children:	You are pulling your ear while you touch your nose.
Teacher:	Is the clown riding the bicycle?
Aide and children:	Yes, he is.
Teacher:	Is he flying a kite, too?
Aide and children:	Yes, he is.
Teacher:	Is he doing both at the same time?
Aide and children:	Yes, he is.
Teacher:	Then what he is doing while he rides the bicycle?
Aide and children:	He is flying a kite while he rides the bicycle.

Things to
Look Out For:

1. You have a lot of freedom in choosing the actions. As long as you can illustrate two actions occurring simultaneously, you can run this drill.

2. Some dialects use *when* rather than *while* in the context of the drill pattern. Follow the local dialect and use whichever is preferred.

3. If the subordinated clause uses the continuum it is possible to delete the pronoun. For example:

R_4: You are pulling your ear while touching your nose.
R_4: The clown is flying a kite while riding a bike.

This situation may be found in some dialects and not in others. If it is used in the children's dialect area, you may wish to drill it. Remember that the full form appears before identical units are deleted.

4. When drilling dialectal variants, it is probably best to check with a local person who has not gone to college to find out whether or not a dialect is used in the area. Going to college often changes people's ideas about the way things can and cannot be said.

LESSON 8.13

Objective: To drill *wh-* replacement clauses as adverbial inserts expressing both place and time, with auxiliaries in the matrix.

Materials: Use the children's knowledge of routine events, recent past events, or events scheduled for the near future.

Basic Drill Pattern:

S_1: $\begin{Bmatrix} DO \\ Modal \end{Bmatrix}$ *(subject)* $\pm$ $\begin{Bmatrix} sometimes \\ always \end{Bmatrix}$ *(verb₁)* $\pm$ *(object)*?

R_1: Yes, *(subject)* $\pm$ $\begin{Bmatrix} sometimes \\ always \end{Bmatrix}$ DO.

S_2: *(Modal)* *(subject)* *(verb₂)* $\pm$ *(object)* then?

R_2: Yes, *(subject)* *(modal)*.

S_3: Tell me $\begin{Bmatrix} when \\ where \end{Bmatrix}$ *(subject)* *(modal)* *(verb₂)* $\pm$ *(object)*.

R_3: *(Subject)* *(modal)* *(verb₂)* $\pm$ *(object)* $\begin{Bmatrix} when \\ where \end{Bmatrix}$ *(subject)* *(verb₁)* $\pm$ *(object)*.

Method: Select two actions which are commonly associated with each other. Some examples are raining and getting wet; washing hands and using soap; or going to the bakery and seeing lots of donuts. Select the more general action (that which determines the other action) and present it as S_1.

Examples:

Teacher:	(demonstrates drill with aide)
Teacher:	Does it ever rain?
Aide and children:	Yes, it sometimes does.
Teacher:	Can things get wet then?
Aide and children:	Yes, they can.
Teacher:	Tell me when things can get wet.
Aide and children:	Things can get wet when it rains.
Teacher:	Will we go to the zoo tomorrow?
Aide and children:	Yes, we will.
Teacher:	Will we see lots of animals then?
Aide and children:	Yes, we will.
Teacher:	Tell me when we will see lots of animals.
Aide and children:	We will see lots of animals when we go to the zoo tomorrow.

Things to Look Out For: 1. You will need to choose vocabulary very carefully for this lesson. The vocabulary should reflect (*a*) causal relationships between actions or events, or (*b*) the co-occurrence of actions or events. See Note 1 in Lesson 8.9.

LESSON 8.14

Objective: To drill *wh-* replacement clauses as restrictive modifiers of the noun in the complement of an equative matrix.

Materials: Pictures of people in familiar role situations; or common objects which have some significant feature, such as a doll that talks, a car that comes apart, or a gun that shoots ping pong balls.

Basic Drill
Pattern:
S_1: BE *(subject)* *(complement)*?

R_1: Yes, *(subject)* BE.

S_2: $\begin{Bmatrix} DO \\ BE \end{Bmatrix}$ *(subject)* $\begin{Bmatrix} verb \\ verb\text{ -}ing \end{Bmatrix}$ $\pm$ *(object)*?

R_2: Yes, *(subject)* $\begin{Bmatrix} DO \\ BE \end{Bmatrix}$.

S_3: Tell me $\begin{Bmatrix} which \\ what \end{Bmatrix}$ *(complement)* *(subject)* BE.

R_3: *(Subject)* BE *(complement)* $\begin{Bmatrix} which \\ who \\ that \end{Bmatrix}$ $\begin{Bmatrix} verb \\ BE\ verb\text{ -}ing \end{Bmatrix}$ $\pm$ *(object)*.

Method: Present the picture or the object with S_1. Then subordinate the clause representing whatever the picture or object does by presenting S_2 and S_3.

Examples:

Teacher	(demonstrates drill with aide)
Teacher:	Is this a man?
Aide and children:	Yes, it is.
Teacher:	Does he deliver mail?
Aide and children:	Yes, he does.
Teacher:	Tell me which man he is.
Aide and children:	He is the man who delivers mail.
Teacher:	(with talking doll) Is this a doll?
Aide and children:	Yes, it is.
Teacher:	Does it talk?
Aide and children:	Yes, it does.
Teacher:	Tell me what doll it is, then.
Aide and children:	It is a doll that talks.

Things to
Look Out For:
1. The head in the complement in S_1 must be nonspecific: *a man* rather than *a mailman* or *the man*. The whole point of this drill is to give the children practice in using a restrictive modifier, and in order to have it mean anything you *must* start off with a nonspecific noun. The restrictive modifier will then supply some uniqueness that can be used to make the head of the complement more specific.

2. Note that this lesson has the restrictive modifier in an equative. A basic drill pattern for drilling restrictive modifiers of the head noun in objects of transitive clauses could be the following:

S_1: DO *(subject$_1$)* *(verb$_1$)* *(object)*?

R_1: Yes, *(subject)* DO.

S_2: DO *(subject$_2$)* *(verb$_2$)* $\pm$ *(object)*?

R_2: Yes, *(subject$_2$)* DO.

S_3: What kind of *(object)* DO *(subject$_1$)* *(verb$_1$)* $\pm$ then?

R_3: *(Subject$_1$)* *(verb$_1$)* *(object)* $\begin{Bmatrix} \text{who} \\ \text{which} \\ \text{that} \end{Bmatrix}$ *(verb$_2$)* $\pm$ *(object)*.

Examples:

S_1: Does this boy have a dog?

R_1: Yes, he does.

S_2: Does the dog have spots?

R_2: Yes, he does.

S_3: What kind of a dog does the boy have?

R_3: He has a dog that has spots.

Note that in the above pattern the subject of S_2 must have the same referent as the object of S_1.

SECTION 9

Past Tense Modals, the Passive Voice, the Perfective, and a Subject Insert

The ninth and last section of TALK begins by drilling the past tense of the modals *can, may, shall,* and *will;* some of these will be drilled for more than one meaning. Following these drills are two more lessons for drilling the formation of questions using the same modals. Next comes the drills on the passive voice and a lesson on questions with the passive, and following these are the drills for the perfective, along with drill on questions using the perfective. Finally, there will be one lesson on drilling a subject insert by using the restrictive modifier as the insert clause. This lesson will end the TALK drills.

Rationale

The topics of the lessons in Section 9 are all being placed here because of their place in the developmental sequence. All appear after questions and the object and adverbial inserts begin to develop. When these lesson plans have been drilled, the learning of the verb phrase should be complete, and the children should be beginning to place insert clauses into the subjects of matrix clauses.

This section is actually quite a bit larger than it may appear at first glance. For the drills on the passive, for example, both the BE *-en* and the GET *-en* fillers of the passive function are specified in the basic drill pattern, but the suggestion is made that these fillers be drilled separately. In effect, then, the passive lessons consist of twice as many as actually appear. The lessons on the questions are also few in number; but the suggestion is made to return to Section 7 for more drill patterns, within which all of the verb phrase functions can be drilled in question form. In other words, there is more to teaching the functions in Section 9 than meets the eye, and you may find that it takes a lot longer to teach these concepts than might be apparent at first. The reason for this is that we are dealing with some extremely complex relationships in this chapter, e.g., the interrelationships between grammar and semantics for the passive voice are probably the most complicated of concepts to appear in TALK. The time relationships for the perfective run a close second, however, and the semantic structure of the past tense modals will be found difficult by many children. To have gotten this far in the program will be a major achievement for many low-functioning children; to complete what is in this section will be beyond what many of us once thought was possible. It is possible, however.

The Lessons

Most of the lessons in this section are relatively straightforward. Many complications that are not specified in the basic drill patterns can be added easily once the children begin to use the specified pattern smoothly. All of the verb phrase function lessons can be negated, for example, even though it might take a little adjustment in the pattern from time to time. Anyone who has been using TALK to this point should have no difficulty in making those adjustments, however.

You will probably find that there are not enough lessons on the questions in this section, but, if you return to Section 7, you will find enough patterns into which the concepts that need drilling can be plugged easily. Do not hesitate to take as long as you need to teach the questions adequately; indeed, drilling the questions concurrently with the declaratives would be very instructive for the children, and you should try to mix them as soon as possible.

LESSON 9.1

Objective: To drill the past tense of the modal, using *could* in the sense of both "ability" and "possibility."

Materials: Talk about familiar events in the children's lives.

Basic Drill
Pattern: S$_1$: (*Subject*) DO + NEG have (*object$_1$*). Can (*subject*) (*verb*) ± (*object$_2$*)?
R$_1$: (*Subject*) could (*verb*) (*object$_2$*) if (*subject*) had (*object$_1$*).
S$_2$: But (*subject*) DO + NEG have (*object$_1$*). Could (*subject*) (*verb*) ± (*object$_2$*)?
R$_2$: No, (*subject*) could not (*verb*) ± (*object$_2$*).

Method: In S$_1$, present two events, one of which depends on the other, e.g., having money and going to the movies; having long arms and reaching the top shelf, etc. The ability to accomplish the second can then be expressed as depending upon the first.

Examples:

Teacher:	(demonstrates drill with aide)
Teacher:	I don't have long arms. Can I reach the clock?
Aide and children:	You could reach it if you had long arms.
Teacher:	But I *don't* have long arms. Could I reach the clock?
Aide and children:	No, you could not reach the clock.
Teacher:	I don't have a car. Can I drive to Indianapolis?
Aide and children:	You could drive to Indianapolis if you had a car.
Teacher:	But I *don't* have a car. Could I drive to Indianapolis?
Aide and children:	No, you could not drive to Indianapolis.

Things to
Look Out For: 1. Be sure that the second event in S$_1$ depends on the first event.

2. Note that R$_2$ uses *could* to express "ability," and R$_4$ uses it to express "possibility." It is quite possible that R$_2$ will give your children a great deal of trouble because of the *if* clause; i.e., there are indications that *if* does not develop until quite late. It does give your children an inordinate amount of difficulty, drop R$_1$ and S$_2$. The basic drill pattern will then drill only "ability":

S$_1$: (*Subject*) DO + NEG have (*object$_1$*). Can (*subject*) (*verb*) ± (*object$_2$*)?
R$_1$: No, (*subject*) could not (*verb*) ± (*object$_2$*).

3. If you use one of the children's names as (*subject*), that child should remain silent for the entire drill, because the group will be talking about that child in the third person, whereas the child would have to talk about himself in the first person. For an individual drill, however, the child should respond for the entire drill:

S$_1$: Johnny, you don't have a hall pass. Can you go to the principal's office?
R$_1$: I could go to the principal's office if I had a hall pass.
S$_2$: But you *don't* have a hall pass. Could you go to the principal's office?
R$_2$: No, I could not go to the principal's office.

LESSON 9.2

Objective: To drill the past tense of the modal, using *might* in the sense of "possibility."

Materials: Talk about familiar events in the children's lives, just as in Lesson 9.1.

**Basic Drill
Pattern:**

S_1: Do you think that (*subject*) will (*verb*) $\pm$ $\left\{ \begin{array}{l} object \\ complement \end{array} \right\}$ (*adverbial*$_{time}$)?

R_1: (*Subject*) might (*verb*) $\pm$ $\left\{ \begin{array}{l} object \\ complement \end{array} \right\}$ (*adverbial*$_{time}$), but we are not sure.

S_2: Let's find out what (*subject*) thinks. (*Name*)?

R_2: (*Appropriate reply.*)

Method: Refer to events that often happen, e.g., classroom duties, going to the movies, riding the school bus.

Examples:

Teacher:	(demonstrates drill with aide)
Teacher:	Do you think that Johnny will clean the blackboard this afternoon?
Aide and children:	He might clean the blackboard this afternoon, but we are not sure.
Teacher:	Let's find out what Johnny thinks. Johnny?
Johnny:	I will.
Teacher:	Do you think that Sally will be here tomorrow?
Aide and children:	She might be here tomorrow, but we are not sure.
Teacher:	Let's find out what Sally thinks. Sally?
Sally:	I think I will.

**Things to
Look Out For:**

1. When one of the children is the (*subject*) in S_1, that child should remain silent for R_1 and respond only to S_2. See Note 3, Lesson 9.1.

2. If you ask about something you yourself might do, leave out S_2 and respond directly to R_1 in an appropriate manner.

LESSON 9.3

Objective: To drill the past tense of the modal, using *should* in the sense of "obligation."

Materials: Same as in Lessons 9.1 and 9.2.

Basic Drill
Pattern: S$_1$: (*Subject*) is supposed to (*verb*) ± $\begin{Bmatrix} object \\ complement \end{Bmatrix}$ (*adverbial*$_{\text{time or place}}$). Will (*subject*) do it?

R$_1$: (*Subject*) should (*verb*) ± $\begin{Bmatrix} object \\ complement \end{Bmatrix}$ (*adverbial*$_{\text{time or place}}$) because (*subject*) is supposed to.

S$_2$: Let's find out. (*Name*)?
R$_2$: (*Appropriate response.*)

Method: This drill is much the same as the drill in Lesson 9.2, and is done in the same manner.

Examples:

Teacher:	(demonstrates drill with aide)
Teacher:	Johnny is supposed to go home this afternoon. Will he do it?
Aide and children:	He should go home this afternoon because he is supposed to.
Teacher:	Let's find out. Johnny?
Johnny:	I am going to.
Teacher:	Sally is supposed to be a snowflake in our play. Will she do it?
Aide and children:	She should be a snowflake in the play because she is supposed to.
Teacher:	Let's find out. Sally?
Sally:	Yes, I want to.

Things to Look Out For:
1. See Notes 1 and 2, Lesson 9.2.

2. Note the ellipses on the infinitives that appear in this drill. You may find that your children need to leave the ellipted portions of the responses intact.

LESSON 9.4

Objective: To drill the past tense of the modal, using *would* in the sense of "characteristic actions."

Materials: Talk about actions that were carried out regularly in the past. Pictures of people playing roles or the activities children remember can be used.

Basic Drill Pattern:

S_1: When (*subject*) $\begin{Bmatrix} verbed \\ was \\ used\ to\ be \end{Bmatrix}$ $\begin{Bmatrix} object \\ complement \end{Bmatrix}$ did (*subject*) (*verb*) ± (*object*) (*adverbial*$_{time}$)?

R_1: Yes, (*subject*) did.
S_2: What would (*subject*) do?
R_2: (*Subject*) would (*verb*) ± (*object*) (*adverbial*$_{time}$).

Method: Hold up the picture of the person playing the role or ask about the remembered event and present the basic drill pattern.

Examples:

Teacher:	(demonstrates drill with aide)
Teacher:	When this man was a mailman, did he deliver mail every day?
Aide and children:	Yes, he did.
Teacher:	What would he do?
Aide and children:	He would deliver mail every day.
Teacher:	When Johnny lived down the street, did he walk to school every day?
Aide and children:	Yes, he did.
Teacher:	What would Johnny do?
Aide and children:	He would walk to school every day.

Things to Look Out For:

1. Adverbials of time that can be used in this drill are those that indicate repeated action, e.g., *every day, all the time, when it was morning*.

2. See Note 1, Lesson 9.2.

LESSON 9.5

Objective: To drill the past tense of modal, using *would* in the sense of "hypothesis" in the matrix clause.

Materials: As in Lesson 9.1, talk about familiar events in the children's lives. As a topic, you can use pictures of children doing nothing in particular, a puppet, or yourself.

Basic Drill Pattern:
S_1: (*Subject*) wants to (*verb*) $\pm$ (*object*$_1$), but (*subject*) DO + NEG have (*object*$_2$).
R_1: That's too bad.
S_2: Do you think (*subject*) would (*verb*) $\pm$ (*object*)?
R_2: Yes, (*subject*) would (*verb*) $\pm$ (*object*$_1$) if he had (*object*$_2$).

Method: As in Lesson 9.1, present two events, one of which depends on the other, e.g., playing outside and having the time (see Lesson 9.1).

Examples:

Teacher:	(demonstrates drill with aide)
Teacher:	This boy wants to buy a watch, but doesn't have enough money.
Aide and children:	That's too bad.
Teacher:	Do you think he would buy a watch?
Aide and children:	Yes, he would buy a watch if he had enough money.
Teacher:	I want to go to Florida, but I don't have the time.
Aide and children:	That's too bad.
Teacher:	Do you think I would go to Florida?
Aide and children:	Yes, you would go to Florida if you had enough time.

Things to Look Out For: 1. See all notes for Lesson 9.1.

LESSON 9.6

Objective: To drill the past tense of the modal in *yes/no* questions.

Materials: Use the experiences of the children, yourself, or the aide as topics for the questions.

Basic Drill Pattern:

S: $\begin{Bmatrix} \text{Let's ask} \\ \text{Ask} \end{Bmatrix}$ *(name)* if *(subject)* $\begin{Bmatrix} \text{could} \\ \text{would} \\ \text{should} \\ \text{might} \end{Bmatrix}$ *(verb)* ± *(object)* ± *(adverbial)*.

R_1: ± *(Name)*, $\begin{Bmatrix} \text{could} \\ \text{would} \\ \text{should} \\ \text{might} \end{Bmatrix}$ *(subject)* *(verb)* ± *(object)* ± *(adverbial)*?

R_2: (Appropriate reply.)

Method: Have the children question you, the aide, or each other about things that *could, would, should,* or *might* happen.

Examples:

Teacher:	(demonstrates drill with aide)
Teacher:	Ask me if I could fly to the moon.
Aide and children:	Could you fly to the moon?
Teacher:	If I had a rocket I could. Let's ask Mr. Jones if he might fly to the moon.
Teacher and children:	Mr. Jones, might you fly to the moon?
Aide:	No chance!

Things to Look Out For:

1. When you or your aide answer the questions, the topics are very flexible. When the children answer the question, however, be sure that only questions they can answer are used.

2. If necessary, break this drill down into separate drills for each modal. If the children can handle all four in one drill, however, do not hold them back from doing so.

LESSON 9.7

Objective: To drill the past tense of the modal in *wh-* replacement questions.

Materials: Use the experience of the children, yourself, or the aide as topics for the questions. You could also use pictures of persons or animals in action, about to engage in an action, or just having completed an action.

Basic Drill Pattern:

S: Ask (*name*) $\begin{Bmatrix} \text{who} \\ \text{what} \\ \text{where} \\ \text{when} \\ \text{how} \end{Bmatrix}$ (*subject*) $\begin{Bmatrix} \text{would} \\ \text{could} \\ \text{should} \\ \text{might} \end{Bmatrix}$ (*verb*) ± (*object*).

R₁: ± (*Name*), $\begin{Bmatrix} \text{who} \\ \text{what} \\ \text{where} \\ \text{when} \\ \text{how} \end{Bmatrix}$ $\begin{Bmatrix} \text{would} \\ \text{could} \\ \text{should} \\ \text{might} \end{Bmatrix}$ ± (*subject*) (*verb*) ± (*object*)?

R₂: (Appropriate reply.)

Method: Question the children about ordinary daily routine or about what is happening in the picture you are showing them.

Examples:

Teacher:	(demonstrates drill with aide)
Teacher:	Ask me who might clean the blackboard today.
Aide and children:	Who might clean the blackboard today?
Teacher:	I think Johnny might, if he keeps on being good.
Teacher:	Ask me what the bulldozer could knock down.
Aide and children:	What could the bulldozer knock down?
Teacher:	It could knock down a big tree.
Teacher:	Ask Mr. Jones where the principal should be.
Aide and children:	Where should the principal be?
Teacher:	He should be in his office.

Things to Look Out For:

1. Notice how the *wh-* words given could replace subjects, objects, complements, adverbials, etc., but that not all *wh-* words fit this pattern. Any of the *wh-* replacement pattern drills from the section on questions could be used to elicit these (or any other) *wh-* word with a past tense modal. Adapt as freely as you need in order to teach the question with past tense modals.

2. See Notes 1 and 2, Lesson 9.6.

Past Tense Modals, the Passive Voice, the Perfective, and a Subject Insert   **431**

LESSON 9.8

Objective: To drill, in the passive, habitual actions using the simple present tense.

Materials: Use pictures of objects that can be used to illustrate actions which the children know are habitual or recurrent.

Basic Drill Pattern:

S_1: $\begin{Bmatrix} \text{What} \\ \text{Who} \end{Bmatrix}$ BE (*complement*)?

R_1: (*Subject$_1$*) BE (*complement$_2$*)?

S_2: What does (*subject$_1$*) do?

R_2: (*Subject$_1$*) (*verbs*) (*object*).

S_3: What happens to (*object*)?

R_3: (*Subject$_2$*) $\begin{Bmatrix} \text{GET} \\ \text{BE} \end{Bmatrix}$ (*verb* -en).

S_4: $\begin{Bmatrix} \text{Who} \\ \text{What} \end{Bmatrix}$ BE (*subject$_2$*) (*verb* -en) by?

R_4: (*Subject$_2$*) $\begin{Bmatrix} \text{GET} \\ \text{BE} \end{Bmatrix}$ (*verb* -en) by (*passive complement*).

Method: Present pictures of people in roles who are in the act of doing something to objects, e.g., a gardener weeding a garden. You can also refer to real objects that have specific functions, e.g., milking machines, movie projectors, a bucket and water.

Examples:

Teacher:	(demonstrates drill with aide)
Teacher:	Who is this man?
Aide and children:	He is an artist.
Teacher:	What does he do?
Aide and children:	He paints pictures.
Teacher:	What happens to the pictures?
Aide and children:	They get painted.
Teacher:	Who do they get painted by?
Aide and children:	They get painted by the artist.
Teacher:	What's that?
Aide and children:	It is a movie projector.
Teacher:	What does it do?
Aide and children:	It shows movies.
Teacher:	What happens to the movies?
Aide and children:	They get shown.
Teacher:	What do they get shown by?
Aide and children:	They get shown by the movie projector.

Things to Look Out For:

1. Other present habitual actions can easily be drilled in this pattern, such as: Trucks get driven by truck drivers; toys get played with by kids; teeth get brushed by toothbrushes.

2. Note the fact that BE -*en* and GET -*en* are shown as alternates in this drill. Begin by drilling GET -*en,* and later, when the children are using it freely in their everyday speech, switch to BE -*en.* This may mean that you will have to go through *all* of the drills on the

passive and on into the drills on the perfective (and maybe the subject inserts as well) before beginning drill on the use of BE -*en*. In this context, S_4 is shown to use the BE -*en* filler of the passive. You will want to use *GET* -*en* at first, and to do so, the dummy DO is used in S_4 as follows:

> Who does the mail get delivered by?
> Who does the truck get driven by?

3. Watch your verbs. Some are highly irregular and may give your children some problems. Included in this category would be verbs such as *cut, hurt, put, hit, sleep, send, bring, teach,* and *think.* It is perfectly all right to use these verbs, but be aware of their irregularity and the fact that it may be easier to drill the pattern with more regular verbs such as *see* and *deliver.* This warning may be especially relevant for the first couple of times you try this drill. Irregular verbs will become less of a problem as you get into the drill.

4. In the basic drill pattern, the (*complement*) in S_1 is the (*subject$_1$*) of S_2 and R_2; also, the (*object*) of S_3 is the (*subject$_2$*) of the passive clause in R_3, S_4, and R_4. See the example provided folowing the basic drill pattern.

LESSON 9.9

Objective: To drill the passive in the simple past.

Materials: Materials are similar to those used in Lesson 9.8, but use only those that can depict completed actions. Pictures should also demonstrate completed actions using the simple past tense, such as a dog going away from a house showing the bone that he left sitting in front of his dog house.

Basic Drill Pattern:

S_1: $\begin{Bmatrix} \text{Who} \\ \text{What} \end{Bmatrix}$ BE *(complement₁)*?

R_1: *(Subject₁)* BE *(complement₁)*?

S_2: What did *(subject₁)* do to *(object)*?

R_2: *(Subject₁)* *(verb* -ed) *(object)*.

S_3: What happened to *(object)*?

R_3: *(Subject₂)* $\begin{Bmatrix} \text{GET} \\ \text{BE} \end{Bmatrix}$ *(verb* -ed).

S_4: $\begin{Bmatrix} \text{Who} \\ \text{What} \end{Bmatrix}$ $\begin{Bmatrix} \text{GET} \\ \text{BE} \end{Bmatrix}$ *(subject₂)* *(verb* -ed) by?

R_4: *(Subject)* $\begin{Bmatrix} \text{GET} \\ \text{BE} \end{Bmatrix}$ *(verb* -ed) by *(passive complement)*.

Method: Completed actions are presented through pictures or demonstrations with toys and objects; drill the children on what just took place. Again, role playing may be used here.

Examples:

Teacher:	(demonstrates drill with aide)

(Teacher demonstrates action, e.g., a bulldozer pushing dirt.)

Teacher:	What is that?
Aide and children:	It is a bulldozer.
Teacher:	What did it do to the dirt?
Aide and children:	It pushed the dirt.
Teacher:	What happened to the dirt?
Aide and children:	It got pushed.
Teacher:	What did it get pushed by?
Aide and children:	It got pushed by the bulldozer.

Things to Look Out For:

1. Examples of other completed actions that can easily fit into this pattern are a cat chased (up a tree) by a dog, cars stopped by a school crossing traffic guard, or any other situation in which an action has resulted in something being accomplished.

2. See Notes 2, 3, and 4, Lesson 9.8.

LESSON 9.10

Objective: To drill the passive in the simple future.

Materials: Similar to those used in Lessons 9.8 and 9.9, except that they must be able to illustrate actions which are going to occur, such as a cat crouching in the grass watching a butterfly.

Basic Drill Pattern:

S$_1$: $\begin{Bmatrix} \text{Who} \\ \text{What} \end{Bmatrix}$ BE (*complement*)?

R$_1$: (*Subject$_1$*) BE (*complement*).

S$_2$: What will (*subject$_1$*) do to (*object*)?

R$_2$: (*Subject$_1$*) will (*verb*) (*object*).

S$_3$: What will happen to (*object*)?

R$_3$: (*Subject$_2$*) will $\begin{Bmatrix} \text{GET} \\ \text{BE} \end{Bmatrix}$ (*verb* -ed).

S$_4$: What will (*subject$_2$*) $\begin{Bmatrix} \text{GET} \\ \text{BE} \end{Bmatrix}$ (*verb* -ed) by?

R$_4$: (*Subject$_2$*) will $\begin{Bmatrix} \text{GET} \\ \text{BE} \end{Bmatrix}$ (*verb* -ed) by (*passive complement*).

Method: Drill this pattern in the same manner as you did Lesson 9.9, but use future actions.

Examples:

Teacher:	(demonstrates drill with aide)

(Teacher shows a picture, e.g., a lumberjack chopping down a tree.)

Teacher:	What is he?
Aide and children:	He is a lumberjack.
Teacher:	What will he do to the tree?
Aide and children:	He will chop down the tree.
Teacher:	What will happen to the tree?
Aide and children:	It will get chopped down.
Teacher:	Who will it be chopped down by?
Aide and children:	It will get chopped down by the lumberjack.

Things to Look Out For:

1. Examples of other future actions that can easily be drilled in this pattern are a snowball about to hit a snowman, Santa Claus about to deliver toys, a dump truck about to dump a load of sand, a boy with a toothbrush in hand on his way to brush his teeth.

2. You may wish to use *going to* as an alternate form to *will*. There should be no problem if you do.

3. Other modals, such as *can* or *must,* fit easily into this drill pattern, and you may use the pattern to drill them if you wish. Note that semantic relationships will change, however:

    The boy will drive the bike.
    The boy can drive the bike.

Otherwise, the basic drill pattern remains the same:

    What is he?
    He is a boy.
    What can he do to the bike?

Past Tense Modals, the Passive Voice, the Perfective, and a Subject Insert   **435**

He can ride the bike.
What can happen to the bike?
It can get ridden.
Who can it get ridden by?
It can get ridden by the boy.

4. See Notes 2, 3, and 4, Lesson 9.8.

LESSON 9.11

Objective: To drill the passive using the present continuum.

Materials: Pictures of people in roles doing things to objects, such as a farmer milking a cow, a plumber fixing a leaky pipe, etc. You may also use the objects that your children use as role playing materials, i.e., objects such as toy milk bottles, farmer's or mechanic's tools, etc. You may also use pictures of actions in which something is being done to something else.

Basic Drill Pattern:

S_1: $\begin{Bmatrix} \text{Who} \\ \text{What} \end{Bmatrix}$ BE (*complement*)?

R_1: (*Subject₁*) BE (*complement*).

S_2: What BE (*subject*) doing to (*object*)?

R_2: (*Subject₁*) BE (*verb* -ing) (*object*).

S_3: What is happening to (*object*)?

R_3: (*Subject₂*) BE $\begin{Bmatrix} \text{get} \\ \text{be} \end{Bmatrix}$ -ing (*verb* -ed).

S_4: What BE (*subject₂*) $\begin{Bmatrix} \text{get} \\ \text{be} \end{Bmatrix}$ -ing (*verb* -ed) by?

R_4: (*Subject₂*) BE $\begin{Bmatrix} \text{get} \\ \text{be} \end{Bmatrix}$ -ing (*verb* -ed) by (*passive complement*).

Method: Run this drill in a manner similar to that of Lessons 9.8–9.10.

Examples:

Teacher:	(demonstrates drill with aide)
Teacher:	What is he?
Aide and children:	He is the farmer.
Teacher:	What is he doing to the cow?
Aide and children:	He is milking the cow.
Teacher:	What is happening to the cow?
Aide and children:	It is getting milked.
Teacher:	Who is it getting milked by?
Aide and children:	It is getting milked by the farmer.

Things to Look Out For: 1. Other examples of similar actions which can fit into the pattern are a farmer picking corn, a cook opening a can, a carpenter hammering nails, a painter painting a house, etc. Use your imagination and go through lots of magazines.

2. See Notes 2, 3, and 4, Lesson 9.8.

LESSON 9.12

Objective: To drill both the *yes/no* and *wh-* replacement questions in clauses in the passive voice.

Materials: Use the same materials used in Lessons 9.8–9.11.

Basic Drill Pattern:

S$_1$: Ask (*name*) if (*subject*) BE being (*verb* -ed) in this picture.

R$_1$: BE (*subject*) being (*verb* -ed)?

R$_2$: $\begin{Bmatrix} \text{Yes} \\ \text{No} \end{Bmatrix}$, (*subject*) BE ± NEG. (If NEG, give appropriate reply.)

S$_2$: Ask (*name*) $\begin{Bmatrix} \text{who} \\ \text{what} \end{Bmatrix}$ (*subject*) BE ± being (*verb* -ed) by.

R$_3$: $\begin{Bmatrix} \text{Who} \\ \text{What} \end{Bmatrix}$ BE (*subject*) ± being (*verb* -ed) by?

R$_4$: (Appropriate reply.)

Method: Using the same pictures and the (by now) familiar passive patterns, have the children ask you, the aide, or the other children questions about the actions in the picture. Vary tense throughout the drill.

Examples:

Teacher:	(demonstrates drill with aide)
Teacher:	Ask me if the cat is being chased in this picture.
Aide and children:	Is the cat being chased?
Teacher:	Yes, it is. Ask me who it is being chased by.
Aide and children:	Who is it being chased by?
Teacher:	By the dog.
Teacher:	Ask Johnny if the dirt is being pushed in this picture.
Aide and children:	Johnny, is the dirt being pushed?
Johnny:	No, it isn't. The bulldozer stopped.
Teacher:	Ask Johnny what it was pushed by.
Aide and children:	What was it pushed by?
Johnny:	By the bulldozer.

Things to Look Out For:

1. Note the optional *being* in S$_3$. This allows you to ask questions about actions that are completed in R$_3$. See examples.

2. Other *wh-* questions are possible, and you may wish to use alternate drill patterns. See Section 7 for possible patterns that can be adapted to the passive.

3. Although this drill specifies only the BE *-ing* filler, GET *-en* should be used at first as is true for the other drills on the passive. Because this is the final drill for the passive, however, Be *-en* is shown throughout the examples to give you an idea of how this (and the other drills for the passive) will sound with the BE *-en* form.

LESSON 9.13

Objective: To drill the present tense of the perfective.

Materials: Pictures of people in action, or common experiences of the children.

Basic Drill Pattern: S: *(Subject)* must *(verb₁)* ± *(object)* before *(subject)* can *(verb₂)* ± *(object)*. $\left\{ \begin{array}{c} \text{Have} \\ \text{Has} \end{array} \right\}$ *(subject)* *(verb₁ -en)* ± *(object)* ± yet?

R: $\left\{ \begin{array}{c} \text{Yes} \\ \text{No} \end{array} \right\}$, *(subject)* $\left\{ \begin{array}{c} \text{Have} \\ \text{Has} \end{array} \right\}$ ± NEG *(verb₁ -en)* ± *(object)*.

Method: Choose two events that are logically connected, i.e., one event must precede another, such as brushing teeth and going to bed; finishing chores and going out to play. Choose pictures that can represent one of the two events so as to elicit an affirmative or negative statement.

Examples:

Teacher:	(demonstrates drill with aide)
Teacher:	This boy must get out of bed before he eats breakfast. Has he gotten out of bed yet?
Aide and children:	Yes, he has gotten out of bed.
Teacher:	This girl must eat her vegetables before she gets dessert. Has she eaten her vegetables yet?
Aide and children:	No, she has not eaten her vegetables yet.
Teacher:	You children must go to gym before you eat lunch. Have you gone to gym yet?
Aide and children:	No, we have not gone to gym yet.

Things to Look Out For:

1. Just as was true of the passives, you may find that some verbs give you more trouble than others. Since the passive has already been drilled, you should be well aware of which ones these are, if any.

2. You may find that you have to break this drill down into two separate drills, one for *has* (used with third person singular subjects) and one for *have* (used with all other subjects). Do not break it down if you do not have to, however.

LESSON 9.14

Objective: To drill the past tense of the perfective in the sense of "completed action" prior to some other "completed action."

Materials: You can use the same type of materials used in Lesson 9.13.

Basic Drill
Pattern: S: (*Adverbial*$_{time}$), (*subject*) had to (*verb*$_1$) ± (*object*) before (*CLAUSE*). Then (*subject*) could (*verb*$_2$) ± (*object*). Did (*subject*) (*verb*$_1$) (*object*)?

R: $\left\{ \begin{array}{l} \text{Yes} \\ \text{No} \end{array} \right\}$, (*subject*) had ± NEG (*verb*$_1$ -en) ± (*object*) $\left\{ \begin{array}{l} \text{before} \\ \text{yet} \end{array} \right\}$ ± (*subject*) (*verb*$_2$) ± (*object*).

Method: For this drill you need three events. The event representing either (*verb*$_1$) or (*verb*$_2$) should be depicted in the picture.

Examples:

Teacher:	(demonstrates drill with aide)
Teacher:	This morning Johnny had to get out of bed before he could brush his teeth. Then he could come to school. Did he get out of bed?
Aide and children:	Yes, he had gotten out of bed before he came to school.
Teacher:	(Holds up picture of girl doing homework.) Yesterday, the girl had to finish her homework before she could eat supper. Then she could eat her supper. Did she eat her supper?
Aide and children:	No, she had not finished her homework.

Things to
Look Out For: 1. All events must be couched in the past time for this drill to work.

2. See Note 1, Lesson 9.13.

3. If NEG is used in the response, the pattern ends with *yet;* if NEG is not used, the pattern ends with "Before (*subject*) (*verb*$_2$) ± (*object*)." See examples provided.

LESSON 9.15

Objective: To drill *yes/no* questions containing the perfective.

Materials: Either use pictures, as in Lessons 9.13 and 9.14, or refer to events in the daily lives of the children.

Basic Drill
Pattern: S: Ask (*name*) if (*subject*) HAVE (*verb* -en) ± (*object*) (*adverbial*).
R₁: HAVE (*subject*) (*verb* -en) ± (*object*) (*adverbial*)?
R₂: (Appropriate reply.)

Method: Tell the children to question you, the aide, or each other about events that may or may not be completed.

Examples:

Teacher:	(demonstrates drill with aide)
Teacher:	Ask me if Johnny has eaten his breakfast yet.
Aide and children:	Has Johnny eaten his breakfast yet?
Teacher:	I think so—it is almost lunchtime. Let's check. Ask Johnny if he had eaten his breakfast before he left home.
Aide and children:	Johnny, had you eaten your breakfast before you left home?
Johnny:	Yes, I did.

Things to
Look Out For: 1. Note how vocabulary is no problem in this drill the way it might have been in Lessons 9.13 and 9.14, because you supply all necessary forms in the stimulus, including the particular form of HAVE and the perfective form of the verb.

2. Also note that you can vary tense freely. All you have to do is to supply the proper form of HAVE.

LESSON 9.16

Objective: To drill *wh-* replacement questions in clauses with the perfective.

Materials: Use the same type of materials used in Lessons 9.13–9.15.

Basic Drill
Pattern: S: Ask *(name)* $\left\{\begin{array}{l}\text{where}\\\text{when}\\\text{how}\end{array}\right\}$ *(subject)* HAVE *(verb* -en) ± *(object)*.

R₁: $\left\{\begin{array}{l}\text{Where}\\\text{When}\\\text{How}\end{array}\right\}$ HAVE *(subject)* *(verb* -en) ± *(object)*?

R₂: (Appropriate reply.)

Method: Tell the children to ask the questions indicated in the basic drill pattern about actions that have been completed already.

Examples:

Teacher:	(demonstrates drill with aide)
Teacher:	Everybody, ask Johnny when he has played kickball.
Aide and children:	Johnny, when have you played kickball?
Johnny:	I played it yesterday.
Teacher:	Ask me when I had been in the army.
Aide and children:	When had you been in the army?
Teacher:	Before I became a teacher.

Things to
Look Out For:
1. See Notes 1 and 2, Lesson 9.15.
2. Other *wh-* replacement drills are possible. See Section 7 for ideas.

LESSON 9.17

Objective: To drill the *wh-* replacement as a restrictive modifier in the subject of the matrix.

Materials: Pairs of pictures depicting two of the same category of people (teacher, actor, doctor, etc.), or two of the same category of things (trucks, balls, etc.). However, the pairs of people or things must differ somehow, either in terms of characteristics or in terms of actions.

Basic Drill Pattern:

S_1: Here are two (*nouns*). This one (*verb$_1$*) ± (*object*), and this one (*verb$_2$*) ± (*object*).

$\left\{ \begin{array}{c} \text{DO} \\ \text{AUX} \end{array} \right\}$ this one (*verb$_3$*) ± (*object*)?

R_1: Yes, (*subject*) $\left\{ \begin{array}{c} \text{DO} \\ \text{AUX} \end{array} \right\}$.

S_2: $\left\{ \begin{array}{c} \text{DO} \\ \text{AUX} \end{array} \right\}$ this one (*verb$_4$*) ± (*object*)?

R_2: Yes, (*subject*) $\left\{ \begin{array}{c} \text{DO} \\ \text{AUX} \end{array} \right\}$.

S_3: Which one (*verb$_{1 \text{ or } 2}$*) ± (*object*)?

R_3: The (*noun*) $\left\{ \begin{array}{c} \text{who} \\ \text{that} \end{array} \right\}$ (*verb$_{3 \text{ or } 4}$*) ± (*object*) (*verb$_{1 \text{ or } 2}$*) ± (*object*).

Method: Alternately indicate one or the other picture. Picture *A* should be characterized by (*verb$_{1 \text{ and } 3}$*), and Picture *B* by (*verb$_{2 \text{ and } 4}$*). For S_3, choose either (*verb$_1$*) or (*verb$_2$*) and have the children form the restrictive modifier using either (*verb$_3$*) or (*verb$_4$*).

Examples:

Teacher:	(demonstrates drill with aide)
Teacher:	Here are two boys. This one (*A*) has a hat, and this one (*B*) does not have a hat. Is this one (*A*) throwing a ball?
Aide and children:	Yes, he is.
Teacher:	Is this one sitting down?
Aide and children:	Yes, he is.
Teacher:	Which one wears a hat?
Aide and children:	The boy who is throwing a ball wears a hat.
Teacher:	Here are two women. This one (*A*) has a child, and this one (*B*) has a dog. Does this one (*B*) carry a shopping bag?
Aide and children:	Yes, she does.
Teacher:	Does this one have a baby carriage?
Aide and children:	Yes, she does.
Teacher:	Which one carries a shopping bag?
Aide and children:	The woman who has a dog carries a shopping bag.

Things to Look Out For:

1. The nouns in the subject of the matrix should be nonspecific, i.e., they should refer to general classes of people or things. The reason we use a restrictive modifier is to make a noun that represents a general class more specific.

2. *AUX* in this drill refers to any auxiliary in the VP other than DO. This symbol allows

for the continuum, modals, etc., to be used freely. In addition, any one of the four clauses could be equative:

> The man who is the tall one is fat.
> The boy who has the fish was at the pond.

3. The following is a possible alternate drill for subject inserts:

Basic Drill Pattern: S_1: BE *(subject) (complement)*?

R_1: Yes, *(subject)* BE.

S_2: $\begin{Bmatrix} DO \\ BE \end{Bmatrix}$ *(subject)* $\begin{Bmatrix} verb_1 \\ verb_2\text{-ing} \end{Bmatrix}$ $\pm$ *(object)*?

R_2: Yes, *(subject)* $\begin{Bmatrix} DO \\ BE \end{Bmatrix}$.

S_3: $\begin{Bmatrix} DO \\ BE \end{Bmatrix}$ *(subject)* $\begin{Bmatrix} verb_2 \\ verb_2\text{-ing} \end{Bmatrix}$ $\pm$ *(object)*?

R_3: Yes, *(subject)* $\begin{Bmatrix} DO \\ BE \end{Bmatrix}$.

S_4: Tell me what you know about *(subject)*.

R_4: *(Subject)* $\begin{Bmatrix} who \\ that \end{Bmatrix}$ $\begin{Bmatrix} verb_1 \\ BE\ verb_1\text{ -ing} \end{Bmatrix}$ $\pm$ *(object)* $\begin{Bmatrix} verb_2 \\ BE\ verb_2\text{ -ing} \end{Bmatrix}$ $\pm$ *(object)*.

Method: Show the children a picture of someone or something that is engaged in an action of some sort *(verb 1)*. Pick out something distinctive about the actor *(verb 2)* and use it for the restrictive modifier. S_2 provides the matrix, and S_3 the insert.

Examples:

Teacher:	(demonstrates drill with aide)
Teacher:	Is this an artist?
Aide and children:	Yes, he is.
Teacher:	Does he paint pictures?
Aide and children:	Yes, he does.
Teacher:	Does he wear a smock?
Aide and children:	Yes, he does.
Teacher:	Tell me everything you know about him.
Aide and children:	The man who paints pictures wears a smock.
Teacher:	Is this a rocket?
Aide and children:	Yes, it is.
Teacher:	Does it take people to the moon?
Aide and children:	Yes, it does.
Teacher:	Is it very big?
Aide and children:	Yes, it is.
Teacher:	Tell me everything you know about it.
Aide and children:	The rocket that takes people to the moon is very big.

References

Note: In front of several of the following references an asterisk (*) will be found. This mark indicates materials that deal directly with teaching technology. Some of these materials are not referenced in the text, but are good enough to warrant inclusion.

*Allen, H. B. (Ed.). *Teaching English as a second language, A book of readings.* New York: McGraw-Hill, 1965.

Bandura, A. *Principles of behavior modification.* New York: Holt, Rinehart, & Winston, 1969.

Bellugi, U. *The emergence of inflections and negations in the speech of two children.* Paper presented at the New England Psychological Association Annual Convention (Cited by McNeill, 1970).

Berko, J. The child's learning of English morphology. *Word,* 1958, *14,* 150–177.

Bloom, L. *Language development: Form and function in emerging grammars.* Cambridge: M.I.T. Press, 1970.

Bloomfield, L. *Language.* New York: Holt, Rinehart, & Winston, 1933.

Braine, M. D. S. On learning the grammatical order of words. *Psychological Review,* 1963, *70,* 323–348.

Brown, R. *A first language: The early stages.* Cambridge: Harvard University Press, 1973.

Brown, R., & Bellugi, U. Three processes in the child's acquisition of syntax. *Harvard Educational Review,* 1964, *34,* 133–151.

Carroll, J. B. (Ed.). *Language, thought, and reality: Selected writings of Benjamin Lee Whorf.* (New York: John Wiley, 1956.

Chappell, E. *A picture test of English inflection.* Unpublished doctoral dissertation, University of Wisconsin, 1968.

Chomsky, N. *Syntactic structures.* The Hague: Mouton, 1957.

References

Chomsky, N. *Aspects of theory of syntax.* Boston: M.I.T. Press, 1965.

Chomsky, N. *Language and mind.* New York: Harcourt, Brace, Jovanovich, 1968.

Cromer, R. F. The cognitive hypothesis of language acquisition and its implications for child language deficiency. In D. M. Morehead, & A. E. Morehead (Eds.), *Normal and deficient child language.* Baltimore: University Park Press, 1976.

*Crystal, D., Fletcher, P., & Garman, M. The grammatical assessment of language disability: A procedure for assessment and remediation. *Studies in Language Disability and Remediation* (Vol. 1). London: Edward Arnold, 1975.

Curtiss, S., Fromkin, V., Krasken, D., Rigler, D., & Rigler, M. The linguistic development of Genie. *Language,* 1974, *50,* 528–554.

*Dacanay, F. R., & Bowen, J. D. *Techniques and procedures in second language teaching* (Philippine Center for Language Study Monograph #3). Dobbs Ferry, N.Y.: Oceana Publications, 1967.

Dever, R. A new perspective for language research. *Mental Retardation,* 1966, *4,* 20–23.

Dever, R. *Language problems of the retarded child.* Paper presented at the National Council of Teachers of English Annual Convention, November, 1968.

Dever, R. A comparison of the results of a revised version of Berko's *Test of Morphology* with the free speech of mentally retarded children. *Journal of Speech and Hearing Research,* 1972a, *15,* 169–178.

Dever, R. Before transformational grammars: The case for data-gathering. *Journal of Special Education,* 1972b, *5,* 119–126.

Dever, R., & Gardner, W. Performance of normals and retardates on Berko's *Test of Morphology. Language and Speech,* 1970, *13,* 162–181.

Dever, R., & Knapczyk, D. The Indiana University preservice undergraduate program for training teachers of the moderately, severely, and profoundly handicapped. *Teacher Education Forum* [Vol. 5 (2)]. Bloomington, Ind.: Indiana University School of Education, 1977.

Dweck, C. S. The role of expectations and attributions in the alleviation of learned helplessness. *Journal of Personality and Social Psychology,* 1975, *31,* 674–685.

Elson, B., & Pickett, V. *An introduction to morphology and syntax.* Santa Ana, Calif.: Summer Institute of Linguistics, 1965.

Ervin-Tripp, S. Language development. In M. Hoffman & L. Hoffman (Eds.), *Review of child development research* (Vol. 2). Ann Arbor: University of Michigan Press, 1966.

*Finocchiaro, M. *English as a second language: From theory to practice.* New York: Simon & Shuster, 1964.

Flavell, J. H. *The developmental psychology of Jean Piaget.* New York: D. Van Nostrand, 1963.

Floor, L., & Rosen, M. Investigating the phenomenon of helplessness in mentally retarded adults. *American Journal of Mental Deficiency,* 1975, *79,* 565–572.

Francis, W. N. *The structure of American English.* New York: Ronald, 1958.

Fries, C. C. *American English grammar.* New York: Appleton-Century-Crofts, 1940.

Fries, C. C. Have as a function word. *Language Learning,* 1948, *1,* 4–8.

*Fries, C. C. *The teaching of English.* Ann Arbor: George Wahr, 1949.

Fries, C. C. On the intonation of Yes–No questions in English. Offprint, n.d.

Fries, P. H. *The uses of the infinitive in the object of the verb in English.* Unpublished Ph.D. dissertation, University of Pennsylvania, 1964.

Fries, P. H. *The English verb phrase: A description of its form.* Mimeo, February, 1966.

Fries, P. H. *Clauses.* Mimeo, November, 1968.

Fries, P. H. On pernicious recursion. *Working papers in linguistics* [Vol. 1 (1)]. Madison, Wisc.: Madison Linguistics Circle, 1970a.

Fries, P. H. On double-function in tagmemic analysis. *Anthropological Linguistics,* 1970b, *12,* 122–135.

Fries, P. H. *Tagmeme sequences in the English noun phrase.* Santa Ana, Calif.: Summer Institute of Linguistics, 1972.

Fries, P. H. Some fundamental insights of tagmemics revisited. In E. Palome, W. Winter, & M. Jazayery (Eds.), *Volume in honor of the retirement of A. A. Hill from the University of Texas, December 1, 1971.* (Reprinted from R. Brand (Ed.), *Advances in tagmemics.* North Holland, Mich.: North Holland Press, 1973a.)

Fries, P. H. *Constructions which are grammatically the same may have quite different semantic interpretations.* Mimeo, 1973b.

Fries, P. H. Problems in the description of the English noun phrase. In L. Heilman (Ed.), *Proceedings of the 11th International Congress of Linguistics, 1.* Bologna, Italy: Societa Editrice il Milano Bologna, 1974.

Fries, P. H. *The notion of hierarchy illustrated with English.* Mimeo, n.d.(a).

Fries, P. H. *Phrase, clause and sentence.* Xerox copy, n.d.(b).

Gatenby, E. V. Conditions for success in language learning. In H. B. Allen (Ed.), *Teaching English as a second language: A book of readings.* New York: McGraw-Hill, 1965.

Gleason, H. *Linguistics and English grammar.* New York: Holt, Rinehart, & Winston, 1965.

Gold, M. Task analysis of a complex assembly task by the retarded blind. *Exceptional Child,* 1976, *43,* 78–85.

Gunter, R. Elliptical sentences in American English. *Lingua,* 1963, *12,* 137–150.

Halliday, M. A. K. Language structure and language function. In J. Lyons (Ed.), *New horizons in linguistics.* Middlesex, England: Penguin Books, 1970.

Halliday, M. A. K. *Learning how to mean.* Paper prepared for E. Lenneberg and E. Lenneberg (Eds.), *Language development in healthy children,* Part II of *Foundations of language development: A multidisciplinary approach.* UNESCO, 1972.

Halliday, M. A. K. *Early language learning: A sociolinguistic approach.* Paper prepared for the IXth International Congress of Anthropological and Ethnological Sciences, Chicago, August–September, 1973(a).

Halliday, M. A. K. *A sociosemiotic persepctive on language development.* Paper presented to the Fifth Child Language Research Forum, Stanford University, April 6, 1973(b).

Heber, R., Garber, H., Harrington, S., & Hoffman, C. *Rehabilitation of families at risk for mental retardation.* Madison, Wisc.: Rehabilitation Research and Training Center in Mental Retardation, 1972.

Hockett, C. D. The origin of speech. *The Scientific American,* 1960 (Sept.), 2–10.

Hunt, K. W. Syntactic maturity in school children and adults. *Monographs of the Society for Research in Child Development,* 1970, *35,* (1).

Itard, J. M. G. [The wild boy of Averyon] (G. Humphrey & M. Humphrey, Trans.). New York: Appleton-Century-Crofts, 1962. (Originally published, 1799.)

Jensen, A. R. How much can we boost IQ and scholastic achievement? *Harvard Educational Review,* 1969, *39,* 1–123.

Joos, M. *The five clocks.* New York: Harcourt, Brace, Jovanovich, 1961.

*Kent, L. R. *Language acquisition program for the severely retarded.* Champaign, Ill.: Research Press, 1974.

Knapczyk, D. R. Behavior change strategies for the retarded. In R. Dever (Ed.), *Proceedings of the Special Study Institute for Teachers of the Trainable Mentally Handicapped.* Frankfort, Kentucky: Kentucky Department of Education, 1974.

Koenigschnecht, Roy. Statistical information on developmental sentence analysis. In L. Lee, *Developmental sentence analysis.* Evanston, Ill.: Northwestern University Press, 1974.

Labov, W. *Finding out about children's language.* Paper delivered to the Hawaii Council of Teachers of English, July, 1970.

*Lado, R., & Fries, C. C. *English pattern practices.* Ann Arbor: University of Michigan Press, 1964.

*Lado, R., & Fries, C. C. *English sentence patterns.* Ann Arbor: University of Michigan Press, 1965.

*Lee, L. *Developmental sentence analysis.* Evanston, Ill.: Northwestern University Press, 1974.

*Lee, L., Koenigschnecht, R., & Mulhern, S. *Interactive language development. Teaching: The clinical presentation of grammatical structure.* Evanston, Ill.: Northwestern University Press, 1975.

*Lee, L., & Canter, S. Developmental sentence scoring: A clinical procedure for estimating syntactic development in children's spontaneous speech. *Journal of Speech and Hearing Disorders,* 1971, *36,* 316–340.

LeFevre, C. A. *Linguistics, English, and the language arts.* Boston: Allyn and Bacon, 1970.

Lenneberg, E. *The biological foundation of language.* New York: Wiley, 1967.

Levy, S., Pomerantz, D., & Gold, M. Work skill development. In N. Haring (Ed.), *Teaching severely/profoundly handicapped individuals* (Vol. 1). New York: Grune & Stratton, 1975.

Liem, N. D. *English grammar: A combined tagmemic and transformational approach.* Linguistics Circle of Canberra Publication [Series C, Vol. 1 (*3*)] Canberra, Australia: Australian National University, 1966.

McNeill, D. Developmental psycholinguistics. In F. Smith & G. A. Miller (Eds.), *The genesis of language: A psycholinguistic approach.* Cambridge: M.I.T. Press, 1966.

McNeill, D. The development of language. In P. H. Mussen (Ed.), *Carmichael's manual of child psychology* (3rd ed.). New York: John Wiley, 1970.

Menyuk, P. *Sentences children use.* Cambridge: M.I.T. Press, 1969.

Menyuk, P. *The acquisition and development of language.* Englewood Cliffs, N.J.: Prentice-Hall, 1971.

Menyuk, P., & Looney, P. A problem of language disorder: Length vs. structure. In D. M. Morehead & A. E. Morehead (Eds.), *Normal and deficient child language.* Baltimore: University Park Press, 1976.

Miller, G. A. The magic number seven, plus or minus two: Some limits to our capacity for processing information. *Psychological Review,* 1956, *63,* 81–97.

References

*Miller, J. F., & Yoder, D. E. A syntax teaching program. In J. McClean, D. Yoder, & R. Schiefelbusch (Eds.), *Language intervention with the retarded*. Baltimore: University Park Press, 1972.

*Miller, J. F., & Yoder, D. E. An ontogenetic language teaching strategy for retarded children. In R. Schiefelbusch & L. Lloyd (Eds.), *Language perspectives: Acquisition, retardation and intervention*. Baltimore: University Park Press, 1974.

Morehead, D. M., & Ingram, D. The development of base syntax in normal and linguistically deviant children. In D. M. Morehead & A. E. Morehead (Eds.), *Normal and deficient child language*. Baltimore: University Park Press, 1976.

Moores, D. F. Psycholinguistics and deafness. *American Annals of the Deaf*, 1970, *115*, 37–48.

Moores, D. F. Non-vocal systems of verbal behavior. In R. Schiefelbusch & L. Lloyd (Eds.), *Language perspectives: Acquisition, retardation, and intervention*. Baltimore: University Park Press, 1974, 377–418.

Moulton, W. G. Linguistics and language teaching in the United States, 1940–1960. In *Trends in European and American linguistics*. Utrecht, Netherlands: Spectrum Publishers [U.S. Government Printing Office Offprint: 1962, 0-652303(17)].

*National Council of Teachers of English. *English for today, books I–VI (Teachers' Editions)*. Champaign, Illinois: National Council of Teachers of English, 508 S. Sixth Street, 1962.

*Norris, M. J. Linguistic science and its classroom reflections. In *Selected articles from language learning, #2: Theory and practice in English as a foreign language*. Ann Arbor: The Research Club in Language Learning, 1963.

Olson, D. R. *Cognitive development: The child's acquisition of diagonality*. New York: Academic Press, 1970.

Olson, D. R. Language acquisition and cognitive development. In H. C. Haywood (Ed.), *Social-cultural aspects of mental retardation*. New York: Holt, Rinehart & Winston, 1971.

Ortony, A. Language isn't for people: On applying theoretical linguistics to practical problems. *Review of Educational Research*, 1975, *45*, 485–504.

Premack, D., & Premack, A. J. Teaching visual language to apes and language-deficient persons. In R. Schiefelbusch and L. Lloyd (Eds.), *Language perspectives: Acquisition, retardation, and intervention*. Baltimore: University Park Press, 1974, 347–376.

Quirk, R., Leech, G., Greenbaum, S., & Svartik, J. *A grammar of contemporary English*. New York: Seminar Press, 1972.

Rosenberg, S. Problems of language development in children: A discussion of Olson's review. In H. C. Haywood (Ed.), *Social-cultural aspects of mental retardation*. New York: Holt, Rinehart & Winston, 1971.

Segall, M., Campbell, D., & Herskovits, M. *The influence of culture in visual perception*. Indianapolis: Bobbs-Merrill, 1966.

Sweet, W. *Latin: A structural approach*. Ann Arbor: University of Michigan Press, 1957.

Trager, G., & Smith, H. *An outline of English structure*. (Studies in Linguistics, Occasional Papers, no. 3). Reprinted. Washington, D.C.: American Council of Learned Societies, 1957.

Sailor, W. Reinforcement and generalization of productive plural allomorphs in two retarded children. *Journal of Applied Behavior Analysis*, 1971, *4*, 305–310.

Weir, R. H. *Language in the crib*. The Hague: Mouton, 1962.

APPENDICES

OBSERVATION CHECKLIST FOR CLAUSAL DEVELOPMENT

1. *Does the child use intransitive and transitive clause constructions?*

	Never	Occasional	Consistent	Comments
a. Intransitive Constructions				
1) imperative (predicate)	—	—	—	_____
2) declarative (predicate–object)	—	—	—	_____
b. Transitive Constructions				
1) imperative (predicate–object)	—	—	—	_____
2) declarative (subject–predicate–object)	—	—	—	_____
c. Adverbial Functions				
1) time	—	—	—	_____
2) place	—	—	—	_____
3) manner	—	—	—	_____
4) instrument	—	—	—	_____
5) accompaniment	—	—	—	_____

Notes:

a. If intransitive and transitive constructions are present, begin listening to equative and transitive with indirect object constructions, and coordinate constructions (**2**).

b. If intransitive and transitive constructions are not present, begin listening to Stage II and IIIa semantic functions (**6**).

c. If intransitive constructions are present but transitive constructions are not, begin teaching with transitive imperatives and declaratives.

d. If declaratives have all obligatory functions filled, assume that imperatives have reached Stage IV even if you do not hear the child using them.

2: *Does the child use equative constructions, transitive with indirect object constructions, and coordinated clause constructions?*

	Never	Occasional	Consistent	Comments

a. Equative Constructions

    1) equative (subject–BE–complement)   — — —   _____

b. Transitive Constructions

    1) with indirect object: (subject –
       predicate – indirect–direct)   — — —   _____

c. Coordinated Clause Construction

    1) clause (*and, so, but*) clause   — — —   _____
    2) deletions of repeated forms in second clause — — —   _____

Notes:

a. If these constructions have all of their obligatory functions filled, begin listening to question constructions (**3**).

b. If any of these constructions do not have all of their obligatory functions filled, branch to verb phrase (**6**). Note that you may need to assess *both* verb phrase *and* these constructions at the same time because of the interaction between them.

3. *Does the child move tense in question constructions?*

	Never	Occasional	Consistent	Comments

a. Questions

    Clauses with Auxiliaries

       Yes/No

	Never	Occasional	Consistent	Comments
1) continuum	—	—	—	_____
2) modals	—	—	—	_____
3) passive	—	—	—	_____
4) perfective	—	—	—	_____

       Wh-

	Never	Occasional	Consistent	Comments
1) continuum	—	—	—	_____
2) modals	—	—	—	_____
3) passive	—	—	—	_____
4) perfective	—	—	—	_____

    Equative with No Auxiliaries

	Never	Occasional	Consistent	Comments
Yes/No	—	—	—	_____
Wh-	—	—	—	_____

    Intransitives and Transitives with Dummy DO

	Never	Occasional	Consistent	Comments
Yes/No	—	—	—	_____
Wh-	—	—	—	_____

Notes:

a. If tense movement occurs except for passive and perfective, branch to subordinates and passive (**4**).

b. If passive and/or perfective appear in questions, and if tense is being moved correctly, you can assume completion of all other question development.

c. If tense is *not* being moved for continuum, modals, equative BE or the dummy DO, branch to the early verb phrase (**6**). If tense is being moved for these functions and not for perfective or passive, branch to the late VP functions (**7**).

d. Teach VP functions in the declarative constructions before teaching them in question constructions.

e. For *wh-* questions, check to get a rough idea of which *wh-* replacements are being used (e.g., subject, object, restrictive modifier) and note them.

4. *Does the child insert clauses in to matrix functions, and is the passive being formed?*

	Never	Occasional	Consistent	Comments

a. Subordinate Constructions

Infinitive Inserts:

1) direct object with *wanna, gonna, gotta, hafta, hasta, lemme,* and *lets* in the matrix
2) direct object with other matrix forms
3) adverbial
4) equative clause subject and/or complement
5) gerunds

Wh- Inserts:

1) direct object
2) adverbial
3) object restrictive modifiers
4) subject restrictive modifier
5) other (specify)
6) optional deletions of *wh-* words

b. Passive

1) GET *-en* filler
2) BE *-en* filler

Notes:

a. Object and adverbial inserts can be assumed to have developed if restrictive modifier or subject inserts have developed.

b. If only object inserts are being used, branch to question (**3**) and verb phrase (**6 and 7**).

5. *If the child uses one- or two-word sentences, which semantic functions are present?*

	Never	Occasional	Consistent	Comments

Stage II: Holophrastic Utterances

Substantive Functions

1) comments — — — ——————
2) greetings — — — ——————
3) vocatives — — — ——————
4) actor — — — ——————
5) action — — — ——————
6) patient — — — ——————

Relational Functions

1) recurrance — — — ——————
2) nonexistence — — — ——————
3) disappearance — — — ——————
4) rejection — — — ——————
5) cessation — — — ——————
6) existence — — — ——————

Stage IIIa: Combinations

1) existence (a, the + substantive) — — — ——————
2) recurrence (more, another, again, + substantive)
3) nonexistence (no, away, all gone, + substantive)
4) rejection (no + substantive) — — — ——————
5) denial (no + substantive) — — — ——————
6) possession (substantive + substantive) — — — ——————
7) attributive (substantive, action + substantive)
8) location (a, the + substantive)
9) dative (action + substantive) — — — ——————
10) accompaniment (action + substantive) — — — ——————
11) instrument (action + substantive) — — — ——————

6 and **7.** *Does the child use the functions and/or fillers of the verb phrase?*

	Never	Occasional	Consistent	Comments

a. Functions

    1) continuum inflection (*-ing*)

    2) continuum auxiliary (*is*)

    3) continuum auxiliary (other forms)

    4) modal (*may, can, will*)

    5) dummy DO (except negative)

    6) modal (other forms)

    7) perfective

b. Negative

    1) in contractions (*can't, won't, don't*)

    2) with other auxiliaries

    3) in equatives with BE

    4) with dummy DO (*doesn't, didn't, don't*)

c. Inflections

    1) regular past (*-T*)

    2) irregular past

    3) regular third singular (-S_3)

    4) irregular third singular (*does, has, says*)

Notes:

a. If perfective is present, assume all other listed VP functions are present and branch to subordinates.

b. Teach equative predicate before concentrating on the modals or the dummy DO.

c. Teach negative along with each function as it is being taught.

d. Begin to teach *yes/no* questions (using each VP function learned) soon after the function appears in declaratives during conversations.

8. *Does the child use the functions and fillers of the noun phrase, and does he know all of the pronouns and when they are used?*

	Never	Occasional	Consistent	Comments

a. Functions

1) determiner$_2$ articles
2) loose-knit modifier
3) limiter
4) determiner$_1$
5) determiner$_2$
6) determiner$_3$
7) close-knit modifier (adverbial)
8) restrictive modifier (adverbial)
9) nonrestrictive modifier (adverbial)
10) complex nominal (of + completion)

b. Inflections

1) regular plural (-S$_1$)
2) irregular plurals
3) possessive (-S$_2$)
4) comparative/superlative (-*er*) and (-*est*)

Notes:

a. If restrictive and nonrestrictive modifiers and complex nominals are being used, assume that all other NP functions have appeared.

Personal Pronouns

	Subject		Object		Comments
	Sg.	Pl.	Sg.	Pl.	

1st: I, we, me, us
2nd: you, you, you, you
3rd: he, she, it, they, them

Possessive Pronouns (det.$_2$)

Sg.	Pl.	Sg.	Pl.

1st: my, our
2nd: your, your
3rd: his, hers, its, their

Possessive Pronouns (nominal)

	Subject		Object		Comments
	Sg.	Pl.	Sg.	Pl.	
1st: mine, ours					
2nd: yours, yours					
3rd: his, hers, its, their					

Reflexive Pronouns

	Sg.	Pl.	Sg.	Pl.	
1st: pro + self/selves					
2nd: pro + self/selves					
3rd: pro + self/selves					

APPENDIX B

GLOSSARY

Adjective   Words that can (a) fill either the complement function in an equative clause or the loose-knit modifier function in the noun phrase; and (b) be inflected for comparison (-er, more) or superlative (-est, most).

Adjectival   The entire class of words or constructions that act like adjectives.

Adjunct   A word or phrase that can be added to the end of a clause at the speaker's option. It carries indispensable information to the hearer, but the information can be carried in other constructions, e.g., indirect objects, complex nominals.

Adverb   Word that (a) can fill an adverbial slot in a clause; (b) can be intensified (very _____); and (c) responds to the questions: How? When? Where? With whom? With what? (d) In addition many adverbs can be inflected for comparison (-er, more) or superlative (-est, most).

Adverbial   (a) An optional slot in the English clause that can be filled by an adverb or a prepositional phrase; (b) any word or construction that acts like an adverb.

Affix   A sound or group of sounds that can be added to the end of a base form, e.g., -s, -ing, -ment.

Aphasia   A condition in which a person is not able to produce all or certain parts of the language spontaneously.

Applied linguistics   The pedagogy of languages.

Article   A closed list of words that fill the determiner$_2$ functions: a, an, the, some, any, no, this, that, these, those.

Assessment   The process of discovering what the learner must learn next.

Auxiliary   The filler of any function in the verb phrase other than the head, e.g., modal, continuum.

Base form   The form considered to be the core of a word to which suffixes can be added.

Clause   The construction in English that has one and one only predicate, filled by a verb phrase. The clause may also have one or more optional functions: sub-ject, indirect object, direct object, complement, adverbial.

Complement   A function in a clause that refers to and complements (completes) another function, normally the subject (subjective complement) or the object (objective complement).

Conjoining   The use of conjunctions to string clauses, phrases, or words together.

Conjunction   Words that join clauses, phrases, or words in coordinate constructions, e.g., and, but, so, because, although.

= ("Consists of")   A symbol used in a tagmemic grammar to indicate that the rule for the construction follows immediately.

Construction   A unit of analysis in a tagmemic grammar. A construction has functions (slots) that appear in a specific sequence.

Content   What the learner must learn to do.

Contraction   Occurs when words are attached to each other in the written language, and one or both lose part of their form, e.g., can't, I'll, they're.

Coordination   A grammatical construction in which (a) two or more clauses are strung together using conjunctions, and (b) in which both clauses have equal grammatical status in the sentence.

Deafness   A condition in which the sense of hearing is not available for the purpose of learning a language.

Declarative   Clause construction in which tense in the verb phrase normally follows the subject of the clause. Semantically, declaratives most often express statements.

Developmental checklist   A list of sequenced behaviors used to (a) discover what a child needs to learn next, and (b) keep records of past and current behavior.

Dialect   The specific form of a language spoken by a group of people in a homogeneous area or social group.

Direct object   Obligatory function in a transitive

459

clause. It ordinarily follows the predicate in the active voice and becomes the subject of the clause in the passive voice.

Discontinuous filler   A filler of a function that appears in two different places, separated by another form, e.g., *am* runn*ing*.

continuum

Discourse   The back and forth interplay in a language.

Echolalia   A form of behavior in which one person repeats all or part of what another person says, apparently unable to do otherwise. The echolalic behavior may be immediate or delayed, partial or complete.

Ellipsis   A linguistic situation in which (*a*) the grammatical structure of a previous utterance supplies the grammatical structure for a following utterance, or (*b*) the context supplies the grammatical structure for an utterance.

Elision   Verbal contractions, e.g., *Jyeat yet?* ("Did you eat yet?").

Equative   A clause type in which (*a*) BE fills the head of the verb phrase in the predicate, and (*b*) no passive is possible.

Feedback   Methods of letting the learner know when he is doing what the teacher wants him to do.

: ("Filled by")   Symbol used in a tagmemic formula to indicate that the forms that follow the symbol fill the function that precedes the symbol.

Fillers   The forms that can go into a slot (function) of a construction.

Form   What actually appears in a language; sounds or groups of sounds recognized as having coherence by the speakers of the language.

Format   The method used to instruct.

Function   A slot in a construction that is filled by one or more forms. When more than one form can fill a slot, all forms that can be used are mutually substitutable.

Gerund   A word that can fill the same functions as can an infinitive, and which has the following construction: *verb -ing*.

Grammar   The rules for sequencing words in a language.

Head   The slot in a phrase that is able to represent the entire phrase. The head is always obligatory in the phrase construction.

Imperative   Clause construction in which the subject is optional and no tense appears in the verb phrase. Semantically, the imperative most often expresses a command.

Inflection   An affix that conforms a word to its grammatical function but does not change its meaning, e.g., *plurality, verb, past*.

Instructional group   Four to seven responding children in a TALK group.

Intonation   The variations in pitch and stress in a language.

Intransitive   A clause construction in which (*a*) only the subject and predicate are obligatory, (*b*) no passive is possible.

Language   For the purpose of this book, this term refers to the American English language.

Language delay   A condition in which a person lags behind his chronological peers in the development of his ability to produce the language spoken in his environment.

Lexicon   The collection of words in a language (as in a dictionary).

Linguistics   The study of languages per se.

Marker   The word that signals ("marks") a construction, e.g., *to* (marker for the infinitive construction).

Matrix   A framework of blanks that can be filled in by following specific rules or procedures.

Mental retardation   A condition associated with delayed development of expected behaviors.

Modifier   An optional or obligatory function in a construction other than the head.

Morpheme   The smallest unit of the language that carries meaning. Morphemes can be words or parts of words.

Morphology   The level of a language on which the smallest units of the language that have meaning (*morphemes*) are found.

Negative   Any form that (*a*) is attached to tense in the verb phrase, and (*b*) fills the negative function.

Nominal   A word or phrase that acts like a noun.

Noun   Words (*a*) that fill the head slot in a noun phrase (a _____; the _____); and (*b*) most of which make a distinction between singular (*dog, man*) and plural (*dogs, men*).

Number   The contrast between singular and plural forms.

+ ("Obligatory")   Symbol used in a tagmemic formula to indicate that the function that follows the symbol is obligatory in the construction.

± ("Optional")   Symbol used in a tagmemic formula to indicate that the function that follows the symbol is optional in the construction.

Participle—Two forms   *Present:* the form derived by adding *-ing* to a verb, e.g., *running, wishing.*

Past: the form derived by adding one of the *-en* inflections to a verb, e.g., *thrown, shaken, wished* (often irregular).

Passive voice   The form of a clause in which the action expressed goes from back to front in the clause, e.g., *The dog was chased by the cat.*

Pattern drill   Drill for instruction of a construction, function, or filler that attempts to get the learner to use a pattern over and over while varying specifics (vocabulary, etc.)

Phonology   Term referring to the sounds of the language. It includes not only the discrete sounds (*phonemes*), but also the musical qualities of the language (*stress, pitch*).

Phrase   Constructions that fill functions (*a*) on the clause level (e.g., *noun phrase, verb phrase*), or (*b*) on the phrase level (e.g., *quantity phrase, numeral comparison phrase*). All phrases have obligatory head functions as well as optional and obligatory modifiers.

Person   There are three persons in English: (*a*) *first person* (the speaker); (*b*) *second person* (the person spoken to); and (*c*) *third person* (the person spoken about). Pronouns and verbs reflect person.

Post nominal   Words or constructions that follow the noun in the noun phrase.

Preclausal constructions   Constructions that occur normally in the course of language development in which one or more obligatory functions of the adult clause are missing.

Predicate   The only obligatory function in all English clauses; filled by a verb phrase.

Prefix   A sound or a group of sounds that can be added to the front of a base form, e.g., *in-, pre-, de-.*

Prenominal   Words or constructions that appear before a noun in the noun phrase.

Preposition   Words like *in, of, for, to.* They are always followed by another word (e.g., a noun) or phrase (e.g., a *noun phrase*) to form a prepositional phrase.

Pronoun   Any form or construction that can fill the same functions as can a *noun phrase.* Forms include *personal pronouns* (*I, you,* etc.); *possessive pronouns* (*our, hers,* etc.); *reflexives* (*myself,* etc.). Constructions vary, e.g., *both* (in "give me *both*"); *all three* (in "*all three* arrived").

Psycholinguistics   The study of the processing of linguistic rules.

Response   What the child does in a TALK drill.

Rules   Statements of regularities in behavior among people.

Question   Clause construction in which tense normally precedes the subject of the clause. *Yes/no questions* seek a "yes" or a "no" in the response; *wh-questions* seek a specific bit of information (*who, what,* etc.); and *tag questions* seek agreement (*You saw that, didn't you?*).

Semantics   The meaning accruing to the various levels of the language.

Sentence   The construction in English that consists of one or more clauses in a single intonational envelope.

Sign language   The manual language used by deaf people. It may or may not closely approximate English in terms of the grammar. Forms of sign that closely approximate English are called, variously, *Signed English,* or *Pedagogical Sign.*

Slot   Alternate term for *function.*

Speech   The use of the spoken language.

Stem   An alternate term for *base form.*

Stimulus   What the child hears in a TALK drill.

Stress   Emphasis that is placed on parts of spoken words or constructions.

Subject   A function in clauses that (*a*) normally appears first in the clause, and (*b*) in active clauses, typically carries the *actor* or *instrument* semantic functions.

Subordination   Occurs when two clauses appear in the same sentence, where one serves as a *matrix* for the *insertion* of the other.

Suffix   A sound or group of sounds that can be added to a base form (see *prefix* and *affix*).

Syntax   Synonym for *grammar.*

System   The collection of regularities that occur in language across people (see *Rules*).

Tag   The part of a *tag question* construction that is ellipted, e.g., That's mine, *isn't it?*

Tagmeme   The correlation between a *slot* and its *filler.*

Tagmemics   A theoretical approach to describing the grammar of a language.

Appendices

Task analysis   The process of analyzing the parts of an instructional task and the manner in which the parts might be taught.

Transcript   An exact written record of the conversation of two or more people.

Transitive   A clause construction (*a*) in which there is an obligatory direct object; and (*b*) the clause can be cast in the passive voice.

Transformation   A statement of relationships between sentence constructions that may involve (*a*) position shifts, (*b*) deletions, or (*c*) additions, e.g.: The declarative-question relationship is such that tense follows the subject in the declarative, whereas it precedes the subject in the question.

Verb   A word that (*a*) can fill the head slot in a verb phrase (*run*); (*b*) contrasts present and past (*throw/*

threw); (*c*) can be inflected for third singular (*hears*), present participle (*wishing*) and past participle (*known*).

Verb phrase   The construction that (*a*) fills the predicate function of a clause, and (*b*) has a verb filling its head function.

Vocative   Semantic function that refers to the person addressed.

Voice   A grammatical category that allows action to be expressed two ways without changing the basic meaning of the sentence (*John loves Mary; Mary is loved by John*).

Word   Term referring to the written language; any form that is separated from other forms by white spaces on either side of the form.

VOCABULARY LIST

This appendix includes lists of words which might prove helpful in those moments during preparation when you cannot think of words which will work well in the lesson. This list is, of course, hardly exhaustive. However this is a "starter list" of nouns, verbs, and adjectives which will give you a springboard now and then when you just cannot think of a word which fits the day's pattern well. It is up to you from here. Note that you can make different words and word classes from one word by adding derivational morphemes: *play, player, playful, playfully,* etc. If these lists are not suggestive enough, you can always go to a thesaurus or a dictionary for help.

Verbs

answer	cough	flap	kneel	pay
ask	count	float	know	pick
bake	cover	fold	knock	play
beat	crack	forgive	lay	please
become	crawl	freeze	laugh	point
begin	cry	fry	learn	pull
behave	cut	gather	leave	push
belong	dance	get	let	quit
bite	dig	give	lift	rain
blow	do	giggle	listen	read
breathe	dress	go	look	remind
break	drink	grab	make	remove
bring	drive	grin	mean	rest
brush	drop	grow	meet	return
button	dust	guess	melt	ride
call	eat	have	mend	rub
catch	empty	hear	miss	run
chase	enjoy	help	mix	saw
chew	enter	hide	mop	say
clean	explain	hit	move	scare
climb	fall	hold	name	scratch
close	feed	hop	notice	see
comb	fill	interrupt	obey	sell
come	find	jump	own	send
cook	fit	keep	pack	sew
copy	fix	kiss	paint	shake

share	watch	bowl	doll	kitchen
shine	wet	box	door	knife
shout	whisper	boy	doorknob	lamp
show	will	bracelet	dragon	leg
sing	wipe	brick	dress	library
sit	wish	broom	duck	lid
skate	wrap	brush	ear	light
skip	yawn	bureau	elephant	lion
sleep	yank	bus	eraser	lip
slide	yell	bush	eye	living room
smell	zip	button	eyebrow	mail carrier
smoke		cabinet	fan	meat
sneeze		cake	farmer	milk
sniff		camera	fence	mitten
snow	**Nouns**	candle	finger	monkey
speak		candy	fire fighter	moon
spill	airplane	candy store	fish	mop
spread	apple	car	flag	motorcycle
stand	arm	card	flat	mouse
stay	baby	carpet	floor	nail
stir	back	cat	flannel board	napkin
stop	bakery	ceiling	flower	neck
swallow	ball	chair	fog	necklace
swap	balloon	chalk	food	nose
sweep	barbershop	cheek	foot	notebook
swell	barn	chicken	fork	nurse
swim	bait	chin	frame	orange
swing	bathroom	church	frog	owl
take	bead	circle	garage	paint
talk	bear	clock	gas station	pan
taste	bed	closet	girl	pants
tear	bedroom	clothing store	glass	paper
tell	bell	cloud	glove	parking lot
think	belt	clown	goat	pen
throw	bib	coat	grass	pencil
tie	bicycle	cookie	green	pet shop
touch	bird	couch	grocery store	picture
try	bite	cow	hair	pig
turn	black	crayon	hammer	pillow
twist	blackboard	cup	hand	pink
undo	block	curb	hat	pipe
undress	blouse	curtain	hinge	pitcher
untie	blue	deer	horn	plate
visit	board	desk	horse	playground
wait	boat	department store	house	playroom
walk	book	dining room	Indian	police officer
want	bookshelf	doctor	jar	porch
wash	boots	dog	key	potato

puppet
puppy
purse
puzzle
rabbit
radio
railroad track
rain
rainbow
ranch hand
record
record player
refrigerator
restaurant
ring
road
rock
roller skate
rooster
rope
rug
ruler
sailboat
saucer
saw
scarf
school
screwdriver
sheep
ship
shirt
shoes
shoe store
shorts
shoulder
sidewalk
sink
skirt
skunk
snake
snow
sock
spoon
square
stair
star
stick
stop sign

stove
street
straw
sun
sweater
switch
T.V.
table
teacher
teeth
telephone
thumb
tie
toe
tongue
train
tree
triangle
tricycle
truck
vase
vegetable
wagon
wall
watch
window
windowsill
zipper

Adjectives

afraid
angry
asleep
awake
beautiful
big
black
blond
blue
brave
brown
bumpy
busy
clear
closed

cloudy
cold
cool
creaky
curly
cute
damp
dark
dim
dry
dull
dusty
fidgety
firm
fluffy
friendly
funny
fussy
gray
gold
good
green
grouchy
handsome
happy
hard
heavy
high
hot
hungry
icy
ill
jumpy
lazy
light
little
long
loud
mad
narrow
nervous
new
noisy
old
open
orange
peppy
pink

plump
pointed
pretty
purple
quiet
rainy
red
rough
round
sad
sharp
shiny
short
sick
sleepy
slick
slippery
small
smoky
soft
square
squeaky
squirmy
straight
strong
sunny
sweet
talkative
tall
thin
thirsty
tiny
tired
unhappy
warm
weak
well
wet
white
wide
yellow
young

SUBJECT INDEX

AUTHOR INDEX